Howard W. Stone

Theological Context for Pastoral Caregiving: Word in Deed

"These essays reveal the mature thinking of a seasoned veteran of both the pastoral counseling clinic and the divinity school classroom. Though respectful of the behavioral sciences, Howard Stone argues that pastoral care and counseling must have a sound theological base or be little more than 'psychotherapy with a twist.' He is concerned that pastoral caregivers have 'sold our theological birthright for a psychological template' and wants us to recognize that theological/spiritual/existential issues, spoken or unspoken, are often the central concern brought to the pastoral caregiver.

Stone offers a theological template that informs our understanding of human brokenness and leads to effective healing. I particularly profited from his clinical suggestions about the pastoral assessment, his description of the place of spiritual direction in pastoral care and counseling, and his discussion of suffering. Pastoral care specialists will be challenged by his creative ideas for constructing a pastoral theological foundation for pastoral care and counseling that informs the clinical practice of ministry."

Andrew D. Lester, PhD
Professor of Pastoral Theology
and Pastoral Counseling,
Brite Divinity School,
Texas Christian University

The Haworth Pastoral Press
An Imprint of The Haworth Press, Inc.

Theological Context
for Pastoral Caregiving
Word in Deed

The Haworth Pastoral Press
Religion, Ministry & Pastoral Care
William M. Clements, PhD
Senior Editor

New, Recent, and Forthcoming Titles:

Growing Up: Pastoral Nurture for the Later Years by Thomas B. Robb

Religion and the Family: When God Helps by Laurel Arthur Burton

Victims of Dementia: Services, Support, and Care by Wm. Michael Clemmer

Horrific Traumata: A Pastoral Response to the Post-Traumatic Stress Disorder by N. Duncan Sinclair

Aging and God: Spiritual Pathways to Mental Health in Midlife and Later Years by Harold G. Koenig

Counseling for Spiritually Empowered Wholeness: A Hope-Centered Approach by Howard Clinebell

Shame: A Faith Perspective by Robert H. Albers

Dealing with Depression: Five Pastoral Interventions by Richard Dayringer

Righteous Religion: Unmasking the Illusions of Fundamentalism and Authoritarian Catholicism by Kathleen Y. Ritter and Craig W. O'Neill

Theological Context for Pastoral Caregiving: Word in Deed by Howard Stone

Theological Context for Pastoral Caregiving
Word in Deed

(Revised edition of *Word of God and Pastoral Care*)

Howard W. Stone

The Haworth Pastoral Press
An Imprint of The Haworth Press, Inc.
New York • London

Published by

The Haworth Pastoral Press, an imprint of The Haworth Press, Inc., 10 Alice Street, Binghamton,
NY 13904-1580

Revised edition of *Word of God and Pastoral Care*, published by Abingdon Press, © 1988.

Library of Congress Cataloging-in-Publication Data

Stone, Howard, W.
    Theological context for pastoral caregiving: word in deed / Howard W. Stone.
        p.   cm.
    Includes bibliographical references and index.
    ISBN 0-7890-0125-X (alk. paper)
    1. Pastoral counseling. 2. Pastoral theology. I. Title.
BV4012.2.S755   1996
253–dc20
                                                                                96-355
                                                                                CIP

For Karen

ABOUT THE AUTHOR

Howard W. Stone, MDiv, PhD, is Professor of Pastoral Care and Counseling at Brite Divinity School of Texas Christian University in Fort Worth, where he has taught since 1979. The author of *Word of God and Pastoral Care* and the co-author of *Christian Caring: Schleiermacher's Practical Theology*, Professor Stone serves on the editorial boards of the *American Journal of Pastoral Counseling,* the *Journal of Religion and Aging,* and the *Journal of Pastoral Care*. He is a member of the American Association of Pastoral Counselors, the American Association of Marriage and Family Therapists, and the Society for Pastoral Theology.

CONTENTS

Preface   xi

Introduction: The Religion Taboo   **1**

Chapter 1. The Distinctiveness of Pastoral Care   **7**

The Historical Breadth of Pastoral Care   9
Pastoral Care in the Twentieth Century   10
The New Shape of Pastoral Care   12
Theology and Pastoral Care   14
The Secular "Theologies"   14
The Mental Health Ethic   16
The Distinctiveness of Christian Care   16
Roadblocks to Correlation   17
Incorporating the Theological into Pastoral Care   19

Chapter 2. Theological Assessment   **25**

The Theological Template   25
A Method of Pastoral Assessment   28
Pastoral Assessment in Practice   33

Chapter 3. The Word   **39**

The Word of God   40
God's Revelation to Humanity   41
Establishing and Extending Relationship   42
Communication of the Faith   43
The Verbal and Visible Word   45
Pastoral Care as Communication of the Word   47
Listening for and Speaking the Word   54
Word and Intervention   58

Chapter 4. Correlating Theology and Ministry   **63**

Cognition and Correlation   65
The Two Hemispheres of the Brain   65

Two Modes of Processing Cognitive Data   67
Hemispheric Dominance   69
Bilateral Cognition   70
Creative Thinking   71
Correlating Intentionally   72

Chapter 5. Spiritual Direction   77

Direction and Correlation   79
History and Terminology   81
Relation to Psychotherapy and Pastoral Counseling   84
Beginning the Process   86
The Contemplative Attitude   89
Writing Activities   91
Structuring the Sessions   92
Spiritual Disciplines   93
The Director   100
Discernment   102

Chapter 6. The Priesthood of All Believers   107

Ministry and Laity   107
Vocation and Priesthood   108
Lay Pastoral Care   112

Chapter 7. Acceptance of Self and Spirit   115

Acceptance   115
Self and Spirit   117
Two Forms of Acceptance   119
Acceptance in Pastoral Care   121

Chapter 8. Suffering   125

Toward a Theology of Theodicy   126
God as Both Loving and All-Powerful   128
God the Creator   129
The Problem of Evil   130
The Tension of Faith   131
God the Redeemer   133
The School of Suffering   136

Suffering and the Christian   138
Pastoral Care and Theodicy   140
Assessing Why Questions   141
Embodying the Presence of the Church   143
The Answers People Give   145
Crises and the Why Questions   147
Talking About Theodicy   147

Chapter 9. Love of God and Neighbor   **153**

A New Relationship in Christ   153
Love of Neighbor   154

Chapter 10. Pastoral Care as Community Endeavor   **161**

Community as Locus of Pastoral Care   164
Community and Scripture   167
Community and Individualized Pastoral Care   168

Index   **171**

Preface

In order for pastoral care and counseling to be more than just psychotherapy "with a twist," it must have a sound theological base that informs its theory and practice, shaping not only the way pastoral care is carried out, but also the actual words a minister speaks in caregiving encounters. At the same time, theology, if it is to be vital and relevant, must be informed by the needs and experiences of people and by the ministry of pastoral care.

In previous books, I have commented briefly on the relationship between the two areas, but pastoral counseling and caring techniques were the first concerns of those writings. In this book, the relationship of pastoral care and theology is my primary concern. Both are important for faithful pastoral care and counseling to occur.

Theological Context for Pastoral Caregiving: Word in Deed is offered to you, the reader, as an introduction to correlating pastoral care and theology. My purpose is neither a thorough elaboration of pastoral care nor a detailed exposition of theology, but the meeting of the two. Assuming that all teaching aims at the developing of skill, the gaining of knowledge, or the influencing of attitude, then this book focuses mainly on the third of these three goals. My hope is that, as an introduction, it will stimulate and enrich your thinking and assist you in your own endeavor to bring together these two fields.

Chapter 1 gives an overview of the state of pastoral care and counseling today, noting some of the major contemporary movements in the field. Chapter 2 focuses on pastoral assessment of the persons served, including assessments of their theological beliefs. Chapter 3 presents my theological understanding of the ministry of pastoral care and counseling. Pastoral care is not to be relegated to the fringes of ministry—as it has been by so many interpreters in the history of the church—but is to be acknowledged as at the heart of the church's proclamation of the Word. Chapter 4 offers suggestions for going about correlating theology and pastoral care. Chapter 5 sets forth spiritual direction as a discipline that can help our pastoral care and counseling ministry regain a solid theological base.

Succeeding chapters explore how several theological concepts might be more explicitly and intentionally related to pastoral care–the priesthood of all believers in Chapter 6, acceptance of self and spirit in Chapter 7, theodicy and suffering in Chapter 8, love of God and neighbor in Chapter 9, and pastoral care as community endeavor in Chapter 10. These issues are of course only a selection, intended to be illustrative but by no means complete.

Carolyn Zerweck and Carol Walther provided valuable help in research for the book, and in addition, Ms. Walther prepared an index for the manuscript. Shirley Bubar carefully typed the manuscript, and Karen Stone gave of her time to the preparation of the text; for this help, too, I express my deep gratitude.

Many of the ideas presented in this book are drawn from my day-to-day clinical practice of pastoral care and counseling. Consequently, the book contains portions of actual case histories. Since confidentiality is essential to pastoral practice, all case descriptions have been altered with respect to name and other particulars in order to preserve anonymity while not distorting the essential reality of the experience described.

Introduction

The Religion Taboo

"It's just that I'm so lonely," the thirty-seven-year-old woman, recently divorced, said to her pastor. "I feel as if God is no longer there."

Pastor: You're feeling abandoned, alone since John left you.
Counselee: Yes, and my prayer life is a big nothing. Talking to God is like talking to the wall.
Pastor: Not having your husband there has left you feeling very much alone.
Counselee: Uh . . . well, yes, but I wish I could pray now and know God's will for me.
Pastor: You want to know what to do.
Counselee: (Pause) I want to know what God has in store for me. (Pause) I've always felt in tune with God's will, but just now I'm having trouble even knowing what to do.
Pastor: Are you dating now?

Religion appears to have replaced sex as the major taboo among pastoral counseling ministers. At any rate, it is certainly the primary taboo I encounter in my supervision of trainees in pastoral care and counseling. Talking about religion, using religious resources with those who come for help, or thinking theologically about their cases makes most students feel uncomfortable and embarrassed.

When in supervised pastoral counseling a counselee says, "I believe it is the will of God" or "What does the Bible say about it?" or "Scripture says it's wrong, doesn't it?" the trainee often is embarrassed, stammers an evasive response, offers Rogerian mir-

---

This chapter appeared as "Religion as Taboo" in the *SPC Journal*, 1986, The Lutheran Council in the USA.

roring, or simply ignores the "religious" comments. Or a trainee may answer with apparent condescension, as an "enlightened" counselor responding to one who is less aware. Rarely do the counselees' feelings or thoughts concerning their faith meet a response as sensitive as that with which other counseling topics are discussed. This religion taboo reminds me of the skittishness about sex that I and other trainees felt several decades ago when I first began doing pastoral counseling. The dynamics are the same; only the sensitive subject has changed.

Does this anti-religion bias exist only among students and trainees? Hardly. For most of us the temptation is strong indeed, when the topic of religion comes up, to change the subject, gloss over the religious issue, and deflect the conversation by asking, "Are you dating now?"

Early in our pastoral care education, most of us were taught some version of "what it means" when counselees talk about religion. They are looking outside themselves for power and rescue. They are avoiding the issues and handing their problems over to a higher authority. Or they are seeking sure and certain answers when there are none. Perhaps they are simply venting their feelings. It may be, even, a sign of psychosis.

Any of these interpretations may be true—*sometimes*, in whole or in part. Equally true is the fact that religious ideation and talk about God, prayer, and faith may be mishandled in pastoral counseling sessions because of the minister's own (perhaps unresolved) feelings about religion. The dynamics of a taboo are likely to be similar whatever the specific issue—be it death, sex, or religion.

People who seek out pastors for care and counsel do not come merely because we are cheap, available, and generally nice people. Such considerations play their part, of course, but the reasons run deeper. Whenever I myself have been in distress, I have chosen a confidant or counselor carefully. I do not bare my soul to just anyone, nor do most people. It seems that a major reason people in need approach a minister is their sense that somehow we pastors have a special tie with the ultimate, that we have faith resources and religious information which they themselves do not possess, but which could be of help. Such feelings are often present, though rarely stated.

How can it be that religion is so often a taboo topic among pastoral caregivers? Whenever I question trainees about their discomfort or embarrassment when discussing religion with counselees, two answers consistently emerge. First, most pastoral care and counseling students, at least in the mainline Protestant seminaries, say they do not want to be mistaken for fundamentalists or archconservatives, giving "pat" answers to difficult questions–a concern that surely cannot be faulted.

Second, the trainees do not want to force beliefs, even their own, on other people; they want their counselees to have the freedom to believe for themselves. This, too, is extremely important. Surely, I do not wish to be put in the same camp as the Hare Krishna missionary at the airport, or the street-corner evangelist, or that former neighbor of mine who could not have a simple conversation without haranguing the other person on matters of scripture and morality.

However, are these the only alternatives–do we talk of religion and therefore be thought of as fundamentalists, or do we cease speaking of religion altogether? Either we force our beliefs on others, or we preserve their freedom by not speaking of religion at all? No! These are false dichotomies that are based on several erroneous assumptions. Let us look more fully at these false assumptions.

First, it is not necessarily true, as some assume, that evangelicals (or fundamentalists) always cram their brand of belief down the throats of other people. This false stereotype about religious conservatives is understandable. There is hardly an evening that I do not read in the paper about the crazy things that some right-wing religionist has said or done that day. It incenses me, even though I know I am reading about a small minority. The fact is that liberal and moderate Christians do not have a corner on the sensitivity-in-interpersonal-relationships market, and I know some liberals who are as dogmatic as the most rigid conservative. Only the dogma is different.

Do we have to allow archconservative religionists to steal our methods (and our message)? Our desire to disassociate ourselves from the televangelists of this world, who not only make the evening papers but are frequently the butt of jokes on talk shows, should not make us forsake our calling. Talking of faith with the faithful, using prayer and scripture in care and counseling, anointing the sick, and offering the Eucharist during a hospital visit are all part of our heritage and of our present-day pastoral care and counseling ministry.

Second, the either-or assumption is without base. Certainly, there is a middle ground between forcing my beliefs onto others and saying nothing. I doubt if most of us believe things because they have been forced on us; rather, we accept certain ideas because they seem right. Parishioners are not of a different species than pastors. People will generally hold fast to a belief because it makes sense, not because it is forced on them by a religious authority. Surely, pastors can talk sensitively about religion and even interject their own viewpoints without being coercive. After all, our goal in pastoral counseling is to help individuals accept more fully their own humanness (and that of others) *and* fulfill their calling as people of God. Regarding faith, we probably can exercise an influence, but surely we are not able to coerce people into believing.

Religion and religious issues can be discussed with a counselee in the same way other issues are handled. If a troubled couple sees a marriage counselor, they expect, and rightly so, that the counselor will draw from a well of professional experience those ideas and methods that can help them strengthen their marriage. The situation is similar for ministers. If people come to us as experts in issues of faith, belief, and meaning, they can anticipate, rightly, that we will speak out of our expertise in this particular area. A marriage counselor does not hand down fiats about how a given marriage should function, but carefully helps counselees look, for example, at alternative patterns of female/male relationships and at different ways of structuring family discipline. Similarly, a minister does not speak in dictums, but helps people look at their present understanding of God and what it means to be a child of that God and consider other ways of coming into contact with the One who is love.

Third, it is also risky business to assume that everyone who wants to talk about faith, or everyone who desires prayer or the Eucharist, will ask for it. Such an assumption is about as valid as telling the recently bereaved, "If there's anything I can do, please let me know." In most instances, the bereaved will not ask for help. They do not want to impose. They do not even know how to ask the right questions. They are not at all sure what *will* help. What they need is the loving offer to do specific things, such as taking a son to his flute lesson, bringing in an evening meal, cleaning the house, or sharing a ride to worship. Similarly, in pastoral care and counseling, we need to develop sensitivity to the various types of religious resources that may be needed in specific situations and then offer them. Of course, people may say no. Or worse, they may tolerate our praying with them when deep down they would rather we did not. Such a risk exists. Since the pendulum in recent care and counseling has swung so far away from pastoral speech about God and from the use of our spiritual heritage, we need to risk erring in the other direction—all the while using our religious resources as sensitively as we use all other resources in the caregiving process.

There is yet another assumption that sometimes hinders pastoral caregivers in their use of spiritual resources. It is the belief that if such resources are not helpful to me personally, they most likely will not be helpful to the people I counsel. ("If prayer is outmoded for me, it certainly will be of little use to others.") Let's face it: for many of us, what piqued our special interest in care and counseling was not only a prior interest in psychology, but perhaps also some personal experience of the benefits of psychotherapy. But not everyone has had the same experiences as we. Not everyone is comfortable with the field of psychology, let alone with the thought of entering psychotherapy. For many people, religious resources have formed the basis of their meaning in life, and returning to them can help re-cement a shaken foundation. Caregivers who discount religious resources can be denying their counselees important forms of pastoral support.

A fifth assumption, often erroneous, is that religious resources should be used only after a relationship is well established. Although care relationships in general should probably begin with periods of listening and attending, in some situations that I have experienced, religious resources were exactly what were needed to help establish (or reestablish) the pastoral relationship from the onset.

I will never forget a recent occasion when I was called to the hospital at eleven o'clock one Sunday night by the family of an elderly woman who was comatose and not expected to live until morning. I was not the family's first choice, but their own pastor was out of town, so they called me. I had a prior acquaintance with only two family members; I had never met the other people gathered outside that intensive care unit. After introducing ourselves and reviewing briefly the woman's condition, the ten of us sat in silence, occasionally exchanging some embarrassed small talk. After about fifteen or twenty minutes, in which I was as uncomfortable as they were, I asked whether they would like to pray. At least seven of them immediately said, in unison, "Yes!" We prayed, and everything changed. The little cluster of assorted friends suddenly became a cohesive unit. For me it became obvious that one of their unspoken reasons for inviting me was that they wanted to pray together as a group but felt unable to do so without a minister (I could lament here about the fact that lay people so often expect the clergy to do their praying for them—but that is hardly the point). In this situation prayer transformed the interrelationships of the people gathered. Immediately, there was a more spontaneous expression of feelings. Several people even sat back and sighed, obviously experiencing at long last a moment of peace in the midst of their difficult crisis.

The religion taboo must be confronted as surely as any other taboo we might hold. The pastoral counseling supervision I received when I was first in training compelled me to face sex as a taboo. My supervisor talked to me about it. He urged me, when counselees broached the matter, to discuss the issues openly with them rather than to change the subject; he even wanted me to initiate questions having to do with sexuality and sexual relations. He urged me to explore my own feelings about sex and the way I developed them. Such a process also can be helpful regarding the religion taboo. We need to be aware of how we feel about it and to learn what in our background has led us to such feelings. We also need to read about it and to discuss the matter with our colleagues. We need to think and talk about it in actual practice, even bring the topic up in our dealings with parishioners. In fact, we need to view other people's desires for religious resources not necessarily as a sign of dependency, but as a reaching out to establish or reclaim meaning in the midst of their present pain.

Chapter 1

The Distinctiveness
of Pastoral Care

The Babylonian Captivity of the Church, a famous Reformation treatise, offered to the church of 1520 a fresh understanding of the sacraments. In it, Martin Luther the theologian joins Martin Luther the pastor in a discussion of some of the "impediments" that had traditionally been thought to justify annulment of a marriage. Detailed consideration is given to the specific case of a woman whose husband is impotent but refuses to grant his wife a divorce. Luther suggests two alternatives:

> Then I would further counsel her, with the consent of the man (who is not really her husband, but only a dweller under the same roof with her), to have intercourse with another, say her husband's brother, but to keep this marriage secret and to ascribe the children to the so-called putative father. The question is: Is such a woman saved and in a saved state? I answer: Certainly, because in this case an error, ignorance of the man's impotence, impedes the marriage; and the tyranny of the laws permits no divorce. But the woman is free through the divine law, and cannot be compelled to remain continent. Therefore the man ought to concede her right, and give up to somebody else the wife who is his only in outward appearance.
>
> Moreover, if the man will not give his consent, or agree to this separation–rather than allow the woman to burn [I Cor. 7:9] or to commit adultery–I would counsel her to contract a mar-

A portion of this chapter originally appeared as "Pastoral Care in the 1980s" in *Religion in Life* (Autumn 1980), pp. 349-359. Copyright © 1980 by Abingdon Press. Used by permission.

riage with another and flee to a distant unknown place. What other counsel can be given to one constantly struggling with the dangers of natural emotions? . . . Is not the sin of a man who wastes his wife's body and life a greater sin than that of the woman who merely alienates the temporal goods of her husband?[1]

Today, blessed with learnings from modern psychology that were unavailable to Luther, we can chuckle over the pastoral care he suggests for the wife of an impotent husband. Luther's proposed resolution of the problem, however, allowing the wife either to have sexual relations with a relative of the husband or to run off to another city with a new husband, at least represented an honest attempt to understand pastoral care from a theological standpoint—the perspective of Christian liberty.

Today, a couple seeking pastoral help for this same problem is likely to learn of additional alternatives, perhaps some of the highly effective therapeutic methods that are currently available. A theological understanding that sends the wife packing to Billings or Paducah with a new husband would be clearly inadequate. The techniques offered by such specialists in sexuality as Masters and Johnson can be of real help to individuals and couples trying to cope with sexual dysfunction.[2]

For those of us who live and work at the interface between theology and pastoral care, however, a new dilemma has arisen. Along with the tremendous benefits that psychology has brought to modern society, to the church, and to ministers doing pastoral care, there also has come an attendant loss. In our actual care of people, we have tended to ignore the basic foundations and full heritage of Christian care throughout the ages; we also have tended to ignore our biblical heritage in theology, ethics, and anthropology. In fact, as I mentioned in the "Introduction," religion seems at times to have replaced sex as the major taboo among pastoral caregivers.

It would seem that pastoral care in recent decades has actually lost its roots. Enthralled by the truly impressive strides made by other scholarly disciplines in our time, it has cut itself off from the historical tradition of church and theology, in at least two important respects: (1) pastoral care has become identified so largely with pastoral counseling as to forget the larger meaning of care in its historically more encompassing aspects; and (2) it has come to accept certain implied values and concepts of humanity in secular mental health practice, thereby loosening its historic ties to Christian theology.

THE HISTORICAL BREADTH
OF PASTORAL CARE

In a brilliant historical analysis, William Clebsch and Charles Jaekle point to four functions of pastoral care in the Christian tradition. Pastoral care is understood historically to embrace the helping acts performed by representative Christians as they facilitate the healing, sustaining, guiding, and reconciling of troubled individuals, people whose difficulties occur within the context of ultimate meanings and concerns.[3] All four of these traditional functions are important.

Healing is the pastoral function that "aims to overcome some impairment by restoring a person to wholeness and by leading him to advance beyond his previous condition."[4] Historically, the function of healing has been carried out through such acts as anointing, exorcism, prayers to the saints, pilgrimages to shrines, charismatic healing, magic, and magic medicine.

Sustaining is the function that helps individuals endure and rise above situations in which a restoration to their previous condition is unlikely. Church history records perseverance, consolation, and visitation of the sick and shut-ins as ways in which this function has been exercised.

The guiding function consists of "assisting perplexed persons to make confident choices . . . when such choices are viewed as affecting the present and future state of the soul."[5] Throughout the centuries, two basic forms of guidance have been used in pastoral care. "Inductive guidance" leads the people cared for to adopt *a priori* sets of values as the basis for making decisions. "Eductive guidance" elicits from people's own lives and values the criteria for decision making. Historically, pastoral guidance has been primarily inductive, at various times involving devil craft, advice giving, spiritual direction, and listening.

The fourth function, reconciling, seeks to reestablish broken relationships between people and between individuals and God. Historically, the function of reconciliation has involved such activities as forgiveness, discipline, penance, confession, and absolution.

PASTORAL CARE
IN THE TWENTIETH CENTURY

Pastoral care in our century has emphasized primarily eductive guiding, with a secondary emphasis on healing the psyche. With the rise of pastoral counseling as the queen of pastoral care functions, eductive guidance has all but displaced the other three functions of sustaining, healing, and reconciling. Today in the pastoral care movement, and especially in the United States, I see three major approaches to pastoral care and counseling that dominate the scene: the traditional method, emphasizing inductive guidance; the nondirective approach, emphasizing eductive guidance; and the revised approach, emphasizing all four functions.

A pastor from my hometown routinely uses the first method. He frequently has criticized me for the amount of time I spend in caregiving and counseling a given individual, and he tells me he is able to accomplish most of his pastoral counseling in just one visit. When a couple comes to him with a marriage problem, he opens his Bible and reads several pertinent verses showing that the wife is to be submissive to her husband. He then prays with them, thanking God that they know where to find the solution to their problem. This pastor claims that he has cured many marriages this way since (small wonder) few ever have returned for a second session. This admittedly extreme example can perhaps serve to illustrate the traditional approach to pastoral care, an approach that many of us inherited.

This traditional method has its advantages. It is quick. It uses religious resources and builds on the community's residual acceptance of pastoral authority. It deals with the family system as a whole. It is action-oriented. Yet, for all its emphasis on inductive guidance–telling people on the basis of scripture what they have to do–this method falls short because there is no listening to a person's pain, little learning from the positive benefits of modern psychology, and little opportunity for individuals to grapple their own way through to needed solutions of their problems.

In reaction to this traditional approach, a new method of pastoral care came on the scene in the 1940s and 1950s. Relying mainly on Carl Rogers, with a smattering of Freud, this method became known as the nondirective approach. This method emphasized the structured fifty-minute interview, the role of unconscious motivation in human behavior, the childhood basis of most adult responses, and insight as the major goal of counseling.

The nondirective approach came to the field of pastoral care like a breath of fresh air. It is an approach that has many advantages. Pastors are trained to talk less and listen more to the people they encounter; this helps establish rapport build a solid pastor-parishioner relationship. The negative aspects of ministerial authority, long associated with the authoritarian *Herr Pastor* image, are avoided.

Despite its obvious advantages over the earlier model, however, the nondirective approach also has its liabilities. The major difficulty is that it focuses almost exclusively on one form of pastoral care–eductive guidance, with its techniques of listening and uncovering, and its emphasis on insight as the goal of pastoral care–while ignoring cognition and behavior.[6] Other disadvantages worth mentioning are its time-consuming interest in exploring past events, its penchant for the fifty-minute hour as the preferred setting, and its tendency to look more at individuals than at full family systems or community.

A revised model made its appearance in 1966 with the publication of one of the most important books that had yet appeared–Howard Clinebell's *Basic Types of Pastoral Counseling.*[7] Clinebell acknowledged the contributions of the nondirective model, but he also cautioned that if it were taken as the sole model, it would greatly limit the opportunities otherwise inherent in the office of pastor.

Clinebell went a long way toward helping pastors return to the historical elements of pastoral care, but now there is both the need and the possibility to go even further. Clinebell's approach tended to focus on counseling more than on care. His methods were still tied to eductive guidance. There was little impetus or direction for correlating the moral and theological tradition with the pastoral care process (although Clinebell, it must be noted, has been a major proponent of social-ethical concerns).

THE NEW SHAPE OF PASTORAL CARE

In an effort to help incorporate the historic tradition into present and future practice, I would propose here ten theses suggestive of the shape that pastoral care can take today. These theses, of course, draw upon both the traditional and the nondirective models, and especially upon Clinebell's revised model, but they attempt also to integrate more fully the four historical functions of pastoral care.[8]

1. Pastoral care recognizes liturgy, ritual, confession, and traditional and contemporary Christian resources as beneficial components. It is not shy about offering prayers and sound spiritual healing for the sick. It draws from the discipline of spiritual direction. It reemphasizes the work of the Spirit.

2. Pastoral care does not view personality change as the primary goal of its work. Sometimes, it is supportive of the person; at other times, it is confrontive. Sometimes, it fosters renewal of relationships; at other times, it facilitates their ending. At all times it helps people stretch to use to the fullest their God-given resources and strengths, while at the same time recognizing that people are finite and that the source of all growth lies outside themselves. Finally, it recognizes that the pastoral care goals of all Christians are growth in faith and loving service to others.

3. Pastoral care is not morally or theologically neutral. It operates from a Christian perspective and, when appropriate and effective, speaks to the parishioner from this perspective. It incorporates moral guidance and spiritual direction. In short, pastoral care does not stop at teaching the skills of effective living; it points also to a moral life, a faithful life of service to neighbor. There is an ongoing engagement in the task of correlating theology and pastoral care.

4. Pastoral care occurs within a Christian context—the "community of saints." It attempts to incorporate those who are cared for into the church. Pastoral care is a community endeavor. It seeks to bridge the gap between people and the gap between alienated individuals and God. Pastoral care's focus is on the individual, the couple, the family, and the community of faith.

5. Pastoral care is not performed only by the pastor. It is a task also for the laity. Taking seriously Luther's belief in the priesthood of all believers, pastoral care empowers the laity to strengthen the caring done by a congregation.

6. Pastoral care has a systemic and social orientation. Although pastoral care is not the same as social change, it is informed–as surely as any other aspect of the church's ministry–by an awareness of the need for social ethical action in specific situations.

7. When pastoral care calls for pastoral counseling, frequently in response to a crisis, that counseling normally is short-term. Ministers need to adopt a brief counseling orientation in their ministerial work, rather than rely upon the long-term perspective true of many in the mental health professions.[9] In the few situations when counseling must take longer, counselees usually are referred to other professionals or agencies within the community.

8. Pastoral care takes seriously the pastor's task and opportunity for initiation. It does not stand by waiting for people to request a counseling session. It takes the risk, once a problem is seen, of offering care even where help has not been sought. It is proactive, not simply reactive, to expressed needs.

9. Pastoral care aims to help people develop not only their feelings and attitudes, but also constructive behaviors and thinking. It recognizes that what a person feels and does greatly depends on what that individual thinks and believes.

10. Finally, pastoral care focuses on coping with contemporary here-and-now issues. Its focus is on the future rather than on extensive analysis of past history. Its orientation is preventive, centered on the strengthening of existing skills, abilities, and relationships rather than on breaking down or uncovering deep-seated problems or defects.

The model of care proposed here involves all four strands of the tradition of pastoral care. The future health of pastoral care and counseling itself depends on our regaining the historic balance and interaction between healing, sustaining, guiding, and reconciling.

THEOLOGY AND PASTORAL CARE

Pastoral care has benefited greatly by twentieth-century strides made in psychology. Unwittingly, however, it also has adopted some of the values and concepts of humanity–the "theologies"–of modern psychology, thereby loosening its ties to Christian theology. When pastoral care is faithful to its historical tradition, it is not theologically or morally neutral, as most psychotherapies claim to be, but seeks to help people grow in effective Christian living. When it is not, it is virtually indistinguishable, in philosophy and in function, from modern psychotherapeutic practice.

Over the past three decades, I have reviewed thousands of case histories, audiotapes, and videotapes of pastoral care and counseling sessions. These sessions seem to be characterized by one major and striking feature: theological constructs exert little influence on the help being offered. The pastor's beliefs about sin, grace, judgment, and forgiveness apparently have little effect on the meeting between pastor and parishioner. Why? Are the ministers so poorly trained? The problem is not that simply stated. A more likely reason is that pastoral care (and especially pastoral counseling) has often adopted the "theologies" implicit in modern psychotherapies and moved away from its own theological roots.

THE SECULAR "THEOLOGIES"

This unwitting embrace of secular mental health suppositions has two consequences. In the first place, the emphasis on eductive guidance by the nondirective pastoral care movement has led pastors to adopt a more neutral stance toward issues of value and meaning. Eductive counseling does not impose on people in need an outside moral ethic or theological solution, but attempts to clarify and reshape the emotional responses of parishioners within their own value framework. Practitioners of psychotherapy have rightly noted that if a counselor is judgmental when trying to establish rapport, the counseling process comes to a sudden halt. Building rapport requires the counselor to be warm, open, and relaxed and to suspend judgment. By adopting the neutral stance of the secular counselor, ministers have often lost sight of their task as spiritual directors, ethicists, and theologians. Our pastoral care has leaned toward "bearing another's burden" while relegating the work of judgment to the sermon, politics, or social ethical issues. Pastoral care has lost that tension between law and gospel, judgment and grace, of which Luther spoke so forcefully.

In the second place, there is no real neutrality anyway among mental health care providers. The concept of humanity implicit in much psychology today (especially humanistic psychology) has a much more positive image of human beings than does a Christian anthropology that recognizes the existence of sin in the world. In this regard, I am reminded especially of Luther's understanding of the person as simultaneously both saint and sinner. Most humanistic psychologies, and many others as well, focus mainly on the saint in each of us; they do not recognize the sinner. They thus ignore evil and our human finitude.

Most psychological theorists and system builders in our century have hidden behind the guise of "scientific neutrality." The truth is, though, that their psychotherapies are not neutral! There is a reason why some psychotherapies set themselves against mores and culture. There is a reason why some types of marriage counseling result in a greater number of divorces than others. Those reasons have to do with underlying value assumptions.

Many therapies, besides describing what the "actualized" or "ideal" person is to be, also detail how life is to be lived. They define what health and happiness are. They spell out the marks of love. However, these matters all involve questions of meaning, and any system that addresses them is functioning theologically.

In many ways psychology has become the new religion. Its ministers purvey its teachings through encounter groups, psychotherapy, pop psychology books, and talk shows. They evangelize the latest psychotherapeutic craze. The consequence is that when pastoral care is cut adrift from its traditional roots and adopts exclusively the eductive method of guidance, secular "theologies," rather than Christian theology, become the base from which pastoral care and counseling is conceived and practiced.

THE MENTAL HEALTH ETHIC

Some years ago in a paper titled "The Mental Health Ethic," I suggested that what was then being required of people by the various psychotherapies was tantamount to a rejection of the Christian ethic in favor of a new one. Uncertain about my thesis, I shared the paper with some of my colleagues. They were unconvinced, even bemused. I filed my paper away and did not look at it again until recently.

The mental health ethic I then described is even more prevalent today. It varies from one school of thought and practice to another—from one ideology to another, if you will. But there also are some common themes: be open and honest; be warm; do what you feel ("Go with your feelings"); be congruent; be assertive; share your innermost feelings; be in touch with your sexuality; get out of your mind and into your feelings.

Now, there is much to be said for most of these admonitions, and the qualities extolled are at least somewhat honorable. Their apologists, however, often tend to be one-sided, studiously avoiding a fully developed Christian ethic. Pastors who segregate the caring portion of their ministry from the rest of ministry, who do pastoral care as if they were not ministers (or even Christians) need to realize the significant differences between pastoral care and the secular care offered in such other disciplines as psychotherapy and social work. Essentially, these differences can be reduced to matters of perspective and of context.[10]

THE DISTINCTIVENESS OF CHRISTIAN CARE

The first thing that makes pastoral counseling unique is the perspective of the pastor. Ministers, of course, use various methods borrowed from secular psychology, but we approach them within a specific theological framework. Christian theology is distinctive in its perspective on what it means to be human, its concept of health, and its understanding of human plight and rescue. It often perceives in the suffering person's words a different struggle and end point. This means that the warmth, openness, and acceptance of the pastor in any pastoral care relationship takes on transcendent meaning. A sound theological perspective influences the whole warp and woof of pastoral care.

A second difference between pastors and secular counselors derives from the fact that pastoral care occurs within the context of the Christian community. The minister-parishioner encounter in a counseling chamber has as its larger setting the community of the church–a faith community. In fact, this context is not just a particular congregation at one point in time, but a long pastoral care tradition embracing the whole church and bridging the generations since at least the first century. This recognition that pastoral care occurs within the "community of saints" helps guard against the privatism or pietism that has often affected secular psychotherapy.

Thus, there is something different about pastoral care, and this "difference" means that the minister who responds to individuals from a Christian perspective and within the context of the Christian community must have grappled with and be working out a theology of such things as sexuality, marriage, reconciliation, health, and death. Theology books and courses are not dry theoretical exercises involving pie-in-the-sky formulations that have no human reference; they help establish the foundation for pastoral care ministry.[11]

ROADBLOCKS TO CORRELATION

It has been said that one distinctive aspect of pastors' care is their perspective, the way they relate theology and their own pastoral practice. There are a number of problems, though, inherent in this correlation of theology and pastoral care. Assuming we agree that such a correlation should occur, and aside from the methodological issues yet to be discussed as to how it can be done, some basic difficulties can hinder any such meeting and interaction. A familiarity with these difficulties alerts the caregiver to potential roadblocks that thwart the much-needed dialogue. The major trouble spots deserve listing.

A first area of conflict involves the matter of territorial rights. Who owns the correlation enterprise? Which "side" gets to speak first–or last? Michael Taylor refers to this as disagreement over the game plan: Who serves first? What is in or out of bounds? How is it scored? What is the agenda?[12] When there are differences, how do we go about settling them? What is the final authority? Scripture? Tradition? Experience? Relevance? Pastors probably remember from seminary days the tensions between the practical and classical fields. Those tensions, and the attendant egos and politics, come into play when the two fields meet.

A second problem involves the question of which theology pastoral care is supposed to relate to. Should it be correlated with one of our historical theologies or a contemporary one? Which of the contemporary theologies–all of them, some of them, or only one? A denominational theology? There are so many voices, so many languages, so many historical periods of varying theological concern.

Furthermore, which pastoral care approach is to take part in the dialogue? Earlier in this chapter, I sketched out the shape pastoral care should take in ministry today, but is my sketch sufficient? One of the things I have learned in my travels, and especially on several extended research leaves in Great Britain, is that there are diverse understandings of pastoral care in our world today. Which one is to take the lead in the much-needed dialogue?

Another related concern is the issue of which school of psychology (if any) underlies the pastoral care. Psychoanalysis and nondirective psychotherapy, as we know, are not the only therapies that can influence pastoral care. A review of books on pastoral care and counseling in the last several decades will reveal that pastoral care has drawn heavily from a host of schools, including Jungian, Psychosynthesis, Transactional Analysis, Integrity Therapy, Gestalt Therapy, cognitive therapy, systems marriage and family counseling, behavioral therapy, and Reality Therapy, to name a few. Contrast orthodox Freudianism with Rational-Emotive Therapy and you will see that the pastoral care which relies on one psychological theory will look quite different from that which relies on another. In any event, to what extent do you allow any particular therapeutic approach to determine the pastoral care offered?

If this dilemma is not sufficiently discouraging, read on. The plot thickens. The understanding of ministry varies considerably from person to person, from denomination to denomination, and from one period of history to another. I happen to be keenly interested in how the great pastoral caregivers of previous centuries did their care;

from them I learn more about how I do mine. Edward Pusey and John Keble of the Oxford Movement, for example, were both sensitive, caring, compassionate priests; their letters demonstrate great concern for others in distress. But their paternalism and relatively authoritarian understanding of the office of the priesthood, especially as it relates to confession, would not be acceptable to most ministers today. There is considerable diversity in the concept of ministry and the role of the minister among modern clerics, as well.

Another difficulty in correlating theology and pastoral care has to do with the extreme complexity of the human beings who are the subjects of care. When we begin to relate theology and pastoral care in concrete situations—with reference to the specific people we encounter—we find that humans are very complex beings. No two caregivers would ever agree completely about given counselees—who they are, what their needs are, and what motivates their behavior. There are simply too many unknowns in our knowing, too many uncertainties about the individuals we seek to help, too much that is shrouded in mystery.

Yet another difficulty: when correlating theology and pastoral care, which doctrines do we consider? It is my impression that some doctrines of the church—anthropology, ministry, soteriology—relate quite readily to the types of situations we encounter in the day-in and day-out practice of pastoral ministry. Others, such as those that speak of the garden or the last things may seem distant and of little value. Which doctrines are to take priority in the process of correlation? Which are to form the starting point of our theology?

Finally, do we consider laypersons as pastoral caregivers? If so, that will change the character of the task as well. For the caregiver without a seminary education, there will need to be a method of correlation that is not so inordinately difficult or obscure as to be useless, yet not so simplistic as to avoid the complexities of the actual enterprise.

INCORPORATING THE THEOLOGICAL INTO PASTORAL CARE

There is a way out of the morass, muddled though it may seem. What is required is that we be prepared, do the necessary spadework, and reflect on our experience in light of the Word. In that way, theology can have an impact on our care. We may not, and probably cannot, resolve all the difficulties just enumerated, but we can be sensitive to them and hold them in tension as we proceed with the task of correlation. We can also recognize that what we finally come up with is likely to be very time- and situation-bound, perhaps applicable to only one specific individual or family, or at best to one particular community.

We shall refer to Chapter 2 for the beginnings of a methodology for correlating theology and pastoral care and to Chapter 4 for a way to do it, but at this point I would simply call attention to some of the issues involved. I see the correlation process actually occurring in concrete situations, perhaps in such pastoral acts as visiting an accident victim in the hospital, counseling an estranged couple, or calling on a lonely widower.

Picture this for a simple example: The doorbell rings and when you answer it the paperboy barks, "Collect!" You leave him on the step, run to the bedroom, and return with a ten-dollar bill, apologizing, "Sorry, I don't have anything smaller." "That's okay, I've got it here," and he gives you a handful of bills and coins in change. You wish him a good evening. On the way back to your bedroom you casually count the money in your hand and realize that he gave you change for a twenty instead of a ten. What do you do? Without a moment's hesitation, you probably run to the door and call him back before he gets too far down the street. You explain that he gave you ten dollars too much and he blurts out a surprised, "Thanks a lot!" before going on his way.

Why did you decide to return the money? You could have kept it—most ministers probably have need of some extra change. The boy's mistake confronted you with an ethical dilemma. Without even weighing alternatives, you made a choice. Not everyone would call the paperboy back in such a situation; in fact, many people would not. Your decision had to be based on something prior, something more than a general free-floating niceness in your nature. Your response was shaped no doubt in the distant past, by values you had learned long ago or grew to hold important. These values and beliefs were probably heightened by your years in seminary and by subsequent study of scripture as you prepared for preaching and teaching.

In addition, these values have been shaped by your own exploration of what it is to be a faithful servant; they have come from the examination of your life and the values you live by. Such beliefs are part and parcel of your faith. You might not be able to articulate them as well as you would like, but your faith and values at times overrule the possibility of some responses, such as the urge to think, "Oh, what's the difference; he has no debts, no mouths to feed, and maybe he will learn something from the loss."

The correlation of pastoral care with theology, though it sounds frightfully like an academic exercise, needs to proceed almost as automatically in the concrete care situation as in your response to the paper boy. Although you will occasionally have the luxury of reflecting on the care you offer, good correlation happens over and over again almost automatically in the way you listen and respond to another's anguish. Our faith, beliefs, and values shape what we say and do, as well as how we respond.

Sound easy? I'm afraid there is a catch. Most pastoral care situations are more complex than the case of the paperboy. Competing values are likely to be involved—one's own ego needs, unexamined assumptions induced by the media, the inadequate values inherent in contemporary psychology, and pressures from family, friends, and even the bishop. Indeed, the competition is so great that it becomes easy for us to respond in pastoral situations, not according to Christian values, but according to our own narcissism or professional pride or the mores of society.

For authentic correlation to occur, the pastor must return over and over again to the primary texts that shape the faith. An ethics course back in seminary may have prepared us well enough for the dilemma of the paperboy, but it may not sufficiently alert pastors to the dangers of an increasing emotional involvement with, and dependency on, a counselee of the opposite sex. So, for correlation to occur, the pastor must repeatedly return to the sources of the faith, read widely in theology and ethics, and have a continuing dialogue with the competing value and belief systems present in our culture.

Besides a continual return to the sources, reflection on present experience also is required. The pastor must reflect not only on former learnings, but also on recent events, and upon the care that is currently being given (Chapter 4 offers suggestions on how this can be done). It is easy for one's theological beliefs to become separated from the material world in which one works. A calm review of experience as it relates to the sources of faith, the people who are being cared for, and one's day-to-day relationship with God is essential if there is to be any ongoing encounter between theology and pastoral care.

Reflection is insufficient, however, if it is done in isolation, outside a communal context. Whether it occurs at the local ministers' weekly breakfast, under the guidance of a spiritual director or pastoral care supervisor, during dialogue and feedback within the congregation, or in intimate talks with friends and family members, the correlation of pastoral care and theology does not develop only from reviewing our private beliefs as individuals, or even the opinions of theologians and writers in pastoral care. It is ultimately formed by the convictions of the community of faith.

To summarize, each person's correlation of pastoral care and theology will first involve a study of the sources of our faith and how they are expressed in theology, and secondly, a reflection on those sources as well as on our present experience with people entrusted to our care and reflection on our relationship with God. Such reflection always is tied to the Christian community.

Ministers must develop a method of theological reflection that best suits their own needs. No two will be exactly alike. The method must be so simple that it can be absorbed and acted upon almost without thinking, and yet so sophisticated that it takes seriously the complexity of individuals, values, and beliefs. In some situations we may indeed have time to think, consult, and devise appropriate pastoral strategies; we can, for example, probably consider at length a plan of treatment for someone who is chronically depressed. But in other situations, we may have to act reflexively, in a way that is comparable to the "muscle memory" we employ while driving a car or playing softball. At such times, we must trust that the Word resides within us, that the faith is so ingrained in our living that it affects our decisions even when we do not have opportunity to think them through.

No correlation is perfect and valid for every situation. We must continually make judgments and act upon them, but these judgments and acts remain our frail attempts at truth. They are necessarily tentative; they must remain open to critique, to correction from the community, and to further insight. Nevertheless, pursuing truth to the best of our ability, we must make real commitments. It is at that point of commitment where reflection ends and the practice of pastoral care and counseling begins. Since at the point of action there is usually not enough time to go through a complicated procedure of correlating theology with pastoral care, a "trenches hermeneutics, " an intuitive approach to the pastoral task, is required.

We are there. We act. If there has been prior reflection on theology and pastoral care, it will inform our practice. As we are attentive to the Word, Christian faith will have its impact on the care we give.

NOTES

1. *Luther's Works*, American ed., vol. 36 (Philadelphia and St. Louis: Fortress Press and Concordia Publishing House, 1955-), pp. 103-104 (hereinafter cited as *LW*).

2. Considerably less technical than the pioneering work by William H. Masters and Virginia E. Johnson, *Human Sexual Inadequacy* (Boston: Little, Brown & Co., 1970), is the useful little "Pocket Counsel Books" volume by David Mace, *Sexual Difficulties in Marriage* (Philadelphia: Fortress Press, 1972).

3. William A. Clebsch and Charles R. Jaekle, *Pastoral Care in Historical Perspective* (Northvale, NJ: Jason Aronson, 1964), p. 4.

4. Ibid., p. 33.

5. Ibid., p. 9.

6. My own book *Using Behavioral Methods in Pastoral Counseling* (Philadelphia: Fortress Press, 1980) is an attempt to correct this tendency to rely on only one primary form of psychotherapy in the practice of pastoral care.

7. Howard Clinebell, *Basic Types of Pastoral Counseling* (Nashville, TN: Abingdon Press, 1966), pp. 27-38.

8. The theoretical justification for these theses is drawn from a number of sources, especially Don S. Browning, *The Moral Context of Pastoral Care* (Philadelphia: Westminster Press, 1976) and *Practical Theology* (New York: Harper & Row, 1982); Alastair Campbell, *Rediscovering Pastoral Care* (London: Darton, Longman & Todd, 1981); Howard Clinebell, *Basic Types of Pastoral Care and Counseling* (Nashville,TN: Abingdon Press, 1984); Gerard Egan, *The Skilled Helper*, 2nd ed. (Monterey, CA: Brooks/Cole Publishing Co., 1982); Charles Gerkin, *The Living Human Document* (Nashville, TN: Abingdon, 1984); Paul A. Hauck, *Reason in Pastoral Counseling* (Philadelphia: Westminster Press, 1972); Andrew Lester, *Hope in Pastoral Care and Counseling* (Louisville, KY: Westminster/John Knox Press, 1995); Thomas Oden, *Pastoral Theology* (New York: Harper & Row, 1983); Howard W. Stone, *Crisis Counseling* (Philadelphia: For-

tress Press, 1993); *The Caring Church: A Guide for Lay Pastoral Care* (Minneapolis, MN: Fortress Press, 1991); and *Brief Pastoral Counseling* (Minneapolis, MN: Fortress Press, 1994).

9. See Howard Stone, *Brief Pastoral Counseling* (Minneapolis, MN: Fortress Press, 1994).

10. See Howard W. Stone, *Suicide and Grief* (Philadelphia: Fortress Press, 1972), pp. 93-94.

11. See Howard W. Stone and James Duke, *How to Think Theologically* (Minneapolis, MN: Fortress Press, 1996).

12. Michael Taylor, *Learning to Care: Christian Reflections on Pastoral Practice* (London: S.P.C.K., 1983), pp. 4-5.

Chapter 2

Theological Assessment

Imagine the scene. Two pastors are animatedly discussing a parishioner with whom one has been counseling. We overhear that part of the conversation when Pastor Phyllis concludes that Pastor Fred's parishioner is "obviously struggling with an endogenous depression exacerbated by low self-esteem . . . he is definitely moving out of an 'I'm not okay, you're okay' position, and if only he can strengthen his adult, he will reach greater wholeness."

Fred nods his assent: "I agree with your analysis of the man's script . . . His weak ego state is related to the fact that he had a father who was an alcoholic, and he never experienced a relationship of basic trust with either parent."

Overhearing their assessment of a counselee receiving pastoral care, we begin to wonder if we are perhaps at a convention of the American Psychological Association or the Academy for the Advancement of Psychotherapy instead of at a gathering of ministers. How do pastors assess the parishioners in their care? Do we construe and interpret their problems in the categories of contemporary psychology, or is our pastoral assessment in terms of the church's theological tradition?

THE THEOLOGICAL TEMPLATE

The human mind seems to have within it indispensable structures that organize and interpret data received by the senses. Psycholo-

---

A portion of this chapter originally appeared as "Theological Assessment in Pastoral Care" in *Dialog*, 21 (Winter 1982), pp. 49-54. Copyright ©1982 by Dialog, Inc. Reprinted by permission. The article was co-authored with John W. Schaub who has granted permission for the present alterations and use.

gists using a Rorschach test, for example, know that the brain organizes the ink-blot design and interprets it in light of a counselee's emotional and intellectual status; for one person, the multi-shaped form brings to mind a beautiful mountain scene, while for another the same shape reveals genitalia. These organizing structures of the mind, which I shall call templates, are essential for organizing information into a manageable whole.

Through years of education, training, and reflection upon experience, the physician acquires a "medical template," without which a diagnosis would be impossible. A patient comes into the office and uses common, ordinary words to describe certain symptoms: "I have been feeling light-headed lately, mostly when I am standing." The physician recalls having previously prescribed medication for high blood pressure, and so responds by asking a few questions in equally simple and easily understood language, questions about body positions and movements, fatigue, stress, and hearing.

When it comes to actually assessing the patient's symptoms, however, the physician moves away from ordinary language and resorts to a "medical template" learned in medical school. Technical terms and highly professional categories spring readily to mind, without any need for conscious recall. There are "indications and contraindications" relative to alternative anti-hypertensive drugs, revised dosage levels to be considered, "orthostatic hypotension," and so forth. The whole bag of analytical terms and descriptive categories constitutes a "medical template" that the physician then places on both the patient's own words and the doctor's clinical observations. The purpose is to determine if the prescribed drug is working properly or if too high a dosage is producing unwelcome side effects. The medical template functions to organize the physician's observations and thinking, thus ensuring a more accurate diagnosis and appropriate treatment.

Other professionals also use templates forged from the body of terms and knowledge that is unique to their particular discipline. Each such template represents a distinctive way of looking at things, a distinct perspective on reality. None of these diverse perspectives, however, is to be regarded as definitive in the sense of having summarized and exhausted all possible interpretations and meanings. Not even the collectivity of templates–the whole range of possible perspectives for organizing data in the mind–could do that.

To suggest that each profession does and should use its own distinctive template is not to suggest that only one template should ever be used. The physician may use several–psychological, sociological, legal, religious–other than the strictly medical template in assessing the patient's condition. But good physicians are not likely to reject or ignore the template they were specifically, and uniquely, trained to use.

In our "post-Christian" era, unfortunately, it seems that the pastor's template has become even more confused than those of the physician and psychologist. Religious conceptuality seems to have lost much of its intellectual credibility. Specifically religious language is rarely used, except by conservative and fundamentalist Christians. Mainline Protestant and Catholic ministers often avoid religious language for fear of appearing less credible or of being associated with the religious "right wing." Because of this credibility issue, many pastors are tempted to discard the theological template altogether in favor of a more contemporary secular template, such as that of psychology. Regrettable in that development is not the pastoral use of such other templates, but the exclusion of a theological template from pastoral care.

Phyllis and Fred (if in fact they did not go on to assess Fred's parishioner theologically) had in a sense sold their theological birthright for a psychological template. In this respect, they do not stand alone. At times we have all done the same thing, and we continue to struggle with such a temptation. It often seems easier to speak in Freudian terms, or in the words of Transactional Analysis, for example, than to use a theological template in our pastoral assessment.

Clearly, there is a need today for the pastor, in a self-conscious way, to regain a theological template that will be unique to pastoral care. Without such a template, spiritual assessment of a troubled parishioner will surely remain confused and will frequently result in an inadequate *pastoral* response.

A theological template does not mean a rigid formula, a conceptual framework that is fixed and inflexible. It simply means a way of organizing the pastor's reflections about what has happened and is happening to the parishioner. Such a framework can help the pastor build on past experiences in working with people who have had similar difficulties. It can be helpful in correlating one's theology with one's pastoral acts in concrete situations. Such integration does not imply the mechanical process of simply applying a preexisting body of doctrine to the specific care situation; rather, it implies the dynamic process of actualizing our theology anew in every moment of conflict and suffering.

Pastoral assessment can and should be done from a theological template. The method to be described here involves the use of a series of questions–which could, of course, vary in number and content–in which the form or structure of the series is the important thing. It is offered in the hope that all pastors will be encouraged to use some theological template in their pastoral assessment.

A METHOD OF PASTORAL ASSESSMENT

Paul Pruyser has helped us affirm the unique perspective of the pastor in the assessment of people.[1] His insights have increased our self-conscious grappling with pastoral assessment and have driven us explicitly to identify various criteria that were otherwise only implicit in the formation of our pastoral judgments. The questions– wonderings–that arise in the back of our minds as we encounter people in pastoral care or counseling are not queries for the troubled to address; they are simply constituent elements in a framework that can help ministers reach a theological understanding of what is happening. We pastors need to ask these or comparable questions of ourselves as we listen to the story any particular individual has to tell. If we can begin to answer these questions, we should have a fuller grasp of the pastoral situation we are encountering.

1. Why Is This Person Coming to Me for Help?

There is a reason why people choose a pastor rather than a doctor, friend, attorney, mate, neighbor, relative, or colleague. When someone comes to you, it is important for you to understand *why* he or she has come specifically to you, of all people, to share a personal burden. What specifically do you symbolize to this person? Perhaps there has already developed, at least in part, the insight that the agonizing problem is basically a spiritual problem, and that surely one can turn to a pastor for help in dealing with a specifically spiritual concern.

2. How Does This Person Understand God?

God is likely to be a focal concern in connection with any spiritual problem. Two aspects of that concern are addressed in this single question.

First, how does this person picture God? What is the prevailing God-concept? Is God thought of primarily as a punitive, capricious, moralistically judgmental, indifferent, distant, uncaring deity; or is God a loving, forgiving, fair, and caring parent who incorporates both judgment and grace? Often, parishioners will give us insight into their view of God by the questions they ask: "Why me?" "Am I being punished?" "How could God allow this to happen to a person so young and so good?" "Why does God let her suffer so?" Questions of this sort often reveal a serious personal struggle to understand how God acts or to find meaning within the situation. They can also provide a clue to the maturity of the person and of that person's understanding of God and self.

Second, we must look not only for what the person *says* about God, but also for the congruence, or lack of congruence, between the statement and actual behavior. Is the God talked about the one to whom allegiance is really given? Where do the ultimate loyalties lie? Although some parishioners may verbalize easily about the God they encounter in Jesus Christ, their behavior may indicate, instead, that they actually worship money—or sex or power or work or anything else that demands and receives their major concern and devotion. The pastor needs to ask, What is the primary value around which this person's life is centered?

3. What Is the Sense of Sin and What Role Does Sin Play in This Situation?

The root meaning and cause of sin for Augustine, as for Paul, is idolatry: we worship the gift rather than the Giver. The question about sin also has two aspects.

First, what is this individual's sense of sin, if any? Does guilt appear to be present? If so, does the guilt refer to identifiable wrongs actually committed, or does it reflect something more general—feelings of unworthiness, a self-deprecating attitude? Does the individual accept personal responsibility or shift the blame to some scapegoat? Is the person's awareness of sin experienced only as a sense of shame or remorse, or does it involve also, in the biblical sense, repentance and the intention to change for the better?

Second, what is the impact of "corporate" sin on this situation? Is the person being deformed or destroyed by group, communal, or societal structures that oppress and dehumanize? Is the individual experiencing social injustice? Is she suffering from the effects of sexual stereotyping and prejudice simply because she is a woman? The pastor must attend to the individual sin on the one hand, and to societal evil on the other, discerning the impact of each on the individual.

4. What Is This Person's Relative Capacity for Faith?

Often it is assumed that every person has a completely adequate capacity for faith. In a sense this is true, for no one is beyond God's ability to reach. It may be overly optimistic, however, for the pastor to assert, "All you need is to have faith."

The depressed teenage boy who was extensively abused as a child and has never lived in one home for more than two years may not sense that the world is indeed hospitable and the people in it good. He may believe that the only good is what he gets for himself, that all of creation is primarily evil, and that no one can be trusted. The scarring that has occurred in such a life should not be ignored or taken lightly.

It would be a tragedy, of course, if all capacity for faith were to be denied. Almost as bad, however, is the easy idealism that embraces unreal expectations for the growth of faith.

5. How Does This Person View Salvation?

Salvation is the central promise of the Christian faith. But how does this particular person view it?

Luther noted that Christian faith lives *sola gratia, sola fide*–by grace alone, by faith alone. He pointed to Paul's claim that salvation is a free gift of God irrespective of what we do. Some people who pay lip service to this belief in God's initiative still act as if their true worth comes only from what they do. For others, salvation is a one-time event to which they can point with assurance, but which has little or no impact on the way they presently live their lives. They do not recognize that life in Christ is not something static, but involves a relationship that constantly needs to be nourished.

Is the salvation this person desires and affirms all-encompassing, or is it narrowly understood? For many people, salvation means little more than deliverance from a terrible marriage, poverty, or physical suffering. In pastoral care, then, we attempt to note what specific shape or form the desire for salvation takes in any given instance, and we evaluate it in light of our theological understanding. Does the salvation being sought here bring freedom and well-being, or will it bring only further bondage?

6. How Adequate Are This Person's Faith-Support Resources?

Beyond the pastoral relationship, which we assume will continue, what other groups of people and what other institutionalized traditions of help are available? To the degree that people live outside a supportive and loving community, their problems usually increase in severity.

The church has at times portrayed the family as the basic unit of spiritual nurture and support. In the case of this individual, how effectively is the family providing such support? Is there an openness to other support groups–neighbors, Alcoholics Anonymous, individual or family therapy groups, the church? Is the congregation willing to provide support through individuals or fellowship groups?

A good support group is important not simply in understanding and appreciating the problem, but also in enabling the individual to build upon personal strengths and come to experience new and healthier relationships. If involved in the life of a congregation, how does this person understand and relate to "the body of Christ?" Finally, how does this person experience community, or the lack of it, through such communal events as prayer, scripture reading and study, meditation, contemplation, worship, and congregational fellowship?

7. *What Sense of Hope Exists?*

How does this person live with the "already now but not yet" tension of eschatological hope? In the midst of suffering, what is concretely expected of self, pastor, and God?

How often we hear some prominent guest on a late-night TV talk show blandly assert: "You can do anything you want, as long as you want it badly enough and work for it hard enough!" How often we have been told that if only we pray fervently enough and have enough faith, God will grant our desires. Such notions abound in popular psychology and in popular religion as well.

Most of us recognize, when we reflect a bit, that we are *not* living the life we once envisioned. We *cannot* become anything we want, nor can we make others into just anything they, or we, want. Just as Paul did, we often stand helpless before that "thorn in the flesh," which is uniquely our own. Eschatological hope recognizes a tension–"already now but not yet." The kingdom of God has indeed come, but it is not fully here, not yet, either for the individual or for society.

Is there in the present instance, we ask, a recognition of this tension? Does that recognition produce a sense of freedom in the acceptance of limits, or does the person continue to pursue aims that are wholly beyond the realm of possibility? Has a recognition of limits led to despair? How, for example, does the gay male respond to his own sexuality and to a world that for the most part despises his sexual preference? How in his close relationships does he live with being labeled as different? What expectations does he place on members of the local or larger Christian and secular communities? Does he give up his vision for life, or hold onto it tenaciously in spite of realities? Is his hope based on realistic possibilities or only on a "pie in the sky?"

Part and parcel of living with this tension–the "already now but not yet"–is the way one responds ethically to this world. God's love, when it comes to us, obliges us to "love the neighbor." How is the person before us responding to this obligation? Responses can run the gamut from amoral anarchy to rigid perfectionism, when people are experiencing broken relationships with God. On the other hand, in people who have a sound relationship with God, there must be at least hints of a healthy sense of filial and agapic responsibility.

8. Does Freedom Exist Between This Person and Me?

The final question brings the focus back to the pastoral relationship. Where once we asked why this person is coming to *me*, now we ask, "Am I providing the greatest amount of freedom possible?"

You think, for example, that the couple before you is not working as hard as you are to prevent their divorce. But does this judgment perhaps reflect a personal struggle to save your own troubled marriage? Does it reflect your own need to be successful as a counselor? We need to ask *ourselves*, "Must I succeed, or can I allow myself to 'fail'?" Or even, "Can my pastoral assessment be wrong?"

Assessment in care, like diagnosis in medicine, is an art as well as a science. It requires education, training, and much experience. We must always be flexible, open, and ready to admit to having misinterpreted the situation. A theological template is not carved in stone. The assessing must be attentive, cautious, and continually up for review.

Finally, in this regard, we ask, "Am I open to allowing this parishioner to minister to me?" The question does not imply confusion about who is pastor and who is asking for help, but it does mean acknowledging that in the course of our ministering, we actually receive as well as give. The ministry we have received from God includes the privilege of receiving another person's trust. And in the faces that look trustfully toward us for help, we experience the face of God. Within the very pain and suffering that comes our way, God comes to us too.

PASTORAL ASSESSMENT IN PRACTICE

These eight questions model a method of pastoral assessment that may be worth trying. A concrete case can illustrate its practicability and keep it from being merely an intellectual exercise. It may even point out the nature and usefulness of the theological template in pastoral care.

On a Sunday afternoon in late October, the telephone rang at the quiet home of Pastor Paul Williams just as he was settling down in a comfortable sofa to watch his favorite team on TV. A distraught male voice at the other end asked to see the pastor as soon as possible. The problem was described only as "a real emergency." Paul agreed to meet the man at the church office in thirty minutes.

When he arrived, the pastor was met by the distraught man, who was accompanied by his wife. Neither Gerald nor Jennie were members of the congregation; they had been referred by a member who was their neighbor. Gerald was a Caucasian, possibly in his late thirties, middle-class in appearance. Jennie, also Caucasian, appeared to be in her mid-thirties, attractive, and well-dressed. Gerald had a distended abdomen, a sickly pale complexion, and seemed physically shaken. His voice trembled as he spoke, and he was on the verge of tears. Jennie was composed and soft-spoken, but the picture of fatigue.

When Pastor Williams asked, "How can I be of help?" Jennie told of her decision to end their twelve-year marriage. She spoke of Gerald's drinking problem over ten of the past twelve years and indicated that her husband was unwilling to admit his alcoholism and his need of help. She concluded by repeating her firm decision to divorce him, "I cannot live a life of watching him drink himself to death." When Pastor Williams asked why she had accompanied her husband here to the office, she acknowledged her desire to be supportive in Gerald's efforts at getting help for himself.

Gerald tearfully responded to the pastor's question, this time addressed to him, by admitting his drinking problem and saying he realized he was losing what he cherished most in life–his wife. He further admitted his desire for help, but made a strong appeal for Jennie to give him another chance. He begged her forgiveness and explicitly reminded her of Jesus' teaching on the need to forgive a person who was truly sorry.

As the conversation continued, Pastor Williams learned that this couple had no children and very few friends; their respective sets of parents lived at opposite ends of the state. Both husband and wife were employed, apparently experiencing successful work relationships. There appeared to be no evidence of Gerald's drinking having interfered with his work.

In summary, their problem was verbalized in two ways. The wife's position was: "I am divorcing him, but I care enough to want him to get help." The husband's position was: "I have a drinking problem, and I want help; but I also want her to stay and give me another chance."

Pastoral assessment began with the first meeting and involved immediate use of a theological template. Paul reflected on question one in order to understand the expectations these people had brought with them to his office.

Initially, at least, it appeared that Jennie regarded the pastor not as a reconciler, but as one through whom her husband might be able to get help for his alcoholism. The couple had no prior acquaintance with Pastor Williams. Perhaps they sought him out because their neighbor had characterized him as an understanding and helpful person. Jennie clearly assumed that a pastor would have ties with other relevant helpers in the community.

Gerald, on the other hand, did not see the pastor primarily as a means of attaining further help with his alcoholism. He responded instead to the image of the pastor as "moral teacher," as potential leverage for persuading his wife not to leave him. In effect, Gerald was saying to his wife, "The pastor will agree with me that you should forgive me." He may also have had some awareness that his (and their) problems were bigger than he could handle and that he needed some form of divine assistance.

Pastor Williams regarded Jennie's expectations as the more realistic of the two. He wondered if Gerald's expectations might be indicative of a style of manipulative relating, although he could not, of course, dismiss altogether the ethical question raised by the husband.

In this first encounter, question two, about God, found little in the way of direct expression. Brief reference was made to Jesus, implying the authority of Jesus' teachings, but only in the context of Gerald's effort to convince Jennie that she was wrong to choose a divorce. What or who was the husband's God? What determines Gerald's decision making? Tentatively, one might answer that Gerald's God was nothing but an idol–the bottle, or whatever the bottle offered him. Gerald's claim that his most cherished relationship was that with his wife seemed to be contradicted by his actual history. Jennie's understanding of God did not become at all apparent in this initial visit.

Question three asks about the role of sin. Gerald's drinking problem and manipulativeness revealed a person who had placed himself at the center of his own existence. His past choices had resulted in the actual destruction of his marriage and the potential destruction of his own body. Guilt was perceived not so much in Gerald's asking his wife's forgiveness as in Jennie's comment that he had been drinking himself to death. What guilt would cause him to inflict such a severe self-punishment? By not taking Gerald at his word the moment he asked for forgiveness, the pastor was demonstrating his own assessment that repentance was not yet at hand.

Pastor Williams believed that the topics of faith and salvation, raised in questions four and five, had not yet been broached, at least as far as the husband was concerned. What was Gerald's capacity for faith? What was his conception of salvation? Had he in fact drunk himself into oblivion? Regarding the wife, the pastor thought he saw some signs of faith; she trusted others to help a person she could no longer help. She may even have been trusting her husband, feeling perhaps for the first time that he was about to choose life over death. She saw her salvation, at this time, primarily as deliverance from the daily exposure to her husband's slow suicide. As with most people in crisis, Jennie was having difficulty seeing beyond immediate relief to larger personal needs.

With respect to question six, the pastor had deep concerns. Both people seemed isolated from any recognizable faith support group; they were not a part of the fellowship of believers. Besides himself, Gerald apparently had only a few nameless and not very close relationships at work that could conceivably constitute any kind of support network.

Question seven, about living within the "already now but not yet" tension, was difficult to answer because neither person showed any clear sense of direction—except for Jennie's wanting to get out. Yet, even in her, the pastor did not detect despair. She seemed to be accepting her finitude realistically, recognizing that after she had done all she could to help change her husband, she now had to abandon him to others. Gerald was still testing his finitude, refusing to recognize limits; there was no clear recognition of God as the provider of all strength and succor for the future, only a slight hint of some movement in this direction signaled by his going to a minister.

Question eight is as important as question one. How did Pastor Williams feel about these people? He did not like being pulled away from the football game. Had anger over losing his personal time perhaps diminished his ability to listen? Had it caused him to be condemning in his judgments? Did the prominence of the drinking problem trigger his apparent sympathy with the wife? Was she viewed in a morally superior light as the long-suffering wife simply because the interview had not produced much data about her as a person? Was the pastor's hope for these people and for their marriage tainted by his frustrations over the long years of marriage counseling with couples who opted anyway for divorce?

These then were some of the initial queries with which Pastor Williams began his assessment process. They helped him focus and apply a theological template to his pastoral care. On the basis of such a theological assessment, he would develop a response that might include a whole range of possibilities: continuing pastoral relationship, medical examination, decision counseling, Alcoholics Anonymous and Al-Anon, involvement with a church fellowship, theological confrontation, spiritual guidance, marriage counseling. His systematic reflection helped him develop a much broader and deeper understanding of Gerald and Jennie than might otherwise have been possible. If his relationship with them did in fact continue, as it was expected to do, Pastor Williams' assessment would undergo repeated refinement through continued use of his theological template.

As pastoral care returns to its roots, it will rediscover the significance of its own theological perspective as a primary frame of reference—as a template for correlating with the specific personal situations encountered in pastoral care. The template suggested here is, of course, only one such framework, but it is offered in the hope that it may prove helpful as a methodological aid for pastors in the self-conscious formulation of their own theological templates. The acknowledgment and active use of the theological template in pastoral assessment will be key to our much-needed correlation of theology and pastoral care.

NOTE

1. Paul Pruyser, *The Minister as Diagnostician* (Philadelphia: Westminster Press, 1976).

Chapter 3

The Word

Protestants today, as part of their legacy from the Reformation, still think of ministry as essentially proclamation of the Word and administration of the sacraments. Unfortunately, in too many instances this notion of a ministry of Word and sacraments has had little influence on current pastoral care theory and practice. In fact, pastoral care in our time has had difficulty recognizing any relationship whatsoever to ministry itself, and particularly to a ministry of Word and sacraments. Fancy verbal footwork has often been required to portray pastoral care as being any more central to the task of ministry than, say, the coaching of a basketball team in the church gymnasium.

The development of nondirective counseling may have contributed to this situation, helping push pastoral care to the fringes of ministry. Developed in the 1940s and 1950s under Carl Rogers, this modern psychotherapeutic model breathed fresh life into a practice that had come to be steeped in an outmoded tradition. The earlier traditional methods of pastoral care had been creating increasing discomfort among its practitioners. Pastors had begun to recognize that their parishioners were no longer satisfied with facile answers, even if taken directly from the Bible. These easy answers did not take seriously the concrete realities of today's human situations. As attitudes toward authority in general began to change, people also grew less willing to accept the authoritative solutions offered by their pastors, authorities who often did not listen carefully to their cries of pain or try to understand the real issues they were confronting; certainly, pastors were not integral to any specific solutions to

This chapter originally appeared as "Word of God and Pastoral Care" in *Encounter*, 44 (Autumn 1983), pp. 369-389. Reprinted by permission.

their problems. It was through the newer nondirective counseling methods that pastors began to learn skills of authentic listening and of establishing rapport. Drawing upon psychology and counseling to further their caregiving abilities, pastors who had been trained in the older methodologies now began to find increasing opportunities for intervening helpfully in the lives of their parishioners. The newer nondirective model proved as popular as it was beneficial. Because it relied so heavily on eductive guidance, however, eliciting from people's own lives and values the criteria for decision making, pastors who were drawn to it also lost to some degree their ministerial identity.[1]

Now the essence of pastoral care, as of all ministry sharing in the legacy of the Reformation, is the proclamation or communication of the Word–that Word which became flesh, lived among us, and died reconciling us with God. Caregiving that is truly pastoral proclaims this message. Therefore, it is not something on the fringes of ministry, but at its very center.

THE WORD OF GOD

What is the Word of God? An understanding of "Word" in biblical parlance involves several considerations.[2]

The Hebrew Bible makes little or no distinction between a word itself and the thing or event implied by that word. *Dabar* (word) could represent an event in history or nature as well as a spoken or written word. When God spoke in the creation story, the world was created: "By the Word of the Lord the heavens were made" (Ps. 33:6). The Word was God's way of acting! The Word was also the typical way by which God's will was made known and providential guidance offered to the world. "Word of the Lord" is an expression used to denote a medium of revelation: Yahweh speaks (e.g., "the Word of the Lord that came to . . .") and the prophet hears.

In the New Testament "the Word" (usually *logos*) takes on additional connotations. James Sanders points to six basic usages: the Old Testament law (e.g., Mark 7:13); a particular Old Testament passage (John 10:35); God's revealed will (Luke 11:28); the word proclaimed by Jesus (Luke 5:1); the Christian message (Luke 8:11);

and the incarnate Christ (John 1:1-14). In this last passage, "Word" is used as a title for Christ himself.[3]

Even a brief review of these biblical understandings of "the Word" helps not only to clarify the concept, but also to provide the basis for viewing pastoral care in terms of the Word. Pastoral care involves both proclamation (or communication) of the Word and a mutual listening for it and speaking it. Our cursory reflection on the meanings of *dabar* and *logos* suggests four key considerations: the Word is God's revelation to humanity; it establishes and extends relationship; it is the mode of communication of the faith; and it is expressed both verbally (as spoken or written) and visibly (as act).[4]

GOD'S REVELATION TO HUMANITY

As the communication of God's will to us, the Word is the incarnation of the Totally Other in our midst. To quote Edward Schillebeeckx,

> In and through His historically conditioned humanity, Christ is the revelation of God in our midst. Thus He is the Word of God: God Himself, the Son, speaking personally to man in the man Jesus. A fellow man, who treats us person-to-person, is personally God, the Son. Each truly human act of Christ is therefore a Word of God directed toward mankind, more strongly so than the Old Testament history of salvation.[5]

C. K. Barrett's commentary on John notes that both in the church and in philosophy, *logos* was a common term describing a process of self-expression.[6] In this sense, the Word is God's ongoing self-communication, God's revelation or reaching out to humanity. It is the communication that takes place in the God-human relationship. It is the word of promise, the promise of redemption. Finally, it is the proclamation that God will forgive our sin, not because we are deserving, but because God is the loving and merciful One who cares for us and desires our fellowship.

Gerhard Ebeling, in summarizing the biblical witness, points out:

> Word of God, according to the biblical tradition, thus seeks to be understood as a word event that does not go out of date but

constantly renews itself, does not create closed areas of special interest but opens up the world, does not enforce uniformity but is linguistically creative. Of course it is startling–but only because it reveals what was hidden. Certainly it is tradition, yet tradition of a kind that sets us free for our own present. Whatever is put forth as Word of God is certainly changed into an antiquated, constricting word that enslaves us, and thus becomes the opposite of what the Word of God is, whenever it is denied responsible participation in the word event.[7]

The Word is thus a living proclamation that occurs in a specific situation. It is not an abstract philosophical concept, a pseudonym for "reason." It is not an impersonal force in the universe. The Word is One who shows personal interest in us–who establishes a relationship with us. As Rudolph Bultmann has said, "If we return to the real significance of 'word,' implying as it does a relationship between speaker and hearer, then the word can become an event to the hearer, because it brings him into this relationship."[8]

ESTABLISHING AND EXTENDING RELATIONSHIP

God addresses us in the Word; in the Word we encounter the One who is indeed with us. This meeting of God and person in the Word has about it a sense of call–the call into relationship. The Word is still God, but God as Word shows an intense interest in each of us. The emphasis is not on a passive word–not marks on parchment–but on a living, active, vital occurrence. The Word enters our lives as a creative force, motivating, prompting, and enlivening us. Through it, we are brought into God's presence; we come to stand before God, as the Reformers put it, *coram deo.*

As in an intimate relationship, in which deep feelings, secrets, hopes, and wishes are shared, so in the Word, God is revealed to us. Thus, revelation is not only general (as in nature) or specific (as in written scriptures), but also intensely personal, tailored to each of us. The Word specifically addresses every individual as individual–as a person possessed of personality, intuition, likes, dislikes, woes, and joys.

God's revelation addresses us in human form—through other people, art, drama, literature, and our own thoughts and visions. Whenever God speaks to us, there is a new incarnation of the Word—one that is directed to us in, through, and by a human word. This Word is God in personal relationship, and the message it brings is an intimate, personalized revelation.

Because of the character of Word as incarnational address to the people of God, every human experience is potentially revelatory. No boundaries of denomination, dogma, or religious practice determine God's self-revelation through the Word. Neither do race, class, social standing, I.Q., educational level, gender, mental health, emotional stability, temperament, cleanliness, or perfect pitch. God's Word can encounter us at any place, in any hour, through any event.

This is why we must listen. We must be prepared to hear the Word in any and every circumstance. The Christian who is obsessed with doing, even the doing of honest and upright things, and has little time either for quiet reflection and meditation or for genuine engagement with others, runs the risk of disregarding the Word and missing what God has to say.

COMMUNICATION OF THE FAITH

Every communication of the gospel involves an appearance of the Word embodied in human form. The term *communication* has two basic meanings: (1) it can refer to the passing along of information, as in a help wanted ad listing the types of employment available at a new industrial plant; or (2) communication can also be understood as personal sharing, including emotional elements as well as intellectual content.

In effect, what distinguishes these two types of communication is commonly conveyed in the prepositional distinction between *about* and *of*. The first type—passing along information—is verbal; whether written or spoken, it involves the conveying of data *about* something that may or may not be useful for the listener or reader to *know*. With the second type—personal sharing—a relationship is established or extended; a part *of* one's self is offered in such a way that what is imparted is available for *experiencing*. In the case of the former, the speaker-listener relationship is strictly "business" (in

Martin Buber's terms, an I-It relationship), with the listener being merely an "object" or observer. In the case of the latter, true encounter occurs between speaker and listener (an I-Thou relationship), and attending concern and compassion are expressed.

Dissociating the two modes of communication may not be altogether helpful, or even possible. For example, an advertisement for a job may communicate more to me than mere information about an available position; it may create within me excitement, hope, and anticipation of a new possibility. Likewise, in the sharing of a personal encounter, facts germane to the relationship in process may also be transmitted. In both instances, the communication has an impact on the listener–the person is somehow altered because of what happens.

In communication of the faith, what happens is an encounter with God the Word. It is a message not merely *about* the Word but *of* the Word:

> When faith and God are put together, we may put it thus: We are not concerned just with a piece of information about God, but with participation in him, that is, with an event in which God himself is communicated. If what I have already briefly said is right, then such a communication would be a true meeting with God, and it would not be in the least preposterous, but perfectly appropriate, that this meeting with God should take place in the word as an event.
>
> Of course, it is not any and every word about God that is a communication of faith, that is, that can communicate the faith which is a participation in God himself. To use the language of the biblical tradition, it is the Word of God alone which can do this.[9]

A word is never merely a "word"; it is also an expression of one's self in relation to another. The power of the word is the power of *being* itself; it embraces emotion, is relational, and addresses our past, present, and future. The followers of Jesus transmitted the word of Christ; they "went about preaching the word" (Acts 8:4). It was not a word *about* Christ but indeed *the* Word that God was embodied *in* Christ.

THE VERBAL AND VISIBLE WORD

Communication is both verbal and nonverbal. Gestures, as well as words, portray meaning. A gentle touch can tell more than a thousand words; a look can communicate an indescribable feeling. Crucial ideas can be made explicit by a gesture, deep meanings by an image. Likewise, God's Word is both verbally articulated and visually presented to us. Robert Jenson makes the point:

> The word in which God—for the present, *any* God—communicates himself must be an embodied word, a word "with" some visible reality, a grant of divine objectivity. We must be able to see and touch what we are to apprehend from God . . . A disembodied, purely linguistic communication, however it might occur and whoever or whatever might be able so to speak, could not reveal God. God's presence must grant an object.[10]

Revelation occurs as the Word is embodied. God reveals God's self (as in Christ) in both spoken and visible form.

"The Word comes to the element; and so there is a sacrament, that is, a sort of visible Word."[11] Augustine's famous sacramental phrase has been interpreted and reinterpreted throughout the centuries. Although understandings of "the visible Word" have varied, one major theme has remained constant: when God speaks to us, the Word comes through some element, some form of visible reality. In terms of the sacrament, the Word of God is the wafer broken or the water gently sprinkled. Augustine seems to suggest that liturgies and rites gain their efficacy from the Word, from God's communication with God's people. The elements in the sacrament are God's way of securing the Word in our sensory world, thus making it accessible to us.

Although Augustine and most of his early interpreters contrasted visible Word and invisible Word, the Reformers shifted the emphasis. They contrasted the visible with the verbal, spoken, or audible Word, focusing on the distinction between hearing and the other senses. Augustine was reinterpreted to say that God speaks to us not only in language symbols, but also in those images and signs that are seen, touched, tasted, smelled, and grasped—by any of the senses.

This Reformation distinction between the verbal and the sensory ultimately can assist us in our clarification of the meaning of pastoral care as communication of the Word, because in every instance of effective communication, some of the things transmitted are put in the form of sentences (the verbal Word) and some are relayed to the senses in other ways–through gestures, imagery, tones, or tactile impressions (the visible Word).

"The verbal Word," of course, includes more than simply preaching; it also encompasses teaching, scripture reading, and the written or spoken sharing of the gospel. Similarly, "the visible Word" includes more than simply administration of the sacraments; its meaning can be extended even to such things as an icon, Brahms' *Requiem*, a jazz mass, an embrace, time freely given to listen to another, a warm smile, a covered dish meal brought to the recently bereaved, one's ministry of presence, or the sign of the cross. These, too, are all crucial ways in which God comes to us. The supreme instance of the visible Word, of course, is the incarnation of Christ.

God is the Holy Other, inaccessible to us; it is through the incarnation of the Word in gestures, rites, and other elements of the sensory sphere that the hidden is revealed and the truth is spoken visibly, in ways that we can apprehend. To quote Jenson, "The Father knows himself in Jesus' body that walked to the cross, and in the objects that are used and used up in the gospel-communication. That is, he knows them as visible *words.*"[12] Or, from Luther: "God . . . sets before us no word or commandment without including with it something material and outward, and proffering it to us. To Abraham he gave the word including with it his son Isaac [Gen. 15:4 ff.]. To Saul he gave the word including with it the slaying of the Amalekites [I Sam. 15:2 ff.]. To Noah he gave the word including with it the rainbow [Gen. 9:8 ff.]. And so on. You find no word of God in the entire Scriptures in which something material and outward is not contained and presented."[13]

The church generally, and especially the Protestant church since the Reformation, is most familiar with the verbal Word. In fact, in churches that are accustomed to less formal services, the sermon has so moved to the fore that worship has become almost entirely a hearing of the audible articulation of the gospel. Although ministry usually has been understood, even in such churches, as a matter of proclaiming (or preaching) the Word and administering the sacraments, the sacraments are often little more than an appendage to the audible Word.

God, however, is really present in both the verbal Word and the visible Word. The sacraments are not just *signs* derived from God; God is truly there. The sermon is patently not just words *about* God but the Word *of* God. A pastor's empathy for the parents of a dying child is not just a sign of God's love; God has promised to be there. God's desire is to communicate with God's people. As Schillebeeckx has noted, "The whole world of creatures became a 'gratia externa,' an exteriorizing of grace, that is, grace itself in visible operation. Within this world-embracing manifestation of the Lord, the ministry of the Word and the rituals of the sacraments are only the glowing focus of the visible presence of grace."[14]

Words or phrases about God can say what they mean only as they are embodied, only as they become a "visible presence of grace"; for it is only as they are acted out and apprehended that they become the Word of God. The often trite and offhand "God loves you" can become truly alive and meaningful to a person when it is the response offered by a minister who has listened and graciously received and shared the turmoil bound up inside that person's being—then the Word has indeed become flesh and dwells among us.

PASTORAL CARE AS COMMUNICATION OF THE WORD

The Primacy of the Word

Hans Asmussen in his 1934 work *Die Seelsorge* described pastoral care as "proclamation of the Word of God . . . the message is told to the individual face to face."[15] More recently, Paul Tillich said much the same thing: "If we assume the rightful claim of the ministry to be that the minister pronounces, preaches, teaches, and in counseling mediates the 'Word of God,' no question can arise about the relevance of ministry for every human being."[16] The German theologian Eduard Thurneysen agrees: "Proclamation of the Word is therefore the beginning and end of all true pastoral care . . . Pastoral care exists in the church as the communication of the Word of God to individuals. Like every legitimate function of the church, pastoral care springs from the living Word of God given to the church. This Word demands to be communicated in various ways."[17] Although they would vary in their understandings of what constitutes the Word, Asmussen, Thurneysen, and Tillich are at one in pointing to the communication of God's Word as the purpose of pastoral care and counseling.

The Reformers emphasized the primacy of the Word of God in all ministry. For them the Word is more than just an audible message preached during worship. In his treatise *On the Councils and the Church,* Luther asserts, "Now, wherever you hear or see this Word preached, believed, professed, and lived, do not doubt that the true *ecclesia sancta catholica*, 'a Christian holy people,' must be there."[18] Ministry, and indeed the church, exists whenever and wherever the verbal and visible Word is proclaimed. Luther performed pastoral care along with all the other tasks of ministry, including his teaching duties, without dissociating such ministry from his service of the Word.[19] He believed that all ministry arises out of and returns to the Word.

Of course, when the sermon is preached or the liturgy intoned, the minister's service is of necessity formal in nature. It cannot be tailored to one specific person or family in the manner of pastoral care. While care and counseling allow for a more private, individualized mode of proclamation, they still retain the fundamental character of proclamation–communication of the Word.

Even care that is addressed to the most isolated and specific of human concerns must be seen as having its relationship to God's Word. Such care involves listening deeply to these concerns, but always in the light of the Word. Thurneysen illustrates this point:

> Pastoral care is a conversation resting on a very definite assumption. It intends to be a conversation that proceeds from the Word of God and leads to the Word of God . . . At first, they [the two people involved in pastoral care conversation] perhaps do not mention this Word of God and its content at all; instead they speak of certain very concrete problems and concerns of their lives. Even so they proceed on the assumption

that the Word of God whereby they are addressed or are to be addressed is important for these very problems and concerns.[20]

If pastoral care is indeed the communication of the Word, then it must also be done in a hermeneutically responsible way. Instead of interpreting the Word while poring over scripture, commentaries, and theological handbooks, however, the minister accomplishes the hermeneutical task while concretely listening to others pour out their distress. Pastors practice a kind of "trenches hermeneutics." They lack the luxury of being able to lean back in a chair and cogitate on what they have been reading. Instead they must listen *to* the person and *for* the Word simultaneously, and they must structure their care in response to the event of the Word. It was pointed out at the end of the previous chapter that in concrete care situations, the correlation of theology and pastoral care frequently happens almost automatically. Indeed, pastors rely on their prior theological reflection—listening to the Word—to shape their present responses to other people.

This task of interpreting God's Word cannot be bypassed in the name of providing concrete, issue-oriented counsel. Psychological counseling, of course, can greatly enhance the quality of the care being offered to specific people, even in the midst of the mutual listening for the Word. However, it can also easily supplant the hermeneutical task of the minister so that God's Word is not heard at all and pastoral care deteriorates from proclamation into social work. Beneficial as it may be, social work is not pastoral care; its purpose is rather different. The purpose of pastoral care is to listen to and speak the Word.

Two Modes of the Word

The Word, I have said, is the communication of God that, addressing us both verbally and visibly, establishes relationships. Verbally, the Word is transmitted through preaching, teaching, and the scriptures; visibly, the Word comes through the sacrament, acts of kindness, and the ministry of presence.

Pastoral care must be alert to this twofold mode of address. In actual practice, it has often ignored one of these two manifestations of the Word. Traditional pastoral care, with its emphasis on inductive guidance and urging the cared-for to adopt *a priori* values as the basis for decision making, elevated the speaking of the Word at the expense of listening deeply to a person's own pain or distress. A legacy from the nineteenth century, it did not take seriously the learnings from contemporary psychology, but instead used as key resources the scriptures, occasional services, and prayer. It frequently consisted of the pastor telling parishioners, ostensibly on the basis of scripture or tradition, what they must do. In effect, it was conversational preaching tailored to the pastor's view of the parishioner's problem. Indeed, it might be said that traditional pastoral care strongly emphasized the verbal Word in a ministry of speaking while often ignoring the visible Word.

The nondirective approach of Carl Rogers, coming as a welcome reaction to this traditional care, helped pastors listen more carefully and establish a solid relationship of rapport. It took more seriously the learnings of modern psychology. The pastor became less of a distant parent figure and more of an emotionally close friend. This warm confidant, at once friend and pastor, changed pastoral care from a ministry of speaking the Word through scripture and prayer to a ministry of compassion. A verbal Word, addressing such matters as sin, grace, and God's intervention in our lives, however, was rarely spoken. It might even be said that nondirective pastoral care strongly emphasized the visible Word in a ministry of presence while often ignoring the verbal Word.

Charles Gerkin has characterized the dilemma common to pastors caught between the traditional and the nondirective approaches:

> Faced with persons suffering the double crisis of chaotic experience and muddled faith, the pastor may well be tempted in two opposite directions both leading toward pastoral identity crisis. Speaking the right words that no longer evoke the expected response becomes a vacuous exercise that leads to the despair of having been rendered impotent. On the other hand, there is the temptation so to identify with the bewilderment and confusion of the doubting victim of crisis that the pastor becomes a victim of that doubt that renders ministry an apology. Somewhere between these two extremes of verbally faithful ministry that fails to communicate, and debilitating doubts

that forsakes the pastoral task, the Christian pastor must find his or her integrity.[21]

While it is easy to be swayed in either one of these two directions, it is difficult, but most essential, to find that elusive middle between the extremes. Recalling that the Word is communicated both verbally and visibly may be the key to restoring integrity to pastoral ministry. Indeed, pastoral care that is faithful to the Word of God attends to both the verbal Word and the visible Word. God communicates to and establishes relationships with people in both verbal and visible ways. Pastoral care that emphasizes only one mode of the Word is less than faithful to God's own manner of communication. We need pastoral care that incorporates both modes of address. Sometimes, a hug, an attending glance, or a listening ear will be just right; at other times, a verbal articulation of God's love in Christ will give impact to the Word.

People exercise considerable discrimination when it comes to choosing the person with whom they will share their burdens. People hurting do not come to their minister primarily because the pastor is available and service is cheap; they do not come only for a listening ear or a fresh affirmation of their personhood. Many come precisely because the pastor symbolizes that Other who, they sense, can somehow help inject meaning into their struggles. Then, if we neglect to speak to them of God, offering only uncritical warmth and affirmation, we give the people a stone rather than the Bread of Life; instead of providing eternal nourishment, we simply nurture good feelings for the short term. When issues of sin, guilt, and reconciliation in Christ are at the root of the matter, we may be proffering nothing but psychological techniques. We must be alert to–caught up in the ministry of–imparting the verbal Word.

Ministers, of course, can easily be too quick with words, too ready with facile solutions. We need to appreciate the power of the visible Word. Bonhoeffer said it well:

> Let us ask why it is that precisely in thoroughly grave situations, for instance when I am with someone who has suffered a bereavement, I often decide to adopt a "penultimate" attitude . . . remaining silent as a sign that I share in the bereaved man's helplessness in the face of such a grievous event, and not

speaking the biblical words of comfort which are, in fact, known to me and available to me. Why am I often unable to open my mouth, when I ought to give expression to the ultimate? And why, instead, do I decide on an expression of thoroughly penultimate human solidarity? Is it from mistrust of the power of the ultimate Word? Is it from fear of men? Or is there some good positive reason for such an attitude, namely, that my knowledge of the Word, my having it at my finger-tips, in other words my being, so to speak, spiritually master of the situation, bears only the appearance of the ultimate, but is in reality itself something entirely penultimate? Does one not in some cases, by remaining deliberately in the penultimate, perhaps point all the more genuinely to the ultimate, which God will speak in His own time?[22]

And in such situations the visual Word can sometimes verify (or refute) the spoken Word.

In pastoral care we stand between the Word and the deeply troubled person. The caregiver has the potential, as Tillich put it, to "mediate" God's Word to this other individual. The situation is similar to our experience at a ballet. The dancers, by their physical movements, express emotion and narrate the story, while the libretto with its text helps clarify and augment these movements, actually enhancing the visual impression. But each needs the other. The movements without the libretto or the libretto without the movements would reduce the total impact that might otherwise be had from verbally reading what the dance is about while visually seeing it in all its raw emotion. The total experience comes from a proper blending of the two. In pastoral care, the dancer's movements may transmit God's love, but the libretto clarifies it and gives it a name—Christ.

The Uncontrollable Word

When we encounter what is not a part of our understanding, as Bonhoeffer suggests, and what we can never know in any given pastoral care situation, is precisely when a penultimate word, whether verbal or visible, may become ultimate. A word or a gesture, a recitation of John 3:16 or a spontaneous embrace, a verbal sharing of the transformation made in our lives by Christ's presence, or a period of quiet empathetic listening–any one or more of these events can become the ultimate Word. Each is potentially transforming. Each can mean the changing of human articulations or gesticulations into the Word of God. The frail, finite presence of the pastor can become a window through which the person in pain catches a glimpse of the infinite.

From the general discussion up to this point, it might perhaps seem as if God's Word would come naturally and automatically to the troubled person through the use of proper care and counseling methods involving both verbal and visible expressions. That impression is quite false. The serious danger in such a view lies in the assumption that it is we ministers who cause the Word to come. As pastoral caregivers, we are right to see ourselves as bearers of Christ to other people, but wrong to assume that we are that because of what we do. Caregivers who hold such a notion have lost sight of the *pneuma* that blows where it wishes and is not controlled by our actions (John 3:8). The Word of God is uncontrollable; we can neither manipulate it nor force it. Faith comes only through the work of the Holy Spirit. Only as the Word of God claims the mannerisms and formulations of our sermon, or the gestures and phrases of our pastoral act, do they become Word–what Bonhoeffer called ultimate.

For Luther, "All that our body does outwardly and physically, if God's Word is added to it and it is done through faith, is in reality and in name done spiritually."[23] Our care becomes spiritual care only when the alien Word transforms it. As God's coworkers, (I Cor. 3:1-9) we reach out and admonish other people (II Cor. 5:20), not as if all is dependent on us, but rather with gentleness, sincerity, and tenderness, as we wait for the One who both wills and does (Phil. 2:13).

John Cobb said it well: "Pastors above all will know that they are at most midwives of God's grace."[24] And the people we serve will know that neither the awareness of sin nor the certainty of forgiveness and reconciliation comes from us; both are awakened–in the pastoral caregiver as well as in the parishioner–solely by God's Word through the moving of the Spirit. Thus, the Word is communicated not *by* the pastor, but *through* the pastor as the Spirit transforms the pastoral care encounter.

LISTENING FOR AND SPEAKING THE WORD

Mutual Listening for the Word

"So faith comes from what is heard" (Rom. 10:17; cf. Gal. 3:2, 5). Paul repeatedly asserts that the hearing of the Word precedes faith. Luther reiterates Paul's stress on hearing: "If you want to obtain grace, then see to it that you hear the Word of God attentively or meditate on it diligently. The Word, I say, and only the Word, is the vehicle of God's grace."[25]

In so many ways, contemporary society places humans at the center of the universe, assuring us that whatever we have or are is determined by what we ourselves do. It is only natural for us, then, in matters of faith, to assume that here, too, we can always attain our own righteousness. This self-centered belief can be changed in only one way–by hearing and accepting the Word of God. For the Word declares firmly and clearly that our justification, in fact, whatever good we do, is wholly the result of an alien Word. It is only as we are addressed from the outside that we are reconciled; it is only as we listen that we can begin to understand God's will for us and be declared righteous.

Pastoral care involves listening for the Word of God. It does not assume that it has authoritative control of the Word. It recognizes, as Luther pointed out, that every Christian must daily "creep unto your baptism."[26] The caregiver's task is not merely to proclaim the Word to the parishioner; caregiver and cared-for alike–both being frail, fragile, and sinful creatures–must mutually and humbly await the address of the Word.

This waiting for the Word does not mean that pastoral care is purely passive. It does not mean that we cannot use the best available psychological methods, although at times we will eschew them. It does not mean that we can avoid the responsibility of preparing ourselves to be the best pastoral caregivers we can possibly be although, at times, it seems that much of our training is for naught. It does not mean that we should not carefully and keenly listen to the other, for what comes to us in and through the other's utterances often is God's Word.

Our mutual waiting for the Word does mean that we cannot predict God's address. It does mean that God may sometimes choose the pain of another as a vehicle of revelation for us. It does mean that as two of us speak in the pastoral care event, as two of us listen to each other, we also listen attentively in order to hear the Word.

This waiting for the Word's address can change for the better many aspects of the care being offered today. Our care need not be so frenzied, so doing-oriented, so worried. Though as pastors we do everything we can to care for other people, ultimate care comes as a gift from the outside—as an alien Word that finds us when and where it will. Faith involves the assurance that God's Word *will* come, but not the knowledge of when or how. As Thurneysen put it, "Listening to our neighbor, we shall at the same time listen to the Word of God and seek to perceive its answer to our neighbor's problem."[27]

Speaking the Word

"When Christians live together the time must inevitably come when in some crisis one person will have to declare God's Word and will to another . . . Nothing can be more cruel than the tenderness that consigns another to his sin. Nothing can be more compassionate than the severe rebuke that calls a brother back from the path of sin."[28] In pastoral care, we wait for the Spirit's address, which meets us in both the visible and the verbal. But, as Bonhoeffer has so eloquently stated, there is a time in the care we offer others when a verbal Word must be spoken, when we must attempt to speak the Word of God to those others—be it a word of judgment or of grace. To be silent, to withhold this word in the name of compassion, would be cruel—a departure from the proclamatory task of pastoral care.

To construe pastoral care in terms of proclamation is not to ignore the difficulty of the task of speaking about God today. Indeed, as we noted in the "Introduction," it may be easier in our time and culture to talk to others about such taboo subjects as sex than it is to speak to them about faith in Christ. If pastoral care is supposed to involve the speaking of God's Word, then it has an onerous and challenging task. Perhaps this is why pastoral care, being obliged to speak of God in a "post-Christian" culture, has tended to fall into one of two camps—communicating either the verbal at the expense of the visible or the visible at the expense of the verbal.

Practitioners of traditional pastoral care speak *about* God but frequently fail to establish rapport with the person to whom they speak; in their stress on the verbal, they neglect the visible Word, forgetting that God communicates to us not mechanically but within the framework of an intimate relationship. On the other hand, practitioners of the nondirective approach, aware that God's Word is incarnate in a relationship, forget that God not only *shows* God's Word, God also secures it *verbally*. Out of deference for the person to whom they speak and for the delicacy of a communication that cannot be forced, they lose the ability to speak about God at all, and distrusting the power of the verbal Word about God, they often say nothing. Gerhard Ebeling pinpoints our exacting task in speaking of God today:

> We must not irresponsibly continue to talk of God, nor irresponsibly stop doing so. Yet to a disquieting extent both things are happening today. And both are poisonous, albeit in different ways . . .
>
> Now, however, we find ourselves in an age in which responsible talk of God has to satisfy extreme demands. Never before was there so great a gulf between the linguistic tradition of the Bible and the language that is actually spoken. Hence, never before was it so easy to suspect that God is merely a matter of tradition. Never before was the task of answering for God in our word put before us so radically. The problem today, seen as a whole, is indeed not that there is any lack of institutions and publications which provide possibilities for speaking of God. On the contrary, the problem is how a genuine Word of God is to be asserted in the midst of this tremendous inflation of existing possibilities.[29]

Ebeling goes on to describe most contemporary God-talk as "ghetto language."[30] Although superficial talk of God is everywhere, the languages of academia, business, and science have become so technical that talk about God seems strangely out of place in those milieus. Thus, apart from some occasional vague reference, language about God is reserved for Sunday worship, Christian education, baptism, marriage (maybe), funerals, and certain religious or "devotional" writings. "Talk of God occupies only one narrow sector, and is itself in turn split into many dialects . . . Outside of the appointed reserves it is extraordinarily difficult even in intimate circles to use the word 'God' at all."[31]

Granted, there is this global dissipation of God-talk in our time. It is nonetheless essential that we speak the Word of God in pastoral care. In asserting this, I do not mean to minimize the problem. Merely updating the language, for example, or reformulating it in alluring jargon, surely will not suffice. Although the systematic removal of "thee" and "thou" may help, and the recasting of our images and metaphors from those of an agrarian society into those of a city culture may serve a valid purpose, such attempts can also belie an uneasiness about the real task—indeed a lack of confidence in God and the Word that may be at the heart of our present difficulty. To recast the Word in modern terms, or heroically attempt to proclaim it in spite of all odds, may be to forget that the power of the Word is from God and not from what we do to parse it, adorn it, disguise it, or even improve it. Ebeling put it this way: "Our own age has largely lost the courage—many even believe it has altogether forfeited the possibility—to speak of God."[32]

The courage to proclaim comes not from our own dauntless attempts to "speak it anyway" or disguise it in modern lingo; it arises from the daily nourishment of our own relationship to God within the community of faith. What is needed in pastoral care today is a new and different kind of listening to the Word's address if we are to proclaim the Word courageously in our acts of care.

Could it be that contemporary pastoring, in its frenzy to meet other people's needs, has so invested itself in *doing* as to neglect its prior responsibility of *listening* to the Word? In a technological society with its emphasis on human capacity to alter anything and everything—the environment, government, economy, genes, other people—is it possible that pastoral ministry has tried to manipulate the Word too, and in so doing, lost faith in the Word's intrinsic power? Could it be that in our earnest attempts to "be with" others in their suffering, we have actually taken on their doubts and confusion? Have we forgotten that God's Word is an alien and uncontrollable Word, a Word that even in coming to us does not relinquish to us its sovereignty?

WORD AND INTERVENTION

How is this communication of the Word to be done? For pastors, the most crucial part of our preparation for speaking the Word of God is for each of us to develop an intimate, daily nourished relationship with the Word, and hence, we will become a ministry that is not burned out in frantic doing. As pastoral caregivers, we can be personally receptive to the power of the uncontrollable Word to change lives radically; therefore, we can speak with authentic confidence out of our own experiences with the Word's address. We can approach our ministry of the Word as people acquainted with the Word.

In an age when people are literally bombarded with words on every side, many of us have learned to ignore words as much as possible and even to mistrust whomever speaks them. This is why the visible Word is often so important at the beginning of a pastoral care relationship; it can help provide receptive soil for our verbal messages. As we approach a person in need of care, it is generally best to focus first on establishing a relationship of trust marked by empathy and temporary suspension of judgment, functioning primarily out of the visible Word in a ministry of compassionate presence. To speak the Word of grace or of judgment prematurely will, in most cases, serve only to alienate the person and close off the possibility of any hearing of the Word. Once a relationship has taken hold, the minister cannot be morally neutral (as most psychotherapists claim to be). In fact, there will be times when the verbal Word must be spoken, either to convict of sin or to proclaim release through the Incarnate One. Verbal proclamation occurs not only in sermons or the study of scripture, it is also a central component of all ministry, not least of all pastoral care ministry.

Certain methods of communicating the Word of God verbally in pastoral care have proven historically to be promising—Hasidic storytelling, recovering forms of church discipline that have contemporary relevance, relating parables, labeling experienced events in a way that recognizes the Word's past and present work in a person's life, sharing the impact of the Word on one's own life ("witnessing" revisited), and using biblical narratives as models for living. All of these and more are best used gently—after a trust relationship has been established. After all, the purpose in our using them is not to manipulate or pressure the other person, but to share something of personal importance to ourselves with this other person for whom we care so deeply.

Verbal expression of the Word in any care situation will, of course, be handled quite differently depending on the caregiver's distinctive personality and unique relationship with God. Such expression will emerge from a stance that involves expectant listening to and for the Word. It may take the form of our gently nudging the person torn by guilt to look toward the source of reconciliation, perhaps as a question, "Did Christ die on the cross for everyone except you?" Or it may involve the bearing of a message of hope and peace to a bereaved family in a way that goes beyond simply "being with" them. It could mean confronting a parishioner involved in soft white-collar crime with the full reality of "stealing," no matter how socially acceptable the practice. Of course, there will be times when the introduction of a spoken Word of God may even be superfluous, as Ebeling suggested:

> The Word receives the most explicit character of a promise when the future of the one addressed is involved, and the speaker himself does not promise this or that, but pledges himself and his own future for the future of the other, gives him his Word in the full sense of giving a share in himself. And here is the reason for the ultimate failure of the Word among men. For what happens when one man promises himself to the other? For the most part the Word becomes the bearer and mediator of egotism, inner emptiness, or lies. Yet even at his best man cannot promise true future, that is, salvation, to the other. Only the Word by which God comes to man, and promises himself, is able to do this. That this Word has happened, and can therefore be spoken again and again, that a man can therefore promise God to another as the One who promises himself–this is the certainty of Christian faith. . . .
>
> Word is expressed anew only when it is heard anew, with tense attention to how the traditional Word manages to make itself understood in the real circumstances to which our lives are exposed.[33]

Our concern in this chapter has been to correlate the Word of God and pastoral care. The Word, communicated to us and through us as God establishes a relationship with us, is God's creative way of acting–of opening our future to us. Ever since Augustine, this Word has been characterized as encountering us both verbally and visibly. Proclamation of the Word of God occurs both through what we do (the visible Word) and in our concrete articulations (the verbal Word). The Word, however, is not something that can be manipulated; it is an uncontrollable Word, a sovereign Word. In pastoral care our response is, with the parishioner, mutually to listen for the Word and then to speak it both verbally and visibly. Finally, the courage to speak the Word of God in a culture where God-talk is passé, and even taboo, is best drawn from the well of our own daily nourished trust relationship with that same Word, the embodiment of God's encounter with humanity. Pastoral care is not a peripheral form of ministry. Like all ministry, it has at its core the proclamation of the Word.

NOTES

1. See Thomas Oden, "Recovering Lost Identity," *Journal of Pastoral Care*, 34, March 1980, pp. 4-23.

2. See, e.g., G. Johannes Botterweck and Helmer Ringgren, *Theological Dictionary of the Old Testament*, vol. III, trans. John Willis and Geoffrey Bromiley, (Grand Rapids, MI: William B. Eerdmans, 1978), pp. 85-125; Gerhard Kittel, *Theological Dictionary of the New Testament*, vol. IV, trans. Geoffrey Bromiley, (William B. Eerdmans, 1967), pp. 69-137; *The Interpreter's Dictionary of the Bible*, vol. IV, ed. George Buttrick, (Nashville, TN: Abingdon Press, 1962), pp. 868-872.

3. J. N. Sanders, "The Word," in *The Interpreter's Dictionary of the Bible*, vol. IV (Nashville, TN: Abingdon Press, 1962), pp. 870-871.

4. Although the various theologians to whom I turned, Thurneysen, Luther, Bultmann, Schillebeeckx, and Asmussen, differ extensively in theological background and opinion, they manifest a remarkable convergence of understanding on this topic.

5. Edward Schillebeeckx, "Revelation in Word and Deed," in *The Word: Readings in Theology*, eds. Gavin, Carney, Charles Pfeiifer, William de Rue, and Gayle Vebelhor, (New York: P. J. Kennedy & Sons, 1964), pp. 257-258.

6. C. K. Barrett, *The Gospel According to St. John* (London: S.P.C.K., 1958), p. 61.

7. Gerhard Ebeling, *God and Word*, trans. James W. Leitch (Philadelphia: Fortress Press, 1967), p. 40.

8. Rudolph Bultmann, *Jesus and the Word*, trans. Louise P. Smith and Erminie H. Lantero (New York: Charles Scribner's Sons, 1958), p. 218.

9. Gerhard Ebeling, *The Nature of Faith*, trans. Ronald G. Smith (Philadelphia: Fortress Press, 1961), pp. 87-88.

10. Robert W. Jenson, *Visible Words* (Philadelphia: Fortress Press, 1978), pp. 28-29.

11. Ibid., p. 3.

12. Ibid, p. 36.

13. *LW,* vol. 37, , pp. 135-136.

14. Schillebeeckx, "Revelation in Word and Deed," p. 262.

15. Quoted in Eduard Thurneysen, *A Theology of Pastoral Care*, trans. Jack A. Worthington and Thomas Wieser (Atlanta, GA: John Knox Press, 1962), p. 15.

16. Paul Tillich, "The Relevance of the Ministry in Our Time and Its Theological Foundation," in *Making the Ministry Relevant*, ed. Hans Hofmann (New York: Charles Scribner's Sons, 1960), p. 22.

17. Thurneysen, *A Theology of Pastoral Care*, pp. 66, 11.

18. *LW,* vol. 41, p. 150.

19. See especially John Baillie, John T. McNeill, and Henry P. Van Dusen, gen. eds., *Library of Christian Classics,* vol. 18 (Philadelphia: Westminster Press, 1955), *Letters of Spiritual Counsel*, ed. and trans. Theodore G. Tappert.

20. Thurneysen, *A Theology of Pastoral Care*, p. 115.

21. Charles V. Gerkin, *Crisis Experience in Modern Life* (Nashville, TN: Abingdon Press, 1979), pp. 15-16.

22. Dietrich Bonhoeffer, *Ethics*, ed. Eberhard Bethge, trans. Neville H. Smith (New York: Macmillan, 1955), p. 126.

23. *LW,* vol. 37, p. 92.

24. John B. Cobb, Jr., *Theology and Pastoral Care* (Philadelphia: Fortress Press, 1977), p. 52.

25. *LW,* vol. 27, p. 249.

26. Quoted in John R. Loeschen, *Wrestling with Luther* (St. Louis, MO: Concordia Publishing House, 1976), p. 31.

27. Thurneysen, *A Theology of Pastoral Care*, p. 128.

28. Dietrich Bonhoeffer, *Life Together*, trans. John W. Doberstein (New York: Harper & Brothers, 1954), pp. 105, 107.

29. Ebeling, *God and Word*, pp. 3-4.

30. Ibid., p. 34.

31. Ibid., p. 35.

32. Ibid., p. 10.

33. Ebeling, *The Nature of Faith*, pp. 190-191.

Chapter 4

Correlating Theology
and Ministry

Parish pastors have been heard to complain: "The trouble with you seminary professors is that you don't know what's going on in the parish. Your ivory tower theology has little to do with the problems I encounter in my daily work. I guarantee that if you spent six months as an assistant here in my parish, you'd soon be teaching things differently."

Professors in the practical fields often echo the complaint: "The problem with so many of my colleagues in the classical fields is that they never make their teachings practical enough to be of help to their students. What good does it do to compare Luther and Barth on law and gospel when what we need is a theology that directly addresses the specific issues of ministry–a theology of death, of social justice, of evangelism, of administration. Theologians must speak to the concrete realities of the parish."

Professors in the classical fields have been heard to respond to such criticisms: "What do I know about psychology, church growth, conflict management, or spiritual formation? It is difficult enough just keeping up-to-date in my own specialty, without reading also in psychotherapy and Christian education. If theology is to have an impact on pastoral ministry, it is you practical types who will have to bridge the gap between the disciplines."

The need for correlation between theology and practice is now widely recognized, but who owns the problem? Whose responsibility is it?

This chapter originally appeared as "Left Brain, Right Brain" in *Theology Today*, 40 (October 1983), pp. 292-301. Reprinted by permission.

Theological thinking involves correlation–that is, the process of bringing two or more discrete entities into mutual relation with each other. The correlation may occur between questions and their proposed answers, or among a variety of answers to a particular question.

The term first came into popular use among theologians with the writings of Paul Tillich, who urged that theology follow a "method of correlation." Tillich's account of the theological task generated considerable interest. It also sparked debate, for many feared that his method of correlation had the effect of trimming Christian theological convictions to fit comfortably with the wisdom of the world. The controversy has since passed into the history of theology, with only an occasional flare-up. This is not the place to speak for or against his method. Yet, the term correlation remains a handy label for a complex process of comparison and contrast that takes place in all theological reflection.

Even though theologians may quarrel with the notion of adhering to a formal method of correlation–and there have been numerous understandings of correlation–the fact remains that they are inevitably correlators. To correlate, then, is simply to bring two discrete entities into mutual relation with each other. Correlating theology with the practice of ministry involves allowing the insights of theological thought to impinge upon, interact with, and influence the actual day-to-day tasks of ministry and vice versa. In other words, theological belief and the theological template discussed in Chapter 2 should make a difference in how we think about the care we offer and in how pastoral care, religious education, and church administration are carried out. But encounters with people in the parish (and their issues raised from contemporary culture) must correspondingly interact with, and influence, theology.

The pastors and seminary professors alluded to above are all concerned about the impact of theology, biblical studies, ethics, and tradition on day-to-day life. Their laments, while here a bit overstated to highlight the issue, are expressive of what appears to be an inherent difficulty–the responsibility for correlating theology and the practice of ministry is often relegated, along with the attendant blame, to somebody else, while few people personally take the challenge and seriously grapple with the task. There is a need for all of us in ministry, whether in seminary or parish, both pastors and professors, to participate in the process.

COGNITION AND CORRELATION

Some, indeed, have begun to address the topic, but in most cases their work until now has focused on developing methods for the task.[1] However, a more basic issue underlying any study of method has to do with the cognitive sets used to process data. Our purpose in this chapter is not to propose yet another method for correlation, but to focus on the two forms of mental organization that are essential if correlation, by whatever method, is to occur. These two cognitive sets must be understood before any system of correlation can be implemented. Our description of them here draws heavily on recent research into the functioning of the human brain.

THE TWO HEMISPHERES OF THE BRAIN

In general, the right side of the brain controls the left side of the body, and the left side of the brain controls the right side of the body. Investigation of patients who, through illness or injury, have suffered damage to one hemisphere of the cerebral cortex has provided considerable information about the separate functions of each of the two lobes.[2] For example, damage to the left lobe causes individuals to have difficulty using language; in some cases, language has been totally lost. Damage to the right lobe, although affecting language very little, precipitates great difficulties in spatial awareness, such as the recognition of faces once familiar. Although speech and logic appear unhindered, the ability to dress oneself also may be greatly affected.

The study of cerebral commissurotomy patients, likewise, has contributed significant data on the different functions of these two lobes. This radical technique was developed in order to treat severe epileptics. It involves a surgical severing of the two hemispheres so that they operate independently. For many patients, the operation has provided great help in the control of seizures; additionally, it has allowed researchers to study the specialized functioning of the cortex's two hemispheres.

Although most of the early research involving interhemispheric commissures was performed on cats (and later on monkeys and chimpanzees), it was the study of human subjects who had undergone cortex-severing surgery that greatly advanced the knowledge of how differently the two lobes of the cerebral cortex function. A variety of ingenuous experiments have been used to detect these divergencies.[3]

An example is the now classic test by Roger Sperry in which a word such as *keycase* is flashed on a screen for 100 milliseconds or less. In a split-brain patient's left visual field (that area to the left of the center point that the subject is viewing), only the letters "k,e,y" are seen; the letters "c,a,s,e" appear only in the right visual field. Since the flashing of the word to split-brain patients is at intervals too quick for the subjects to move their eyes, the letters "k,e,y" are presented only to the left eye (and thus to the right hemisphere) while the letters "c,a,s,e" are presented only to the right eye (and thus to the left hemisphere). When patients were asked at one point in the experiment what they saw, they reported only the word case. However, when Sperry asked them to place their left hands in an opaque bag filled with various objects and by touch alone retrieve the object they had just seen flashed on the screen, they removed a key.[4]

Michael Gazzaniga comments on the results of such tests:

The thrust of this work demonstrates there is a sharp breakdown in communication between the hemispheres of visual, somato-sensory, motor, and cognitive information. Information presented to the left hemisphere was normally named and described while information presented to the right was nameless, and the left hemisphere was unable to say what the right hemisphere was seeing or doing.. . . The studies went on to show that there were suggestions of marked differences in the way the hemispheres processed information. . . . More recent work suggests the intriguing possibility that problems that can be solved by either mode are handled by quite different cognitive strategies as a function of which hemisphere works on the task.[5]

TWO MODES OF PROCESSING COGNITIVE DATA

The results of such studies help sketch a clearer picture not only of how the brain functions, but also of how human cognition works. The findings seem to indicate that each hemisphere thinks in fundamentally different ways, with each having its own memory. Each hemisphere has different information-processing rules, which lead to *two different modes of knowing*. Before discussing these, let us look more closely at the differences in functioning between the two methods of thinking.

For most individuals (98 percent of all right-handed and about two-thirds of all left-handed people), the left hemisphere of the brain processes information sequentially. It functions logically (although it can be illogical!) and analytically. It compares, measures, analyzes, and judges. It names things; in fact, both verbal and written language are functions of this hemisphere. The left brain, working on a linear scale, creates time; it distinguishes between past and future.

Thomas Blakeslee, referring to a conversation between two people, provides a good illustration of the differences between the left brain and the right brain:

> The left brain generally responds to the literal meaning of the words it hears and will not even notice the meaning of inflection. The right brain perceives different aspects of the same conversation: tone of voice, facial expression, and body language are noticed while the words are relatively less important. This is a two-way process. The words are coming from the other person's left brain, and the tone of voice, facial expression, and body language are coming from his right brain. Thus, the conversation is going on simultaneously on two levels. In fact, when two people interact, they actually form two separate relationships: the memories and impressions formed by the left and right consciousnesses may be completely different.[6]

The right hemisphere processes body image and the body's orientation in space; it includes recognition of people by their physical features. As Blakeslee points out, it translates paralinguistic and body language. Thus, the right hemisphere processes information holistically rather than sequentially. It receives and considers a large mass of information in a parallel way, without separately considering each individual factor. It performs a synthetic-Gestalt organization of sensory data such as is performed in the perception and interpretation of a painting or photograph.

Because of its parallel processing of information, the right hemisphere has been described as the center of intuition, imagination, and creativity. It appears that many scientific discoveries originate with a right brain "insight."

Max Planck, an early investigator in quantum theory, believed that the scientist, to be creative, needs "a vivid intuitive imagination for new ideas not generated by deduction, but by artistically creative imagination."[7] Robert Nebes states:

> The organization and processing of data by the right hemisphere is in terms of complex wholes, the minor hemisphere having a predisposition for receiving the total rather than the parts. . . . [It] probably provides the neural basis for our ability to take the fragmentary sensory information we receive and construct from it a coherent concept of the spatial organization of the outside world—a sort of cognitive spatial map by which we plan our actions.[8]

Each lobe of the cortex has the potential for many functions, and both participate in most activities. They work in partnership in order to assure the total functioning of the person. Each hemisphere, however, also has the ability to inhibit the other in order to solve a particular problem. In fact, since confusion would often result if both hemispheres gave simultaneous readings of an event or problem, one or the other, according to Robert Ornstein, usually takes over:

> How do these two modes interact in daily life? My opinion, and that of David Galin, is that in most ordinary activities we simply alternate between the two modes, selecting the appropriate one and inhibiting the other. It is not at all clear how this process occurs . . . Clearly each of us can work in both modes—we all can move in space, we all can do both at once . . . The two modes of operation complement each other, but do not readily substitute for one another.[9]

Discoveries about the differences between the two hemispheres of the cortex have been used to support all sorts of outlandish conclusions. Many interpreters have superimposed on the left or right lobe all that they think is wrong with other people. To some the left brain has become the hemisphere of an "uptight" society characterized by rigid military types and impersonal bureaucrats, with its preference for doing over being and for thinking over feeling. The right brain, on the other hand, has become associated with the counterculture, with hippies and flower children, followers of Eastern religions, artsy dilettantes, or with those warm, open folk who say wonderful things but hardly ever get anything done.

In truth, the so-called "clerk mentality," rigidly and mechanically following procedures without question, is no more an example of the left-brain cognitive set than is the drifting and unproductive "dreamer" an example of the right-brain approach. Both distortions are equally irresponsible, perhaps better if facetiously labeled "no brain." The real promise of our new learnings about right-brain and left-brain modes is not in excusing "no brain" mentalities by giving them socially acceptable generic names, but in enabling individuals to make fuller use of their innate capacities in both hemispheres.

HEMISPHERIC DOMINANCE

It appears that by the time they have reached adulthood, most individuals are predisposed in their cognitive functioning to be dominated by one or the other of their two hemispheric lobes (a majority by the left lobe). This predilection to dominance raises interesting questions for the pastors and professors mentioned earlier. Could it be that certain disciplines, such religious studies as the Germanic schools of biblical criticism and other classic academic fields, tend to attract individuals who are dominated by left-brain cognitive processes? Rigorous scholarship often requires examination of minute details, splitting the whole into many pieces in order to complete a thorough sequential analysis. Maybe the classical fields of theology, while they can and do use right-hemisphere cognitive functioning, rely *primarily* on the left-hemisphere style of thinking.

On the other hand, such practical fields as liturgics and pastoral care may seem to draw individuals who are dominated by right-hemisphere processes. The forte in pastoral care, for example, is likely to be listening, empathizing, "being with," and offering warmth and openness. The words of a deeply troubled person cannot be split, parsed, and analyzed like a third-century text; they must be heard as a whole. The caregiver's empathy and emotional closeness take the place of analysis; words of comfort replace critical objectivity. While it cannot be denied that the left hemisphere also functions in pastoral care, perhaps it does so to a lesser extent than in the classical fields of theology. The question is one of dominance.

Is there, indeed, a kind of hemispheric physiological predestination involved here? The age-old environment-versus-heredity argument has certainly surfaced again in recent studies on brain function. Although genetic structure cannot be ignored in understanding hemispheric dominance, most recent findings suggest that environment also is significant. Joseph Bogen states the position of most brain researchers: "It is likely that some anatomical asymmetry underlies the potential for hemisphere specialization; but it is also clear that the extent to which the capacities are developed is dependent upon environmental exposure."[10] Artisan and accountant, biblical scholar and pastoral care specialist—individuals in various occupational groups cannot be differentiated by the pattern of their hemispheric cognitive processes (that is, they do not use totally different modes of thinking). Rather, these groups are distinguished by the degree to which they use (and possibly by their ability to use) the cognitive functions of one or the other of their hemispheres. Thus, although most adults have a hemispheric predisposition, it is one derived primarily through learning. The powerful influence of environment must be given its due.

BILATERAL COGNITION

Since our hemispheric predispositions are not only genetic, but also to a great extent learned, it seems reasonable to assume that a change in environmental conditions can lead to a change in our style of cognitive functioning. To some extent we may have to live with a tendency toward either a right-hemisphere or a left-hemisphere style of information encoding; however, it also is possible to create conditions within our environments and schedules whereby the fullest possible use is made of all our cognitive capacities.

Marcel Kinsbourne hypothesizes that the development of cerebral hemispheric proclivity evolves by increases in proficiency and, in each hemisphere, learning to give attention to contralateral stimuli.[11] In several studies undertaken to verify this thesis, it was observed that giving the left lobe a verbal task reduced the left-eye-field superiority for recognizing faces; additionally, presenting a face recognition problem to the right lobe reduced the right-eye-field visual superiority for words.[12] Therefore, one way to counteract a tendency for left-hemispheric dominance is to "prime the pump" of the right hemisphere by looking at pictures or listening to music. Likewise, for the right-hemisphere-dominant person, reading a book or listening to a lecture will set the stage for greater left-hemisphere activity. In such a way, one can momentarily lessen the dominance of one side of the brain and allow greater freedom for the other to apply itself, and its particular system for encoding data, to a given problem.

A key to effective correlation of theology and the practice of ministry is to set up the conditions that lead to facility in both right-brain and left-brain processes—in other words, to bilateral cognition. The goal is to permit each hemisphere to handle those particular data processing situations that are most suited to its particular style rather than allowing one or the other hemisphere to dominate most of the time. This is especially important since the lobe that is dominant inhibits the functioning of the other, and when one side is "running the show," the other (which is superior in its own type of information processing) is suppressed. Bilateral cognition leads to more comprehensive thought since it allows each hemisphere to think in the manner for which it was designed.

CREATIVE THINKING

One way to understand bilateral cognition is to look at Graham Wallas' outline of the process of creative thinking.[13] Wallas describes four stages of creative thought: preparation, incubation, illumination, and verification. During preparation, relevant information is collected and the problem is narrowed until the issues that must be dealt with are brought into focus. In the incubation stage, out-of-conscious forces work on the problem; although the individual periodically concentrates on it for short periods of time, there can be no movement toward resolution since this is strictly a time of germination, during which nothing appears to be happening. Illumination then occurs spontaneously or as a consequence of a conscious undertaking; here, the intuitive functioning of the brain takes over, and frequently the results occur instantaneously rather than following a series of logical steps. Finally, the verification stage requires logical validation of intuitive discoveries and the construction of an organized method for presenting the results.

Clearly, it can be seen that left-lobe cognitive functioning is required in preparation and verification, while the right lobe will dominate during incubation and illumination. The cooperative functioning of the left brain and the right brain is aptly illustrated in any author's writing process. After completing library research for a book or article and reviewing various conflicting publications on the subject, the writer does best to let the project rest for a time, without pressuring for immediate results or even a detailed outline. Then, perhaps during sleep, the long drive to work, a choir anthem, or even a class lecture, the thesis may come in a flash. That burst of enlightenment must be listened to and trusted. Only after it occurs does the author take pen and paper in hand, or keyboard and word processor, and put the insight into written form.

CORRELATING INTENTIONALLY

What makes the results of split-brain research significant for correlating theology and the practice of ministry is not so much the functional difference between the two hemispheres as the two different cognitive ways data is processed. For a person's theology to have an impact on ministerial practice (and vice versa), both sides of the brain are required. The process of correlation involves a back-and-forth movement between the cognitive processing systems of each hemisphere.

In pastoral care, for example, the left-hemispheric task of preparation is required to help the minister understand basic theological dogma and develop a theological template; the systematic analysis and sequential thinking of this lobe form categories and draw a system of beliefs from scripture and the traditions of the church. The right-hemispheric tasks of incubation and illumination allow the richness of personal experience, as it comes to the pastor in concrete care and counseling situations, to exist side by side with the prior theological constructs. Since the right lobe processes data in a parallel rather than sequential manner, a wide variety of seemingly dissonant information can be processed at the same time. The "genius" of the right hemisphere is its ability to absorb cognitively such diverse things as the deep pain expressed by a suffering human being and the more abstract insights of a biblical or theological theme in such a manner as to give meaning to both of them.

The left-hemisphere verification stage of cognition is required to help put these right-hemisphere insights into words. The parishioner is thereby helped to understand what is experienced. Such verbal processing is also important for the minister. Unless the right hemisphere's output is cycled back and reintegrated with the conceptual constructs, our theological belief systems, only sequentially developed, will become arid, devoid of the richness of parallel-processed experience. The danger in ministry is that we may venerate either the left-hemisphere or the right-hemisphere encoding strategies and not allow bilateral cognition to proceed. Reflection on theology and experience requires both.

It is possible to intentionally structure stages in experience and reflection–to shape our environment–in ways that will require *both* lateral functions of the brain, thus allowing for a dialogical flow of insights between our theology and our practice of ministry. Individuals who find themselves more prone to left-hemisphere modes of information processing need to stop the incessant analyzing that often paralyzes and stifles creativity. They need to be receptive to insights that arrive while they are not overtly working on a specific problem and to trust and nurture these solutions.

Listening to music, gardening, meditating, walking–even such a "mindless" undertaking as turning the crank of a mimeograph machine, if your church still has one–can inhibit left-brain activity and allow the right hemisphere to process information. The disciplines of spiritual direction can be of great benefit. Structuring one's schedule to include such right-hemisphere "pump priming" activities will enhance right-brain functioning. And when the insight comes, often in a flash, it must not be lost. The inspiration can come in a variety of forms–a visual image, a sudden recollection, a burst of ideas. In a pastoral care visit, it may arrive as a mental picture, a parable, or a story from scripture bubbling to the surface of consciousness. Structuring one's schedule to make room for such insight includes a readiness to receive and grasp it.

On the other hand, those whose bias is toward right-brain functioning will be able to include the benefits of left-hemisphere cognition by balancing their approach with disciplined scholarship (preparation) and with logical, measurable verification of insights. Individuals especially interested in pastoral care frequently fail to give adequate attention to the preparation stage, even dismissing it out of hand as a purely head-level operation. As a result, theological constructs often have had little or no effect on the pastoral care offered. To assist in the preparation stage, left-brain "pump priming" can be fostered by reading daily in scripture and theology. Likewise, some practitioners may neglect the crucial verification stage. In this connection, left-hemisphere activity can be fostered by the simple method of putting one's insights into written form. The experiences of ministry are indeed raw material for theological formulation, but only if the pastoral caregiver takes the time–if necessary, scheduled and rigorously observed–to articulate and test insights gained from the caregiving experience. Verification is further enhanced through sharing our reflected insights with others who might profit from them.

Recent research into the functioning of the cerebral cortex thus suggests that we think in two distinct ways. These cognitive sets–one processing data sequentially, the other in a parallel and holistic manner–are both needed for an effective correlation of theology and the practice of ministry. Intentionally creating an environment and structuring a schedule in such a way that both left-hemisphere and right-hemisphere styles of processing are nourished can only enhance the impact of theology upon ministry and allow our day-to-day experiences of ministry to inform and shape our theology. The results of such intentionally enhanced correlation will be seen in the enriched meanings that begin to gather around specific themes once, perhaps, considered as being discretely *either* theological or practical.

NOTES

1. For further information on the method of correlating theology and the practice of ministry see Don Browning, *A Fundamental Practical Theology* (Minneapolis, MN: Fortress Press, 1991); Donald Capps, *Pastoral Care and Hermeneutics* (Philadelphia: Fortress Press, 1984); Larry Graham, "Dimensions of Theological Interpretation in the Practice of Ministry," *The Iliff Review*, 37(3), 1980, pp. 3-11; Walter J. Lowe, "Method Between Two Disciplines: The Therapeutic Analogy," *The Journal of Pastoral Care*, September, 1981, pp. 147-156; John Patton, "Clinical Hermeneutics: Soft Focus in Pastoral Counseling and Theology," *The Journal of Pastoral Care*, September, 1981, pp. 157-168; John Patton, *From Ministry to Theology* (Nashville, TN: Abingdon, 1990); Robert A. Preston, "Hermeneutic Processes and Pastoral Care," *Lexington Theological Quarterly*, October, 1977, pp. 128-136 Charles R. Stinnette, Jr., "The Pastoral Ministry in Theological Perspective," *Criterion*, Winter 1965, pp. 3-9; and Herbert W. Stroup, Jr., "Psychology, Theology, and the Parish or Where the Twain Do Meet," *Dialog*, Spring 1977, pp. 123-127.

2. For a more extended discussion of the two hemispheres of the cerebral cortex see J. E. Bogen, E. D. Fisher, and P. J. Vogel, "Cerebral Commisurotomy: A Second Case Report," *Journal of the American Medical Association*, 1965, pp. 1328-1329; Joseph E. Bogen and Michael S. Gazzaniga, "Cerebral Visuospatial Functions," *Journal of Neurosurgery*, 1965, pp. 394-399; J. E. Bogen and P. J. Vogel, "Cerebral Commissurotomy in Man: Preliminary Case Report," *Bulletin of Los Angeles Neurological Society*, 1962, pp. 169-172; Michael S. Gazzaniga, *The Bisected Brain* (New York: Appleton-Century-Crofts, 1970); Michael S. Gazzaniga, "Brain Mechanism and Behavior," in *Handbook of Psychobiology*, eds. Michael S. Gazzaniga and Colin Blakemore (New York: Academic Press, 1975), pp. 565-590; eds. Steven Harnad, Robert W. Doty, Leonide Goldstein, Julian Joynes, and George Krauthamer, *Lateralization in the Nervous System* (New York: Academic Press, 1977); Robert D. Nebes, "Direct Examination of Cognitive Function in the Right and Left Hemispheres," in *Asymmetrical Function of the Brain*, ed. Marcel Kinsbourne (London: Cambridge University Press, 1978), pp. 99-137; Merlin C. Wittrock, "Education and the Cognitive Processes of the Brain," in *Education and the Brain*, seventy-seventh yearbook, Part II, National Society for the Study of Education, eds. Jeanne S. Chall and Allan F. Mirsky (Chicago: University of Chicago Press, 1978), pp. 61-102; Merlin C. Wittrock, Jackson Beatty, Joseph E. Bogen, Michael S. Gazzaniga, Harry J. Jerison, Stephen D. Krashen, Robert D. Nebes, and Timothy Teyler, *The Human Brain* (Englewood Cliffs, NJ: Prentice-Hall, 1977).

3. For a history of recent brain research, see especially Gazzaniga, "Brain Mechanism and Behavior," pp. 565-573.

4. Roger W. Sperry, "Hemisphere Deconnection and Unity in Conscious Awareness," *American Psychologist*, October, 1968, pp. 723-733.

5. Gazzaniga, "Brain Mechanism and Behavior," p. 567.

6. Thomas R. Blakeslee, *The Right Brain: A New Understanding of the Unconscious Mind and Its Creative Powers* (Garden City, NY: Anchor Press; Doubleday, 1980), pp. 28-29.

7. Ibid, p. 49.

8. Robert D. Nebes, "Man's So-Called Minor Hemisphere," in *The Human Brain*, ed. Merlin C. Wittrock, pp. 102-104.

9. Robert E. Ornstein, *The Psychology of Consciousness* (San Francisco, CA: W. H. Freeman, 1972), p. 62.

10. Joseph E. Bogen, "Some Educational Implications of Hemispheric Specialization," in Wittrock, *The Human Brain*, pp. 144-145.

11. Marcel Kinsbourne, "Cerebral Dominance, Learning, and Cognition," in *Progress in Learning Disabilities*, vol. 3, ed. Helmerr Myklebust (New York: Grune & Stratton, 1975), pp. 201-218; and Kinsbourne, "The Control of Attention by Interaction Between the Cerebral Hemispheres," in *Attention and Performance*, vol. 4, ed. Sylvan Kornblum (New York: Academic Press, 1973), pp. 239-256; also, Kinsbourne, "The Mechanism of Hemispheric Control of the Lateral Gradient of Attention," in *Attention and Performance*, vol. 5, ed. Patrick M. A. Rabbitt and Stanislav Dornic (New York: Academic Press, 1975), pp. 81-97.

12. Danny Klein, Morris Moscovitch, and Carlo Vigna, "Attention Mechanisms and Perceptual Asymmetries in Tachistoscopic Recognition of Words and Faces," in *Neuropsychologia*, 1976, pp. 55-66.

13. Graham Wallas, *The Art of Thought* (London: Butler & Tanner, 1926).

Chapter 5
Spiritual Direction

Theology, in one of its simplest definitions, is the study of the relationship between God and humans. Unfortunately, theological scholarship, by its very nature, can contribute to a distancing of the theologian from the very God who is the subject of study. How this can happen is understandable. Included among the tools of modern scholarship are such enterprises as the painstaking examination of manuscript fragments, the historical probing of minute details, and the defining and interrelating of a myriad of concepts. Most theological education divides the task of ministry into such discrete segments as biblical studies, dogmatics, languages, history, theological ethics, social ethics, public speaking, psychology, sociology, pastoral care, religious education, and church administration.

In seminary, students experience a broad range of courses, each having a particular slant, each affording a different sense of the gospel and of ministry. Each course is offered by an expert who has delved more deeply into that particular subject area than you or I ever will. Much of the scholarship has been performed for us. Thus, the study of theology carries with it an implicit problem: the methodologies inherent in most of its disciplines–form-critical, historical, archaeological–lend themselves to a distancing from the content. This distancing must occur. A critical stance is necessary if one is to gain a more accurate understanding of the object being studied, but there can be an attendant loss. The intimacy of the God-person relationship can be displaced by the methodological tendency to segment, parse, and observe from an objective distance. Wolfhart Pannenberg comments on this loss in academic theology:

This chapter originally appeared as "Spiritual Direction and Pastoral Counseling" in the *Journal of Pastoral Counseling*, 21(2) (Spring-Summer 1986), pp. 60-75. Copyright by Iona College Graduate Division of Pastoral Counseling. Reprinted by permission.

> But authentic theology has always been distinguished . . . by its ability to speak to central motifs of the Christian faith. These are not simply matters of doctrine, such as the Trinity, the cross and resurrection of Jesus Christ, God's kingdom, and faith itself. Such doctrinal issues are indeed related to the dynamic life of Christian faith, but when treated in separation from their experiential roots they can represent little but the deadwood of an old tradition.[1]

His comment is not intended as a criticism of theology or of theological scholarship. There is no implication that "if only the seminaries would teach this or that," then such problems would be resolved. The scholarly methodologies are needed. They give us a clearer grasp of scripture and its message and of the world to which that message is addressed.

Indeed, the problem is not so much the methods employed in contemporary theology as the lack of correspondingly effective methodologies by which Christians can foster the development of their relationship with God. Where the "experiential roots" to complement rigorous theological reflective methods are lacking, a serious gap results. Don Browning has pointed out that in previous eras of the church, methods of Christian living were relied upon to feed spiritual growth and moral development, and that the absence of such methodologies within the church today presents a real crisis.[2]

I would not advocate a return to the era of pietism, when often an individual's relationship with God was considered the only important aspect of faith. Reinvolvement in social ministry and social justice issues was desperately needed if the church was to regain its prophetic role in the world. However, as critical as it surely is for Christians to take a stand on issues that affect society and the natural world, if we lose touch with our "base"—our faith in and our intimate relationship with that world's Creator and Redeemer—then our pronouncements will be empty and our solutions temporary, and we will be dangerously subject to the vagaries of social and political fashion, speaking a word, rather than the Word, to our troubled time.

Given the modern de-emphasis on the Christian's relationship with God, however, and the dearth of methods for fostering spirituality, the church and its clergy are in danger today of moving toward a pre-Reformation orientation in which the pastor authoritatively tells the faithful what to believe and do, while the faithful themselves abdicate their responsibility of striving to hear the Word (the minister does that for them!).

Such a shortcut has its advantages, for confusion and disagreement easily occur when a whole congregation is trying as individuals to discern the Word and will of God. Certainly, it is clearer if the task of discernment is undertaken only by the minister, the faith specialist. But the shortcut of specialization is also dangerous. All Christians need to grow in the Spirit; all need to listen carefully for the Word. And, given this age's lack of methodologies for Christian living, all Christians need assistance in accomplishing that task.

God is always present to us; we operate each day in the face of God. Throughout its history the church has depended on "spiritual direction" to help heighten people's awareness of that presence. Spiritual direction, in brief, is concerned with awareness of and growth in one's relationship with God. It has reference to a place–a person, actually–where Christians can go to talk specifically about that relationship. It suggests a method of pastoral care that sensitizes people to that presence of God that already exists, in which we live.

DIRECTION AND CORRELATION

If the correlation of theology and pastoral care is our purpose, then spiritual direction must be our concern. It is an important bridge between theology and care. It focuses on our relationship with God–that factor in human experience from which we draw meaning, the courage to be, and the power to live an authentic life. For the ministers, spiritual direction may provide a way whereby we can return to the sources of our faith, reflecting on theology and on our experience of God. It prepares us for the automatic responses that are required in the care we give. Spirituality is not a matter of detached reflection, as some may think; it involves a relationship, a gift of grace. That relationship is determined by the Giver, yet is dependent on the recipient's active response to the gift.

Spiritual direction reminds us that a relationship with God is the overarching concern that focuses all others (while not negating or replacing them), that helps us rise beyond our basic human needs and wants to follow the Spirit's leading. In fact, spiritual direction is one method by which what is discussed in theology classes or read in theological discourses can have a direct impact on the ministry we offer. It is a place where doctrines such as sin, finitude, forgiveness, and grace can be discussed and experienced. Frequently, the pastor helps parishioners recognize that what they are going through–for example, release from guilt over a certain offense–is what the liturgy, sermon, and scripture are really talking about, in this case, forgiveness. Thus, spiritual direction serves an interpretive function in pastoral care.

The point was made in Chapter 1 that pastoral care and counseling have benefited tremendously from learnings in psychiatry, psychotherapy, and psychology over the last sixty years. These learnings have revolutionized the care we offer. Psychology has taught us much about underlying motives, human development, how people change, and how relationships are established. Through such learnings our care has become more sensitive. The current resurgence of attention to spiritual direction can have a similar impact on pastoral counseling and care. It can provide tools to assist us and our parishioners in our quieting and centering, so that we all become more receptive to others, the universe, and the Word. It can teach us effective ways of using such spiritual resources as scripture, prayer, journals, and meditation. People who are obsessed with themselves and their own problems can benefit from becoming absorbed, instead, in faith's larger concerns.

Whether or not pastors actually do spiritual direction as such, its influences, like the influences of psychology, can infuse our entire ministry to people. Certainly, it can help us regain a lost or forgotten part of our ministerial heritage, diffuse the criticism that pastoral counseling is nothing but "warmed-over psychology," and enable us to guide people's growth in the most important relationship of life, their relationship with God.

Such growth has been a concern of the church from the very beginning. Paul distinguishes between the *nepioi*, those beginners in the faith ("babes in Christ") who are fed only milk, and the *teleioi*, those more "mature" Christians who can receive solid food (I Cor. 3:1-2, cf. 2:6, 13-16; Eph. 4:13-15; cf. Col. 1:10). In my view, the church today, especially among Protestants, may be focusing too intently on the *nepioi*. We hear too many introductory lectures, too much, "This is what we should be doing [in our lives, the ghetto, Central America]." There is not enough nourishing of the faithful to a deeper understanding of the gospel and a more significant relationship with God.

Spiritual direction, however, and the learnings that flow from it, can help people grow and mature in their faith. Such growth is essential; the *teleioi* are those who have moved from the way of the flesh to the way of the spirit, transforming self-centeredness into compassion and a sense of unmerited gift. The *teleioi* are hopeful for the full revelation of God, a hope that encourages patience in suffering. If our pastoral care is aimed solely toward meeting people's needs, then our ministry will be dominated by the most obvious needs that come before us—people in situational crises who may want only a quick bandage put over their wounds so they can go on their way. But, as C. W. Brister has noted, pastoral care ministry comes out of both the push and the pull of the faith. It requires us to respond to people's needs, of course, but also to help people face the needs and commands of the gospel.[3] Surely, pastoral care ministry is offered to the *nepioi*, but it must foster spiritual growth for the *teleioi* as well.

HISTORY AND TERMINOLOGY

In the Roman tradition, and to a considerable degree in the Anglican, the practice of giving care for the life of the spirit has generally come under the rubric of spiritual direction (its theoretical companion variously classed as ascetic, mystical, or spiritual theology). In most of Protestantism there has been no regularly accepted term for the same reality. "Faith development" or "formation" perhaps come closest. Historically, the church has referred to the person of the spiritual director as: spiritual friend, spiritual companion, spiritual guide, soul friend, ghostly counselor, and spiritual mother or father. "Spiritual direction" and "director" (or simply pastor) will be used here because they are most commonly accepted. In the field as a whole, there are a variety of perspectives, or schools, of spiritual direction, such as Franciscan, Eastern, and Carmelite.[4] I am impressed, above all, with the Ignatian perspective, though I have also learned much from contemporary directors trained in pastoral counseling and psychotherapy.

Spiritual direction, especially in the form of contemplative or meditative prayer, has a centuries-old history. Its roots go as far back as the devotional life of ancient Jewish communities such as the Therapeutae and the Essenes. Spiritual disciplines also are found in the contemplative practices of many Eastern religions. Indeed, early Christian techniques for relaxing, stilling, and breathing, have their parallels in the practices and rites of a number of peoples, such as the Northern Plains Indians in the United States, nomadic Eskimos in Canada and Russia, and several tribes in Africa.

The spiritual disciplines of the church can be traced back as far as the fourth-century desert fathers and mothers. In Egypt, Syria, and Palestine, the early Christians sought out hermit monks as guides for the godly life. Since then, each century has had its cherished guides: Jerome, Catherine of Siena, John of the Cross, Ignatius of Loyola, Teresa of Avila, Martin Luther, Francis de Sales.

Pastoral care has long focused on the parishioner's relationships—with self, family, other people, the universe, and God. Spiritual direction concentrates particularly, though not exclusively, on the relationship with God. The purpose of this chapter is to provide a brief sketch of spiritual direction, especially for those whose previous experience with it may have been quite limited.[5]

As has already become apparent, for pastoral care, two terms bear special importance in any understanding of spiritual direction: "religious experience" and "relationship with God." Religious experience is not altogether familiar to many of us late-twentieth-century travelers. For one thing, most of us have probably given more attention to ethics or action than to the interiority of the religious life. Then too, movements into psychological interiors or toward more abstract theological articulation have tended to ignore spirituality. A different language is needed—a terminology that is relational because it talks about relationships, religious because the relationships in question involve God, and concrete because the focus is on the specific reality of that particular relationship.

By "relationship with God" I mean that we are creatures, whether we know it or not, and God is our creator. If we are unaware of our createdness, we may experience it as rootlessness, loneliness, or a sense of being lost. The lack may also show itself positively, in a yearning for some deeper sense of meaning in life that cannot be named. Spirituality always has at its base a relationship in which God reaches out to us. William Barry puts it this way:

> It should be obvious that this kind of spiritual direction makes a radical assumption in faith; namely, that the Lord is actually and actively engaged now with his people as individuals, that he desires their intimacy, and that his people can experience that intimacy. Moreover, it assumes that such a desire for intimacy is for the benefit of his people.[6]

Thus, spirituality begins with God–God as gift. Spiritual direction is the art of helping others discern that gift and respond to it. Such direction usually occurs in a one-to-one, contractual relationship between director and directee, though there are historical and contemporary precedents for group direction. Most group guidance has been for families or celibate associations. Prayer groups also have sometimes served not only to bring human concerns to God, but also to train people in prayer and the life of the Spirit. Some directors even believe that group guidance may be the most important form of spiritual care, from the standpoint of using time efficiently and of building community.

William Connolly furthered our understanding of spiritual direction when he wrote:

> "Spiritual" does tell us that the basic concern of this kind of help is not with external actions as such, but with the inner life, the "heart," the personal core out of which come the good and evil that men think and do. It includes "head," but points to more than reason and more than knowledge. It also reminds us that another spirit, the Spirit of the Lord, is involved. "Direction" does suggest something more than advice giving and problem solving. It implies that a person who seeks direction is going somewhere, and wants to talk to someone on the way. It implies, too, that the talk will not be casual and aimless, but have to help him find his way.[7]

In spiritual direction one has a companion who supports and confronts, a guide who helps form one's life with God, with other people, and with the universe. Its focus is on the inner life. Its result is to transform our living and to lead to action, responsible service, and moral living.

Such direction helps people search for and find meaning, the lack of which is a major cause of modern malaise. Carl Jung noted that much neurotic behavior in people over the age of thirty-five results from ignoring experiences of meaning. Indeed, Jung states, one of the reasons he studied this area of experience so extensively was because he could not find clergy who were equipped or willing to deal with it.[8] Spiritual direction enables individuals to get beneath their own surface conventions and attitudes about life. Its focus is heavily upon experience; though not anti-intellectual, it is primarily a school of the heart. Direction is a place where the God-person relationship can be talked about seriously, a rare thing in our post-Christian culture, where such talk is often experienced as an embarrassment. Indeed, to quote William A. Barry and William J. Connolly: "Spiritual direction may be considered the core form from which all forms of pastoral care radiate, since ultimately, all forms of pastoral care and counseling aim, or should aim, at helping people to center their lives in the mystery we call God."[9]

RELATION TO PSYCHOTHERAPY AND PASTORAL COUNSELING

In many ways, spiritual direction is similar to pastoral counseling and psychotherapy. Gerald May has suggested a helpful way to highlight the comparison and contrast. He offers three short monologues—one from humanistic psychotherapy, one from pastoral counseling, and one from spiritual direction.[10]

In psychotherapy one might say, "I bring all that I am into this relationship with you. For the time we are together, I attend to you with all my heart and with all my expertise. I give my attention to our being together in the hope that this will facilitate your growth and health."

In pastoral counseling the parallel statement might be, "In the name of God I am here for you. I give my attention to you and to our being together as a representative of God's love and care for you. I am a broken human expression of that love, but you have my attention and care while we are together, and my prayers while we are apart."

In spiritual direction the statement might be, "My prayers are for God's will to be done in you and for your constant deepening in God. During this time that we are together I give myself, my awareness and attention and hopes and heart *to God for you. I surrender myself to God for your sake.*"

These monologues may be oversimplified. After all, every director practices the art in a unique way, usually from the perspective of one of the various "schools" of spiritual direction, and refined explorations of the similarities and differences are available; however, May's simple monologues make vivid some crucial ways in which spiritual direction is unlike either pastoral counseling or psychotherapy.[11]

The most significant distinction of spiritual direction is its focus on developing and strengthening one's personal relationship with God. Relationships with therapist, spouse, family, friends, colleagues, and others in one's life, though not ignored, are all secondary.

Shaun McCarty notes a second difference: "The focus in counseling is more on problem solving, on effecting better personal integration and adjustment in the process of human maturation. The focus in spiritual direction, on the other hand, is more on growth in prayer and charity."[12] In other words, the criteria by which success is judged are also different. In counseling or therapy, success is based primarily on achieving the counselee's wishes, meeting agreed-upon goals, or attaining a certain level of mental health (unless, of course, the counselee wants to achieve something utterly unrealistic or perhaps even illegal). But in spiritual direction, the criteria for judgment are faithfulness to the call of God, Christian virtues such as Paul frequently listed in his letters, service to the entire Christian community, and above all, a heightened sensitivity to the inner murmurings of God's Spirit.

Other differences between spiritual direction and therapy/pastoral counseling might also be mentioned, such as the director's training, charismatic office, and distinctive techniques. That direction also bears resemblances to the other two forms of help, of course, can never be denied. Especially in recent years when directors have begun receiving psychological training, the lines between them have even become somewhat blurred. Robert Rossi makes the point: "Granted the important distinctions, what makes for good counseling makes for good direction: expertise with warmth. When the director's theological and spiritual insight is coupled with his psychological sensitivity, he stands ready to effectively exercise the *cura animarum.*"[13]

For pastoral care, the ideal would seem to be a pastor trained in pastoral counseling who has learned from psychotherapy and has developed skill in spiritual direction. Pastors so equipped, while they may infrequently offer classical spiritual direction, will be better able to ascertain in their care and counseling just what the seeking person needs and just where to begin. My vision is that ministers, particularly Protestant pastors who are not very familiar with spiritual direction, will discover it, learn from it, grow in their own disciplines of prayer, and allow these disciplines to affect the care they offer. Spiritual direction can constitute an excellent environment for the correlating of pastoral care and theology, for unhurried reflection on the experience—and source—of our own faith. By reincorporating spiritual direction into its practice, pastoral care and counseling can significantly realign itself with its religious heritage.

BEGINNING THE PROCESS

Jung's observation that many people in the second half of life struggle with issues of meaning certainly applied to Charles Monti, the forty-nine-year-old owner of a hardware store in a small midwestern town. Monti's wife had died four years earlier, about the time his second and last son left for college in the East. Her death had left Monti with many questions. Outwardly, life continued as usual. His business, managed now by his first son, was running smoothly. At long last he had the leisure to do things he had always wanted to do but previously could not because of family and business. He made regular trips to Minnesota and Canada for fishing and to Wisconsin for deer hunting. He had always been a believer, an active church attender and supporter, and had taught church school classes on and off for years. He liked working with young people and, while his two sons were teenagers, assisted as a sponsor of the youth group. Monti was the type of church member every pastor likes to have in the congregation. Whether you needed a helping hand or something from his store, he always said "yes."

So it was with some surprise that Pastor Karen Jonsered, on asking the widower if he would help organize a church clean-up day, heard him say, "I'd like to talk with you sometime, I mean if you've got the time."

"Sure, I've always got time for you, Chuck. What is it?"

"Oh, it's hard to explain. I'm a little confused, and I'm not sure what I should do."

Pastor Jonsered could not imagine what was on Charles Monti's mind; he did not seem upset or confused. In fact, during the last few years, he had appeared more relaxed and at peace than she ever remembered. They made an appointment.

Once in the pastor's office, Monti poured out his story. True, he was more relaxed than ever. He was doing things he had always dreamed of doing–and even now was planning a fishing trip to Alaska for the following summer. He liked having more recreational opportunities, missed his wife, dated now and then ("But how many women are you going to find in a small town like this?"), but had no plans for marriage. "Ever since we finished the Bethel Bible Series," he said, "I've wondered if something is missing in my life. I really liked the study of the Bible and sometimes wish I could become a better Christian. Sometimes, I feel empty inside and wish that I felt more like I was doing what God intends for me."

Already, pastoral assessment was taking place. Pastor Jonsered pondered some possibilities: Is Chuck suffering from a stalemated grief? Depression? Guilt for some secret past or present sin? Is he just bored with all of his new free time? Is his a case of mid-life crisis? Is he too dependent? Is the problem a matter of vocational crisis? Does he want to go into the ordained ministry? Maybe none of the above? Actually, the pastor found traces of all of the above in Monti's expressions of uneasiness, but none seemed of significant weight. She met with him several times to try to sort things out.

Pastor Jonsered had become interested in spiritual direction while attending seminary and had received two years of direction from an Episcopal priest. She soon began to wonder if direction might not be helpful to Monti, for already by their second visit together he was repeatedly raising questions about prayer, his feelings toward God, and his concerns about not being active enough in the church. Pastor Jonsered suggested that they spend some time helping him develop his life of prayer. "I think you're searching. You seem to be looking for something more in your relationship with God and the church than what you have right now." Monti agreed. "I'd like you to consider spiritual direction," she went on. "It helps people grow in their prayer life and their relationship with God."

When people come specifically in quest of guidance for their spiritual life or "to be closer to the Lord," it is crucial, as in all pastoral counseling, that the pastor determine what really has prompted their appearance. This does not mean that their first expressions of desire for spiritual help should not be taken seriously–to the contrary–but it is always important for ministers to ascertain whether those first-stated desires for help are accurate, or are only a way of asking for something else (perhaps money, prayers, help in dealing with guilt, legal or medical care, or just a listening ear). In addition to asking what must obviously be asked first in theological assessment, "Why are they coming to *me*?" it is necessary to ask, "Why are they coming *now*?" (See Chapter 2.) It is also good to get some sense of what they expect to receive from the spiritual help they are requesting.

Clearly, pastors who offer direction must determine whether the individual is capable of undertaking spiritual direction. This is not to say that only the fit, educated, and emotionally healthy can be involved in spirituality. The history of the church would argue against that; some of the most notable saints, after all, were known to skirt the borders of craziness. However, not all people are able or willing to take the step of entering direction. They may lack sufficient belief in God and prayer or the ability to experience their inner world; they may be incapable of reflection on experience or unable to relax sufficiently to listen for the still small voice; or they may have pressing problems in life that make it difficult to focus on anything else.

A first session in spiritual direction can begin very much like a first session in pastoral counseling, a process that I have described elsewhere.[14] The pastor seeks first to establish a solid relationship with the parishioner, one that allows give-and-take between the two. By the time Charles Monti decided to enter into spiritual direction, he and Pastor Jonsered could already build not only on their years of friendly association, but also on the several counseling sessions in which they had explored the reasons for his bewildering uneasiness. Instead of continuing to discuss his "problem," Monti now talked with the pastor about his decision to proceed. He shared with her some background of his life and faith. Such sharing is important. Pastors cannot assume that their prior association with a parishioner active in the church automatically gives them insight into that individual's faith and inner struggles.

In general, people who have come for direction are not beginners in the faith; most have attained some degree of maturity. The pastor begins by trying to help them focus on and clarify their past religious experiences. Most people are rather inarticulate when they first try to express their deeper feelings and beliefs. The request to "tell me about your relationship with God in prayer" can totally stump some people, even those who are able to speak concretely and subjectively about their relationships with other people. Frequently, directees will rely on purely objective descriptions or theological formulas learned long ago. This inarticulateness poses a barrier that may crumble only slowly; the process can rarely be accelerated. Early on, therefore, parishioners need help in learning to look at, notice, and then actually express what they "see" in the world of their own experience. This began for Charles Monti, as it usually does in spiritual direction, with those initial explorations of what caused him to ask for help. Only after some discussion of his seemingly barren prayer life could director and directee get at the concrete facts about who God is to him and how he responds to God.

THE CONTEMPLATIVE ATTITUDE

One of the most important initial tasks of the director is to help new directees form a "contemplative attitude," i.e., pay attention to their own inner experience. The contemplative attitude includes a looking for and listening to another voice. It means an attentiveness to the Word, to the presence that already exists but needs to be recognized. This approach to prayer represents a major shift in attitude for many people. It means a movement away from self-absorption toward immersion in the Other. It involves listening a good deal less to one's own self-talk or obsessions and more to the presence of God. Without such a contemplative attitude, growth in spiritual life will be stunted. Most efforts to enhance our spiritual life through various disciplines are, like the growing branches on a giant pine, dependent on this base of receptiveness and openness to the movements of the Spirit within us–the sunshine and rain of God's presence in our lives.

Some methods of helping people develop the contemplative attitude can backfire. The person intentionally trying to pray and "get closer to God" can easily end up frustrated and even more self-obsessed. A way to circumvent this frustration is to urge directees to do things they enjoy, things that are naturally engaging. Such activities may include walks on the beach or in the woods, listening to Bach, looking at a sunrise or sunset, watching a thunderstorm run its course, playing a musical instrument, or even long-distance running. The activity must be one that is greatly absorbing. For me, walking quietly in the woods or fishing (staring for hours at a bobber that doesn't move) have been just such activities. They seem to foster contemplation.

Situations in which I find myself have also been catalytic at times. A number of years ago, I started arriving a day early to any conference I planned to attend. The American Association of Pastoral Counselors usually met in big cities that were unfamiliar to me, so I would hit the streets immediately after arrival, and except for sleep, I'd walk for the next twenty-four hours without saying a word to anyone. In the midst of all the hustle and bustle, people rushing this way and that, I would walk aimlessly–observing, listening, thinking, feeling, without a word. I miss those walks, now that they are no longer possible. Such contemplative moments can be redemptive. Each of us will find our own ways to open up and forget about ourselves.

Such experiences seemed already built in so far as Charles Monti's life was concerned. The pastor encouraged him to "let the Lord share these experiences with you." She expressed confidence that God would make God's presence known in time, that Monti only needed to listen for it and be aware of it when it happened. She reassured him, "God is a friend who will be with you in every experience of life. God is the kind of presence you might feel with a close personal friend, only it is *always* there." Monti was urged to adopt a let-it-happen attitude, without trying to force anything. Unlike Charles Monti, some people may be knotted up with tension and anxiety; relaxation or breathing exercises such as I have described elsewhere,[15] may help them become more receptive.

After periods of involvement in each naturally engaging activity, directees are asked to reflect on just what has happened. They need not expect fantastic or deeply moving religious experiences, but only review honestly and openly what actually occurred–thereby learning to be aware of and to reflect on the quiet movements of the Spirit. People learn that God speaks not only when they are on their knees, but also in life's daily events. Experience comes first, then reflection. They are led to ask: "How has God made God's presence known to me? In what ways did the Spirit speak?" Parishioners need to know that this shift in our orientation to prayer takes time, because most of us tend to pray in ways that do not actively foster awareness of God; usually, our lives are so busy that we do not pause to reflect on God's activity in our midst. The contemplative attitude needs nurturing. New skills and disciplines are not developed overnight.

WRITING ACTIVITIES

In some instances, it is a helpful practice at the outset for directees to write a history of their spiritual journey. They should have no worry that they have not been "holy" enough; rather, they are simply to write about their life of faith, including their practice of prayer. Such writing enables the pastor to become better acquainted with their spiritual life, and in turn, directees are stimulated to begin the process of remembering and reflecting on their inner experience.

While such writing activities may be positive for some parishioners, the director will want from others a more extensive background before proceeding with the direction process. In such cases a variation of Ira Progoff's written dialogue process could prove helpful.[16] The pastor may ask the directees to close their eyes and try to image their own spiritual journey as that of a person other than themselves, then open their eyes and write a script of the journey. This is to be done as rapidly as possible, until the writing comes to a natural break or pause. They can then share with the pastor any or all of the written material, as they wish, and it can be used to explore meanings in the directees' lives.

In the case of Charles Monti, he had done little or no writing in his entire lifetime, short of a note scrawled on an invoice or a brief message to one of his employees. His wife had always taken care of the family's correspondence, and his outside interests were far from the literary realm. Surprisingly, perhaps because of its very unfamiliarity, writing became, for Monti, a way to express ideas and emotions he had never verbalized. Through his writing, he discovered much about his own spirituality that he had not previously recognized or understood.

STRUCTURING THE SESSIONS

Once the "getting to know you" period is over and spiritual direction is well underway, a typical session usually begins with silence—perhaps five to ten minutes of silence—during which a spiritual discipline is used (we will mention some of them in the sections that follow).

Pastor and parishioner talk about their reactions to whatever discipline was used in the period of silence and then move on to a discussion of developments in the person's relationship with God, as experienced since the previous session. Special attention is often given to one's prayer experiences. The pastor may then reflect aloud on what has been expressed, as in a pastoral counseling session.

Frequently, such discussion and reflection are all that is required. At other times, the director may make suggestions to assist with the person's growth in prayer. Recommended may be the use of additional disciplines or specific portions of scripture that could be of help in attempts at contemplative prayer. At times, pastors will help the individual through a particular spiritual crisis, such as emotional dryness in prayer.

Spiritual direction sessions generally occur less frequently than counseling sessions. Indeed, after a few initial weekly meetings at which pastor and directee are getting acquainted, direction is likely to take place only once every three or four weeks.

SPIRITUAL DISCIPLINES

A variety of disciplines–methods, techniques–have already been mentioned as being useful in connection with spiritual direction. They facilitate openness in one's relationship with God. Prayer, journals, scripture, and meditation serve such purposes. Each can be a fruitful resource for developing the contemplative attitude. There is not room here to cover these disciplines in the detail they deserve but only to introduce them.

Prayer

Prayer is the most important of the disciplines. In fact, some practitioners think of spiritual direction as essentially a school of prayer. Many people have great difficulty praying; they think of prayer in a stylized manner, and as a result, find it a barren experience. Some ways of praying are helpful while others are not. Prayer motivated by obligation or duty rarely leads to wholeness, and life is often smothered in the tedium or boredom that ensues. Similarly, prayer that is primarily a matter of petitions, thinking, or making resolutions does not lead to the enthusiasm of a love relationship. Indeed, for many people, prayer is so concentrated on self–on one's own sins, problems, strivings, wants, or wishes–that they are prevented from really listening and seeing. If a man overwrought with grief and guilt for "bringing my marriage down by having an affair" is obsessed by his own wrongdoing, he will have difficulty seeing the great deeds that God has done, the forgiveness that God offers, and the new life that comes as a gift.

It can take considerable time and much practice to make the shift from self-centered prayer to openness and listening. Prayer should cease being a matter of duty and become instead a joy, a looked-for event. It is not a chore, like doing the dishes or being audited by the IRS. The woman who still prays like an eight-year-old will not easily tell God her rage at the loss of her husband. She needs guidance in her relationship with God, not glib suggestions to "get your anger out." Years of habit and training cannot be undone in a week. It may be helpful to refer such people to the psalmists' expressions of anger and impatience at God, or to biblical examples of "improper" requests (such as the story of the blind Bartimaeus in Mark 10). Such people need painstaking and compassionate help as they gradually become aware of unwanted feelings toward God and toward creation, and are increasingly able to speak to God about the truth they discover.

Relationships develop only when the parties involved pay attention to each other. Christian tradition assures us that God does God's part, attending always to each of us. The believer, therefore, if relationship to God is to be developed, must attend to God. We human beings have enough trouble even noticing, let alone caring for, anyone else without the added difficulty of paying attention to the invisible, mysterious God. Contemplative prayer means becoming increasingly absorbed in God and the person of Jesus.

Pastoral caregivers have a keen eye for the quality of an individual's relationships. The pastor doing direction likewise keeps an eye on the character of the relationship between the directee and God, as evidenced in prayer. Many of the same dynamics that affect communication in marriage also affect communication between people and God. The pastor skilled in relationship counseling will, for example, be able to discern when an individual is keeping certain feelings or issues hidden, or keeping God at a distance by using words that are highly impersonal. In fact, a person's words (especially the words of address) often disclose a great deal about how that person views God—as an angry and distant parent, a good but impotent friend, a time-management expert who watches our every move, or even a "typical male."

Prayer time is not always a peaceful time. In my experience, prayer can be quite troubling, unnerving, and discomforting. Parishioners who are mature in their faith and have moved beyond God as a bad parent commonly tell of a relationship that appears dry, flat, even distant, of the kind one sees when relatives gather unwillingly for some obligatory family occasion. They are uncomfortable, uninterested in the other people and cannot wait until they get seated for dinner. Some of them sit around in overstuffed chairs with dazed and faraway looks on their faces while others attempt a little pained and awkward small talk.

When this dreadful kind of relationship infects the life of prayer, the pastor must gently question directees to determine causes of the distance and dryness. "What are your feelings now?" "What are the things you are not saying to God?" Questions can often open up the channels of communication and insight. When it appears that emotions will not flow easily, I have sometimes used a Gestalt chair dialogue, with God occupying the empty chair. Once people begin to unload to the pastor and express feelings, it is helpful to suggest that they say these things to God. What they thought they were saying only to the pastor, they now find they are communicating to God–that is prayer! Prayer must mean something significant to us, or it amounts to no more than party chitchat or the selfish requests of a child.

Methods that help ease our experience of dryness in relationship with God are not to be regarded as magical potions. Winter seasons are to be expected in the life of prayer, whether we are in spiritual direction or not, and they will not always change to summer as quickly as we might wish.

In human relationships, intimacy is fostered by regular engagement. So too with prayer. A person wishing to share an intimate relationship with God may need to develop a discipline of prayer, such as setting aside a regular time where the mind's clutter subsides and a listening for the Word occurs. Such a set time period may be especially helpful during the early months of direction. Those who never have mastered daily prayer might be invited initially to undertake a consistent pattern, one that can be continued on a permanent basis later. They should be cautioned, however, that the most common mistake is to start big. In terms of both frequency and length of prayer periods, a small undertaking is best, one that can be sustained on a regular, perhaps daily, basis. More important than how often and how long is the attitude with which we approach this separate time. We should approach it as an opportunity simply to "be" and appreciate the gift of life, allowing our striving egos to relax and our overtaxed feelings to experience calm.

Words are not absolutely essential in prayer. Some beginners on the journey of prayer may not be able to move from voiced petitions to wordless prayer immediately–nor need they ever. In some cases a monologia may be helpful, that is, a prayer consisting of just one word, a few words, or a phrase–repeated over and over again. Many times the right word or phrase will be apparent to the pastor or parishioner after some discussion about the relationship with God. At other times, traditional words such as "Jesus" or "Savior" may be used. Phrases such as the Kyrie or the Jesus Prayer ("Jesus Christ, Son of God, have mercy on me a sinner") are helpful.

Since the exhaling of breath often has a calming effect, tying in the monologia to one's breathing is worthwhile. A monologia that I value is the Kyrie, spoken in Greek–mentally saying "Kyrie" on the inhale and "eleison" on the exhale. Another consists of saying nothing on the inhale, and in my mind repeating "Savior" on the exhale. The Jesus Prayer can be used in similar fashion by inhaling on "Jesus Christ, Son of God" and exhaling on "have mercy on me a sinner." The use of a monologia suggests the great freedom and creativity that can be applied to one's prayer life.

It is, finally, important to remember that there are desert periods, when prayer seems nothing more than a confrontation with tightly locked steel doors that never open to our knock. Most people who have engaged in regular prayer over a large portion of their lives describe times when they do not feel like praying, or when it seems as if no one is listening. But there are other times when prayer is like a walk through the lushest rain forest–full of sights, sounds, and scents rich in beauty and unending in variation. The pastor can help directees understand, and expect, both kinds of experience.

Scripture

Through the Bible, Christians today still hear the Word, as saints through the centuries have always done. Scripture can be vibrant and alive to people; it need not be an antiquated piece of parchment, as it seems to be for some. It also can effectively help structure the prayer experience.

In our caring ministry, we may wish to introduce a variation of the *Lectio Divina*, assuming that counselees already have become familiar with spiritual direction and the contemplative attitude. First, the directees need to quiet themselves, perhaps by way of relaxation exercises, imaging, or regularized breathing. For those who already are fairly relaxed, a breathing exercise done with the eyes closed can be a good way to begin. They may count their breaths, or mentally say, "I am," on the inhale and "calm" (or "relaxed") on the exhale. After a few minutes, they can move to using the Jesus Prayer or some monologia, again in concert with their breathing.

Calm, mentally receptive, and relaxed, the directees next begin to read slowly a short passage from Scripture. They read the same selection several times, again slowly. Usually, the pastor and parishioner have agreed in advance on the series of scripture selections to be used. The Psalms are a good place to begin, as is a system of readings that follows the pattern set forth in Ignatius' description of a religious retreat.[17] When reading the indicated portion of scripture, directees are to reflect on the passage and listen for the Word being spoken to them. Sometimes, it is helpful to ask questions of the selection, so that it may begin to speak. The process should not be forced, however; it is important to stay in the receptive mode, to have patience, and to restrain from demanding or striving for immediate, earthshaking revelations.

The final step requires that parishioners close their eyes and again be aware of their breathing. Now, instead of repeating the Jesus Prayer or some monologia, they use phrases from the given scripture selection to coordinate with their breathing. For example, Psalm 23 (NEB) might be used, beginning as follows:

Inhale: The Lord is my shepherd;
Exhale: I shall want nothing.

Inhale: He makes me lie down in green pastures,
Exhale: I shall want nothing.

Inhale: [He] leads me beside the waters of peace;
Exhale: I shall want nothing.

Inhale: He renews life within me;
Exhale: I shall want nothing.

What is actually occurring here is the formation of a prayer from those phrases of the scripture passage that seem especially compelling. It is not necessary that the directee have a photographic memory or worry about forgetting some sections. The most striking portions of the passage will be remembered in their essence, and they will become the prayer. Directees are instructed to let these remembered passages (now a prayer) speak to them–whether in feelings, images, ideas, or memories–and thus listen for the Word, for God present and speaking. After having repeated these phrases for a period of time, directees are told and they come to experience that the passage continues to speak to them even after they are no longer reciting it. The speaking continues, too, as directees repeatedly reread and "pray" the scripture in the ensuing days and weeks.

Instead of being used to create a litany, scripture can find other functions in spiritual direction. For example, after practicing some of the preparatory quieting exercises just described, directees may be asked to form an image of the biblical scene in their mind's eye. Then, after reading the passage several times, they close their eyes, and using their eyelids as a screen, they imagine themselves part of that scene–as Zacchaeus up in the tree, or as one of the lambs beside the still waters of Psalm 23. They are to smell the smells, hear the sounds, and taste the food and drink. It is not necessary to move the scene's characters around as a stage director would do, but in a receptive attitude, simply let happen whatever happens. Directees can also allow themselves to say or do things that are not precisely described in the passage.

The goal of such an exercise is to allow the scripture reading to come alive. Psalms, parables, and narrative sections of the Gospels are particularly appropriate for such usage. Having once visualized a passage in this way, directees can return again and again to the same image and allow it to continue to speak.

The Journal

Not all parishioners are willing to keep a journal. Some are paralyzed by a fear of writing even though they are told that they will not have to show it to anyone, not even the pastor, and that they should not concern themselves with handwriting, punctuation, neatness, syntax, or grammar. Parishioners willing to write, however, will find it beneficial to keep an ongoing journal in which they record their reflections on their own religious experience. Written reflection can give us a sense of the grace that is always operating in our life. It can foster an understanding of the patterns of grace and help us relax our striving.

Journal entries can include poetry, prose, dialogue, or pictures—anything, whether spontaneous or focused. They can deal with feelings, thoughts, dreams, and intuitions; with past, present, or future. The writing should be casual in style; if it is too "well done," too full of insight, our ego becomes involved, and we try energetically to make something happen rather than receptively allowing the Spirit to flow through us.

The frequency of journal entries is strictly an individual matter. For the beginner, daily entries during the first few weeks or months may be helpful for establishing the writing habit. Later entries can be more sporadic—as one is moved. The amount of time devoted to journal writing can vary from a minute to an hour, depending on the need of the moment. What has been written must not be publicly disclosed lest such disclosure damage the crucial sense of freedom needed to express oneself with complete openness and honesty.

Putting into words these feelings that overwhelm and the images that terrorize or inspire can give us perspective on what we experience. Journal writing can significantly facilitate the process of reflection in that, as Morton Kelsey states, it puts distance between self and experience: "It gives a space to deal with the cause of inner turmoil. We can bring many problems and fears into the open and deal with them face to face in honest combat. In a journal, we can distinguish between friends and foes."[18] No one has done more to popularize journal writing in recent years than Ira Progoff. At his Intensive Journal Workshops, he teaches people to use writing as a way of exploring their inner worlds. With a little adaptation, a number of his techniques can be useful to the spiritual director.[19]

Other Disciplines

A host of other exercises can also be useful in the direction process.[20] People who have a legalistic sense of discipline may be helped by something simple and spontaneous to lighten things up. Others who are inexperienced and hungry for discipline may benefit from structure. Sometimes, a focus on the body is required; when a tense and tired body blocks our attentiveness to grace, the use of yoga, sports, walking, biofeedback, or guided relaxation may be beneficial. Directors should beware, however, of touching the surface of too many disciplines without giving sustained attention to any one of them.

THE DIRECTOR

Regarding the spiritual director, Connolly writes:

> Often, when I hear someone describe himself as a spiritual director, I picture an ageless, emaciated chap in a cowled robe, with his eyes cast down and his hands hidden in flowing sleeves. He sits in a whitewashed, cramped room with one small, barred window high on the wall beside him. Opposite him, wearing dun-colored traveling-dress and bonnet, sits a seventeenth-century French lady. Between them is a table bearing a skull and a guttered candle. She is describing the miseries of managing the family estate with her husband away at Court for much of the year. He is murmuring about being alone with the Alone, or dictating an honorarium that will enable her to bring a measure of monastic order and piety into her life.[21]

One almost can smell the dusky odors of Connolly's scene, depicting as it does a hierarchical social and religious life that no longer exists. One has the impression of a spiritual director out of contact with the real world, parlaying an antiquated theology. The medieval dogma apart, just think of the connotations conveyed by the word "spiritual" to our scientific age, or the word "direction" to an age steeped in freedom and individuality. The perceptions and misperceptions people bring to spiritual direction today can make the pastor's work in this connection harder to accept than, say, psychotherapy. In the Eastern tradition, the need for a guide–sage or guru–is much more widely valued.

It is obvious from the beginning that certain prerequisites are necessary for the pastor who seeks to offer spiritual direction to modern Christians. Pastors may already possess some of them. Others will need to be cultivated.

First, there is the skill to establish, maintain, and deepen relationships. This is a primary requirement for any pastoral caregiver whether making hospital visits, offering pastoral counseling, or visiting a shut-in. The spiritual guide first befriends directees, receives them warmly, listens to them eagerly, is "with" them, and only then, in relationship, assists in their spiritual journey. People coming for direction must feel that they are accepted before they can give their confidence to the director. The old image of the director as one who is uniquely "spiritual," aloof and removed from the world, holy and above sin, can hardly commend a growth process to most congregants today. Indeed, all of the interpersonal characteristics that foster effective pastoral counseling—warmth, openness, respect, listening skills, attending behaviors—are needed by the pastor who offers direction. As a directee, I must trust and respect my guide; I must know that my director hears me before I can entrust myself to the journey toward spiritual growth.

A second requirement for a pastor doing direction is an understanding of the spiritual life. As Barry and Connolly put it, "They do not need doctorates in spirituality to be competent, but they do need to have more knowledge than personal experience and common sense alone can supply."[22] Teresa of Avila and John of the Cross both emphasized this point; they railed against ignorant directors who relied only upon their own experience and knew little of the rich tradition of spiritual practice and direction.

The knowledge required of a spiritual director includes a solid grasp of theology an informed understanding of the faith, of spirituality, of varieties of spiritual experience and methods, and of scripture (including the tools of modern biblical scholarship). Also helpful is a base of knowledge gained from modern psychology and psychotherapy.

Seminary training in spirituality can be of great assistance. Classics such as the desert fathers and mothers, Ignatius, John of the Cross, Teresa of Avila, and Marie of the Incarnation provide rich and deep orientation. Contemporary writers such as Barry, Connolly, Edwards, Jones, Kelsey, LaPlace, Leech, May, and Merton are also useful. We need to reflect on our own prayer experience and learn from it, but we need also to relate it to that of others whom we have met or read.

A third crucial requirement for the pastor who wishes to give spiritual direction is personal religious experience. This may seem obvious, but frequently the parish demands so much of pastors that, caught up in all the activity, we have scant energy or time left for prayer and meditation. Workaholics in the parish, however, offer a negative model for other church members. They pattern a style of life that leaves little room for listening to the Spirit.

It is vital that ministers themselves experience the ebbs and flows of the Spirit's movement, the summers and winters of prayer, so that we know with confidence where hope is to be found and are persuaded that God is indeed with us–God's constant presence, whether perceived by us or not. Ministers need to have faced their own fears, wrestled with their own demons, and known for themselves the undergirding love of Christ. We require experience, and we need to have reflected on that experience.

The director should not be seen by counselees as a superhuman miracle worker and problem solver. Surely, it is important that the pastor act as one in whom Christ is present, who lives daily in faith, who, like Moses, has spoken with God "face to face, as [one] speaks to [a] friend" (Exod. 33:11). But pastors also must communicate that we do not have special powers, a "direct line" to God, or the correct solutions for all problems. Faithful pastors have experienced the Ground of Being, to be sure, but as human beings we are still finite and fallible beings ourselves.

Many other requirements for those who would offer spiritual direction could be listed. These three seem crucial to me. But effective spiritual direction has never required ordination or a special degree. The skill for it always has been seen rather as a charism not possessed by all. Like good pastoral counselors, effective directors tend to be discovered by the Christian community. They need, in summary, skill in establishing and maintaining relationships, an understanding of the spiritual life (and of theology, psychology, and psychotherapy), and their own personal religious experience. Pastors who have these, and the charism, will be ready not only to see spiritual direction influence their care and counseling, but actually to offer spiritual direction as well.

DISCERNMENT

A final issue facing the director, already alluded to earlier, is the ability to assess growth in the directee's spiritual life–classically referred to as discernment of the Spirit. Both pastor and parishioner must decide whether the change that is occurring, and the voice they are listening to, is from God or not. Some directors have maintained that only criteria of the inner world are acceptable in making such judgments. Ignatius, however, was correct when he argued that unless a Christian is experiencing a heightened sense of God's love and unless the increased capacity to love others brings that experience into action in the world about us, spiritual exercises are not complete. Without an appropriate return to full and conscious participation in the wider community, no amount of spiritual direction is fully beneficial.

How does the pastor know that an individual is growing into a deeper life in the Spirit? Although discernment is partly an intuitive matter, there are certain behaviors that give evidence to the Spirit's work. In several of his epistles, Paul lists them: "But the fruit of the Spirit is love, joy, peace, patience, kindness, goodness, faithfulness, gentleness, self-control; against these there is no law" (Gal. 5:22-23).

Barry and Connolly make the point that these signs are not absolutes, but always in the process of development, and when their origin is indeed an action of God's Spirit, they appear not sequentially, but simultaneously. Patience does not make its appearance long after love and joy; it appears, at least in some form, along with them. "The fruits appear as unified growth, not a clutch of conflicting elements. And where there is conflict between the elements, or where one is totally lacking, the director must suspect illusion."[23] The Catholic tradition has long been suspicious of the authenticity of mystical prayer when the mystic cannot take time out to scrub pots and pans. Evidence, not of how directees *think* they respond, but of how they actually *do* respond–how they interact with others– can be helpful as a gauge of how accurately they assess their inner life.

Some descriptions make it seem as if spiritual direction has reference exclusively to the inner world, but it does not. Indeed, spiritual direction is not a matter of inner versus outer. It involves both. It is a movement between the two. There is a reciprocal interaction between inner life and external reality. As Jean Stairs has put it:

> Our relationship with God will feed our enthusiasm to improve the quality of life around us. Prayer will clarify our vision of

the world and will reflect a disposition that is willing to be critical–critical enough to be able to question the conventions and politics of our world.[24]

Our task as directors and directees alike is to listen to the inner for what our vocation (in the theological sense) should be in the outer. In this way, spiritual direction serves the correlation of pastoral care and theology. If we fail to relate the two, the external world becomes a substitute for the inner world, "doing" replaces our hearing of the Word, and we can scarcely guess as to what God's Word is for our lives. Only by listening and remaining receptive to the movements of the Spirit can we realize our true vocation and, in our finite way, be faithful to God's call.

NOTES

1. Wolfhart Pannenberg, *Christian Spirituality* (Philadelphia: Westminster Press, 1983): p. 13.

2. Don S. Browning, *The Moral Context of Pastoral Care* (Philadelphia: Westminster Press, 1976), pp. 116-130.

3. C. W. Brister, *Pastoral Care in the Church* (New York: Harper & Row, 1964), p. 7.

4. David L. Fleming offers a good description of spiritual direction in his article, "Models of Spiritual Direction," *Review for Religious*, 1975, pp. 351-357.

5. For a more extensive treatment, the reader may wish to consult: William A. Barry and William J. Connolly, *The Practice of Spiritual Direction* (New York: Harper & Row/Seabury Press, 1983); Tilden Edwards, *Spiritual Friend* (Mahwah, NJ: Paulist Press, 1980); Carolyn Gratton, *Guidelines for Spiritual Direction* (Denville, NJ: Dimension Books, 1980); Alan Jones, *Exploring Spiritual Direction: An Essay on Christian Friendship* (New York: Seabury Press, 1982); Jean LaPlace, *Preparing for Spiritual Direction* (Chicago: Franciscan Herald Press, 1975); Kenneth Leech, *Soul Friend: The Practice of Christian Spirituality* (New York: Harper & Row, 1980); Henri J. M. Nouwen, *Making All Things New: An Invitation to the Spiritual Life*, 1st ed. (New York: Harper & Row, 1981); *Handbook of Spirituality for Ministers,* ed. Robert Wicks (New York: Paulist Press, 1995), see especially Chapter 20.

6. William Barry, "Prayer in Pastoral Care," *Journal of Pastoral Care*, June, 1977, p. 94.

7. William Connolly, "Contemporary Spiritual Direction: Scope and Principles," in *Studies in the Spirituality of Jesuits* (St. Louis, MO: American Assistancy Seminar on Jesuit Spirituality, 1975), p. 99.

8. Morton Kelsey, "Pastoral Counseling and the Spiritual Quest," *Journal of Pastoral Care*, June, 1978, p. 95.

9. William Barry and William Connolly, *The Practice of Spiritual Direction* (New York: Seabury Press, 1982), p. 11.

10. Gerald May, *Care of Mind, Care of Spirit: Psychiatric Dimensions of Spiritual Direction* (New York: Harper & Row, 1982), p. 99.

11. See especially Robert Rossi, "The Distinction Between Psychological and Religious Counseling," *Review for Religious*, 1978, pp. 546-571; Ruth Tiffany Barnhouse, "Spiritual Direction and Psychotherapy," *The Journal of Pastoral Care*, September, 1979, pp. 149-163; Tilden Edwards, *Spiritual Friend* (Mahwah, NJ: Paulist Press, 1980), p. 130.

12. Shaun McCarty, "On Entering Spiritual Direction," *Review for Religious*, 1976, p. 858.

13. Rossi, "The Distinction Between Psychological and Religious Counseling," p. 568.

14. Howard W. Stone, *Crisis Counseling* (Philadelphia: Fortress Press, 1993).

15. Howard W. Stone, *Brief Pastoral Counseling* (Minneapolis, MN: Fortress Press, 1994), pp. 138-154.

16. Ira Progoff, *At a Journal Workshop* (New York: Dialog House, 1977).

17. Saint Ignacio de Loyola, *The Spiritual Exercises of St. Ignatius* (St. Louis, MO: Institute of Jesuit Sources, 1978).

18. Morton T. Kelsey, *Adventure Inward* (Minneapolis, MN: Augsburg, 1980), p. 25.

19. Progoff, *At a Journal Workshop*. Other useful methods can be found in Kelsey, *Adventure Inward*.

20. Morton T. Kelsey, *The Other Side of Silence: A Guide to Christian Meditation* (Mahwah, NJ: Paulist Press, 1976), has contributed to the field of contemporary spiritual direction through his work on meditation. He suggests five methods for meditation and gives examples of how it can be used to foster growth in the life of the Spirit. The reader who is interested in meditation is referred to Kelsey's writings on the subject.

21. Connolly, "Contemporary Spiritual Direction," p. 98.

22. Barry and Connolly, *The Practice of Spiritual Direction*, p. 131.

23. Ibid., p. 109.

24. M. Jean Stairs, *Be My Companion: A Study of Spiritual Direction* (Toronto: Image Publishing, 1982), p. 51.

Chapter 6

The Priesthood of All Believers

Some churches have begun the practice of listing their church staff in a new way in their Sunday bulletin:

Ministers: All the members of the congregation
Pastor: The Rev. _____
Organist: _____

The opening line may be overly cute, and affording it such priority may be arguable. Not to be ignored, however, is the acknowledged fact that the laity also share in the church's ministry. If prominence in the new listing can get that across, it may be worthwhile, for the fact itself surely deserves repeated emphasis, especially in our day.

MINISTRY AND LAITY

The place of the laity in the church would not have been a major issue in the church of New Testament times. Although a precise picture of what the church was like in the first century cannot be drawn, it is quite clear that there were no sharp divisions between clergy and laity.[1] Alan Richardson describes a lay person in the New Testament ethos as someone who:

This chapter originally appeared as a portion of "Lay Pastoral Care from a Theological Perspective," which was Chapter 2 in *The Caring Church: A Guide for Lay Pastoral Care*. Reprinted by permission from *The Caring Church* by Howard Stone, ©1991 Augsburg Fortress.

Is certainly not (as he tends to be in modern usage) a church-member who has no ministerial responsibility, one who has handed over his functions of evangelism and pastoral care to certain professional Christians who are paid to perform them. All the laity . . . if we use the term in the biblical way, are priests and ministers of the Church of Jesus Christ; and all the "ministers" are equally "laymen."[2]

This point is made dramatically in I Peter 2:9: "But you are a chosen race, a royal priesthood, a holy nation, God's own people, that you may declare the wonderful deeds of him who called you out of darkness into his marvelous light." In the original Greek, the word used here for "people" is *laos*–laity. As Herman Stuempfle writes, "The people, the new race, the Christian 'folk'–without differentiation here with regard to office–were quite simply, the laity."[3]

Some differentiation between clergy and laity began to arise almost before the New Testament authors had completed their writings. Just where and when the division between them occurred is hard to document with precision, for it involved an evolutionary process. With the passage of time, however, the differentiation became increasingly pronounced–to the point where it finally became a highly controversial issue.

VOCATION AND PRIESTHOOD

The sixteenth-century reformers argued that ministry is not just for a special class of Christians, but for all people in the church. Two theological themes that helped the Reformation churches understand ministry can also help us today. Martin Luther referred to them as (1) vocation or calling–one's station in life, and (2) implicit within it, the priesthood of all believers.

One's Station in Life

As Christians, our first calling, according to Luther, is to the state–the lot, status, station, or office–in which we find ourselves.

Our vocation is not to extraordinary careers of piety, but to the common tasks that devolve upon us right where we are.

In the seventh chapter of First Corinthians, Paul mentions several of these states (verses 17-24). We should be able to accept whatever unchangeable life situation we find ourselves in and "lead the life which the Lord has assigned."

Luther bracketed within this first type of vocation one's occupation (as teacher, seamstress, poet, engineer, or firefighter), one's status (single, husband, wife, child), and one's place in life (rich, poor, blind, sighted). Included in our calling are thus our everyday tasks, our occupations, our studies, our daily routines. In this regard, Stuempfle suggests:

> Every Christian, no matter what his office or status in church or world, lived out his life under God's call. . . . Each could equally be the place of service to the neighbor, and thus to God. Luther, I think, would have liked the man who, when asked by a perfervid evangelist, "what he did to serve the Lord," responded without blinking an eye: "I bake bread."[4]

From his understanding of Paul in First Corinthians, Luther argued that every station in life is equal; no one status is higher than another: "The housemaid on her knees scrubbing the floor is doing a work as pleasing in the eyes of Almighty God as the priest on his knees before the altar saying the Mass."[5] We are called to perform our daily tasks as best we can, whatever our life situation, and realize that in our particular place, we can perform a ministry of service to those around us.[6] Thus, ministries vary according to our status in life, but all Christians, meaning specifically all laity, do minister in their particular places.

The Priesthood of All Believers

The second vocation or calling of every Christian is as a member of the priesthood of all believers. A key aspect of priesthood, since biblical times, has been the function of mediation. Under the Mosaic covenant, all the people of Israel were to be a "kingdom of priests" (Exod. 19:6 ff.; Lev. 11:44 ff.; Num. 15:40; Isa. 61-6). God is a holy God; and since human holiness is imperfect, the people of Israel needed someone to intercede for them before God. That was the function of the high priest—mediating between God and the people.

In the New Testament, the terms "priesthood" and "priest" do not refer to the office of ministry. First Corinthians 12 (28 ff.) and Ephesians 4 (11 ff.) contain lists of offices and responsibilities in the church without even mentioning priests. The New Testament refers to only two types of Christian priesthood—the priesthood of Christ (Heb. 6:20; 7:26 ff.) and the universal priesthood (I Pet. 2:9; Rev. 5:10).

Thomas Wilkens describes with great clarity Luther's understanding of our priestly vocation:

> It is a calling with, so to speak, both vertical and horizontal dimensions. Vertically, the calling grants the privilege of free access to God with the potential of faith and salvation. Horizontally, the calling occasions the responsibility of sharing the Gospel through concrete priestly functions or ministries of the Word. These are ministries of love of the first order. Yet there is another aspect of this horizontal dimension of loving ministry; that is, meeting not only one's fellow priest with the spiritual ministries of the Word but also one's neighbor—fellow priest or not—in love within the total context of his temporal situation and human need.[7]

In his understanding of the universal priesthood, Luther tried to recapture the original biblical understanding of laity. Luther and Bucer urged the mutual cure of souls by all members of the Body of Christ. Later, pietists practiced it more widely than during Luther's lifetime. This theme of *Seelsorge aller an allen* (the care of all for the souls of all) emphasized that the gifts of the Holy Spirit moved through all of the people of God and each had a responsibility for the mutual guidance and spiritual sustenance of the others. As John T. McNeill points out, [For Luther] "all Christians are functioning members of one living body, exercising toward one another a spiritual or priestly office."[8] Four consequences of Luther's thinking help clarify this second sense of calling.

- The phrase "priesthood of all believers" simply advances the view that every Christian is a minister in Christ's church. Priestly functions–such as evangelism, visiting the sick and lonely, giving spiritual counsel, praying with the dying, comforting the bereaved, speaking the word of forgiveness–are not reserved for clergy. To quote Luther, "Let everyone, therefore, who knows himself to be a Christian, be assured of this, that we are all equally priests, that is to say, we have the same power in respect to the Word and the sacraments."[9]
- We are initiated into this priesthood by the washing of baptism: "Through baptism we have all been ordained as priests."[10] For each of us, baptism, because it incorporates us into Christ's suffering, death, and resurrection (Rom. 6:3 ff.), marks our entrance into the community of faith. As such, it is also our induction into the universal priesthood. The sprinkling of water, not the donning of a stole, is what makes every Christian a minister.
- The primary task of the priest is to mediate. In the Hebrew Bible, the priest stood before God and interceded for the twelve tribes. On the cross of Golgotha it was Christ, the new high priest, who stood before God and interceded for us. In the same manner we, when we mediate with our neighbor–when we go to our neighbor in love, interceding as Christ has done for us–become, as Luther puts it, "little Christs."[11] The phrase suggests not a disestablishment of priests, but an expansion of their number to include all Christians.
- In addition to the task of mediating, there are a variety of ways in which the role of priest–minister to others–can be fulfilled. While each Christian is a member of the royal priesthood, it would lead to chaos if all were involved in the *public* preaching of the Word and administration of the sacraments. For this reason, the church calls and ordains certain members of the universal priesthood to serve the functions of public ministry. Clergy and laity differ only in function; they do not constitute separate orders. Luther, therefore, saw the Christian, any Christian, as one who hears confessions, shares burdens, consoles, prays, listens, visits the bereaved, gives assurance of forgiveness, and performs the other tasks of ministry. Calvin

required that visitation of homes be carried out not only by the pastor, but also by the elders. This certainly goes beyond the usual delimitation of the laity's work today; it includes many areas that in more recent years have been reserved for clergy—and at times clergy specialists.

LAY PASTORAL CARE

Most Christians, laity and clergy alike, have no quarrel with the notion of lay ministry, whether that means involvement in acts of love toward others or a sharing in the universal priesthood of the church. However, there often appears to be a discrepancy between what Christians think and what Christians do. Some clergy seem reticent to recognize and encourage lay church members in doing pastoral care. And some lay people seem paralyzed by fear when it comes to putting their faith into action in the form of a neighbor-loving pastoral care ministry.

Those who preach on love of neighbor can get annoyed when parishioners are slow to respond in ways that seem appropriate. Yet, some ministers actually inhibit lay people from becoming priests to one another, particularly in the area of pastoral care, which is sometimes regarded as a distinctively ministerial preserve.

When Sandra tells Pastor Tim about Alice being in the hospital as the result of an auto accident, Tim's first reaction might be: "Why is the minister always the last to know?" He feels resentful as he dashes off to the hospital. Now, that is a good thing insofar as it shows how much the pastor really cares—for Alice.

But Sandra needs care too; she needs help to grow in her own pastoral caring. Tim might have responded differently: "Oh, Sandra, I'm sorry to hear that. How is she doing? Have you been to see her yet?" Then, he might affirm Sandra's visit and relate it to their *common* ministry: "Will you be able to continue visiting her? Do you think other members of the choir might want to know and visit her too? Would you be willing to get word to them?"

Sandra may have thought she was only doing a friendly thing when she visited Alice at the hospital. The pastor can turn the moment of his learning about it into a teaching moment. He can help Sandra see her own priesthood, her own neighbor love, and also her continuing potential for pastoral care and for facilitating the care of other parishioners.

Pastoral care is not a job for pastors only. It belongs to the whole community. It assumes—expresses and fosters—the universal priesthood. Ministry can take the form of one-on-one counseling, but it can also involve visiting, bringing food, doing dishes, cleaning house, running errands, or just listening.

Recently, in the church there has been a renewed emphasis on the pastoral care ministry of lay people. A number of churches have teams of trained lay pastoral care visitors who call on the sick, shut-in, bereaved, and troubled. The training of laity in pastoral care methods is designed to reduce fears, enhance skills, provide methods, heighten awareness of the task, and above all, to instill confidence and the conviction that even the simplest acts of caring are commissioned by God. It is a way to help parish members become active responders to God's love. It can provide an easily grasped means for unleashing their love of others within the framework of their particular status and vocation. Lay pastoral care training assists all Christians to share in the ministry to which we have all been called.[12]

Thus, all Christians have two callings, two vocations. The first is to our station in life; the second is to the universal priesthood. In these callings, we are to love and serve our neighbor (Chapter 9). Pastoral care is a ministry that encompasses much of what we do for our neighbor. It is one way in which God's love is communicated to the people about us.

NOTES

1. See Ernst Kasemann, "Paul and Early Catholicism," *New Testament Questions of Today*, trans. W. J. Montague and Wilfred F. Bunge (Philadelphia: Fortress Press, 1969), pp. 246-247; and Herman G. Stuempfle, Jr., "Theological and Biblical Perspectives on the Laity" (pamphlet published by the Lutheran Church in America, Division for Mission in North America, 1973).

2. Alan Richardson, *An Introduction to the Theology of the New Testament* (New York: Harper & Brothers, 1959), pp. 301-302.

3. Stuempfle, "Theological and Biblical Perspectives on the Laity," p. 2.

4. Ibid, p. 6.

5. Ibid, p. 6.

6. Accepting one's lot does not mean, as some have maintained, that certain people–women, ethnic groups, the physically challenged–are therefore to be exploited and held in their place by the prevailing establishment. Each person has the responsibility to determine what can and cannot be changed.

7. Thomas G. Wilkens, "Ministry, Vocation, and Ordination: Some Perspectives from Luther," *The Lutheran Quarterly*, Fall 1977, pp. 75-76.

8. John T. McNeill, *A History of the Cure of Souls* (New York: Harper & Brothers, 1951).

9. *LW 36,* p. 116.

10. Quoted in Paul Althaus, *The Theology of Martin Luther*, trans. Robert C. Schultz (Philadelphia: Fortress Press, 1966), p. 314.

11. Quoted in Stuempfle, "Laity," p. 4.

12. For further information on the training of lay persons in pastoral care, see Howard W. Stone, *The Caring Church: A Guide for Lay Pastoral Care* (Minneapolis, MN: Fortress Press, 1991).

Chapter 7

Acceptance of Self and Spirit

Rarely do I read a book on mental health, pastoral counseling, or ministerial practice that does not emphasize the importance of acceptance. In these fields, a clarion call over the last several decades has been: "Be accepting of others." Rogers, Carkhuff, Ivey, Clinebell, Oates, and many others have made it eminently clear that if one is to develop effective pastoral relationships, one must manifest appropriate attending behaviors, careful reflective listening, suspension of judgment, and other expressions of acceptance.[1]

This call for acceptance in the interpersonal relationships of ministry is usually acknowledged and received with appropriate nods and knowing smiles. I have often sounded the same call myself.[2] Who could possibly disagree? Who indeed could possibly favor nonacceptance, rejection, or a therapeutic cold shoulder? In fact, the acceptance of acceptance is now so common as to deserve fresh reflection and critique.

ACCEPTANCE

Recently, while listening to a lecture on pastoral counseling in the parish, I heard again the familiar call: "The key to doing good pastoral counseling is that you really accept people." The comment

A version of this chapter originally appeared as "Pastoral Care as Acceptance of Self and Spirit" in *Perkins Journal*, 37 (Summer 1984), pp. 21-26. Reprinted by permission from the Archives, Bridwell Library, Perkins School of Theology, Southern Methodist University.

from the podium triggered, for me, a reflective detour. What did the speaker really mean when he made that assertion? What did he understand "acceptance" to be?

Tuning in to the lecturer once again, I soon began to get a clearer picture of his meaning: Acceptance requires the caregiver to value, to listen carefully, and to believe in and work with individuals in spite of what they have or have not done. No condition for such acceptance can be laid out in advance. Acceptance is not something awarded to people only after they have "cleaned up their act," nor is it grounded in their prior subscription to a particular code of ethics. The speaker was clearly advising me to just accept people as they are, in spite of what they have or have not done. I half expected to hear strains of "Just As I Am" in the background; instead of a hymn, however, there flowed quotations from Carl Rogers and other psychotherapists to buttress the point. Only belatedly, almost as an afterthought, did the lecturer also refer to theologian Paul Tillich's sermon "You Are Accepted."[3]

Now, there are good reasons for stressing the importance of acceptance in pastoral care. The emphasis represents a legitimate correction of certain historic, and even contemporary, forms of ministry in which the approach to others often conveyed an almost overbearing parental attitude: You must do what God wills (meaning, "as I say"). In reality, few of the choices we face in life are simple, clear-cut, black-and-white choices; most fall into various shades of gray. Furthermore, our situation today is marked by a radically changed attitude toward authority: *Herr Pastor* is out, "Pastor Bill" is in. Our attending and listening to parishioners is valued, but our telling them what to do is not because most people prefer to discover the answers for themselves.

I personally have experienced acceptance by another and been grateful for it. Probably nothing has a more powerful influence on your life than to know that someone is *for* you–through thick and thin, whether you act appropriately or not. Such acceptance serves as a center, a home base out of which all of life can flow. Its absence, in some cases, can generate a frantic drive to gain acceptance by any means possible and at whatever cost; it can even lead to the lethargy of depressive seclusion as we anxiously seal ourselves off from others. The speaker who recently triggered my reflection was surely correct in asserting that acceptance is a key component in pastoral care. Nonetheless, I for one still find the notion a bit unsettling.

My uneasiness perhaps arises from the way in which unconditional acceptance is often meted out in actual practice. As applied, our acceptance of people as they are rarely seems to include any valuing of the transcendent, any reverence for spirit.[4] For those who are theologically concerned about pastoral care this should give pause.

Rather than simply adopting wholesale the sound psychotherapeutic principle of acceptance, we need to examine carefully its meaning and to broaden our understanding of it to the point where people are accepted not only as they *are,* but also as they can *become* in the life of the Spirit. We dare not assume that an "as is" acceptance on our part will naturally lead someone to transcend self[5] for life in the Spirit–experience simply does not support such an easy assumption. We need, instead, to take a fresh and hard look at acceptance, particularly as it relates to our understanding of self and spirit.

SELF AND SPIRIT

The "self" is the organizing center of human response and activity within each of us. Rogers thinks of self as that "organized consistent conceptual gestalt" composed of various perceptions of the "I" or "me" in relation to the world and other people, and the values that are placed on these perceptions.[6] This self has been variously designated as ego, soul, heart, or "I." Whatever the name, the reference is clearly to the locus of perception, organization, decision making, and response. The self is the internal regulatory system of human mentation and activity.

In most forms of psychotherapy and pastoral care, the purpose of counseling is to strengthen the self. Expressions such as "weak ego-strength" or "lack of self-esteem," technically not synonymous, are typically used by mental health professionals to describe an individual with a weak or undeveloped self. Although psychological approaches to treatment are diverse in the way they describe their goals, most do focus on this center of organization, and their purpose is to strengthen the self and foster some form of self-actualization.

The "spirit," on the other hand, is that facet of the individual wherein God is most directly encountered. "It is the Spirit God" (Rom. 8:16). In the Bible, "spirit" (usually *pneuma* in the New Testament and *ruach* in the Hebrew Scripture) is used variously to describe God, incorporeal beings, manifestations of God, and the divine power in human beings.[7] This last understanding is the one that concerns us here.

Ernst Kasemann believes that of all the New Testament writers, Paul has the most complete, "thoroughly thought-out doctrine" of person.[8] It is in Paul's doctrine of person that the significance of spirit is made prominent. For Paul, the term "spirit" designates the new power, summoning to faith, that comes to Christians in their rebirth. In Galatians 2:20 he characterizes their new situation: "It is no longer I who live, but Christ who lives in me." Baptism marks the death of the old person and the beginning of new life, which is grounded in the resurrection.

Reinhold Niebuhr, in discussing the self/spirit distinction, maintains that in the New Testament "the Hebraic sense of the unity of body and soul is not destroyed while, on the other hand, spirit is conceived of as primarily a capacity for and affinity with the divine."[9]

For Paul, spirit means the entire being as it is physically and spiritually related to God as the center of identity. Spirit is not a repudiation of the flesh (appetites and emotions), but a centering of them and all else in God. Eduard Schweizer puts it this way:

> Paul thinks wholly in terms of the work of the Spirit of God and perceives that the whole existence of the believer is determined thereby. For Paul the Spirit of God is not an odd power which works magically; the Spirit reveals to the believer God's saving work in Christ and makes possible his understanding and responsible acceptance thereof. For this reason the pneuma, though always God's Spirit and never evaporating into the pneuma given individually to man, is also the innermost ego of the one who no longer lives by his own being but by God's being for him.[10]

Paul invites Christians to an existence that is responsive to the summons of the Spirit. His call is for an attentive openness to the Spirit whereby believers allow their selves to be molded by God (Rom. 8:6, 14; Gal. 5:16). Life in the Spirit means a self that is oriented body and soul to God, an identity that is centered in God. "Spirit" has reference not to a portion of me but to all that I am, my whole being, as focused on hearing and responding to the Word.

The self as organizing center for a person's activity tends to respond to the individual's needs, drives, wants, cognitions, and perceptions of reality. It has difficulty looking beyond these primary stimuli. But when the spirit is attentive to God, transcendence of self becomes possible because self is now centered in the Word.

Self is not necessarily identical to spirit. The spirit's task is to transform the self into a likeness of Christ (Rom. 8:29). The spirit presupposes and works with the abilities and attributes we have and enhances them; it does not negate the structures of selfhood, but provides them with a capacity that they hitherto lacked, namely, a certain possibility for life in God's Spirit. The change that occurs when God's Spirit resides in human spirit is always an eschatological change—an "already now but not yet." The power of the self remains in tension with that of the spirit.

Self and spirit become identical only when spirit fully apprehends the self. As John Cobb writes, "The self is spirit only when the self as the organizing center transcends the emotions and other aspects of the psychic life."[11] Only as the self takes responsibility for one's whole life, and orients it in its entirety to the Word, do self and spirit coalesce.

TWO FORMS OF ACCEPTANCE

The "as is" acceptance so common in psychotherapy has reference to self, not spirit. What is appropriate in psychological counseling, however, is not sufficient for the ministry of pastoral care. Psychotherapy's "as is" acceptance raises a whole range of theological concerns. It contains no ethical components; for example, it allows one to listen primarily to one's own needs and desires rather than to the Word of God; it relies on a limited kind of acceptance (by the caregiver) while ignoring the only complete and perfect acceptance (that which comes from God); and it tends to turn one's attention more inward (toward self) than outward (toward neighbor). Our major concern here, however, has to do with the fact that "as is" acceptance typically does not recognize spirit; hence, it is not responsive to God's call for a life in the Spirit.

Diana Wing, a young and intelligent management trainee, was overwhelmed with doubts about her own capabilities. Psychotherapy assisted her to overcome these doubts and to appraise her skills and abilities more realistically, but it did not address the "winning is everything" ethos that shaped her life in both job and family. In fact, her therapist's nonjudgmental acceptance, by neglecting review of these ethical values, was tantamount to an affirmation of them. Therapeutic acceptance tended to deny to Diana the possibility of transcending self and of extending love beyond self. While, for her, self was indeed strengthened, spirit was not. Although she now feels better, functions more effectively on her job, and is more realistic about herself–all good things, to be sure–there is no movement toward a new life informed by the spirit.

Acceptance in pastoral care values both self and spirit. It not only affirms the person who *is,* but also appreciates who that person can *become* in Christ. Pastoral acceptance of this sort exists in an ongoing tension between the desires of the self and the summons of the spirit, between the "as is" of the present and the lure or call forward of the future (as some process theologians have described as the invitation of the Spirit of God).[12]

This call forward, as it is played out in the minister's acceptance of others, is significantly different from a parental no, a scripture-quoting condemnation, or a conditional "I'll accept you when you shape up." It is actually a more complete kind of acceptance in that it not only recognizes present realities, but it also has a vision of future possibilities in the Spirit. There is not only a present story, but also a future story.[13] It maintains that who we *really* are is far more than what we are just *now.* We have not yet received or incorporated all that God has to give, nor have we wholly apprehended God's intention or mission for us. The Spirit compels us to look toward Jesus as a pattern for what we are *becoming* and, thus, to know by God's grace what we *truly* are. Theologically responsible acceptance in pastoral care is eschatological to the core.

ACCEPTANCE IN PASTORAL CARE

The pastoral care that functions out of an acceptance of self *and* spirit is likely to differ in significant ways from the psychotherapy or pastoral counseling that proceeds on the basis of "as is" acceptance. There are concrete ways in which ministers can work to incorporate both self and spirit in their pastoral acceptance. Four areas are worth immediate mention: refocusing the pastor's perspective to more fully include spirit; restructuring care methods to more completely address spirit; speaking to issues of spirit during the care process; and revitalizing the minister's own personal openness to spirit.

Perspective will surely be a key characteristic distinguishing the ministerial counselor from the psychologist. How the pastor views a person's plight and rescue will significantly affect the care offered. From the very beginning, ministers with an understanding of self/spirit acceptance will look and listen for the subtle movements of spirit betokened by the other person's words. We cannot assume that people respond only out of their own needs or wants, drives or compulsions; we will instead recognize each faint hint of aspirations that may lead to transcendence of self. We may, for example, discern (and comment on) a parishioner's impulse to love others that goes beyond any personal assessment of (physical or psychic) attractiveness and approaches a kind of selfless or unselfish love. As pastors, we can try to refocus our perspective, and that of the people we serve, to include spirit as well as self.

A second way to broaden pastoral acceptance is to recognize that, in self/spirit acceptance, care of spirit is at least as important as actualization of self. As a result of such recognition, our methods of care may well begin to take on aspects of spiritual direction (which aims at strengthening the relationship with God) while relying less exclusively on aspects of psychological counseling, which tends primarily to address problems of self. In addition, we will not assume, as much pastoral counseling still does, that self must be responded to *prior* to spirit. Each is a legitimate area of counseling concern, each a possible starting point for care. In fact, pastoral care best addresses both areas–the whole person–at once rather than concentrating on either one to the exclusion of the other. There is always the danger that where issues of self are more recognizable and obviously pressing to the parishioner, they will easily take first priority and sometimes become the only issue addressed. To deal with spirit only "as time permits," however, often means in practice to ignore spirit altogether.

A third way of broadening pastoral care so that it includes both self and spirit is to recall that the Spirit's revelation occurs as the Word of God is embodied. God is revealed in both spoken and visible form. The Word of God is expressed both verbally (in preaching, teaching, scripture reading, and other written and spoken sharing of the message of Christ) and visibly (in the sacraments, an icon, Brahms' *Requiem*, an embrace, a listening ear, a warm smile, the sign of the cross, a meal brought to the mourners' home, one's ministry of presence). (See Chapter 3.) Pastoral care must be alert to this twofold address of the Word. God communicates and establishes a relationship with God's people in both ways, and pastoral care needs to emphasize both in the help it offers.

In pastoral care, the Word is made manifest or visible in the dignity and respect with which the pastor treats the person. The finite worth of the individual is articulated not only in *what* is said, but also in the *way* things are said and in the way the person is treated. Pastors accept the person *and* act out that acceptance, valuing not only who that person is now, but also who that person can become in the unfolding of the spirit.

The verbal Word is proclaimed in that moment of the care process when the minister helps interpret what the unfolding of spirit could mean for the person. As rapport is established and a relationship develops, there will come times when the minister can speak prophetically—not only expressing love "as is," but also helping the person discover what life in the Spirit can be. As Cobb has pointed out, there is a difference between desires and aspirations:

> We *desire* to gain ends that are set by our emotions. But our spiritual aspirations are for the change of our desires. . . . They deal with the motivations of our actions. For example, we may aspire to become people who act out of disinterested love for others rather than out of emotional desires. Such disinterested love is possible in principle only at the level of spirit.[14]

Pastoral care speaks to people concerning this difference between desires and aspirations in order that self can be informed by spirit in the decisions that are faced. The prophetic and interpretive components of ministry are integral to pastoral care in which the minister verbally encourages individuals in their openness to spirit and their aspirations of disinterested love.

Finally, in the realities of parish life, these prophetic and interpretive insights may be hard to come by. As we are scurrying about from meetings to appointments, worried about newsletter deadlines, sermon preparation, negative cash flow, and people's urgent cries for help, it is easy to be caught up–no, it is hard *not* to be caught up–in so many activities and demands that one's *own* spirit is ignored. Pastoral care that is open to spirit requires a minister who is open to spirit, who is not so dragged down by a myriad of activities as to have no time left for quiet listening and prayer. Only through a disciplined, daily, open attentiveness to God's voice is one enabled to sense the sometimes ever-so-slight stirrings of spirit in one's own life and in the lives of others. It is difficult to share with others our insights and directives about spirit when our own spirit is tranquilized by inactivity.

Acceptance in pastoral care is thus broader than acceptance in psychotherapy, which also has a concern for the wholeness of people. The wholeness to which pastoral care ministry aspires requires that the minister accept both self and spirit. Pastoral acceptance that recognizes only the self ("as is" acceptance) and does not value the call of spirit is inadequate, for the fundamental goal of the Christian is a life in the Spirit of Christ. Ministers who would assist others to be attentive to the Spirit's call must themselves be attentive to the Spirit *and* accept others not merely as they are now but as they can be, as they are becoming, as God intends them to be.

NOTES

1. See Robert Carkhuff, *The Art of Helping*, (Amherst, MA: Human Resource Development Press, 1987); Howard Clinebell, *Basic Types of Pastoral Care and Counseling* (Nashville, TN: Abingdon Press, 1984); Gerard Egan, *The Skilled Helper*, 5th ed. (Monterey, CA: Brooks/Cole Publishing Co., 1994); Carl R. Rogers, *Client Centered Therapy* (Boston: Houghton Mifflin Co., 1951).
2. See especially my books *Crisis Counseling* and *The Caring Church*.

3. Paul Tillich, *The Shaking of the Foundations* (New York: Charles Scribner's Sons, 1948), pp. 153-163.

4. Carl R. Rogers probably has done the most theoretically to define acceptance for psychological counseling. Acceptance or "unconditional positive regard" he describes as "a warm, positive and acceptant attitude toward what is in the client. . . . It involves the therapist's genuine willingness for the client to be whatever feeling is going on in him at that moment–fear, confusion, pain, pride, anger, hatred, love, courage, or awe. . . . He does not simply accept the client when he is behaving in certain ways, and disapprove of him when he behaves in other ways. It means an ongoing positive feeling without reservations, without evaluations." *On Becoming a Person* (Boston: Houghton Mifflin Co., 1961), p. 62.

5. To "transcend self" here means to perceive the self accurately and take responsibility for it, as well as to lose oneself in commitment to the greater concerns of the larger group.

6. Carl Rogers quoted in C. H. Patterson, *Theories of Counseling and Psychotherapy* (New York: Harper & Row, 1966), p. 407.

7. S. V. McCasland, "Spirit," in *The Interpreter's Dictionary of the Bible*, vol. IV, ed. George A. Buttrick (Nashville, TN: Abingdon Press, 1962), pp. 432-434.

8. Ernst Kasemann, *Perspectives on Paul* (Philadelphia: Fortress Press, 1971), pp. 1-2.

9. Reinhold Neibuhr, *The Nature and Destiny of Man*, vol. 1 (New York: Charles Scribner's Sons, 1949), p. 152.

10. Eduard Schweizer, "Spirit," in *Theological Dictionary of the New Testament*, vol. 6, ed. Gerhard Friedrich, trans. Geoffrey W. Bromiley (Grand Rapids, MI: William B. Eerdmans, 1968), p. 436.

11. John B. Cobb, Jr., *Theology and Pastoral Care* (Philadelphia: Fortress Press, 1977), p. 12.

12. See John B. Cobb, Jr., *The Structure of Christian Existence* (Philadelphia: Westminster Press, 1967) and *God and the World* (Philadelphia: Westminster Press, 1969); see also Gordon E. Jackson, *Pastoral Care and Process Theology* (Washington, DC: University Press of America, 1981).

13. Andrew D. Lester, *Hope in Pastoral Care and Counseling* (Louisville, KY: Westminister John Knox Press, 1995).

14. Cobb, *Theology and Pastoral Care*, p. 16.

Chapter 8

Suffering

Like several other graduate student families nearing the end of their stay at Claremont, my wife Karen and I decided to have a child. I had completed my comprehensive exams, and the dissertation was coming along nicely. Underfoot already was a five-year-old, and if ever we were to have a second child, this was the time.

Karen was in excellent health, and the first half of her pregnancy went smoothly. She had just begun wearing her old corduroy maternity clothes when the problems began. At the time, I did not understand completely what the obstetrician had to say, but one phrase came through clearly: "I'm not sure the fetus is developing as it should."

The next few weeks were a time of anxiety and waiting. Finally, the word came: "The fetus is dead." Period. The doctor did not know what went wrong; he could only surmise that "the fetus was abnormal in some way and would most likely have been born with defects, or worse."

For several more weeks, Karen carried our loss around with her, literally. Finally, in a middle-of-the-night emergency operation six months after conception, the remaining tissue was removed along with our dreams for this dearly wanted child.

The doctor was perfunctory. "Wait six months to a year and you can try again," he cheerfully advised. To him we had lost a fetus; to us, it was the baby we had put off having, the one who was never to be. I was not interested in some future possibility. (Today, the five-year-old who was underfoot back in 1970 is still our only child.)

Miscarriages are difficult enough to accept in the first month or so

---

The second part of this chapter originally appeared as "Theodicy in Pastoral Counseling" in *Journal of Pastoral Psychotherapy*, 1(1) (Spring 1987), pp. 47-62.

of pregnancy, but we had begun to think of this baby as part of our family. Karen had started feeling, as she drove around town on errands, that she was not alone–that she had brought that other person along with her.

The response of our family and friends was overwhelming. They rallied around, expressed their love, cleaned, cooked, and listened. We grieved.

Why did this happen? How could a loving God allow this? If God is all good and all powerful, why did God let this occur? Where is God when I need God? *Why?*

I was too "sophisticated" theologically to voice any of these questions out loud. Nevertheless, I secretly wondered about a God who had promised always to be with us but did not seem to be around just when we needed God. I never voiced those questions to anyone, and no one broached the issue of theodicy with either of us. I did talk to friends about the pain in my heart, but I also would have liked to talk about the "whys" ricocheting in my head.

The loss of our wished-for child led me to much reflection and to reading books that addressed my questions. The question of "theo-dicy"–the justification of God's righteousness in the face of so much implausible evil and suffering–has been posed by many thoughtful people in every age, yet it continues to be the Gordian Knot of monotheism and a hard problem for all who proclaim such faith. We ministers need to craft a theological understanding of the issue and an approach to addressing it in the concrete situations of ministry.

TOWARD A THEOLOGY OF THEODICY

In any context, ministers address the why of suffering with great trepidation, knowing that whatever we say will at best be only partially adequate. Yet address the question we must, since theodicy is one of the most important theological issues affecting pastoral care: "No profession faces the direct question of the meaning of suffering more frequently than ministry," says Thomas Oden. "And no theological dimension of the pastor's work is more difficult. Theodicy remains among the most perplexing, practically pressing, and difficult of the theological issues of pastoral practice. Ultimately, it affects every other dimension in one's ministry."[1]

In the seminary environment where I teach, I discovered that students discussing pastoral cases or reviewing video tapes of counseling sessions invariably find it difficult to respond to the issue of seemingly needless suffering. They view on tape a person in severe pain, dying of cancer, and then I question: "Now assume that you are there actively listening, showing acceptance. How would you respond?" The replies are almost predictable: "I don't know what to say"; "I don't have anything to say." At first I thought that my students were inarticulate in such situations because they were new and inexperienced in the field of pastoral care. But then I began to examine how I respond to the why questions, and I discovered that I had a repertoire of fairly safe ways for ignoring them or changing the subject. We all know the paralysis experienced in the face of such a frightening, and sometimes devastating, topic.

From other pastoral counselors and from seminary colleagues, however, I was able to receive much help for my own reflections on theodicy as a pastoral counseling issue. The reflections presented here on suffering in a Christian context will focus primarily on the personal suffering most commonly encountered in pastoral care, suffering connected with such events as death, divorce, job loss, disability, and terminal illness. This is not to gainsay the Christian concern for societal and global suffering but only to focus and limit the present chapter. In addition, many interpretations of suffering ignore the distinction between the suffering we can end and that which we cannot. We will speak here only of the latter, the suffering that arises out of inevitable or irreversible events that do not readily yield to social, political, medical, or even charitable solutions.

The attempt in this chapter is not to recapitulate the variety of theories concerning theodicy, but rather to put forward some ideas that have been helpful for me in shaping my own understanding of it.[2] In these few pages, I will construct the skeleton of a theology of theodicy that I hope will assist readers in further shaping their own theological viewpoint.

The New Testament offers no formal theodicy except for the eschatological reassurance that for the faithful "all things work together for good" (Rom. 8:28 KJV). Yet, as Langdon Gilkey points out, "For many sincere Christians, both the intellectual question of evil and vivid personal experiences of evil, in war and disease, in sin and death, have done more to shake their faith in God than anything else."[3] Indeed, most of us do not even think much about theodicy—except in the midst of suffering, at a point when dispassionate exploration and reflection is nearly impossible because we are in much pain or are called to serve someone in pain. Even then, people, like myself, may not raise the question out loud, "How can God allow such a tragedy?" But they will ponder it, trying to make sense of the perceived incongruities.

The question confronts us with several major issues. If God is both loving and all-powerful, how can evil exist? What is the distinction between moral and natural evil? Do humans cause all evil, or just moral evil? Is God's relationship to creation a close one, emphasizing active involvement, or a loose one, emphasizing human freedom? What effect does the Cross, our redemption, have on an understanding of suffering? Finally, is suffering necessary in order for one to be Christian?

GOD AS BOTH LOVING AND ALL-POWERFUL

First, the basic problem of theodicy is this: *either* God is all-powerful but refuses to abolish evil (and therefore is not loving), or God is loving but unable to abolish evil (and therefore is not all-powerful). Three variables exist here: God is love, God is all-powerful, and evil exists. The problem is that Christian faith affirms what all reason and logic deny–the concurrent validity of all three.

Now, if there is no God, the solution is easy: We simply say the world is evil. Then, responding to people in suffering, we do not have to ask why–that's just the way it is.

For twentieth-century Christians who believe in God, the easiest way to resolve the problem may be to view God not as all-powerful, but as one who, after creating the world, stands back from creation and does not presently govern it. Such a view assumes that God has little or nothing to do with the daily course of events. A difficulty with this position, however, is that the scriptures witness to a God of history; Christianity is unique in its emphasis on the incarnation, on God active in history, bringing us redemption.

Another possible solution to the theodicy problem is to deny the all-loving quality of God. Even to conceive of God as unloving, however, or uncaring, would be difficult for most contemporary Christians. Alternatively, there is the interpretation that conceives of evil in the world as not being *really* evil; "bad" events being somehow God's will are not *really* bad. Our suspicions of this position are buttressed every day; as we read the paper or watch the newscasts, it is difficult to hold that the events being reported are unequivocally good. Besides, if evil were not real, would we have the Cross?

GOD THE CREATOR

To try to resolve this apparent contradiction–an all-powerful and all-loving God coexisting with evil–we must look at God's relationship to creation. To what extent is God involved in all that happens around us and to us? How active, or removed, is God?

One view sees God as actively involved in creation: God is the primary cause of everything that occurs. God is involved in the skinning of my knee. The things that happen, do so because they are God's will–hurricanes, flowers, birth, death, and my skinned knee. If I need plane fare to visit my ailing grandmother and I pray about it, then when the money turns up, God's hand has been in it; it is an answer to prayer. The danger in such a view is that it can lead to human attempts to manipulate God. On the positive side, though, such a view does allow for petitionary prayer; I can pray for material things and even for the healing of someone who is ill since God is intimately involved in all that happens. This view of God's active involvement strongly emphasizes the immanence of God.

But there is also the view that sees God as removed from the world: I skin my knee, not by God's design or will, but by my own foolhardiness in not looking where I was going. God is not active in everything, or anything, that occurs. Pushed to its extreme, this is the position of Deism, in which God "the clockmaker" wound up the world and then withdrew to let it tick away unattended. This view acknowledges that people get cancer because of the multiplying of bad cells; hurricanes are spawned by winds interacting with one another.

An advantage of this view is that it does not lay evil at God's doorstep; evil occurs because of natural causes or because of our misuse of freedom. This view of God's aloofness strongly emphasizes God's transcendence. A disadvantage is that prayer, as a consequence, effects little more than psychological side benefits; it can bring me peace perhaps, or inner strength, or calm the storm within, but there is no use praying for divine intervention. I can ask God to be with those who are ill, but I cannot ask for their healing, except as God would allow the physicians to use their natural talents.[4]

In terms of Christian theology, there is no definitive answer to the question of God's involvement or lack of involvement in the world. Cogent arguments can be made for both positions. My personal view is closer to the second than to the first, though with a stronger sense of God's continuing agency in the world. A view of a God as being only loosely tied to creation is helpful for the modern mind because it embodies a firmer understanding of natural causation within the world.

When someone asked Jesus why a certain man was born blind, Jesus turned the question aside and then healed the man; God's will is not directly linked to everything that happens. However, I do not believe we can support the view of an impotent God; rather, God freely chooses to limit God's power in order to allow humans freedom of action, without which there can be no real love. But God can alter God's choice at any time; God can, and does, act not only in creation and incarnation, but also in our lives. In this view prayer becomes a way to hear God's Word for us, and petitionary prayer has a place in pastoral care: God is still the God of history.

THE PROBLEM OF EVIL

It seems to me that, however fancy our theological footwork, evil cannot be denied. Classically, theologians have spoken of two types of evil–natural evil and moral evil. Natural evil means that all things are created intrinsically good, yet can themselves be the cause of immense devastation and suffering. For example, winds can lead to hurricanes; growth, to cancer; water, to floods; and fire, to destruction. God is not the cause of such natural evil; God only allows it.[5] In other words, God is the basis of the possibility for evil in creation, but not its cause. So far as natural evil is concerned, God is removed from the world. God can and does intervene in the natural order of things, but only occasionally, as an exception to the rule, for in the creation, God deliberately limited God's self, allowing natural processes such as winds and growth, hurricanes and cancer, to occur as they do. Contemporary Christians, therefore, generally do not place religious significance on a specific calamity or illness; natural evil is absurd, that is, without explanation, and to blame it on God would be ludicrous, however much insurance companies may refer to such losses as "acts of God."

It is interesting that the Gospels never speak of God expunging natural evil from human existence; instead, they address questions of moral evil.[6] By moral evil theologians have traditionally meant that evil which results from the misuse of human freedom, that freedom with which we are created as beings separate from God. It is called "sin." This is what Paul writes about in his letters to the early Christian churches. He sees each person as having free choice, and in the exercise of that freedom, making actual choices that lead away from God. There can be no freedom at all without the freedom to say no to God. Murder, child abuse, rape–all are examples of how humans misuse their freedom and cause suffering. Every day millions of people, created in the image of God, are acting and reacting to their physical environment and to other people. Out of these interactions, or lack thereof, evil erupts and widespread suffering results, and the world, created good, is jolted by its consequences, indeed may someday be annihilated by them.

Thus, God is surely omnipotent and loving, but limits God's self, out of love, both in relationship to nature and in relationship to human freedom. As creator, God is the *basis* for all that happens, both good and evil, but not its *cause*. As part of the created world, humans are participants in its beauty and goodness, but also subject to its ugliness and suffering; as free agents we are contributors to both.

THE TENSION OF FAITH

How then do we understand the why questions, the issue of theodicy, the cause and meaning of suffering? There is no clear answer. The New Testament's answer is essentially, "wait and see." Not much help to many of us today perhaps, but there it is.

Søren Kierkegaard stresses that, to make sense of suffering, a transition is required from scientific thinking to the religious mode of belief and faith. When most people ask why, they are asking scientific rather than religious questions. We seek root causes. Of course, most of us would deny that we can use scientific methods to prove the existence of God, yet we forget that when we ask why questions in the face of suffering, we are actually employing scientific cause-and-effect thinking.[7] Kierkegaard writes:

> But that the heavy suffering is good is something that must be *believed*, because it cannot be seen. Perhaps we can see afterwards that it *has been* good, but at the time of suffering we can neither see it, nor, even though ever so many people with the best of motives keep on repeating it, can we hear it spoken; it must be believed. It is the thought of faith we need, and the earnest, confident, frequent expressing of this thought to ourselves. . . . But when one looks on unmixed misery all around, then by faith to see the joy: yea, this is meet and proper. It is meet and proper so to speak of faith, for faith is always the reference to what is not seen, whether the *invisible* or the *improbable*.[8]

So the Christian in the midst of suffering is compelled to ask why because faith insists on holding together in irreconcilable tension three things that logically do not stand together: God is love, God is all-powerful, and evil exists.

It is right and proper for believers to raise questions of theodicy, to wonder about suffering as the ending of the book of Job implies. Ultimately, though, all analogies and metaphors fail. The choice God made in creating the world the way it is, and in continuing to respond to it the way God has, is beyond our human conception. This does not mean that we should not try to understand it, or that we should cease asking questions; it means only that our quest will never be finally successful. Our answers will always be tentative, our perspective finite. The resolution to our despair and anger will have to take the form not of an intellectual conclusion, but of a renewal in faith, hope, and love. Indeed, just when Job sulks, screams, and pleads with God for an answer to the why, he does not get one–at least not the answer he expects. God does not give a defensible answer that could be reviewed and critiqued academically. Instead, God replies, in effect: "Job, who do you think you are? You can't know. You can't judge what is best, only I can. You're a human and I am God, and that is the difference of night and day." The question is not really answered, but Job nonetheless rests in the answer, for he is not God; he cannot view things from God's vantage point. Only in faith can we understand–and then only in a very limited way.

GOD THE REDEEMER

If the question of theodicy is not answered as we might have hoped, what is God's response? God's answer is Christ. Not only is God the creator who limits God's self, God is also the redeemer who enters life as a sharer in our suffering. God does not remain aloof. God is intensely engaged, suffers, and is the first to enter into the resurrection. Incarnation and crucifixion are not so much an answer to the question as they are a redefinition of the world, and of our relationship to God in it, such that the question itself comes to mean something different.

Elie Wiesel, a survivor of the Holocaust, was brought to Auschwitz when he was not quite fifteen years old. In his book *Night* he recalls how the experience devastated his once deep faith:

> Never shall I forget that night, the first night in camp, which has turned my life into one long night, seven times cursed and seven times sealed. Never shall I forget that smoke. Never shall I forget the little faces of the children, whose bodies I saw turned into wreaths of smoke beneath a silent blue sky. Never shall I forget those flames which consumed my faith forever.[9]

Wiesel writes of being forced to witness the execution by hanging of three people–two men and a young boy who he said had a face like a sad angel.

"Long live liberty!" cried the two adults.

But the child was silent.

"Where is God? Where is He?" someone behind me asked. . . .

The two adults were no longer alive. . . . But the third rope was still moving; being so light, the child was still alive.

For more than half an hour he stayed there, struggling between life and death, dying in slow agony under our eyes. . . .

Behind me, I heard the same man asking:

"Where is God now?"

And I heard a voice within me answer him:

"Where is He? Here He is–He is hanging here on this gallows."[10]

Francois Mauriac talked with Wiesel about the experience while Wiesel was still a young man, working as a journalist in Paris. In the Foreword to *Night* Mauriac writes of their talk:

And I, who believe that God is love, what answer could I give my young questioner, whose dark eyes still held the reflection of that angelic sadness which had appeared one day upon the face of the hanged child? What did I say to him? Did I speak of that other Jew, his brother, who may have resembled him–the Crucified, whose Cross has conquered the world? Did I affirm that the stumbling block to his faith was the cornerstone of mine, and that the conformity between the Cross and the suffering of men was in my eyes the key to that impenetrable mystery whereon the faith of his childhood had perished? . . . We do not know the worth of one single drop of blood, one single tear. All is grace. If the Eternal is the Eternal, the last word for each one of us belongs to Him. This is what I should have told this Jewish child. But I could only embrace him, weeping.[11]

Jewish thought does, in fact, view God in God's empty and debased form as sharing the torment of people in exile, in prison, in martyrdom. This is implied in the Hebrew understanding of *shekinah*–the "indwelling presence of God in the world"; God suffers wherever people suffer.

As Christians, we see in Christ's suffering and death on the cross

God's response to the question, "Did God create evil?" God did not create evil (although certainly the possibility for it), but endures it along with us. God is not the hangman, not a spectator–an aloof deity; but rather God suffers, and through Christ, is with us in our suffering. The gospel is that in Christ we are saved not only *out of* our suffering, but also *through* it. This is not to say that God is concerned only for the broken and undone; surely, God is concerned also for health, happiness, and a good quality of life. But in suffering, which is inevitable, we are united with the Christ. There is one who has gone before us, not in power and strength, but in weakness, humbled and abused. In the pain and isolation of Jesus' cry, "My God, my God, why have you forsaken me?" he becomes one with us.

A resurrected God who rose from the dead after dying peacefully in his bed of old age, without any suffering whatever, would be a different divinity from the Christ. What comes after always somehow includes what went before. At no point can you ever be as though you had not experienced the previous years of your life. One can be forgiven all that has gone before, but one can never erase it. The same is true of the resurrection; it does not cancel the death that preceded it. After the resurrection, Jesus bore in his hands and sides the marks of his violent death. Today he still carries them, as well as the suffering, transformed but not canceled.

So, even though we may picture God the Creator as somehow more removed from the world than actively involved in its day-to-day affairs, in God the Redeemer we see a different picture–of a God who walks with us along our lonely paths. The gospel does not picture God as the totally other depicted in the creation story; instead, it shows Christ as the totally involved one who suffers beatings, abuse, hunger, thirst, pain, loneliness, and finally a death in which he is seemingly forsaken by God.

The Greeks believed that if a god suffered–and even love was a suffering kind of passion–that god's perfection was negated. But according to New Testament faith it is in God's very suffering and subsequent resurrection that God's perfection is made evident. In the case of Jesus, God's perfection was revealed, not negated, by the scandal of the passion. To the amazement of disciples and enemies alike, God's power manifested itself in Jesus' self-giving love, in weakness and vulnerability. Gilkey writes, "Truly here was one of the most radical transformations of values in all historical experience: not the avoidance of suffering, but its willing acceptance in love, became the deepest clue to divinity."[12]

Many people who have experienced suffering have done so without knowing God as the one who suffers. They may have looked to God for power and strength and miracles, but not for this! The school of suffering, however, requires meeting the Savior where he is, in weakness, seeing the scars, feeling the nail holes. Suffering is the precursor to resurrection. To recognize Christ's face in one's impending death will be no mean feat, and for some may be impossible. Nevertheless, when the "whys" have subsided and the listening and looking begin, then possibly–just possibly–one can get a glimpse of the mystery that is God.

THE SCHOOL OF SUFFERING

A fifteen-year-old boy has too many beers, loses control of his motorcycle, crashes, and dies. In the aftermath, his father, an alcoholic of twenty years, a has-been engineer frequently laid off from his job, an irascible and disagreeable character, cleans up his act. He gets off the bottle, dedicates himself anew to the church he had rejected as a teenager, takes a fresh interest in his wife and family, and becomes responsible again on the job. Out of a son's death comes a transformation of a father's life.

Now, it would be cruel and utterly absurd to say that God used the boy's death to teach the father a lesson. True, the father has turned his life around, but at what expense, the life of his child? Even such a remarkable turnabout can never justify such suffering and death. Suffering is simply inevitable. No one would ever wish for such a tragedy, but tragedies do occur. Suffering is a school where we can learn about ourselves, about our lives, and about God; it can ultimately serve as a foundation for maturation.

Suffering, from a Christian perspective, has two components–the anguish itself, and the reflection or learning that occurs in response to the pain. Søren Kierkegaard writes, "When a man suffers and is willing to learn from suffering then he constantly learns about himself and his relationship to God; this is the sign that he is being trained for eternity."[13]

Suffering is part of being human. The struggle to learn from suffering, to reflect on its depths, helps bring meaning to one's life. As undesirable as suffering is, it is a key to personality development and personal maturity. Certainly, this has been a major theme in existential psychology, especially in the work of Victor Frankl.[14] Untold pastoral counseling sessions have begun with individuals describing some horror or tragedy, some physical or spiritual suffering, and almost in the same breath telling how it has changed their lives for the good.

The danger in suffering is that the disorganization and personality disintegration it brings may lead not to growth, but to despair and cynicism. There is always that potential. People who suffer do not invariably mature in the faith; some abandon it. Where suffering is concerned, the question is one not of bad versus good—all suffering is bad—but only of wasted suffering versus the contemplated anguish that brings depth and growth. The suffering itself and the evil that produces it is not what brings the good; if good there be, it is due to our active response that results in new learnings.

Ministers in particular have surely noted this. Some people we endeavor to help want only an adhesive bandage to cover the wound so they can go on as if little or nothing had happened. There are others, however, who desire not only to be relieved of the pain, but also to learn from it. Learning from suffering is thus one hoped-for outcome in pastoral care. Suffering is a school that each Christian is called to attend. Again, Kierkegaard writes of what we learn there:

> Suffering itself is, from the human point of view, the first danger, but the second danger, which is still more terrible, is that we should not learn obedience. Suffering is a lesson full of danger; for, if we do not learn obedience—then it is as terrible as if the most efficacious of medicines had the wrong kind of effect! In such danger man needs help; he needs the help of God; else he learns not obedience.[15]

The academy of obedience does not teach us stoicism, a folding of the arms, a gritting of the teeth, and an emotional distancing from others; rather, it teaches us an open-armed acceptance of our lot. Dorothee Soelle puts it this way:

The Christian idea of the acceptance of suffering means something more than and different from what is expressed in the words "putting up with, tolerate, bear." With these words the object, the suffering itself, remains unchanged. It is borne–as a burden, suffered–as an injustice; it is tolerated, although intolerable; borne, although unbearable. "Put up with" and "tolerate" point to stoic tranquility rather than to Christian acceptance.[16]

SUFFERING AND THE CHRISTIAN

In the apocalyptic books of Scripture, the last stages of the world are characterized by terrible suffering: "tribulation" is the term applied to this aspect of apocalyptic chronology. The message is that the world, even the universe, is steadily degenerating from its original state at creation. Things are getting progressively worse. As we approach the end of time and enter this period of tribulation, the righteous will have to suffer, they above all. Why the righteous? Because in the last days the powers of evil gain the ascendancy, and the ruler of this world (as the devil is called in John 12:31; 14:30; 16:11) is determined to afflict the righteous in every way possible. The suffering of the righteous, then, far from being illogical or unexpected, is precisely what Christians must be prepared to face in the last times. Suffering will be the distinguishing mark of the Christian.

Although in scripture suffering is at times tied to one's sins, in the Beatitudes it is portrayed as a gift. Certainly, what is meant here is not that we are to ignore suffering or pretend it does not exist, but simply that suffering that enhances communion with Christ is a source of joy, hence a gift. In Matthew 5 the Greek *makarios*, which is usually translated "blessed," may well mean "happy": "blessed" (or "happy") are those who suffer.

In his instructions to Christians (who happened to be slaves), the author of First Peter reminds them that they must suffer and endure pain, as God in Christ endured pain while suffering unjustly. The message again is that we must suffer. Suffering is a part of being Christian. God left us an example in Christ, who suffered for us, and we are to follow in his steps (I Pet. 2:11-25).

For Paul, ministry, to which all Christians are called, is not merely to speak the gospel, but also to live it. Since the heart of the gospel is the death and resurrection of Jesus, suffering is an integral part of the believer's ministry. We read much about the law of love; indeed, it is one of the key concepts of the New Testament that in Christ the old bonds of the law are broken and the new law of love established. But what is often overlooked in twentieth-century Christianity is its companion, the law of suffering. As redeemed people of God, we are charged to love others, but we also are called to suffer with Christ. Suffering is not only the lot of all humans; it is the particular calling of all Christians. To suffer is not good, for all suffering is indeed undesirable, but it is nevertheless right and proper. A hidden assumption that frequently lurks behind the theodicy question is the belief that somehow we Christians have a right *not* to suffer! On the contrary, suffering is to be expected, especially by Christians, since we are specifically called to follow the example of Christ. As Alastair Campbell points out:

> Often the Christian churches put on the appearance of power and success, denying with their show of comfort and self-confidence, the bleeding and despised body of their Lord. But new life can come to suffering people when they find themselves in the company of those who, like Paul, are not ashamed to bear "the marks of Jesus branded on [their] body" (Gal. 6:17 NEB). Healing comes within a community of sufferers, because there, where weakness is freely acknowledged, the power of God's love can enter in.[17]

For Paul Tillich faith requires that we "accept suffering with courage, as an element of finitude, and affirm finitude in spite of the suffering that accompanies it."[18] Courage enables us to extract meaning out of suffering. Courage means facing existence and accepting suffering as a part of it. Our faith is that, in spite of the suffering, the way of the Spirit will be realized. Courage comes not out of strength but, strangely, out of weakness. It is the alternative to despair. As Dorothee Soelle puts it: "We don't have the choice of avoiding sufferings and going around all these deaths. The only choice we have is between the absurd cross of meaninglessness and the cross of Christ, the death we accept apathetically as a natural end and the death we suffer as a passion."[19]

PASTORAL CARE AND THEODICY

> All extreme suffering evokes the experience of being forsaken by God. In the depth of suffering people see themselves as abandoned and forsaken by everyone. That which gave life its meaning has become empty and void: it turned out to be an error, an illusion that is shattered, a guilt that cannot be rectified, a void. The paths that lead to this experience of nothingness are diverse, but the experience of annihilation that occurs in unremitting suffering is the same.[20]

This comment of Dorothee Soelle reminds us of what we face in the ministry of pastoral care. How do we respond to suffering in a real-life situation, when a grieving person asks, "Why did God let this happen to me?" The question is hard, insistent, even paralyzing.

Even those ministers who are especially facile with words may find themselves hemming and hawing when confronted by the apparent conflict between God's goodness, on the one hand, and our seemingly needless human anguish, on the other. There are no simple solutions to the conflict, nor can we avoid facing it. It might be helpful at this point to suggest some technical considerations that can perhaps assist us in responding to issues of theodicy as a part of our pastoral care, and so translate the earlier theological discussion into the idiom of human relationships.

Ministers need to be prepared to face the issue of theodicy, for it will be encountered invariably and often in pastoral care and counseling situations. Therefore, it is imperative that we consider our own personal struggles and losses, and that we reflect on the theological issues they raise. In addition to such soul searching about our own suffering, and discussion with colleagues, I have found it helpful to practice responding to specific cases, whether hypothetical or real, where the why question is raised. The case to be considered should be as realistic as possible. It is not easy, but it is beneficial, to act or try to act as the representative presence of the church, verbalizing one's own understanding of theodicy in concrete situations. Such preparation and practice may reduce the uneasiness we all feel in a crisis situation; not that ministers should have all the answers, but as interpreters and proclaimers of the faith, we must be able to help others make sense out of this theological issue. Ministers who have reflected on the issue and discerned their own basis of hope may be less likely to become ensnared in the parishioner's confusion and loss, and they may be better enabled to offer the presence of the church, which is faith and hope, rather than simply compound the despair.

ASSESSING WHY QUESTIONS

Why questions are bound to be asked in pastoral care situations. When they are asked, two immediate dangers arise.

In the first place, there is the temptation for the caregiver to provide immediate answers without first establishing a solid relationship with the troubled people and listening to their pain. Such answers may be spoken from a conservative theological stance, by restating some of the traditional responses to suffering; or they may be a liberal refinement or rebuttal of such traditional notions, by offering (for example) a process view of theodicy. In either event, to launch too quickly into a discourse on suffering and theodicy, no matter how astute, is to ignore people's pain, while perhaps not even answering their *real* questions.

At the other extreme, there is the danger of simply reflecting or mirroring the question back to the questioner, the classical nondirective approach. The peril in such a response is that we may overlook the person's *real* questions, the ones that demand real answers. Frequently, though, the why question is itself a truly serious one. If the pastor nondirectively ignores it, that could ultimately affect the pastor-parishioner relationship in a negative way. At the very least, it might suggest to the parishioner that the minister is not comfortable with these serious theological issues.

What is important is not that ministers rush in prematurely with facile answers, or nondirectively evade the questions altogether, but that they bring to the situation their own prior reflection. Reflection upon our own suffering is part of the caring that listens to others' anguish. Our listening is the crucial thing, and it is not offered condescendingly by haves to the deprived have nots; rather, it is a self-conscious participation in the common suffering of humanity.[21] As Campbell puts it:

> The wounded healer heals, because he is able to convey, as much by his presence as by the words he uses, both an awareness and a transcendence of loss. . . . The wounded healer heals because he, to some degree at least, has entered the depth of his own experiences of loss and in those depths has found hope again.[22]

In Chapter 2 on theological assessment, it was noted that the why questions can often help ministers gain a clearer understanding of the parishioner's implicit and explicit theological assumptions. Discussion of a person's questions can disclose much about his or her views of God, sin, faith, and salvation.

When the why question is first raised, pastors must try to discern whether the individual truly wishes to discuss a theological issue, or whether the why question is rather a vehicle for expressing a sense of loss. Does it reflect a desire to understand what does not seem to be understandable, or is it a way to communicate one's pain? In my experience the questioner rarely intends either one or the other; rather, a mixture of both is involved. As pastor it is my job, however, to discern which of the two is pressing for priority at any given time.

Many of the whys counselees raise are actually *poetic questions*. They are symbolic or metaphoric ways of expressing depths of misery. Indeed, many parishioners may find it easier to ask, "Why did God do this?" than to say, "I have had an immense loss and am feeling utterly devastated by it." As a rule during shock or in the early phases of reacting to a recent or impending loss, most people use why questions primarily to voice their own anguish. This does not mean that the theodicy question is not also of concern–perhaps even their *real* concern–but only that in most cases emotional pain, rather than curiosity, is the driving force at the moment.

A helpful way to determine whether the why is poetic or literal is tentatively to assume that people are in fact expressing emotional hurt, and then operate first on that basis. The response to "How could God let this happen to me?" may be something like "John's death is really a great loss for you." This approach assumes that implicit within the why question being asked is a profound expression of grief, and that the pastor's task is to help the individual discern and express it. The individual who then replies with a verbal or implied "yes, *but*" is most likely a person genuinely searching for some sort of adequate answer to the why; indeed, some people seem emotionally unable to express grief until they have seriously and thoughtfully wrestled with the theodicy issue.

If, on the other hand, the individual latches onto the pastor's basically empathetic response, it is sensible to follow that track and facilitate the expression of feelings. In such cases, however, it is important that the minister not ignore or pass over the why question altogether, but consciously return to it at a later time. Although theodicy concerns may eventually diminish in emotive intensity after the person has had a chance to express sorrow—especially after some days, weeks, or months of becoming accustomed to the loss—the question usually will not go away by itself. In fact, as the intensity of the loss diminishes, the theodicy issue may come to the fore even more forcefully. The pastor who initiates a return to the question at a later session can provide an important opportunity for growth in the faith.

EMBODYING THE PRESENCE OF THE CHURCH

A pastor who sits with people whose world has been turned upside down serves as a representative presence of the church in that situation. Where pastor and parishioner are gathered together at such times, there the church resides. The presence of one who believes, who has been redeemed by the Lamb, who rests in the gospel's hope, who is seen as a representative of God and the church on earth, can provide succor to the person who is troubled and hurting. The ministry of presence, including the listening ear and the dynamic power of the visible Word can be, for the person in suffering, a door that opens onto new meaning in what had otherwise seemed a barren and meaningless situation.

In the pastor's patient listening, the person in pain can often sense this presence of the church. Allowing the expression of emotions felt about the tragedy can be a loving and helpful thing, for thinly veiled by the articulated whys may well be a consuming anger. As the church's representative, the pastor needs to expect and be prepared to meet a barrage of rage, all of which is basically directed against God.

I had just such an experience when I was still in college. Married and poor at that time, I routinely accepted almost any part-time job that could put food on the table. Near campus, in the center of Minneapolis, was a church that needed canvassers. I agreed to knock on doors in the neighborhood on their behalf, ask a few demographic questions, and inquire whether each resident had a church home. The job lasted only a week or two.

One beautiful spring afternoon, a tall and intimidating man with two days' growth of beard opened the door of his run-down duplex. He was wearing a heavy scowl and a dirty T-shirt. His very appearance stopped me cold for a moment. I quickly asked my questions, staring all the while at my clipboard. After barking a few terse one-word answers, he suddenly asked, "Are you a Christian?" I meekly responded that I was. He said, "Come in. I want to talk with you." We canvassers had been instructed that, after asking the survey questions, we should be willing to discuss faith or the church with anyone who wanted to do so. I loathed the idea of talking with this man but did not see a way out, so I followed him into his living room and sat on the couch.

After the door closed, the man began to storm for some fifteen or twenty minutes, which to me at the time seemed like an eternity. He raged on about the hypocrisy of Christians and screamed that God does not even exist, because if there were a God, God would not let innocent children be hurt and destroyed. Then the man told me how his own son had been run over by a car only six weeks earlier. He railed at me, "How could God allow my boy to be killed right in front of my own house?" Terrified by the sheer bulk of the man and the intensity of his anger, I stared feverishly at my lap, glancing up only occasionally to look for an escape route. There was none. I was trapped. Suddenly, the man did something that was even more uncomfortable for a young college student to witness. He began to cry, in fact to sob, "You are the first person who has listened to me."

I could take no credit for listening. In fact, I had heard little of what he said and would have slipped eagerly out into the street if I could have. But sitting there on the couch, I learned something: The why questions and the angry epithets about Christian hypocrites were simply this man's way of telling how devastated he was by the death of his young son. He was still trying to make sense of the tragedy. He may have had real questions about the existence and goodness of God too, but for some six weeks now the primary issue was his grief and sorrow. Pastors who would embody the loving presence of the church at such a time need to be prepared to face anger and to help in getting that anger expressed.

THE ANSWERS PEOPLE GIVE

Over the years, while making pastoral care visits–especially hospital visits–I have sadly encountered many people whose well-meaning friends and acquaintances have responded to their why questions with theological answers that left them terribly upset and proved actually to be destructive: "This is God's punishment on you for your sins." "This is God's will; you have to accept it." "This has happened to bring you to the Lord." "God wanted your dear one with him in heaven." "If you hadn't skipped out on your wife, this wouldn't have happened." "If you had stayed home with your children where God wants you to be, they wouldn't have started taking drugs."

More recently I have also come across another whole class of answers–more psychological than religious–to the theodicy issues: "You are responsible for your illness." "You are sick because of your destructive thoughts." "The cancer inside you is pent up anger; you've got to release it to get well." "You are what you eat; if only you had cut out fat and exercised more." Some people are so eager to give their answers that they scarcely wait for the questions to be asked. The results are often quite grim.

When I first began pastoral care work, I would have thought such pronouncements were rare, or occurred only in the more conservative denominations. Not so! Things such as this happen everywhere, regardless of the conservative or liberal orientation. Simplistic and damaging answers flow from well-meaning people at a time when their hearers are in considerable distress, vulnerable, and unable to talk back. I raise the issue here because if ministers care only for people's emotional pain and do not respond theologically to the issue of theodicy, parishioners will inevitably get their theological education elsewhere, and it may not be the kind we would have wished for them. In other words, if ministers will not respond, sooner or later, to the vital questions of theodicy, neighbors and friends are likely to do so, and not always in a helpful manner.

Another assumption I carry into pastoral care visits where theodicy may be an issue is that the person has already received a medical explanation. In the loss that Karen and I experienced, it ran as follows: "The fetus was abnormal in some way and most likely would have been born with defects, or worse." Medical responses are usually offered by physicians, but they too can be voiced by other people, medical personnel as well as friends. The variety of such medical explanations is endless: "You are young; you can have another." "He's out of pain now, and that's a blessing." "Better that she went quickly." "They would have suffered, or had brain damage, the rest of their lives."

Sound medical explanations are often helpful; they can contribute to an improved understanding of what actually has happened or is happening. But such explanations also pose a problem: they do not deal adequately with theodicy. The why question has to do with meaning, and as such, requires a theological answer.

It is important to remember that many people do not verbalize their why questions (I did not). This does not mean they are not thinking about them—and hearing spurious advice about them. When counseling after a divorce, for example, we are careful to sense whether the individuals are experiencing guilt, even if they are saying "everything is fine." Likewise, we need to be aware that in many pastoral care situations where simple faith in God's goodness clashes with the fact of personal suffering, people may not speak of it—they do not wish to "offend" the pastor—but their inner world is likely to be in desperate turmoil as they attempt to understand how a loving God can coexist with evil, can allow such suffering. Answers will mushroom all about them—answers that are superficial, possibly harmful, and surely fall short of the church's hope-filled message.

CRISES AND THE WHY QUESTIONS

Researchers in the area of human crises have pointed out that an acute crisis situation not only can affect an individual emotionally, physically, and intellectually, but also can turn one's values and sense of meaning upside down. In a previous book on crisis intervention, I wrote:

> Besides causing upheaval in an individual's emotional, physical, and intellectual life, a crisis also can upset a person's values and sense of meaning. . . . Ministers or counselors who deal with the emotional, physical, or intellectual life and ignore the spiritual core of crises are not responding to the whole person. During crises, because of their heightened psychological accessibility, people may be especially receptive to issues of faith if they are sensitively portrayed.
>
> Conversely, during a crisis, upstanding members of a congregation may question in their faith what they had previously affirmed. The minister needs to remain emotionally with them at such times. The helper's sensitivity and ministry of presence can aid them in weathering their uncertainty.[23]

We have to assume that in crisis and loss situations profound issues of meaning and theodicy are being raised, whether or not they are articulated. The suffering experienced in such situations can be so immense that one of the first tasks of pastoral care is to help people put what they are going through into words. Such a "language of lament" can help them speak the unspeakable, to ask why, and thereby begin to move in the direction of needed acceptance and change.

TALKING ABOUT THEODICY

How do we then talk about theodicy, once we have discerned that the major pain is not primarily emotional, but flows from a real desire to understand God and God's connection with tragedy? To speak of God and suffering requires great pastoral artistry and a careful listening for the Word and to the Word. Although it is not primarily a matter of technique, pastors may want to be aware of the following technical considerations when they talk to suffering people about theodicy.

Ministers must have done prior reflection; they must know what they themselves believe. We have said this before, but it cannot be emphasized enough. Moreover, we are not to coerce others into adopting our religious views, but to enable them to achieve a better understanding of scripture and of their own faith. Surely, it is a false dichotomy to suggest: *Either* I force my views on others *or* I say nothing to them at all. There is plenty of middle ground between these extreme authoritarian and laissez-faire positions. Ministers who would find and occupy that middle ground need only function in one of the standard pastoral roles–as prophet, proclaimer of the Word, as enabler, or teacher. Parishioners need and want to know what the church has to say about theodicy; they probably will not have the privilege unless pastors care, proclaim, and educate to provide it.

An understanding of suffering requires not scientific questioning, but faith and belief. Whatever methods of pastoral visitation and care are appropriate to the person's situation and religious tradition can also help that person to be grasped by the core of the gospel and gain insight into the whys. For if Kierkegaard is correct, that only out of faith can we understand suffering, then whatever nourishes faith also addresses the issue of theodicy. It may well be impossible for any minister to address the whys of someone perennially hostile to the church and to faith. For ultimately the issue of theodicy is resolved only within the gospel, not outside of it.

The why questions are real questions, bubbling up from the deepest center of one's being. They should not be turned into casual, abstract, ideological debate. Since each individual raises the questions in a slightly different way and out of a slightly different position in life, each needs to be addressed in a unique way. Stock answers will not suffice. Our response always must be contextually based–the result of a dialogue between the Word and the specific situation. Ministers who have worked out their own views on theodicy will recognize the uniqueness of each person they encounter and tailor a response to that particular person. In my experience, not all people are helped by the same set of metaphors about theodicy.

Our task is to help counselees search for those specific metaphors that hold truth for them.

Crisis intervention theorists have taught us that people who are in crisis, experiencing a loss or threat of loss, go through a period of heightened psychological accessibility. Their mistrust diminished, they undergo an increased openness toward learning from people who are there to help them. Thus, a crisis can be a turning point in a person's emotional, intellectual, and spiritual well-being. Wilbur Morley's diagram of a crisis describes graphically this state of heightened psychological accessibility (see Figure 1).

In the first diagram, a triangle represents the person who is *not* presently in crisis. Things are fairly stable. One of the three sides of the triangle is solidly planted somewhere on the continuum between mental health and the absence of mental health. A large portion of the person's psyche is fairly stable and can be relied on when the person is not in crisis, though a necessary consequence of such stability is that the person is less open to change. In normal day-to-day living people require this sizable degree of personality stability.

The second diagram shows a person who *is* in crisis, indicated by the triangle tipped up on end. Much less of the individual's personality is firmly planted on that line between mental health and the absence of mental health. The person is in a period of "upsetness" and vulnerability. The natural urge is to reestablish stability, so the person is more open to any influence—whether from inside or outside—that can aid in the resolution of the crisis. One time for people to learn to deal with

FIGURE 1. Morley's Diagram of Crisis

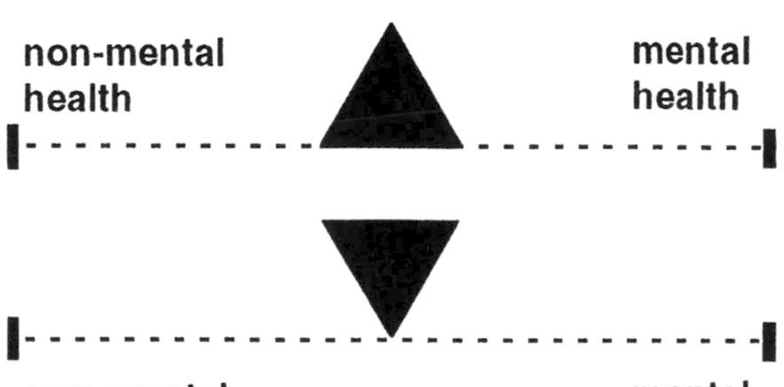

theodicy is when they raise the issue at a time of crisis. Since there is heightened psychological accessibility, the person is more open to new viewpoints than when the triangle is on its base. Frequently, after the most immediate and basic emotional needs are addressed, the issues of why can be discussed at a time when there is still this increased openness toward help from others.[24]

When we talk with parishioners about why questions, it is best to begin by asking what they think, or have thought, rather than verbalizing our own views. We need to draw out their thinking, the answers they have heard from others, and the answers that have made sense to them. As in any other area of care or counseling, it is best to explore first the feelings and thoughts of the counselee. We should listen carefully before responding. Sometimes it is helpful to ask direct questions: "Is that how you've always thought about it?" "What's troubling or confusing you now?" "What answers have other people suggested to you?" "What do you think of these answers?" "How has this episode shaken your faith?"

In our discussion of why questions, and especially as we try to help individuals find meaning in what at the moment seems to make no sense, we need to be careful not to imply that they *must* feel any particular way. When people are already feeling guilty for even raising a question about the goodness of God, if the pastoral caregiver badly asserts that one ought to view suffering as a blessing, they may end up feeling doubly guilty–not only for raising the question, but also for viewing their suffering as bad. We should help people acknowledge their own feelings and bless them when they do. Frequently, it is in the discussion of these feelings and related ideas, as they pertain to Scripture, that individuals begin to wrestle seriously with theodicy.

When speaking of our own understanding, our faith response to the why questions, it may be helpful to speak in image language. The worst possible response would be to start quoting a term paper on theodicy written back in seminary, for the faith-talk in which we are here engaged is not a theological discussion as expressed technically in the classroom. Our purpose is to speak simply, personally, and directly without jargon (though not condescendingly), while at the same time giving people the cognitive tools they need to help them begin making sense of their own plight. Many times this can be done through stories, parables, and Scripture. The most helpful approach is to speak from your own experience of loss, your own struggle with the question of theodicy, sharing what has helped you, or others, in times of pain.

When we speak of the potential for growth and meaning that rises out of suffering, we should try to avoid the hard sell. Suffering is not a thing to be desired. It is a given that comes as a part of our finitude, not good, but nonetheless inevitable—one that we can use for good or for ill.

A final thought. When we speak about suffering as a potential source of good, we cannot hope to wrap up the whole discussion by the end of the first meeting. At best we can only provide some initial material for continuing cogitation. Our task is not to convince vulnerable people who are in pain, but to help them shift their thinking just enough to look at their experience in a slightly different way, open to the possibilities of new interpretation.

When all is said and done, more Christians will probably get through the experience of evil and suffering with the help of a believer's quiet assurance of faith, rather than with a scholar's discussion and critique of their theology. But both provide ways in which God can speak the verbal and visible Word—both the clear discussion of why questions and the loving presence of the church—through the minister. As we mature in the Christian faith, we arrive at ever deeper understandings of the relationship between human suffering and God's power and love. In the meantime, faced with evil, we may be able to do more than stammer, say a few words, and clam up. We may find it possible to be with them, to cry and feel helpless, but also to speak trustingly of the presence of a loving God who, though not the cause of their sorrow, can in its midst be their strength and release.

NOTES

1. Thomas C. Oden, *Pastoral Theology: Essentials of Ministry* (New York: Harper & Row, 1983), p. 223.

2. Ibid., for a short synopsis of the historical understandings of theodicy, pp. 223-248.

3. Langdon Gilkey, *Maker of Heaven and Earth* (New York: Doubleday & Co., 1959), p. 210.

4. I am indebted to my colleague Dr. David Gouwens for his help in elucidating the issues discussed here.

5. The Deuteronnomic writer argued that God prospers the righteous and punishes the wicked. Therefore, if evil occurs, it is God's punishment of one's wickedness. For example, see Psalm 1.

6. Gilkey, *Maker of Heaven and Earth*, pp. 225-226.

7. Søren Kierkegaard, *The Gospel of Our Sufferings*, trans. A. S. Aldworth and W. S. Ferrie (London: James Clarke & Co., 1955), pp. 30-37.

8. Ibid., pp. 32-33.

9. Elie Wiesel, *Night*, trans. Stella Rodway, with a foreword by Francois Mauriac (New York: Farrar, Straus, & Giroux, 1960; Bantam Books, 1982), p. 32.

10. Ibid., pp. 61-62.

11. Ibid., pp. x-xi.

12. Gilkey, *Maker of Heaven and Earth*, p. 255.

13. Kierkegaard, *The Gospel of Sufferings*, p. 66.

14. Victor Frankl, *Man's Search for Meaning* (New York: Washington Square Press, 1963), pp. 105-116.

15. Kierkegaard, *The Gospel of Sufferings*, p. 55.

16. Dorothee Soelle, *Suffering*, trans. Everett R. Kalin (Philadelphia: Fortress Press, 1975), p. 103.

17. Alastair V. Campbell, *Rediscovering Pastoral Care* (London: Darton, Longman & Todd, 1981), p. 45.

18. Paul Tillich, *Systematic Theology*, vol. 2 (Chicago: University of Chicago Press, 1957), p. 70.

19. Soelle, *Suffering*, p. 157.

20. Ibid., p. 85.

21. Henri Nouwen, *The Wounded Healer* (New York: Doubleday & Co., 1979).

22. Campbell, *Rediscovering Pastoral Care*, pp. 42-43.

23. Howard W. Stone, *Crisis Counseling* (Philadelphia: Fortress Press, 1993), pp. 29-30.

24. Stone, *Crisis Counseling*, pp. 21-32.

Chapter 9

Love of God and Neighbor

I have often been moved by the answer to the first question in *The Westminster Shorter Catechism*, which asks, "What is our chief end?" The response beautifully expresses the joy of our redeemed relationship with God: "Our chief end is to glorify God, and to enjoy God forever."

A NEW RELATIONSHIP IN CHRIST

The foundation of the new life transformed by Christ's suffering and resurrection–and our primary reason for glorifying God–is our justification by faith. Through the incarnation in Christ, God has inaugurated new life and called us into an intimate relationship. This reconciled relationship liberates us from all concern over gaining our salvation or even doing what is right to please God. We are free people. God wants it that way and does not intend that we do anything to achieve this relationship, but offers it freely, as a gift. It is an exciting and joyful thing!

Not only are we free from worry over making ourselves right with God and from long lists of "do's and don'ts" ruling our lives, but our fears, anxieties, and energies are also loosed to be channeled into appreciating, honoring, even *enjoying* God, as the *Westminster Catechism* so perfectly claims. In the midst of the suffering and uncertainty of this life there is one who is certain, and upon whom we can rely.

Portions of this chapter were first published in Chapter 2 of *The Caring Church: A Guide for Lay Pastoral Care*. Reprinted by permission from *The Caring Church* by Howard Stone, ©1991 Augsburg Fortress.

Luther commented on the new life in Christ, "A Christian is a perfectly free lord of all, subject to none. A Christian is a perfectly dutiful servant of all, subject to all." [1] Our Christ-relationship does not exempt us from good works, as Luther pointed out, but rather from false understandings of them, from needless attempts to gain salvation through anything we do. As Paul Althaus has written, "Christian behavior, therefore, however imperfect and sinful it may be in and of itself, is good because it is grounded in the assurance of a prior 'yes,' in that divine approval which the Christian does not have to seek because it has already been given. This is why the Christian can go ahead and act in confidence and joy, even though his works are still impure and imperfect."[2] It is the foundation of pastoral care ministry–indeed, all ministry.

Martin Luther explained the interrelationship of love of God and love of neighbor by comparing it to a water fountain. His image shows God's love flowing into us and then flowing out to our neighbor. Faith, which accepts God's love coming to us, and love of neighbor, which passes on, are part of the same process, Althaus contends:

> Because the Christian's activity flows out of his experience of God's love and since this activity is in itself love, it shares all the characteristics of God's own love. God wants his people to act spontaneously, freely and voluntarily, happily and eagerly. Where the Spirit and faith do their work, the Christian does not respond compulsively or artificially to his neighbor; rather, he acts with an inner necessity comparable to the natural processes by which trees bear fruit.[3]

This is the task of every Christian and the natural fruit of our redeemed life in Christ–to care for those who are near us. It is not only the responsibility of the ordained; the ministry of pastoral care for the neighbor is one in which all Christians are participants.

LOVE OF NEIGHBOR

To comprehend better what the new Testament meant by love of neighbor, which informs pastoral care ministry, let us examine it briefly. The *law of love*, also referred to as the love command or the love ethic and expressed in such phrases as "love your neighbor," "love your brothers and sisters," "love one another," or even "love your enemy," is most clearly portrayed in the Synoptics, in Paul's letters, and in John.

The double command to love God and neighbor is found in all three Synoptic Gospels (Matt. 22:34-40, Mark 12:28-34, and Luke 10:25-37), but in Matthew (5:43-48) and Luke (6:27-36) the love ethic is radicalized; we are told to love our *enemies*. The following discussion will very briefly review all of the above texts and will examine Reformation insights in the recapturing of these biblical themes.[4]

Synoptic Gospels

In the time of Christ, rabbis were frequently challenged to sum up the 613 commandments of the law. The scribe in Mark's version of the double command (12:28-34) makes such a request of Jesus, apparently in a nonabrasive way. He is told by Jesus that to love God and neighbor are the quintessence of the law. To love one's neighbor and to love God are treated as belonging to a class apart from all the other commandments; each is an integral part of the *chief commandment*. It is interesting to observe in Matthew's version (22:34-40) that the questioner is a lawyer rather than a scribe and that his question is phrased to "test" Jesus, to put him on the spot. Matthew's account of Jesus' response also emphasizes the relatedness of the two commands (22:38-39). Love of God is put forth as the "great and first commandment" but love of neighbor is "like" it. He goes on to say that "all the law and the prophets" depend on the double command (22:40).

Both Matthew's and Mark's reports of the double command to love God and neighbor emphasize the supreme importance of *both* commandments—which would in effect delimit the significance of the ceremonial laws of the time (especially among the scribes and Pharisees) and elevate the importance of caring for one's neighbors.

In Luke's discussion of the double command, it is crucial, for an understanding of love of neighbor, to include the parable of the Good Samaritan that follows it (6:30-37). With priest and Levite refusing to help while a hated Samaritan gives assistance, Jesus'

parable emphasizes that simply knowing what is right is insufficient. Action is required, and obedience to the law of love breaks
down artificial boundaries of sex, age, caste, nation, or race. Furnish
comments on the parable:

> Obedience in love establishes relationships where none were
> conceivable or possible before. Thus, the problem of neighbor
> is not one of definition but of performance, and where there is
> performance, where one's deeds are moved and shaped by
> love, there is neither time nor reason to ask, *"Who* is my
> neighbor?" . . . Concrete deeds of love, not casuistic defini-
> tions of love's limits, should be of concern.[5]

Both love of God and love of neighbor are inextricably linked
parts of one and the same response to God's grace and to God's
claim upon our lives. To love one's neighbor is to love God; Christ
said, "As you did it to one of the least of these . . . you did it to me"
(Matt. 25:40). The symbiosis between the two is expressed, in one
way or another, in each of the Synoptics. We owe to our neighbor
the same selfless love that we undeservedly receive from God and
gratefully return in worship, in prayer, and in love to our neighbor.

Paul

The law of love is also articulated in the writings of Paul
(although there are no explicit parallels to the double command as
found in the Synoptics).[6] The love ethic of Paul is stated from the
viewpoint of his "theology of the cross." According to Paul, Christ
is no mere prophet or teacher; in his life, death, and resurrection, he
is the very embodiment of the promise that God had been acting out
with the children of Israel, throughout antiquity–the promise of
redemption and new life. At the same time he embodies the new
law: to give oneself totally in the service of love.

Since believing in Christ is not to assent to a dogma but to be
joined with him and to become a participant in his suffering, death,
and resurrection, the Christian is thereby released from the bondage
of desire and self-will and is instead bound by the freedom of God's
grace to serve and care for others.

John

A key to understanding the law of love as revealed in the Gospel of John is provided by the "farewell discourses" (chapters 13-17). In this section of John the emphasis is on love within the Christian community: "By this love you have for one another, everyone will know that you are my disciples" (13:35). Serving others, noted in the Synoptics and Paul, is here transformed into discipleship. We are to follow Christ's example—"you also should do as I have done to you" (13:15). The high point of the thirteenth chapter of John articulates the author's understanding of Christ's law of love: "A new commandment I give to you, that you love one another" (13:34). The shackles of the old law are broken and there is a new law; following Christ means emptying oneself, serving and caring for others within the community.

The Reformers

The theology of the Reformation was strongly directed by the law of love and service to one's neighbor. To paraphrase Martin Luther, *a Christian lives in Christ through faith and in the neighbor through love.* By faith, the Christian is caught up beyond oneself into God. By love, the Christian sinks down beneath oneself into the neighbor.[7]

According to Luther, it is inevitable that a stream of loving service should flow from the spring of a life redeemed by and committed to Christ—who told us he "came not to be served but to serve" (Mark 10:45). Luther's only concern was that Christians should avoid the error of, on the one hand, releasing the bonds of love's law or, on the other hand, binding the free, redemptive act—God's gift of grace received through faith.

The double command of love found in the Synoptics is molded into one by Luther. He maintains that any love we have for God is properly offered to others. Thus, he contends that in the suffering and needy neighbor we find and love God; we serve the neighbor whenever we want to serve God: "Thus the commandment to love God is fully and completely subsumed in the commandment to love our neighbor."[8]

Our responsibility as Christians to love and serve others is in spite of the inherent limitedness of our response in faith. Though the bondage of sin and alienation has been broken in Christ, we are each still "both saint and sinner," and all attempts at loving others–including pastoral care–will remain fragile and sometimes weak. Rather than becoming discouraged by these realities, Luther urges, we should remind ourselves of Christ's command to go, serve, and care, with the assurance that our liberation, meted out by Christ through his power, gives us the capability of caring for others.

It is vital to add that God does not expect all Christians to obey the law of love in the same way. As Luther writes, "It is God's firm intention that all the saints are to live in the same faith, and be moved and guided by the same Spirit; but in external matters carry out different works."[9] In Luther, then, the love command is not confused with redemption, but is seen as the natural response of the Christian to the neighbor, taking on various forms of service depending on the needs of the other and the talents of the Christian.

Summing up some of the major themes from Paul, the Gospel authors, and the reformers, I suggest several points that can serve as a foundation for the pastoral care we offer.

- Pastoral care is a task to which we have been charged; we are *commanded* to love others, no matter how difficult that might be. Although we love each other freely, spontaneously, and in gratitude to God for God's grace toward us, our Christian freedom does not allow us to sit down on the job.
- Our ministry of loving and caring for others is based on our prior acceptance and love by God. God welcomes us back into a right relationship (reconciles us) and frees us to serve. All care for others flows out from God's love for us.
- In this new relationship the old law is replaced by the *law of love*. Caring for God and neighbor becomes the criterion by which our actions are assessed. This does not mean that the old law has no import, but that it must be weighed against the law of love. Luther explains, "In all his works he should be guided by this thought and look to this one thing alone, that he may serve and benefit others in all that he does, having regard to nothing except the need and advantage of his neighbor."[10]

- One way to love God is to love one's neighbor. God would sooner have us invest our time and energy in serving our neighbor than in spending extensive time on acts of worship or scrupulous introspection. To quote Luther again: "God would much rather be deprived of his service than of the service you owe your neighbor."[11] This in no way demeans the worship, honor, and "enjoyment" of God or the Christian's sense of awe and wonder in God's presence; but it recognizes that service to our sisters and brothers is a central feature of our life "in Christ."

- The love and care we address to others is given to other Christians (especially as seen in John), to those who are not members of the Christian community "whether Jew or Greek," and even to our enemies. Kierkegaard, discussing love of others, defined neighbor by saying that if there are only two people, the other person is the neighbor; "If there are millions, each one of these is the neighbor."[12] Pastoral care and counseling then is not only for the middle class who give to the church or pay for sessions; it is for all people.

- Luther's analogy of the love of God channeled through us as through a fountain emphasizes that we can be used to carry God's love to others. (It is not something we control but is dependent on the Spirit.) On such occasions our care is transformed and we become Christ for the other.

- Each member of the Christian community has a different configuration of gifts. All of us have a responsibility to use those particular talents that we have been given. We are not to covet others' gifts but rather enhance and use our own unique talents to their fullest extent.

- Love of neighbor is not just the correct attitude or the right belief. It is not simply knowing what to do or feeling affection and compassion. It is all of these, but it is also *action*–faith, active in love.

Love of God and neighbor prompts our pastoral care ministry. We love God *and* neighbor when we respond to those in need who are around us. But love of God and neighbor is not only what serves to motivate the care that we as pastoral carers offer; it also should be a goal for the parishioner to strive for as well. One of the distinguishing marks of pastoral counseling (vis-á-vis psychotherapy) should be that it tries not only to free up people *from* their problems, but also free them *for* something; they are freed to love God and neighbor themselves. Therefore, love of God and neighbor is not only an objective for the ministering person but also an aim for those who are being helped.

NOTES

1. Martin Luther, *Martin Luther: Selections from His Writings*, ed. John Dillenberger (New York: Doubleday Anchor, 1961), p. 53.

2. Paul Althaus, *The Ethics of Martin Luther*, trans. Robert C. Schultz (Philadelphia: Fortress Press, 1972), p. 6.

3. Althaus, *Ethics of Martin Luther*, pp. 14-15.

4. In discussing the law of love, I am not trying to detail a total ethic. For example, there is no attempt to address the ethical distinction between meeting the neighbor's *needs* and doing what the neighbor *desires*; that would be beyond the scope of this book. Rather, the aim is to articulate one part of an ethic that relates to pastoral care.

5. Victor Furnish, *The Love Command in the New Testament* (Nashville, TN: Abingdon, 1972), pp. 44-45.

6. The "law of Christ" (Gal. 6:2), the "principle of faith" (Rom. 3:27), and the "law of the Spirit of life in Christ Jesus" (Rom. 8:2) are possible references to the dual love command.

7. Martin Luther, *Works of Martin Luther*, ed. Henry Jacobs (Philadelphia: 1915-1943), vol. 2, pp. 342-43.

8. Martin Luther, *D. Martin Luthers Werke*, gen. ed. J. K. F. Kraake, Kritische Gesamtausgabe (Weimar, Germany: Bohlaus Nachfolger, 1883-), vol. 17:II, p. 99.

9. Luther, Weimar edition, vol. 8, p. 588.

10. *LW*, vol. 2, p. 335.

11. Luther, Weimar edition, vol. 10:III, p. 249.

12. Søren Kierkegaard, *Works of Love*, trans. David F. Swenson and Lillian M. Swenson (Princeton, NJ: Princeton University Press, 1949), p. 18.

Chapter 10

Pastoral Care
as Community Endeavor

Take a look at a typical pastoral care relationship in a North American congregation, and this is what you are likely to find: one pastor, one parishioner. (Or one pastor, one family.) They meet in the pastor's office, the home, the hospital room. Conversations are kept private. Oftentimes, unless there is a death, arrest, or similar public event, other members of the congregation have little or no knowledge of the struggle facing that lone person or family.

What, if anything, is wrong with this picture? Certainly a great deal of good comes from these private pastoral encounters. But the community of saints is conspicuous by its absence. The model for these one-to-one pastoral care relationships clearly is not the dominant one in the tradition of the church, and even less from its Hebrew roots where community was paramount. Instead, the Western practice of pastoral care reflects the style of our society, and seems to have been drawn from a highly individualistic medical and psychotherapeutic model—which is itself under challenge today. In business, education, and even medicine, emphasis is shifting from an individualistic and often competitive mode of operating to cooperation, shared learning, and collaboration.

The individualistic model may be a natural extension of our society, but it is not always beneficial for isolated and often alienated people. It may even be unhealthy. Our concern for privacy and self-reliance often leaves us on our own when we desperately need the support of others. The pastor cannot move in with troubled

Portions of this chapter were first published as "Sojourn in South Africa: Pastoral Care as a Community Endeavor" by Howard W. Stone in the *Journal of Pastoral Care*, vol. 50, no. 2 (Summer 1996), pp. 207-213. Reprinted by permission.

parishioners to guide them through their dark times. The pastor is not even available at every time of need.

There is another way. I discovered an example that illumines the possibilities of community-based pastoral ministry during a recent trip to South Africa. I had been invited by Julian Müller of the Theological Faculty at The University of Pretoria. Over the years we have talked about the differences in the practice of pastoral care in South Africa and the United States. He said if I was ever to understand pastoral care in his country, I needed to come and see it firsthand. Finally, I did. I did not go to lecture on "how it's done in America." Rather, I went to observe and to listen. I wanted to carry back from South Africa ideas that would inform my pastoral care ministry.

My aim had been to find out what special problems they might encounter in pastoral care (especially crisis intervention) during a time of rapid sociopolitical change; what I found was an attitude toward pastoral ministry that has answered my nagging concerns with a picture of how pastoral care as community endeavor might look.

Among the many rural, urban, black, and white congregations we visited, my wife and I went to Tshilidzini, a Christian mission in what was once the Venda Homeland in northern Transvaal. (In the new South Africa, the homelands–self-governing regions where black Africans of certain tribes were forced to live during the darkest years of apartheid–are no longer independent entities. Venda is no longer "Vendaland," but it is still there.)

The Rev. Wilhelm van Deventer is a pastor of the Dutch Reformed Church of South Africa; his wife Claire is a doctor who trains nurse practitioners to bring basic medical care to the people of this extremely poor, rural, but densely populated area.

They drove us around their parish. The Tshilidzini church (*Tshilidzini* is a Venda word meaning "God's grace") is made up of twenty-nine small congregations scattered throughout the region. There are one part-time and two full-time pastors serving these twenty-nine outposts. Each of the congregations has worship every Sunday; when the pastor is not there, the lay people preach, lead worship, and share in the responsibility of pastoral care. On Sunday we worshipped with them, sitting on rows of bricks under the shade of a spreading fig tree. It was a moving service, full of spontaneity, music, and participation.

Pastor Van Deventer sees pastoral care as not just a responsive task that reacts to the problems and needs that people bring to him, but as a proactive one. In this time of new freedom, he believes that pastoral care is the key to ministry in the Venda congregation. And if pastoral care and counseling is the major task of ministry, and if it is the task of all the people of the congregation, then the leaders of the church need to have a vision for bringing Christ's care to all members, and a plan to go about it. Several years ago the elders of the Tshilidzini church met with the pastor and mapped out how they would go about this pastoral care task. For the first two years, the elders decided, the ministry was to be was based upon Matthew 28–that is, to help each church member recognize that in Christ each one of them is a precious, worthful person. After decades of repression that realization may have been slow in coming; but–as Julian Müller expressed it–after the free elections of 1994, it was as if a dam had burst. People began to see themselves and each other in a new light.

The opening chapters of Ephesians is a key to the second phase of pastoral care ministry in Venda, where the church is now. The focus of these two years will be to help people recognize that they are free to care for others. Each person has unique gifts. These gifts are for the good of the community, and each person is called to exercise them. Christians are not to wait for others to take the lead, but to actively express God's love by ministering to others. They have been set free to help each other. The emphasis, in other words, is on every person not only as a precious child of God, but as a leader taking responsibility for the care of others–for praying with them, offering solace, and helping them in whatever way is needed. Each Christian is the leaven of the community.

Although it is too soon to predict with certainty the direction of subsequent phases of the pastoral care ministry at Tshilidzini, family problems are serious in Venda and very likely will be the next focus of ministry. Aside from their obvious poverty, some of the major problems facing the families are alcoholism and spouse abuse.

Pastor Van Deventer and I discussed pastoral care in this traditional African setting. He said that with South Africa's new beginning, under a government elected by all of the South African people, the initial task of his ministry has been accomplished. Black South Africans are freed from the rule of a white minority, though not yet from the poverty and inequality that the old system fostered. Now, he said, his task is to help people recognize their own humanity and worth, and to accept their freedom. They are not only to recognize God's concern for them, but they are to express that love to those around them.

That sounds much like a pastoral care or counseling task that American ministers often face; the difference is that *every* single person in the Tshilidzini congregation must grapple with the same issue. It probably will take generations for the wounds of apartheid to heal and for black Africans to accept more fully their own worth and their own gifts of ministry to others. Neither the pastor nor the members of the congregation seemed to feel hopeless or over-whelmed by the task, but they are cognizant of its enormity and take it very seriously.

COMMUNITY AS LOCUS
OF PASTORAL CARE

Pastoral care as it is practiced in Tshilidzini—and as I found through-out the country—is primarily a function of the church as a whole and not the pastor's exclusive role. It is the task of all the people. The minister is a facilitator, a teacher, and a leader in pastoral care, but most of the work is done in the community by the community.

The understanding of pastoral care and counseling in South Africa, and especially in traditional African communities, struck me as being quite different from the more individualized and special-ized ministries of pastoral care and pastoral counseling in North America. It is not pastoral psychotherapy, but rather the support, prayer, correction, and sustenance of the Christian community for each member. For example, one of the goals in Sunday worship at the Tshilidzini congregations is to learn who has a problem, a grief, a difficulty, and then arrange for members of the congregations to pray for and visit that person during the following week.

Pastor Van Deventer illustrated the community pastoral care orientation of the African people by telling a story of the first time he set out to make house to house visits. He arrived early in the morning at the first hut. After he finished visiting with them, the people from the first house accompanied him to the second house;

and when he went to the third house, the people from the first and second houses also joined him as he continued the visitation. By the evening he had with him the families of all the people he had visited throughout the day. Pastoral care visitation was a total community undertaking.

Among the African people, according to Julian Müller, pastoral care and counseling is done mainly by the church as community. The idea of going to a pastor with a personal problem is somewhat foreign to many white South Africans, and only quite recently have the educated middle and upper-middle classes sought psychotherapy and counseling. This is true of black Christians as well–even more so than Afrikaners (whites of Dutch background).

Here is a noticeable difference between Christian ministry in South Africa and in the United States. In South Africa, pastoral care is not so much a task of the individual minister (and certainly not of private pastoral counseling agencies or pastoral psychotherapists) as it is a responsibility of the entire congregation. Lay pastoral care is very much a part of its tradition.

Among blacks, the extended family carries on most of the pastoral care tasks. As a case in point, in Atteridgeville (a black township near Pretoria), two pastors reported that although unemployment is high and poverty is almost universal, you will virtually never see a homeless person in their community. Whether you live in a luxurious home, a nice bungalow, or a corrugated metal shack, "there is always room for one more." The nuclear family, the extended family, or the church as the family of God, spreads its arms and takes in those who are without. There is some concern reported in the South African press that urbanization will result in the breakdown of these strong extended family units and leave, especially, the elderly poor without support. At present, however, the extended family (which often includes distant relatives and friends) is the primary social unit in the black African community, providing most of the sustenance and social services that Westerners have come to expect from counselors, ministers, social workers, schools, and public agencies.

White South Africans live in a more individualized, western culture. Nevertheless, according to Dr. Müller, the emphasis of pastoral care in South Africa's Christian churches is strongly upon the congregation's role in the care of souls, and not upon the pastor as a

Lone Ranger "treating" an individual or family. This emphasis is consciously promoted in the teaching of pastoral care and counseling in the seminaries of the church.

Daniel Louw is Professor of Pastoral Care and Counseling at the University of Stellenbosch, near Capetown. In his book *Illness as Crisis and Challenge: Guidelines for Pastoral Care*, he emphasizes the importance of community in South African churches:

> Writers on pastoral care within an African context agree that pastoral care must be seen as a social and community issue. In the traditional [Western] approach of pastoral counselling, the individual stands in the center of a network of relationships. In the African context, pastoral counselling must undergo a metamorphosis, as the community and network of relationships are in the center and the individual at the periphery.[1]

Professor Louw goes on to point out that a person's role in society "determines who one is and it is of greater importance than one's personal qualities and individual needs. Role fulfillment becomes more important than personal self-actualization."[2]

A danger whenever moving back and forth between one culture and another is to idealize aspects of the one while ignoring its problems. (In anthropology there has always been the danger of perceiving the customs of indigenous peoples as correctives to the presumed ills of the anthropologist's own culture.) The problems in traditional South African cultures cannot be ignored; a number of them have already been referred to in this chapter. Crime, spouse abuse, alcoholism, poverty, and unemployment are only a few of the most compelling ones. In addition, the community's exemplary participation in pastoral care cannot hide a weakness (from this American pastoral caregiver's perspective) in basic pastoral counseling skills on the part of some of the ordained clergy. For example, I asked several pastors what they do to help a family burdened with alcoholism or spouse abuse. Their answer: they tell people that they should not hit their wives, that it is better to drink in moderation, and that they should not neglect their children. Such a prophetic approach is appropriate in some cases, but dealing with these prob-

community. The called share collectively in a partnership with Christ and the Holy Spirit, in grace, and sufferings and comfort."[7]

COMMUNITY AND INDIVIDUALIZED PASTORAL CARE

In recent years, the field of pastoral theology in the United States has been calling upon those who practice pastoral care and counseling to move away from its rather individualized model and take seriously a more communal perspective. Still, most American pastoral counselors have been so heavily schooled in individual psychology–no matter what stripe–that the suggestion has not, for the most part, taken hold. It sounded good in theory, but the advocates of community-based pastoral care have supplied little detail to clarify the vision and offer strategies for accomplishing it. I have to include myself in those numbers. Back in 1976 I wrote, "The congregation is an instrument through which God's love is translated to those in need. As a caring community, the church is singularly well suited for responding to people in crisis."[8] In 1983 I wrote an entire book on lay pastoral care, arguing that each Christian is a mediator of God's grace through their caring for neighbor.[9]But what I proposed in those texts was primarily an individual response, from one Christian to another. In South Africa I have seen one-to-one pastoral care, but it always occurs under the aegis of the body of Christians who share a responsibility to care for each other. Pastoral care is a community-based, not an individual-based, endeavor. In this matter, I believe that the practice of pastoral care in North America can learn much from South Africans.

What might this mean? More reliance on elders or deacons of the church to perform pastoral tasks? Reorganization of large congregations into small cells of Christians who learn from and minister to each other? Moral development taking a more serious part of pastoral care and counseling? Private practice and pastoral counseling center care tied more directly to the community of faith? The relinquishing of "star" status for ordained clergy? Increasing use of lay ministry? Convincing church members to accept their brothers and sisters as competent caregivers? South African churches provide some models; we will have to find our own ways.

*   *   *

Under the fig tree in Tshilidzini, worship drew to a close with a final prayer, hymn, and benediction. The members greeted each other with something like the traditional passing of the peace, clasping hands and moving around until every person had greeted every other worshipper. During the greetings, a sixteen-year-old girl who regularly attends church told the pastor that her mother had committed suicide the previous Tuesday. The father is nowhere to be found; she will now be mother and father to her younger brothers and sisters.

The little congregation was called to gather back together. Clustered in a tight knot around the girl, we were told what had happened to her and asked to offer help and prayers. We sang a familiar hymn of comfort, each in our own language. The pastor and the elder prayed with their arms around the girl, then called on the congregation to offer their prayers. Everyone began praying *at once*, in their own words and their own languages. It was not cacophony, but a soothing tide of human sound washing over the group. After the prayers, the pastor and elder organized people to visit the family every day during the coming week (according to Venda tradition, the funeral would be Saturday). The elder told us, "She will have the strength to get through. I have been training her since she was young; she is strong in the Lord. She will be able to survive. We will always be here for her."

The night before we had spoken of pastoral care and counseling as the task of the community. The pastor had told me how the people cared for each other. Suddenly, I was experiencing it. I could see in action what he was describing to me: pastoral care as a community function. The depth of emotion to which my wife and I were moved during this simple, spontaneous event may reveal a hunger for a sense of belonging to the body of Christ that our individualized lives have left unfed.

*   *   *

It is possible to reclaim, to a greater extent, the spirit of community that thrived in the early church. For those who offer pastoral care and counseling in our alienated and sometimes fractured American society, it is not too soon to begin. Although the ethos of community in North American and African society is different—as it is different from that of Israel or the early church—our pastoral care can begin to take on more of a community focus. Through sermon, study of scripture, and teaching, we as congregations can examine ways in which we can become more of a caring community—responding to each other as individuals and as the total community of faith.

NOTES

1. Daniel Louw, *Illness as Crisis and Challenge: Guidelines for Pastoral Care* (Doornfontein, South Africa: Orion, 1994), p. 21.

2. Ibid.

3. See volume 2 of *Theologie of the Old Testament* by Horst Dietrich Preuss, trans. Leo Perdue (Louisville, KY: Westminster/John Knox, forthcoming 1996), Chapter 12.

4. Ibid.

5. See Abraham J. Malherbe, *Paul and the Thessalonians: The Philosophic Tradition of Pastoral Care* (Philadelphia: Fortress, 1987).

6. Abraham J. Malherbe, "Traditions and Theology of Care in the New Testament," in *Dictionary of Pastoral Care and Counseling*, ed. Rodney Hunter (Nashville, TN: Abingdon Press, 1990), p. 791.

7. Ibid., p. 789.

8. See the revised edition of *Crisis Counseling* (Minneapolis, MN: Fortress Press, 1993), final chapter.

9. See the revised edition of *The Caring Church: A Guide for Lay Pastoral Care* (Minneapolis, MN: Fortress Press, 1991).

Index

Abraham, 46
Acceptance, 4,16,32,115-123,
    127,158
Acceptance of self, 115-117
Althaus, Paul, 154
Asmussen, Hans, 47
Assessment, theological, 25,37
Augustine, 45,60

Barrett, C.K., 41
Barry, William, 83,84,101,103
Barth, Karl, 63
Behavior, 11,13,29
Belief(s), 4,20-22,31,54,73,88,89,
    132,148,159
Bible, 1,10,39,40,56,87,118
Blakeslee, Thomas, 67
Bogen, Joseph, 70
Bonhoeffer, Dietrich, 51,53,55
Brain function, 65,70
Brain, right, left, 67,69,72,74
    hemispheres, 65-66
Brahms, 46
Brister, C.W., 81
Browning, Don, 78
Buber, Martin, 44
Bucer, Martin, 110
Bultmann, Rudolph, 42

Calvin, John, 111
Campbell, Alastair, 139,141,142
Carkhuff, Robert, 115
Catherine of Siena, 82
Centering, 80
Clebsch, William, 9
Clinebell, Howard, 11,115
Cobb, John, 53,119,122

Cognition, 11,67
    bilateral, 71,73
Cognitive sets, 65,74
Communication, 41,43-46,48,49,51,
    56,66,94,95
Community, 11,12,17,31,32,35,83,
    103,113,139,157,161-170
    Christian, 17,22,32,85,102,157,159
    faith, 12,17,22,57,111,168
    of Saints, 12,17
Connolly, William, 83,84,100,101,103
Contemplative attitude, 89-91,93,96
Correlation of theology and pastoral
    care, 8,11,12,17,19-23,28,37,
    49,79,86,104

de Sales, Francis, 82
Discernment of the Spirit, 103

Ebeling, Gerhard, 41,56,57,59
Eductive guidance, 9-11,14,15,40
Edwards, Tilden, 101
Ethic, Christian, 16
    love, 155,156
    mental health, 16
Ethics, 8,64,82,116
    social, 77
    theological, 77
Evil, 15,30,83,128-131,137,146,151

Faith, 2,4,12,21-23,30-32,36,41,43,
    44,53-55,78-81,83,89,91,101,
    102,110,112,118,128,132,
    133-135,137,139,141-143,
    146-148,150,151,153,154,
    157,158,167,170

False assumptions, 3-6
Frankl, Victor, 137
Freud, Sigmund, 11

Galin, David, 68
Gazzaniga, Michael, 66
Gerkin, Charles, 50
Gilkey, Langdon, 127,135
Grace, 14,15,31,47,53-55,58,79,
    80,98,120,134,156-158,
    162,168
Gospel, 15,43,46,63,77,81,110,135,
    139,143,148
Guiding, 9,10,13
Guilt, 30,36,51,80,87,88,93,140,
    146,150

Healing, 9,10,12,13,129,130,139
Human, 16,133,137,139
Humanity, 15,41,142,164

Ignatius of Loyola, 82,97,101,103
Inductive guidance, 9,49

Jaekle, Charles, 9
Jenson, Robert, 45
Jerome, 82
Jesus Prayer, 96,97
John of the Cross, 82,101
Jones, Alan, 101
Journal, 80,93,98,99
Jung, Carl, 84,86

Kasemann, Ernst, 118
Keble, John, 19
Kelsey, Morton, 99,101
Kierkegaard, Søren, 132,136,137,
    148,159
Kinsbourne, Marcel, 71

Leech, Kenneth, 101
Laity, 107-109,111-113
LaPlace, Jean, 101
Lay ministry, 112,168
Lay pastoral care, 13,19,113,165,168
Lectio Divina, 96
Love of God and neighbor, 154-156,
    159,160
Luther, Martin, 7,8,13,15,48,53,54,
    63,82,108-111,154,157-159

Malherbe, Abraham J., 167
Marie of the Incarnation, 101
Mauriac, Francois, 134
May, Gerald, 84,101
McCarty, Shaun, 85
McNeill, John T., 110
Meditation, 31,80,93,102
Mental health, 9,14,15,85,117,149
Merton, Thomas, 101
Ministry, 13,16-19,33,39,46-48,50,
    57,58,60,63-65,73,74,77,81,
    107-113,115,116,127,139,
    140,162-164,167
Ministry of presence, 46,49,122,
    143,147
Monologia, 96,97
Morley, Wilbur, 149
Moses, 102

Nebes, Robert, 68
Niebuhr, Reinhold, 118
Noah, 46
Nondirective approach, 10-12,14,39,
    40,50,56,141

Oates, Wayne E., 115
Oden, Thomas D., 126
Ornstein, Robert, 68

Pannenberg, Wolfhart, 77
Parable, 74,98,151,155,156
Pastoral assessment, 33-37,87

Paul, 54,80,85,103,109,118,119,131, 139,155,156-158,167
Planck, Max, 68
Pneuma, 53,118
Poetic questions, 142
Prayer, 2,6,12,31,51,80,82,83,85,86, 88,89,91-96,98,101-103,123, 129,130,156,164,169
Priesthood of all believers, 13,107-111 universal, 111-113
Progoff, Ira, 91,99
Pruyser, Paul, 28
Psychology, 5,8,10,14,15,18,21,32, 40,50,63,77,80,101,102, 137,168
Psychotherapy, 5,14-16,63,80,82, 84-86,100-102,117,119-121, 123,160,164,165
Pump-priming, 73,74
Pusey, Edward, 19

Quieting, 80

Reconciling, 9,10,13
Religion, 1,2,3
Religion as taboo, 1-3,6,8
Religious experience, 82,98, 101,102,167
Resources, Christian, 12 faith, 2 religious, 1,5,6,10 spiritual, 5,80
Revised model, 10,12
Richardson, Alan, 107
Rogers, Carl, 11,39,50,115-117
Rossi, Robert, 86

Sacraments, 7,39,45-47,111,122
Salvation, 30,31,36,41,59,110,142
Sanders, James, 40
Saul, 46
Schillebeeckx, Edward, 41
Schweizer, Eduard, 118

Scripture, 3,10,18,20,31,42,46,49,50, 58,73,74,78,80,92,93,96-98, 101,122,128,138,148,150, 151,154,170
Self, 29,32,43,90,117,119-121,123
Self and spirit, 115,117-123
Sin, 14,15,29,30,35,41,51,53,55, 58,80,87,93,101,130,138, 142,145,158
Soelle, Dorothee, 137,139,140
Sperry, Roger, 66
Spirit (Holy), 12,53,55,79,80,90,91, 99,102-104,110,117-120,122, 123,139,154,158,159
Spiritual direction, 12,73,77,79-89, 92,93,95,96,98,100-104,121
Spiritual director, 15,22,81,99-104
Spiritual disciplines, 82,93
Spirituality, 78,82,83,88,92,100,101
Stairs, Jean, 103
Station in life, one's, 108,109,113
Stuempfle, Herman, 108,109
Suffering, 31-33,125,127,128, 130-141,143,146-148,150, 151,153,156,157,168
Sustaining, 9,10,13

Taylor, Michael, 17
Teresa of Avila, 82,101
Theodicy, 126-129,131-133,139-143, 145-148,150,151
Theological constructs, 14,73,74
Theological template, 27,28,33,35, 37,64,72
Theology, 8,17,18,20-22,63,64,69,70, 72-74,77-81,100-102,151,157 Christian, 9,14-16,130
Thurneysen, Eduard, 47,48,55
Tillich, Paul, 47,52,64,116,139
Traditional method, 10,12,50,56

Values, 9,14,20-22,29,120,147
Verbal word, 41,45-47,49-52,55,56, 58-60,122,151

Visible word, 41,45-47,49-52,55,56,
        58,60,122,143,151
Vocation, 108,109,113

Wallas, Graham, 71
Wiesel, Elie, 133-134

Wilkens, Thomas, 110
Word, 20,22,23,39-60,78-80,89,
        95-98,104,110,111,119,122,
        130,147,148
Wounded healer, 142

JAVA
Quick Reference

Michael M. Afergan

Credits

President
Roland Elgey

Publisher
Joseph B. Wikert

Publishing Manager
Fred Slone

Senior Title Manager
Bryan Gambrel

Editorial Services Director
Elizabeth Keaffaber

Managing Editor
Sandy Doell

Director of Marketing
Lynn E. Zingraf

Acquisitions Editor
Angela C. Kozlowski

Production Editor
Thomas Cirtin

Product Marketing Manager
Kim Margolius

Assistant Product Marketing Manager
Christy M. Miller

Strategic Marketing Manager
Barry Pruett

Technical Editor
Mark Robinson

Technical Support Specialist
Nadeem Muhammed

Acquisitions Coordinator
Bethany A. Echlin

Software Relations Coordinator
Patty Brooks

Editorial Assistant
Andrea Duvall

Book and Cover Designer
Nathan Clement

Production Team
Marcia Brizendine
Amy Gornik
Daryl Kessler
Paul Wison

Indexer
Cheryl Dietsch

Composed in Frutiger and ITC Kabel by Que Corporation.

About the Author

Michael M. Afergan (**mikea@ai.mit.edu**) began working with Java during the Spring of 1995 through his research at the Massachusetts Institute of Technology AI Labs. Since then, he has carefully studied its growth, developing practical applets for large businesses as an independent consultant. Michael is a founding member of TeamJava, a network of Java professionals, and is also a weekly contributor to *Digital Espresso,* Java's online digest. Michael was a contributing author for Que's *Special Edition Using Java*, and wrote a chapter on multi-user environments for *Java Unleashed,* Sams Publishing.

Although only 18 years old, Michael has been programming for 10 years and has even taught Java overseas and a computer science class at MIT. He is currently attending Harvard University where he was accepted for early admissions. His official Web page is at **http://www.ai.mit.edu/people/mikea/resume.html**.

We'd Like to Hear from You!

As part of our continuing effort to produce books of the highest possible quality, Que would like to hear your comments. To stay competitive, we *really* want you, as a computer book reader and user, to let us know what you like or dislike most about this book or other Que products.

You can mail comments, ideas, or suggestions for improving future editions to the address below, or send us a fax at (317) 581-4663. For the online inclined, Macmillan Computer Publishing has a forum on CompuServe (type **GO QUEBOOKS** at any prompt) through which our staff and authors are available for questions and comments. The address of our Internet site is **http://www.mcp.com** (World Wide Web).

In addition to exploring our forum, please feel free to contact me personally to discuss your opinions of this book: I'm **75703,3504** on CompuServe, and I'm **akozlowski@que.mcp.com** on the Internet.

Thanks in advance. Your comments will help us to continue publishing the best books available on computer topics in today's market.

Angela C. Kozlowski
Product Development Specialist
Que Corporation
201 W. 103rd Street
Indianapolis, Indiana 46290
USA

To my parents, for supporting me no matter which paths I choose to take.

To Papa Bert, for inspiring me to march down all paths with determination and dedication.

To Dan, for always being awesome.

Contents at a Glance

Introduction   1

API Reference   5

Syntax Reference   307

Action Index 327

Index of Fields 333

Index of Methods 345

Index of Classes and Interfaces 415

Table of Contents

Introduction 1
What Does This Manual Contain? 1
How to Use This Manual 2

API Reference 5
java.applet 9
    Class 10
    Interfaces 16
java.awt 19
    Classes 20
    Interfaces 116
java.awt.image 119
    Classes 120
    Interfaces 139
java.io 145
    Classes 147
    Interfaces 187
java.lang 191
    Classes 192
    Interfaces 245
java.net 251
    Classes 252
    Interfaces 270
java.util 273
    Classes 274
    Interfaces 294
Exceptions 297
    java.awt 299
    java.io 299
    java.lang 300
    java.net 301
    java.util 301
Errors 303
    java.awt 304
    java.lang 304

Syntax Reference 307
Abstract 309
Break 309
Catch 310
Class 310

Java Quick Reference

Continue	311
Do...While	311
Else	312
Extends	313
Final	313
Finally	314
For	315
If	315
Implements	316
Import	316
Instanceof	317
Modifiers	317
Native	318
New	319
Package	319
Public	319
Private	320
Return	320
Super	321
This	321
Throw	322
Throws	322
Static	322
Static	323
Switch	323
Synchronized	324
Try	324
While	325
Action Index	**327**
Animation	329
Applets	329
Applications	330
Communication	330
Image Processing	330
Input and Output	331
Math	331
User Interfaces	332
Index of Fields	**333**
Index of Methods	**345**
Index of Classes and Interfaces	**415**

INTRODUCTION

What Does This Manual Contain?

The Java language consists of two parts: the *syntax* and the *libraries*. The Java syntax closely resembles that of C++ as it defines the structure of your programs. The Java API (application programming interface) libraries are the resources that you, as a programmer, have to work with. By using the libraries according to the rules of the Java syntax, you are able to develop programs.

The API

The largest part of this book is devoted to the Java API libraries. These libraries were written by the developers of Java to enable you to create full-blown applets and applications.

The API libraries are made up of several packages, each containing several classes that are grouped by functionality. These classes are composed of *fields* and *methods*.

This manual lists and explains every *class* and *interface* as well as their respective fields and methods. The classes are in alphabetical order by package, and the summaries of many classes include examples of their use as well as the output of the code. In addition, every component has a picture, so you know how your interface will look before you even begin.

Indexes

To make this manual easy to use, there are several indexes that organize the "API Reference" section in various manners. At the end of this book, you will find indexes of all classes, methods, and fields. Each entry provides you with the full package and class name as well as the page number directing you to a detailed summary of the class.

Furthermore, you will also find at the back of this book the "Action Index," which not only lists several of the major tasks that Java is used for, but also lists the classes necessary to accomplish those tasks.

How to Use This Manual

Designed as a handy reference, this manual can be used in a myriad of ways as described in the following sections.

API Reference

This section serves as the primary source of information for the manual. Each class, interface, exception, and error used in Java programming is listed here and explained in depth. In addition, every method and field within these classes and interfaces is explained in detail. For easy reference, they are in alphabetical order and grouped by package. Furthermore, to give you a jump start on your task, several classes have complete applets that serve as code examples.

Due to their unique natures, *exceptions* and *errors* are listed separately after the classes and interfaces. They too are in alphabetical order and grouped by package.

Syntax Reference

Even the most experienced programmer sometimes forgets the exact usage of a certain keyword or construct. Arranged alphabetically, this section provides you not only with an explanation of each keyword in the Java language, but also a general definition of the syntax and a specific example.

Action Index

Few programs can be written using only one class. The task-related "Action Index" provides you with a list of the several common uses of Java along with the packages, classes, and methods necessary to accomplish these tasks and the page numbers for finding these packages, classes, and methods in the "API Reference" section. Therefore, the "Action Index" enables you to learn not only what classes you need to use, but also how to use them.

Index of Classes and Interfaces

Because you may not always know the package of a class based solely on its name, this index lists all classes in alphabetical order and provides their complete names and page numbers. Conveniently located at the end of the manual, this index can also be used even if you do know the package of a class.

Index of Methods

Just because you know of a method doesn't mean that you know where it came from. This index enables you to look up a method based on its name and find its class as well as its page number.

Index of Fields

Similar to methods, it is not always clear which package a field belongs to. This index enables you not only to find the page on which the field is explained, but also the class to which it belongs.

API
REFERENCE

API REFERENCE

This reference presents and explains the entire Java API. The API, which stands for *Application Programming Interface,* is a set of classes and interfaces that outline a set of platform-independent behaviors that establish the foundation of all Java applets and applications. Although any program depends on the strategies of the programmer, these classes and interfaces are the tools that all programmers use in creating Java applications.

JAVA.APPLET

CLASSES AND INTERFACES

 **JAVA.APPLET**

The `java.applet` class provides you with only one class and three interfaces, but it is one of the most used packages because it lays the foundation for all applets. The `Applet` class is most important because it is required when you create an applet. Also useful is the `AppletContext` interface, which is employed to interact with the browser.

Class

Applet Extends java.awt.Panel

This class is the heart of every Java applet. Derived from the `java.awt.Pannel` class, the `Applet` class possesses all the methods found in the `java.awt.Container` class that enable you to create a powerful and appealing user interface. Every applet that you create *must* extend the Applet class.

As stated above, in order to create a Java applet, you must create a class that extends the `java.applet.Applet` class. However, to run the applet, you must embed it in an HTML page. This is done with the `<APPLET>` tag, which specifies the name, height, and width of the applet. You may also specify additional parameters—information that the applet can obtain. The HTML page shown in figure 1 specifies two parameters: NAME and KEY (see Listing 1).

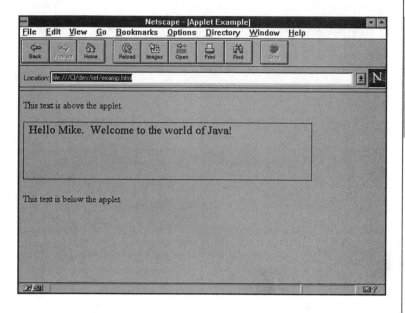

Fig. 1 A simple applet produced by the code and HTML file in Listing 1.

Listing 1   Sample HTML Page for an Applet

```
<HEAD>
<TITLE>Applet Example</TITLE>
<BODY>
This text is above the applet.<P>

<applet code="examp.class" width=500 height=100 >
<param name=NAME value="Mike">
<param name=KEY value = "j">
</applet>
<P>This text is below the applet.<P>
</BODY>
```

This document will load the `examp` class that will be stored in a file named `examp.class`. Listing 2 is the complete source code for that class.

Java Quick Reference

Listing 2   Sample Applet

```java
import java.applet.Applet;
import java.awt.*;

public class ExampleApplet extends Applet
{
    String userName;
    char favoriteKey;
    int appletWidth, appletHeight, fontHeight;
    Font fontToUse;
    FontMetrics fm;

    /* This class will be called before the applet is
       started.  As a result, it can be used to perform
       preparatory operations. */

    public void init() {
      userName = new String();// creates a new, empty string
      appletWidth = this.size().width - 2; // uses
                           //Component.size()
      appletHeight = this.size().height - 2;
      fontToUse = new Font("TimesRoman", Font.PLAIN, 20);
                           // creates a new Font object
        fm = getFontMetrics(fontToUse);     // obtains the
                                  //FontMetrics for the font
        fontHeight = fm.getMaxAscent(); /* maximum size that
                          one of the font's characters may
                                      extend upwards    */
        getInfo();     // gets info from HTML tag   }


    /* This method uses the getParameter() method to obtain
         the information passed to the applet in the applet
        tag.  This method assumes that there will be two
        tags, titled "NAME" and "KEY" in the HTML page. */

    void getInfo() {
      userName = getParameter("NAME");
      favoriteKey = getParameter("KEY").charAt(0);
      // we want the first character in the returned string
      }
```

```
/* This method is automatically called whenever the
   mouse is depressed within the applet */

public boolean mouseDown(Event evt, int x, int y) {
  showStatus("Mouse Click at ("+x+","+y+")" );
  return true;
}

  /* This method is automatically called whenever a key is
     depressed within the applet */
public boolean keyDown(Event evt, int key) {
  if (key == favoriteKey) {
    showStatus("You pressed " + favoriteKey +
                              ", my favorite key!");
    return true;
  }
  return false;
}

/* This method is automatically called whenever the
   applet needs to be drawn */

public void paint(Graphics g) {
  g.setFont(fontToUse);
  g.drawRect(0,0,appletWidth, appletHeight);
  g.drawString("Hello " + userName +
    ".  Welcome to the world of Java!",10,fontHeight + 3);
}

}
```

The classes used in this example, `Font`, `FontMetrics`, and `Graphics`, are explained in the AWT package section. However, you should note that of the five methods in this applet, only one, `getInfo()`, is explicitly called by the applet. The others will be called by either the browser or by one of the classes on which the `java.applet.Applet` class is based. Methods, such as `init()`, are called by the browser itself at particular times. Methods, including `keyDown()` and `mouseDown()`, are called to handle specific user events within the applet. More such methods can be found in the `java.awt.Component` class.

Methods

◆ **void destroy( )**
This method may be used to perform any cleanup necessary
after execution of the applet. It is empty by default; thus,
you must override it if you want the method to do anything.
The method is automatically called by the browser when the
applet is stopped.

◆ **AppletContext getAppletContext( )**
Returns the `AppletContext` of the applet. This is the
browser (i.e., Netscape or Appletviewer) used to view the
applet.

◆ **String getAppletInfo( )**
This can be used to return such information as version
number or the author's name. If you do not override it, a null
string is returned.

◆ **AudioClip getAudioClip(URL url)**
Loads the audio clip residing at the specified URL.

◆ **AudioClip getAudioClip(URL url, String clipname)**
Loads an audio clip with the specified URL and name.

◆ **URL getCodeBase( )**
Returns the URL of the applet, and is usually the URL of the
page containing the current applet without the document
name.

◆ **URL getDocumentBase( )**
Returns the URL of the page on which the current applet
resides.

◆ **Image getImage(URL url)**
Loads the specified image, which may not be an immediate
process inasmuch as it may take some time to actually load
the image.

◆ **Image getImage(URL url, String imagename)**
Loads the specified image, which may not be an immediate process inasmuch as it may take some time to actually load the image.

◆ **String getParameter(String labelname)**
Returns the parameter specified in the HTML page.

◆ **String[ ][ ] getParameterInfo( )**
Returns all parameters from the HTML page.

◆ **void init( )**
This method may be used to perform some preparatory actions. While the method is naturally empty, this method is usually used to perform preparatory tasks—such as to create streams and to load information. This method is always called by the browser.

◆ **boolean isActive( )**
Returns true if the applet is currently running.

◆ **void play(URL url)**
Plays the specified audio clip.

◆ **void play(URL url, String audioClipName)**
Plays the specified audio clip.

◆ **void resize(int width, int height)**
Resizes the applet to the specified dimensions. In Netscape, this method has no effect. To set the size of an applet, use the width and height parameters in the applet HTML tag.

◆ **void resize(Dimension d)**
Resizes the applet to the specified dimensions. In Netscape, this method has no effect. To set the size of an applet, use the width and height parameters in the applet HTML tag.

◆ **void setStub(AppletStub stub)**
Sets the AppletStub of the applet. This task is performed

automatically by the browser. Therefore, you should have no reason to use this method.

◆ **void showStatus(String msg)**
Displays a message at the bottom of the browser. This is usually the simplest way to communicate with the user.

◆ **void start( )**
By overriding this method, you can perform some tasks immediately after the applet is created. This method is automatically called by the runtime system.

◆ **void stop( )**
By overriding this method, you can perform tasks once the applet is stopped. This method is automatically called by the runtime system. It is not used often, but can be harnessed to perform some cleanup operations.

Interfaces

AppletContext

The AppletContext interface provides you with a means to interact with the browser. Every applet can obtain its AppletContext through the getAppletContext() method. Although the inner workings of the AppletContext depend on the browser, you are guaranteed that it will be capable of performing the following tasks.

▶ *See Listing 18, "Runnable Example—HTML," p. 246*

Methods

◆ **Applet getApplet(String name)**
Returns the applet with the given name.

◆ **Enumeration getApplets( )**
Returns a set of all applets on the given page.

◆ **AudioClip getAudioClip(URL url)**
Returns the specified audio clip.

◆ **Image getImage(URL url)**
Returns the specified image.

◆ **void showDocument(URL url)**
Shows the specified document in the current context.

◆ **void showDocument(URL url, String target)**
Requests that the browser show the specified document in a particular location—either a browser window or a Netscape frame.

Options for `target` are shown in the following table:

Value	Document Display
"_self"	Current Frame.
"_parent"	Parent Frame.
"_top"	Top-most Frame.
"_blank"	In a new and unnamed browser window.
"aNameofYourChoice"	Creates a new browser window with the specified name. You may later display other documents in this window by using the same name as the target.

◆ **void showStatus(String mesg)**
Displays a string at the bottom of the browser.

AppletStub

The `AppletStub` interface is primarily used when creating an applet viewer. However, it is used by the `Applet` class to retrieve information and interact with the browser. Because all of this interaction is already handled by the `Applet` class, there is generally no need for you to use the `AppletStub` class.

Methods

◆ **void appletResize(int width, int height)**
   This method is called when the applet wants to be resized.

◆ **AppletContext getAppletContext( )**
   Returns the applet context.

◆ **URL getCodeBase( )**
   Returns the base URL without the document name.

◆ **URL getDocumentBase( )**
   Returns the current URL.

◆ **String getParameter(String name)**
   Returns the specified parameter.

◆ **boolean isActive( )**
   Returns `true` whenever the applet is running.

AudioClip

The `AudioClip` interface is a high-level representation of the behavior of an audio clip. While interface objects cannot be created, objects that extend the `AudioClip` interface may be handled through this interface. Consequently, while the `getAudioClip()` in the `Applet` class returns an object we know little about, knowing that it implements the `AudioClip` interface enables us to make use of the `loop()`, `play()`, and `stop()` methods.

Methods

◆ **void loop( )**
   Begins to play the audio clip and loops to the beginning upon reaching the end of the clip.

◆ **void play( )**
   Plays the audio clip.

◆ **void stop( )**
   Halts playing of the audio clip.

JAVA.AWT

CLASSES AND INTERFACES

 **JAVA.AWT**

The Java Abstract Window Toolkit (AWT) consists of resources to enable you to create rich, attractive, and useful interfaces in your applets. Possessing managing tools, such as `LayoutManager` and `Container`, the AWT also has several concrete interactive tools, such as `Button` and `TextField`.

Classes

BorderLayout Implements LayoutManager

A `BorderLayout` is a class that may be used for designing and managing components within your user interface. A `BorderLayout` is a landscape onto which you may place up to five components. Components may be anchored by specifying either `"North"`, `"South"`, `"East"`, `"West"`, or `"Center"`, when adding the component to the layout.

Methods

◆ **BorderLayout( )**

Creates a new `BorderLayout` with a `hgap` and a `vgap` of 0. The `hgap` and `vgap` fields determine the amount of padding between components in the layout.

◆ **BorderLayout(int hgap, int vgap)**

Creates a new `BorderLayout` with the specified `hgap` and `vgap`. The `hgap` and `vgap` fields determine the amount of padding between components in the layout.

◆ **void addLayoutComponent(String location, Component comp)**

Adds a component to the layout at the specified location.

Options for `location` are as follows:

"North"

"South"

"West"

"East"

"Center"

- ◆ **void layoutContainer(Container target)**
  Reshapes the components in the `target` container in accordance with a `BorderLayout`.

- ◆ **Dimension minimumLayoutSize(Container target)**
  Returns the minimum size necessary for the components in the specified container. This value is based on the minimum sizes of the components added to the amount of spacing for the container.

- ◆ **Dimension preferredLayoutSize(Container target)**
  Returns the "preferred size" of the container. This is based on the preferred size of each component as well as the amount of spacing specified.

- ◆ **void removeLayoutComponent(Component comp)**
  Removes the specified component from the layout.

- ◆ **String toString( )**
  Returns a string detailing the `hgap` and the `vgap`.

Button Extends Component

The `Button` class creates a standard button for use in your interfaces (see fig. 2). A `Button` is a standard component that may be added to any of the layout manager classes. The label string for each button serves not only to identify the button to the user, but to the programmer as well. Whenever a button is depressed, an `ACTION_EVENT` will be posted to the container in which the button resides. To distinguish between the various buttons on the screen, the Event will contain an `arg` string containing the label of the button that was depressed.

▶ *See Listing 6, "GridbagLayout Example," p. 74*

Fig. 2 A Button in Windows NT.

Methods

◆ **Button( )**
Creates an unlabeled button.

◆ **Button(String label)**
Creates a button with the specified label. This will also serve as the arg value in the Event created when the button is depressed.

◆ **synchronized void addNotify( )**
Creates a peer for the button.

◆ **String getLabel( )**
Returns the label of the button.

◆ **protected String paramString( )**
Returns a string specifying the label of the button.

◆ **void setLabel(String label)**
Sets the label of the button.

Canvas Extends Component

The Canvas class provides you with a simple background on which you can build. As is, the Canvas class establishes a peer and paints a simple gray background. However, if you choose to extend the Canvas class, you are able to create your own custom components—something very useful.

Methods

◆ **Canvas( )**
Creates a new canvas.

◆ **synchronized void addNotify( )**
Creates the canvas's peer.

◆ **void paint(Graphics g)**
Paints the canvas. By default, this method simply paints a
blank background having the same color as the background.

CardLayout Implements LayoutManager

A `CardLayout` enables you to scroll through a series of
components. Generally, the "cards" are containers—each with a
specific theme. Each card is referred to by a title and is furthermore sequentially indexed. Therefore, you are to scroll through
the cards either in order or by selecting a specific card by name.

The code in Listing 3 was used to create the applet shown in
figure 3. As you can see, the applet uses a `Choice` component
to enable the user to scroll through the various cards.

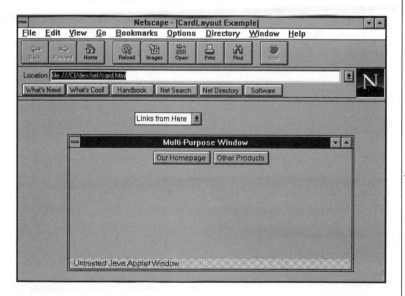

Fig. 3 `CardLayout` Example.

Listing 3   CardLayout Example Source Code

```java
import java.awt.*;
import java.applet.Applet;

public class CardLayoutExample extends Applet {

    Frame sidecard;
    private static String LINKS = "Links from Here";
    private static String ORDERFORM = "Order Form";

    public CardLayoutExample() {
        Choice selector = new Choice();  // creates a selector
                                         // on the original page
        selector.addItem(LINKS);
        selector.addItem(ORDERFORM);
        add(selector);

        sidecard = new Frame("Multi-Purpose Window");
                                // creates the side frame
        sidecard.setLayout(new CardLayout());

        Panel p = new Panel();  // create the individual panels
        p.add(new Button("Our Homepage"));
        p.add(new Button("Other Products") );
        sidecard.add(LINKS, p);

        p = new Panel();
        p.setLayout( new FlowLayout() );
        p.add(new TextField("Name", 20));
        p.add(new TextField("Address", 50) );
        p.add(new TextField("Phone", 20) );
        p.add(new Button("Order") );
        sidecard.add(ORDERFORM, p);

        sidecard.show();          // shows the side frame
    }

    public boolean action(Event evt, Object arg) {
        CardLayout display;
```

```
if (evt.target instanceof Choice) { /* if the event
                                occurred in a Choice */
  display = (CardLayout)sidecard.getLayout();
                    // obtains control of the frame
  display.show(sidecard,arg.toString());
      // displays the panel with the corresponding title
   return true;
   }
   return false;
}

public synchronized boolean handleEvent(Event evt) {
  if (evt.id == Event.WINDOW_DESTROY) {
    this.hide();
        return true;
  }
  return super.handleEvent(evt);
  }
}
```

Methods

◆ **CardLayout( )**

Creates a new CardLayout manager.

◆ **CardLayout(int hgap, int vgap)**

Creates a new CardLayout manager with the specified hgap and vgap—the spacing between components.

◆ **void addLayoutComponent(String name, Component comp)**

Adds the component to the container with the specified name.

◆ **void first(Container parent)**

Displays the first card in the layout.

◆ **void last(Container parent)**

Displays the last card in the layout.

◆ **void layoutContainer(Container parent)**
Arranges the `parent` container based on the `CardLayout`
parameters.

◆ **Dimension minimumLayoutSize(Container parent)**
Returns the minimum size necessary for this layout. This
value is based on the minimum size of the parameters.

◆ **void next(Container parent)**
Displays the next card.

◆ **Dimension preferredLayoutSize(Container parent)**
Returns the preferred size of the layout in the `parent`
container. This is based on the preferred size of the components in the container.

◆ **void previous(Container parent)**
Displays the previous card.

◆ **void removeLayoutComponen(Component comp)**
Removes the specified component from the layout.

◆ **void show(Container parent, String cardname)**
Shows the specified card in the parent container.

◆ **String toString( )**
Returns a string detailing the `hgap` and `vgap` values for this
layout.

Checkbox Extends Component

A checkbox, as shown in figure 4, provides you with an easy
way of obtaining input from the user. It resembles a standard
checkbox: a text label and a box on the client's machine.

Fig. 4 A simple checkbox.

▶ *See "CheckboxGroup," p. 28*

▶ *See "CheckboxMenuItem Extends MenuItem," p. 28*

▶ *See Listing 6, "GridbagLayout Example," p. 74*

Methods

◆ **Checkbox( )**
Creates an non-labeled checkbox.

◆ **Checkbox(String label)**
Creates a checkbox with the specified label.

◆ **Checkbox(String label, CheckboxGroup group, boolean state)**
Creates a checkbox with the specified label and places it in a CheckboxGroup. The state parameter determines whether or not it is initially checked.

◆ **synchronized void addNotify( )**
Creates the peer of the checkbox.

◆ **CheckboxGroup getCheckboxGroup( )**
Returns the CheckboxGroup of which the current checkbox is a member.

◆ **String getLabel( )**
Returns the label of the checkbox.

◆ **boolean getState( )**
Returns the state of the checkbox (true if checked, false if not).

◆ **protected String paramString( )**
Returns a string detailing the checkbox's parameters—such as its status and location.

◆ **void setCheckboxGroup(CheckboxGroup g)**
Sets the CheckboxGroup for the current checkbox.

JAVA.AWT

♦ **void setLabel(String label)**
   Sets the label of the checkbox.

♦ **void setState(boolean state)**
   Sets the state of the checkbox (checked or unchecked).

CheckboxGroup

By employing a CheckboxGroup, you are able to create a radio button group—a set of Checkboxes, only one of which can be selected at a time. This is useful for exclusive choices (the user can only choose one of the options), such as "How do you want to pay for your purchase?"

To employ a CheckboxGroup, first create and layout your checkboxes as you normally would. Then assign them to the CheckboxGroup by using the setCheckboxGroup() method.

▶ *See "Checkbox Extends Component," p. 26*

Methods

♦ **CheckboxGroup( )**
   Creates a new Checkbox group.

♦ **Checkbox getCurrent( )**
   Returns the currently selected checkbox.

♦ **synchronized void setCurrent(Checkbox box)**
   Sets the specified checkbox to be the selected checkbox.

♦ **String toString( )**
   Returns a string detailing the currently selected checkbox.

CheckboxMenuItem Extends MenuItem

A CheckboxMenuItem is a MenuItem whose status may be toggled (see fig. 5). Placed within a Menu column, a CheckboxMenuItem will display a check mark when selected.

▶ *See "Checkbox Extends Component," p. 26*

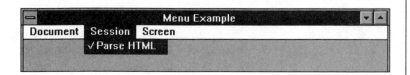

Fig. 5 A `CheckboxMenuItem` in Windows NT.

Methods

◆ **CheckboxMenuItem(String label)**
Creates a new checkbox menu item with the specified label.

◆ **synchronized void addNotify( )**
Creates the checkbox menu item's peer.

◆ **boolean getState( )**
Returns the current state of the checkbox.

◆ **String paramString( )**
Returns a string detailing the checkbox's value.

◆ **void setState(boolean state)**
Sets the state of the checkbox.

Choice Extends Component

The `Choice` component creates a standard pop-up menu, as shown in figure 6, from which the user can select one item.

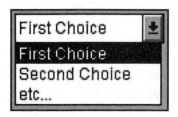

Fig. 6 A `Choice` in Windows NT.

▶ *See Listing 6, "GridbagLayout Example," p. 74*

JAVA.AWT

Methods

◆ **Choice( )**
Creates a new choice component.

◆ **synchronized void addItem(String label)**
Adds a selection to the choice listing with the specified label.

◆ **synchronized void addNotify( )**
Creates the choice's peer.

◆ **int countItems( )**
Returns the number of items currently existing in the choice's listing.

◆ **String getItem(int pos)**
Returns the label of the choice in the specified position in the choice list.

◆ **int getSelectedIndex( )**
Returns the index of the currently selected item.

◆ **String getSelectedItem( )**
Returns the label of the currently selected item.

◆ **protected String paramString( )**
Returns a string including the label of the currently selected item.

◆ **void select(String label)**
Selects the item with the specified label.

◆ **synchronized void select(int pos)**
Selects the item at the specified position.

Final Color

The `Color` class provides you with the various colors that you can employ in your programs as well as the capability to create and customize your own colors.

▶ *See "Abstract Graphics," p. 62*

Fields

▶ **final static Color black**
▶ **final static Color blue**
▶ **final static Color cyan**
▶ **final static Color darkGray**
▶ **final static Color gray**
▶ **final static Color green**
▶ **final static Color lightGray**
▶ **final static Color magenta**
▶ **final static Color orange**
▶ **final static Color pink**
▶ **final static Color red**
▶ **final static Color white**
▶ **final static Color yellow**

Methods

◆ **Color(int rgb)**

Creates a new color represented by the passed integer. Bits 0–7 represent the blue component, 8–15 the green component, and 16–23 the red component.

◆ **Color(float red_value, float green_value, float blue_value)**

Creates a new color with the specified values ranging from 0 to 1.0.

◆ **Color(int red_value, int green_value, int blue_value)**

Creates a new color with the specified values ranging from 0 to 255.

◆ **Color brighter( )**

Returns a brighter version of the current color by dividing each integral component of the color by 0.7.

◆ **Color darker( )**

Returns a darker version of the current color by multiplying each integral component of the color by 0.7.

◆ **boolean equals(Object otherObject)**
Compares a `Color` to another `Object`. They can only be
equal if the other object is also a `Color`.

◆ **int getBlue( )**
Returns the blue component of the color.

◆ **static Color getColor(String name)**
Returns a Color assuming that `name` refers to a color
specified in the system properties. If the property is not
found, the method returns `null`.

◆ **static Color getColor(String name, int default)**
Returns a Color assuming that `name` refers to a color
specified in the system properties. If the property is not
found, the method returns the color represented by
`default`.

◆ **static Color getColor(String name, Color default)**
Returns a Color assuming that `name` refers to a color
specified in the system properties. If the property is not
found, the method returns `default`.

◆ **int getGreen( )**
Returns the green component of the color.

◆ **static Color getHSBColor(float hue, float saturation,
float brightness)**
Creates a `Color` based on the specified HSB (hue, saturation, and brightness) values ranging from 0.0 to 1.0.

◆ **int getRed( )**
Returns the red component of the current color.

◆ **int getRGB( )**
Returns the rgb value of the current color as one integer. Bits
0–7 are blue, 8–15 are green, and 16–23 are red.

◆ **int hashCode( )**

Returns the `hashcode` for the current color. This value is the same as the integer returned from `getRGB( )`.

◆ **static int HSBtoRGB(float hue, float saturation, float brightness)**

Creates a single integer representation of the color defined by the specified hue, saturation, and brightness. In the integer, bits 0–7 are blue, 8–15 are green, and 16–23 are red.

◆ **static float[ ] RGBtoHSB(int red, int green, int blue, float hsbvals[ ])**

Returns hue, saturation, and brightness values for the color defined by the red, green, and blue values. In the array, `hsbvals[0]` = hue, `hsbvals[1]` = saturation, and `hsbvals[2]` = brightness.

◆ **String toString( )**

Returns a string, including the red, green, and blue components of the color.

Abstract Component Implements ImageObserver

The `Component` class is the basis for the various components in the AWT that may be employed, such as `Button` and `Scrollbar`. While the specific components possess methods pertinent to their function, the `Component` class provides them with a myriad of methods designed to facilitate a base functionality—such as event handling.

You will also note that the `Component` class relies heavily on the `java.awt.peer` classes for much of its implementation because the system commands to create a component on UNIX machines are different from those to create the component on Windows-based machines. Instead of directly interacting with these methods, the peers serve as intermediaries, translating your Java-based code into platform-dependent commands.

JAVA.AWT

Methods

◆ **boolean action(Event evt, Object what)**
Called by `handleEvent ( )` when an action occurs in the component. This method should be overridden if you want to gain more control over events occurring in components or containers. It returns `true` if the event is handled successfully.

◆ **void addNotify( )**
"Notifies" the component that it must create a peer.

◆ **Rectangle bounds( )**
Returns the boundaries of the component.

◆ **int checkImage(Image image, ImageObserver observer)**
Returns the status of an image being displayed on the screen. This value is either obtained from the component's peer or the current `Toolkit`. The specified `ImageObserver` will be notified of the status of the `Image`.

◆ **int checkImage(Image image, int width, int height, ImageObserver observer)**
Returns the status of an scaled image being displayed on the screen. This value is either obtained from the component's peer or the current `Toolkit`. The specified `ImageObserver` will be notified of the status of the `Image`.

◆ **Image createImage(int width, int height)**
Creates an off-screen image with the specified width and height.

◆ **Image createImage(ImageProducer producer)**
Creates an image from the information supplied by the specific `ImageProducer`.

◆ **void deliverEvent(Event e)**
"Delivers" an event to the component.

◆ **synchronized void disable( )**
Disables the current component. The component will not be able to respond to user events.

◆ **void enable(boolean cond)**
If `cond` is `true`, this method enables the component. Otherwise, it disables the component.

◆ **synchronized void enable( )**
Enables the component.

◆ **Color getBackground( )**
Returns the current background color.

◆ **synchronized ColorModel getColorModel( )**
Returns the `ColorModel` used when creating the component.

◆ **Font getFont( )**
Returns the font of the component. If the component does not have a font, this method returns the font of the parent container.

◆ **FontMetrics getFontMetrics(Font font)**
Returns the `FontMetrics` of the component. Returns null if the component currently is not available.

◆ **Color getForeground( )**
Returns the foreground color of the component. If none exists, this method defaults to the foreground color of the parent container.

◆ **Graphics getGraphics( )**
Returns the graphics context used in creating this component. As of the 1.0.2 JDK release, this method was only implemented for `Canvas` components.

◆ **Container getParent( )**
Returns the parent container in which the `Component` resides.

◆ **ComponentPeer getPeer( )**
Returns the peer of the component.

◆ **Toolkit getToolkit( )**
Returns the component's `Toolkit`.

◆ **boolean gotFocus(Event evt, Object what)**
This method is called whenever the component receives the input focus (usually the result of a mouse movement). The `what` parameter represents the argument of the event. (`what` is equal to `evt.arg`.)

◆ **boolean handleEvent(Event evt)**
This method is called whenever an `Event` is posted to the component. By default, it calls a series of more specific methods, such as `mouseDown( )` and `keyUp( )`.

This method returns `true` if the event has been handled successfully. If you override this method but still want to employ the component's default method handling abilities, call `super.handleEvent(evt)`.

◆ **synchronized boolean inside(int x, int y)**
Determines if the specified coordinates are inside the current component.

◆ **synchronized void hide( )**
"Hides" the component by making it no longer visible.

◆ **boolean imageUpdate(Image img, int flags, int x, int y, int width, int height)**
Repaints the specified image if and when the image is changed. The `flags` are constants, such as `FRAMEBITS` and `ALLBITS` found in the `java.awt.image.ImageObserver` interface.

This method will be called by the system when more information becomes available about the `Image`. Therefore, this method should only be used if you want to add some functionality to the method.

◆ **void invalidate( )**

A component is invalid if it needs to be laid out. This method makes the current component invalid, forcing it to be laid out again.

◆ **boolean isEnabled( )**

Enables a component to interact with the user. This method returns `true` if the component is enabled and `false` otherwise.

◆ **boolean isShowing( )**

Returns `true` if the component is visible to the user. This requires that the component be visible in a container that is also visible.

◆ **boolean isValid( )**

A component is invalid if it needs to be laid out. This method returns `false` if the component is invalid and `true` if it is valid.

◆ **boolean isVisible( )**

Returns `true` if the component is visible.

◆ **boolean keyDown(Event evt, int key)**

Called by `handleEvent( )` when a key is depressed. The `event` parameter is the complete event posted. The `key` parameter is the key depressed.

◆ **boolean keyUp(Event evt, int key)**

Called by `handleEvent( )` when a key is released. The `event` parameter is the complete event posted. The `key` parameter is the key released.

◆ **void layout( )**

Correctly positions the component in the layout.

◆ **void list( )**

Prints out the current parameters to the standard output stream.

◆ **void list(PrintStream out)**
Prints out the current parameters to the specified
`PrintStream`.

◆ **void list(PrintStream out, int indent)**
Prints out the current parameters to the specified
`PrintStream`, starting from the specified indentation.

◆ **Component locate(int x, int y)**
Returns the component occupying the specified location.

◆ **Point location( )**
Returns a `Point` containing the x- and y-coordinates of the
component in its container.

◆ **boolean lostFocus(Event evt, Object what)**
Called by `handleEvent( )` when the component looses
the input focus.

◆ **boolean mouseDown(Event evt, int x, int y)**
Called by `handleEvent( )` when the mouse is depressed
in the component.

◆ **boolean mouseDrag(Event evt, int x, int y)**
Called by `handleEvent( )` when the mouse is dragged in
the component. (A drag is considered a mouse movement
while the mouse button is down.)

◆ **boolean mouseEnter(Event evt, int x, int y)**
Called by `handleEvent( )` when the mouse enters the
component.

◆ **boolean mouseExit(Event evt, int x, int y)**
Called by `handleEvent( )` when the mouse leaves the
component.

◆ **boolean mouseMove(Event evt, int x, int y)**
Called by `handleEvent( )` when the component looses
the input focus. (A *move* is a mouse movement while the
mouse button is up.)

◆ **boolean mouseUp(Event evt, int x, int y)**
Called by `handleEvent ( )` when the component looses the input focus.

◆ **Dimension minimumSize( )**
Returns the minimum size necessary to display the component.

◆ **void move(int x, int y)**
Moves the component to the new location and causes the component to become invalidated.

◆ **void nextFocus( )**
Advances the focus to the next component. This is useful in such applications as forms in which the user wants to go from one component to the next.

◆ **void paint(Graphics g)**
Paints the component.

◆ **void paintAll(Graphics g)**
Paints the component and all its subcomponents.

◆ **protected String paramString( )**
Returns a string containing information about the component including its location, and whether it is visible, valid, and/or enabled.

◆ **boolean postEvent(Event e)**
Posts the specified event to the component, resulting in a call to `handleEvent ( )`. If the component does not successfully handle the event, the event will be passed to the component's parent container.

◆ **Dimension preferredSize( )**
Returns the preferred size of this component. This value is supplied by the component's peer.

Java Quick Reference

◆ **boolean prepareImage(Image image, int width, int height, ImageObserver observer)**

This method "prepares" a scaled image to be displayed. This process includes loading the image and preparing the screen where the image is to be displayed. The `imageUpdate( )` method in the specified `ImageObserver` will be informed of the status of this process.

◆ **boolean prepareImage(Image image, ImageObserver observer)**

This method "prepares" and image to be displayed. This process includes loading the image and preparing the screen where the image is to be displayed. The specified `ImageObserver` will be informed of the status of this process through the `imageUpdate( )` method.

◆ **void print(Graphics g)**

"Prints" the component. By default, this method simply calls the `paint( )` method.

◆ **void printAll(Graphics g)**

"Prints" the component and its subcomponents. By default, this method paints the component and its subcomponents.

◆ **synchronized void removeNotify( )**

Disposes of the component's peer.

◆ **void repaint(int x, int y, int width, int height)**

Repaints a portion of the component.

◆ **void repaint(long delay, int x, int y, int width, int height)**

Repaints a portion of the component after waiting the specified number of milliseconds.

◆ **void repaint(long time)**

Repaints the entire component after waiting the specified number of milliseconds.

◆ **void repaint( )**
  Repaints the entire component.

◆ **void requestFocus( )**
  Request the input focus.

◆ **synchronized void reshape(int x, int y, int width, int height)**
  Moves the component to the specified coordinates and reshapes it to the specified size. This will cause the component to become invalidated.

◆ **void resize(Dimension d)**
  Resizes the component to the specified dimensions—width and height. This will cause the component to become invalidated.

◆ **void resize(int width, int height)**
  Resizes the component to the specified width and height. This will cause the component to become invalidated.

◆ **synchronized void setBackground(Color c)**
  Sets the background color for the component.

◆ **synchronized void setFont(Font f)**
  Sets the font for the component.

◆ **synchronized void setForeground(Color c)**
  Sets the background color for the component.

◆ **void show(boolean cond)**
  Displays the component if the `cond` parameter is `true`. If the `cond` parameter is `false`, the component is hidden.

◆ **synchronized void show( )**
  Displays the component.

◆ **Dimension size( )**
  Returns the size of the component.

JAVA.AWT

◆ **String toString( )**
Returns a string containing the component's parameters.
This consists of the name of the component as well as the
values returned by `paramString( )`.

◆ **void update(Graphics g)**
This method is called as a result of a call to `repaint( )`. It
can be used to perform management tasks associated with
updating the component.

◆ **void validate( )**
Makes the component valid. This means that it does not
need to be laid out.

Abstract Container Extends Component

The `Container` class is a basic class that may hold other
`Components`. The `Container` class serves as the basis for the
other container-type classes such as `Frame`, `Panel`, and
`FileDialog`. Note that you cannot create a `Container`
explicitly, but rather must either use one of the derived classes or
create your own `Container` class.

Methods

◆ **synchronized Component add(String info, Component comp)**
Adds the component to the container. The use of the
information supplied in the string depends on the
`LayoutManager` for the `Container`.

◆ **synchronized Component add(Component comp, int pos)**
Adds the component to the container at the specified
position.

◆ **Component add(Component comp)**
Adds the component to the end of the container.

◆ **synchronized void addNotify( )**
Creates the container's peer.

◆ **int countComponents( )**
Returns the number of components in the container.

◆ **void deliverEvent(Event evt)**
Delivers the specified event to the appropriate component. If the event does not occur in one of the components belonging to the container, the event is handed over to the `java.awt.Component.postEvent( )` method.

◆ **synchronized Component getComponent(int num) throws ArrayIndexOutOfBoundsException**
Returns the component at the specified index. Throws an `ArrayIndexOutOfBoundsException` if there are fewer than `num` components in the container.

◆ **synchronized Component[ ] getComponents( )**
Returns an array containing the components residing in the `Container`.

◆ **LayoutManager getLayout( )**
Returns the layout manager used in creating this container.

◆ **synchronized void layout( )**
Organizes the components in the container according to the conventions of the layout manager.

◆ **void list(PrintStream out, int indent)**
Displays the standard component information (name and parameters) as well as the components within the container. Begins printing at the specified indentation point.

◆ **Component locate(int x, int y)**
Returns the component that occupies the specified coordinates.

◆ **synchronized Dimension minimumSize( )**
Returns the minimum size necessary for this component. This value is based on the minimum sizes for the individual components.

JAVA.AWT

◆ **void paintComponents(Graphics g)**
Paints the components in the container. Identical to the
`printComponents( )` method in this class.

◆ **protected String paramString( )**
Returns the information supplied by the
`java.awt.Component.paramString( )` method in
addition to the layout manager of the component.

◆ **synchronized Dimension preferredSize( )**
Returns the preferred size of the container. This is based on
the values returned from the `preferredSize( )` methods
for the individual components.

◆ **void printComponents(Graphics g)**
Displays the components in the container. Identical to the
`printComponents( )` method in this class.

◆ **synchronized void remove(Component comp)**
Removes the specified component from the container.

◆ **synchronized void removeNotify( )**
Removes the container's peer.

◆ **void setLayout(LayoutManager mgr)**
Sets the layout manager for the component.

◆ **synchronized void validate( )**
Valid components do not need to be laid out. This method
makes the container and all its components valid.

Dialog Extends Window

A `Dialog` is a type of `Window` that is used to accept user
input. A `Dialog` must exist in a `Frame` object.

A modal `Dialog` is a type of `Dialog` that will capture all the
input from the user.

Methods

◆ **Dialog(Frame parent, String title, boolean modal)**
Creates a new `Dialog` in the specified `Frame` and with the specified title. If the `modal` parameter is `true`, the `Dialog` will be modal.

◆ **Dialog(Frame parent, boolean modal)**
Creates a new `Dialog` in the specified `Frame` that will have no title. If the `modal` parameter is `true`, the `Dialog` will be modal.

◆ **synchronized void addNotify( )**
Creates the `Dialog`'s peer.

◆ **boolean isModal( )**
Returns `true` if the `Dialog` is modal.

◆ **boolean isResizable( )**
Returns `true` if the `Dialog` is resizable.

◆ **protected String paramString( )**
Returns a string containing the parameters of the `Dialog`, including its title whether or not it is modal.

◆ **void setTitle(String title)**
Sets the title for the `Dialog`.

Dimension

The `Dimension` class provides you with a simple way of handling the dimensions of graphical tools. Most often, the `Dimension` class is used to enable a single method to return two values: `width` and `height`.

Fields

▶ **int height**
▶ **int width**

Methods

◆ **Dimension( )**

Creates a new `Dimension` object.

◆ **Dimension(Dimension d)**

Creates a new `Dimension` object with the same values as an already created `Dimension` object.

◆ **Dimension(int width, int height)**

Creates a new `Dimension` object with the specified width and height.

◆ **String toString( )**

Returns the width and height of the `Dimension` in the form of a string.

Event

The `Event` class, used as a means of responding to user interactions, delivers a lot of information about a user event in a single object. Through its constants and instance variables, each `Event` object is capable of providing you with many specific details regarding each event.

All final fields serve as constants against which you may compare information contained in the `Event` objects that you receive. In general, the fields fall into two categories: those that represent certain keys (e.g., `F1` and `HOME`) and those that represent certain events (e.g., `GOT_FOCUS` and `KEY_PRESS`).

▶ *See Listing 3, "CardLayout Example Source Code," p. 24*

▶ *See Listing 7, "Menu Example," p. 94*

Fields

▶ **final static int ACTION_EVENT**

A flag representing a broad umbrella of event types. An `ACTION_EVENT` will cause a call to `action( )`.

▶ **final static int ALT_MASK**
Will be placed in the `modifiers` field if the ALT key is down. It should be tested for using the AND operator.

▶ **Object arg**
An optional argument dependent on the type of event. Most components set the `arg` equal to their titles.

▶ **int clickCount**
Tracks the number of consecutive mouse clicks.

▶ **final static int CTRL_MASK**
Will be placed in the `modifiers` field if the CTRL key is down. Should be tested for using the AND operator.

▶ **final static int DOWN**
▶ **Event evt**
A reference to another `Event` object. This can be used to create a linked list of `Event` objects.

▶ **final static int F1**
A possible value for the `key` field.

▶ **final static int F2**
▶ **final static int F3**
▶ **final static int F4**
▶ **final static int F5**
▶ **final static int F6**
▶ **final static int F7**
▶ **final static int F8**
▶ **final static int F9**
▶ **final static int F10**
▶ **final static int F11**
▶ **final static int F12**
▶ **final static int GOT_FOCUS**
Created when the `Component` gets the input focus. It calls `gotFocus( )`.

▶ **final static int HOME**
A possible value for the `key` field.

▶ **int id**
The id of the event. It can be compared to such static constants as `ACTION_EVENT` or `MOUSE_DOWN`.

▶ **int key**
Contains the key that was depressed.

▶ **final static int KEY_ACTION**
Created when the user presses a function key. It causes a call to `keyDown( )`.

▶ **final static int KEY_ACTION_RELEASE**
Created when the user releases a function key. It causes a call to `keyUp( )`.

▶ **final static int KEY_PRESS**
Created when the user presses a standard `ASCII` key. It causes a call to `keyDown( )`.

▶ **final static int KEY_RELEASE**
Created when the user releases a standard `ASCII` key. It causes a call to `keyUp( )`.

▶ **final static int LEFT**
A possible value for the `key` field. It represents the left-arrow key.

▶ **final static int LIST_DESELECT**
Called when the user deselects an item on a `List`. The `Event` will also contain an `Integer` as its `arg` field representing the item that was deselected.

▶ **final static int LIST_SELECT**
Called when the user deselects an item on a `List`. The `Event` will also contain an `Integer` as its `arg` field representing the item that was deselected.

▶ **final static int LOAD_FILE**
   Created when a file is loaded.

▶ **final static int LOST_FOCUS**
   Created when the Component looses the input focus. It
   causes a call to lostFocus().

▶ **final static int META_MASK**
   Will be placed in the modifiers field if the META key is
   down. It should be tested for using the AND operator.

▶ **int modifiers**
   Represents the status of the modifier keys: Alt, Ctrl,
   Meta, and Shift. It can be compared against the static
   constants defined within the class using the AND operator.

▶ **final static int MOUSE_DOWN**
   Created by a mouse click. It causes a call to mouseDown().

▶ **final static int MOUSE_DRAG**
▶ **final static int MOUSE_ENTER**
▶ **final static int MOUSE_EXIT**
▶ **final static int MOUSE_MOVE**
▶ **final static int MOUSE_UP**
▶ **final static int PGDN**
▶ **final static int PGUP**
▶ **final static int RIGHT**
▶ **final static int SAVE_FILE**
▶ **final static int SCROLL_ABSOLUTE**
   Created when the user moves a scrollbar marker to a specific
   location within the scrollbar.

▶ **final static int SCROLL_LINE_DOWN**
   Created when the user clicks on the down arrow in a
   scrollbar.

▶ **final static int SCROLL_LINE_UP**
▶ **final static int SCROLL_PAGE_DOWN**
▶ **final static int SCROLL_PAGE_UP**

▶ **final static int SHIFT_MASK**
Will be placed in the `modifiers` field if the Shift key is down or if Caps Lock is on. It should be tested for using the AND operator.

▶ **Object target**
The object at which the event was directed.

▶ **final static int UP**
▶ **long when**
The time at which the event occurred.

▶ **final static int WINDOW_DEICONIFY**
A possible value of the `id` field.

▶ **final static int WINDOW_DESTROY**
A possible value of the `id` field. It is used when the user tries to close a `Window`.

▶ **final static int WINDOW_EXPOSE**
A possible value of the `id` field.

▶ **final static int WINDOW_ICONIFY**
A possible value of the `id` field.

▶ **final static int WINDOW_MOVED**
A possible value of the `id` field.

▶ **int x**
The x-coordinate of a mouse click.

▶ **int y**
The y-coordinate of a mouse click.

Methods

◆ **Event(Object target, int id, Object arg)**
Creates a new `Event` with the specified target, id, and arg values.

◆ **Event(Object target, long when, int id, int x, int y, int key, int modifiers)**

Creates a new `Event` with the specified target, time stamp (when), id, x, y, key, and modifier values.

◆ **Event(Object target, long when, int id, int x, int y, int key, int modifiers, Object arg)**

Creates a new `Event` with the specified target, time stamp (when), id, x, y, key, modifiers, and arg values.

◆ **boolean controlDown( )**

Returns `true` if the Control key is down.

◆ **boolean metaDown( )**

Returns `meta` if the Control key is down.

◆ **protected String paramString( )**

Returns a string containing the values of all the `Event`'s instance variables.

◆ **boolean shiftDown( )**

Returns `true` if the shift key is down.

◆ **String toString( )**

Returns the `Event` object's name as well as the information returned from the `paramString( )` method.

◆ **void translate(int x, int y)**

FileDialog Extends Dialog

A `FileDialog` creates a window to provide the user with a selection of files. The `FileDialog` itself will resemble the appearance of file dialog boxes on the client's machine.

The `FileDialog` shown in figure 7 was created with the code in Listing 4. Although the code is obviously too simple to serve as a complete applet, it nevertheless demonstrates the technique for creating a `FileDialog`.

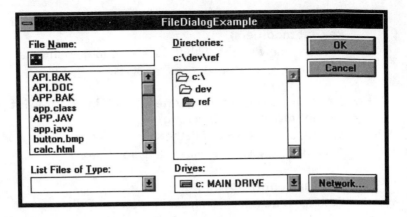

Fig. 7 A file dialog box in Windows NT.

Listing 4   FileDialog Example

```java
import java.applet.Applet;
import java.awt.*;

public class FDialogExample extends Applet {

    public void init( ) {
        Frame f;
        f = new Frame( );

        Dialog d;
        d = new FileDialog(f,"FileDialogExample");

        f.show( );
        d.show( );
    }
}
```

Fields

▶ final static LOAD

This constant is used to define the mode of the
FileDialog. If the mode equals LOAD, then the
FileDialog is designed to load files.

▶ **final static SAVE**

This constant is used to define the mode of the
`FileDialog`. If the mode equals `SAVE`, then the
`FileDialog` is designed to save files.

Methods

◆ **FileDialog(Frame parent, String title, int mode)**

Creates a `FileDialog` with the specified mode.

◆ **FileDialog(Frame parent, String title)**

Creates a `FileDialog`, setting the mode to `LOAD`.

◆ **synchronized void addNotify( )**

Creates the `FileDialog`'s peer.

◆ **String getDirectory( )**

Returns the current directory.

◆ **String getFile( )**

Returns the file name selected by the user.

◆ **FilenameFilter getFilenameFilter( )**

Returns the `FilenameFilter` used by the user in selecting
the file.

◆ **int getMode( )**

Returns the mode of the `FileDialog`—either `LOAD` or
`SAVE`.

◆ **protected String paramString( )**

Returns the attributes of the component including the
directory and the mode.

◆ **void setDirectory(String dir)**

Sets the directory in the `FileDialog`.

◆ **void setFile(String file)**

Highlights the specific file in the `FileDialog`.

◆ **public void setFilenameFilter(FilenameFilter filter)**
Sets the filter for the dialog to be employed by the user in selecting the file.

FlowLayout Implements LayoutManager

The `FlowLayout` class is a relatively simple layout manager. It places components in rows and continues on the next line when the current line becomes full.

Fields

▶ **final static int CENTER**
Aligns the components with the center.

▶ **final static int LEFT**
Aligns the components on the left.

▶ **final static int RIGHT**
Aligns the components on the right.

Methods

◆ **FlowLayout( )**
Creates a new `FlowLayout` with an alignment of `CENTER`.

◆ **FlowLayout(int align)**
Creates a new `FlowLayout` with the specified alignment.

◆ **FlowLayout(int align, int hgap, int vgap)**
Creates a new `FlowLayout` with the specified alignment. `hgap` and `vgap` specify the amount of spacing around the component.

◆ **void addLayoutComponent(String name, Component comp)**
This method is required inasmuch as this class implements the `LayoutManager` interface. However, it does absolutely nothing.

◆ **void layoutContainer(Container target)**

Arranges the specified container according to its
`FlowLayout` parameters.

◆ **Dimension minimumLayoutSize(Container target)**

Returns the minimum size necessary for the components in
the specified container. This value is based on the minimum
sizes of the components added to the amount of spacing for
the container.

◆ **Dimension preferredLayoutSize(Container target)**

Returns the preferred size necessary for the components in
the specified container. This value is based on the preferred
sizes of the components added to the amount of spacing for
the container.

◆ **void removeLayoutComponent(Component comp)**

Removes the specified component from the layout manager.

◆ **String toString( )**

Returns a string containing the layout's name, the alignment, the `hgap`, and the `vgap`.

Font

The `Font` class serves as an intermediary between your code
and the client's machine, providing you with specific styles for
your text. Although it will not affect the appearance of the
output to the output streams (e.g., `System.out`), the current
font will determine the appearance of any text created in
displaying a `Component`—particularly an `Applet`.

▶ *See Listing 2, "Sample Applet," p. 12*

> **Note** To actually change the display font, you must first
> create a new `Font` and then set the current font. This is done
> using either the `java.awt.Component.setFont( )` or
> `java.awt.Graphics.setFont( )` method.

Fields

▶ **final static int BOLD**
A possible value for `style` indicating a bold font.

▶ **final static int ITALIC**
A possible value for `style` indicating an italic font.

▶ **protected String name**
The name of the font.

▶ **final static int PLAIN**
A possible value for `style` indicating the standard font.

▶ **protected int size**
The size of the font.

▶ **protected int style**
The style of the font.

Methods

◆ **Font(String name, int style, int size)**
Creates a new font with the specified name, style, and size.

◆ **boolean equals(Object anotherobject)**
Compares two fonts for equality. The return value will
always be `false` if the second object is not a `Font`.

◆ **String getFamily( )**
Returns the name of the family to which the font belongs.
This value depends on the system itself.

◆ **static Font getFont(String name)**
Returns the font possessing the system-dependent font
name.

◆ **static Font getFont(String name, Font defaultfont)**
Returns the font possessing the system-dependent font
name. If the font cannot be found, the method returns the
`defaultfont`.

◆ **String getName( )**
Returns the name of the font.

◆ **int getSize( )**
Returns the size of the font.

◆ **int getStyle( )**
Returns the style of the font.

◆ **int hashCode( )**
Returns the `hashcode` of the font, a value dependent on the font name, style, and size.

Returns the name of the font.

◆ **boolean isBold( )**
Returns `true` if the font is bold.

◆ **boolean isItalic( )**
Returns `true` if the font is italic.

◆ **boolean isPlain( )**
Returns `true` if the font is plain (neither bold nor italic).

◆ **String toString( )**
Returns a string containing information on the font, including its name, style, and size.

FontMetrics

The `FontMetrics` class provides you with information regarding a given font. This class is very useful for such tasks as animation of text because it is often necessary to know exactly where each character will be. By creating a `FontMetrics` for the font and then using the accessor methods to obtain information, you can determine the exact size of your characters and strings.

▶ *See "Font," p. 55*

Java Quick Reference

> **Note**   To employ a `FontMetrics` in your program, declare an instance of a `FontMetrics` and then use the `java.awt.getFontMetrics()` method to provide the `FontMetrics` with information.

Field

▶ **protected Font font**

The font on which the `FontMetrics` is based.

Methods

◆ **protected FontMetrics(Font font)**

Creates a new `FontMetrics`.

◆ **int bytesWidth(byte data[ ], int offset, int len)**

Returns the width of a set of bytes. The `offset` parameter specifies the index at which the measurement begins and the `len` parameter specifies the number of terms to be considered in the measurement.

◆ **int charsWidth(char data[ ], int offset, int len)**

Returns the width of a set of characters. The `offset` parameter specifies the index at which the measurement begins, and the `len` parameter specifies the number of terms to be considered in the measurement.

◆ **int charWidth(char ch)**

Returns the width of a single character.

◆ **int charWidth(int ch)**

Returns the width of a single character.

◆ **int getAscent( )**

Returns the amount of space between the x-height (the height of the main body of lowercase letters) and the top of a character in the font.

◆ **int getDescent( )**
Returns the amount of space between the baseline (the imaginary line on which the type sits) and the bottom of a character in the font.

◆ **Font getFont( )**
Returns the font.

◆ **int getHeight( )**
Returns the amount of space between the top and bottom of a character in this font.

◆ **int getMaxAdvance( )**
The advance is defined as the space between two characters (actually between the bottom of one character and the top of the next). This method returns the maximum advance for any character in this font.

◆ **int getMaxAscent( )**
The ascent is the distance from the x-height to the top of the letter. This method returns the maximum ascent for any character in the font.

◆ **int getMaxDescent( )**
The descent is the distance from the baseline to the bottom of the letter. This method returns the maximum descent for any character in the font.

◆ **int[ ] getWidths( )**
Returns an array containing the width of the first 256 characters of the font.

◆ **int stringWidth(String str)**
Returns an integer representing the width of the specified string.

◆ **String toString( )**
Returns a string containing information about the class, including the class name, font name, ascent, descent, and height.

Frame Extends Window Implements MenuContainer

A `Frame` is a `Window` that has added capabilities. In terms of appearance, a `Frame` possesses a border and a title. In terms of functionality, you can add a menu to a `Frame` and specify the image that appears when the `Frame` is minimized.

▶ **See "MenuBar Extends MenuComponent Implements MenuContainer," p. 93**

▶ **See "Window Extends Container," p. 115**

> **Tip** When using a `Frame`, remember to invoke the `show()` method. Otherwise, your frame will be invisible!

Fields

▶ **final static int CROSSHAIR_CURSOR**
▶ **final static int DEFAULT_CURSOR**
▶ **final static int E_RESIZE_CURSOR**
▶ **final static int HAND_CURSOR**
▶ **final static int MOVE_CURSOR**
▶ **final static int NE_RESIZE_CURSOR**
▶ **final static int NW_RESIZE_CURSOR**
▶ **final static int N_RESIZE_CURSOR**
▶ **final static int SE_RESIZE_CURSOR**
▶ **final static int SW_RESIZE_CURSOR**
▶ **final static int S_RESIZE_CURSOR**
▶ **final static int TEXT_CURSOR**
▶ **final static int WAIT_CURSOR**
▶ **final static int W_RESIZE_CURSOR**

Methods

◆ **Frame( )**
Creates a new Frame without a title.

◆ **Frame(String title)**
Creates a new frame with the specified title.

◆ **synchronized void addNotify( )**
Creates the `Frame`'s peer.

◆ **synchronized void dispose( )**
Disposes the resources used by the `Frame`.

◆ **int getCursorType( )**
Returns the cursor type for this `Frame`.

◆ **Image getIconImage( )**
Returns the `icon` for this frame. The `icon` is an inaccessible variable that defines the appearance of the `Frame` when it is minimized.

◆ **MenuBar getMenuBar( )**
Returns the current `MenuBar` for this `Frame`.

◆ **String getTitle( )**
Returns the title of this `Frame`.

◆ **boolean isResizable( )**
Returns `true` if the `Frame` can be resized.

◆ **protected String paramString( )**
Returns a string, including the title of the `Frame` and the word *resizable* if the `Frame` is resizable.

◆ **synchronized void remove(MenuComponent m)**
Removes the specified `MenuBar` from this `Frame`.

◆ **void setCursor(int cursorType)**
Sets the appearance of the cursor for this `Frame`. The parameter value may be any one of the above listed constants.

◆ **void setIconImage(Image image)**
Sets the icon for this `Frame`. The icon will be displayed when the `Frame` is minimized.

◆ **synchronized void setMenuBar(MenuBar mb)**
Sets the `MenuBar` for this `Frame`.

JAVA.AWT

- ◆ **void setResizable(boolean resizable)**
  Makes the `Frame` either resizable (`true`) or not resizable (`false`). All `Frames` are initially resizable.

- ◆ **void setTitle(String title)**
  Sets the title for the `Frame`.

Abstract Graphics

The Graphics class provides you with a wide variety of graphical tools, ranging from the generic drawing tools, such as `drawLine( )`, to editing tools, such as `clipRect( )`.

If you are creating an applet, the creation of a graphics object will be done for you by the browser environment. Therefore, you can use the `Graphics` objects passed as parameters to the `paint( )` and `update( )` methods without worrying about how `drawLine( )` actually does its chore.

▶ *See Listing 2, "Sample Applet," p. 12*

The `Graphics` class provides you with a wide variety of graphical tools to create attractive interfaces (see fig. 8). Listing 5 gives a brief sample of these tools and demonstrates the form for creating graphics.

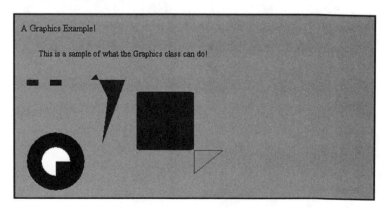

A Graphics Example!

This is a sample of what the Graphics class can do!

Fig. 8 An example of the `Graphics` class capability.

JAVA.AWT

Listing 5 Graphics Example

```java
import java.applet.Applet;
import java.awt.*;


public class GraphicsExample extends Applet
{

   public void paint(Graphics g) {

     g.setFont( new Font("TimesRoman", Font.PLAIN, 14) );
              // sets the font for the drawString() statement
     g.drawString("This is a sample of what the Graphics class
➥can do!",30,20);

       g.setColor(Color.red);

       g.fill3DRect(10,60,20,10,true);
       g.fill3DRect(50,60,20,10,false);
       int xpoints[] = {120,130, 150, 140, 180 };
                          // x-coordinates for polygon
       int ypoints[] = {60,50, 90, 170, 60};
       g.fillPolygon( xpoints, ypoints, 5);

       g.fillRoundRect(200,80,100,100,10,5);
       g.setColor(Color.blue);
       g.fillArc(10,150,100,100,0,360);

       g.setColor(Color.white);
       g.fillArc(35,175,50,50,0,270);

       g.setColor(Color.magenta);
       g.drawLine(300,180,350,180);
       g.drawLine(300,180,300,220);
       g.drawLine(300,220,350,180);
   }

}
```

Methods

◆ **protected Graphics( )**
   Creates a new `Graphics` object.

◆ **abstract void clearRect(int x, int y, int width, int height)**
   Clears the specified rectangle with the background color.

◆ **abstract void clipRect(int x, int y, int width, int height)**
   Sets the clipping rectangle for the graphical operations. Only
   those graphics within the specified area will be displayed.

> **Tip**   Be careful when setting the clipping area. Once this is
> done, it cannot be undone! Therefore, it is often wise to
> create a temporary `Graphics` object with the `create( )`
> method. You can set the clipping area and paint with this
> new object. When you want to display on the full screen
> again, you can revert to the original `Graphics` object.

◆ **abstract void copyArea(int x, int y, int width, int width,
   int height, int dx, int dy)**
   Copies the area defined by the x- and y-coordinates and the
   `width` and `height` dimensions. This region will then be
   moved `dx` pixels horizontally and `dy` pixels vertically.

◆ **Graphics create(int x, int y, int width, int height)**
   Creates a new `Graphics` object. This object will be identical to the current `Graphics` object except for the fact that
   its clipping area will be set to the specified coordinates and
   dimensions. This is useful inasmuch as once the clipping area
   is set it cannot be reset. Therefore, by creating a new
   `Graphics` object, you are able to employ a clipping area
   without destroying the original `Graphics` object.

◆ **abstract Graphics create( )**
   Creates a new `Graphics` object identical to the current
   object. Because both the original and the new copy may
   paint to the same region, this is often useful when you are
   making temporary yet irrevocable changes to the `Graphics`
   object—such as setting the clipping area.

◆ **abstract void dispose( )**

Disposes of the resources used by the graphics context.

◆ **void draw3DRect(int x, int y, int width, int height, boolean raised)**

Creates a 3-D rectangle with the specified location and size. Setting the `raised` parameter to a value of `true` gives the rectangle a brighter color—making it appear three-dimensional.

◆ **abstract void drawArc(int x, int y, int width, int height, int startAngle, int arcAngle)**

Draws the outline of an arc at the specified coordinates with the given size. The `startAngle` and `arcAngle` are measured in degrees and represent the angle at which the arc begins and ends (i.e., an arc from 0 to 360 is a complete circle).

◆ **void drawBytes(byte data[ ], int offset, int length, int x, int y)**

Displays bytes from the `data[]` array. The `offset` value represents the index of the first byte to be drawn; `length` is the number of bytes to be drawn; and `x` and `y` are the coordinates at which the bytes will be drawn on the screen.

◆ **void drawChars(char data[ ], int offset, int length, int x, int y)**

Displays characters from the `data[]` array. The `offset` value represents the index of the first character to be drawn; `length` is the number of characters to be drawn; and `x` and `y` are the coordinates at which the characters will be drawn.

◆ **abstract boolean drawImage(Image img, int x, int y, int width, int height, Color bgcolor, ImageObserver observer)**

Draws an image at the specified location with the specified size. `bgcolor` is the color that will be drawn "behind" the image—visible if there are any transparent pixels in the image. `observer` is the `ImageObserver` that monitors the progress of the image.

Java Quick Reference

> **Note** The `java.awtComponent` class implements the `ImageObserver` interface. Therefore, in most applets, you may use the `this` keyword as the `ImageObserver`.

◆ **abstract boolean drawImage(Image img, int x, int y, Color bgcolor, ImageObserver observer)**
Draws an image at the specified location with its normal size. `bgcolor` is the color that will be drawn "behind" the applet—visible if there are any transparent pixels in the image. `observer` is the `ImageObserver` that monitors the progress of the image.

◆ **abstract boolean drawImage(Image img, int x, int y, int width, int height, ImageObserver observer)**
Draws an image at the specified location with the specified size. `observer` is the `ImageObserver` that monitors the progress of the image.

◆ **abstract boolean drawImage(Image img, int x, int y, ImageObserver observer)**
Draws an image at the specified location with its normal size. `observer` is the `ImageObserver` that will monitor the progress of the image.

◆ **abstract void drawLine(int x1, int y1, int x2, int y2)**
Draws a line between the given points.

◆ **abstract void drawOval(int x, int y, int width, int height)**
Draws the outline of an oval at the specified coordinates with the specified size.

◆ **void drawRect(int x, int y, int width, int height)**
Draws the outline of a rectangle at the specified coordinates with the specified size.

◆ **abstract void drawRoundRect(int x, int y, int width, int height, int arcWidth, int arcHeight)**
Draws the outline of a rectangle at the specified coordinates having the specified size. `arcWidth` and `arcHeight` determine the size and shape of the corners of the rectangle.

◆ **void drawPolygon(Polygon p)**
Draws the polygon defined by the specified `java.awt.Polygon` object.

◆ **abstract void drawPolygon(int xPoints[], int yPoints[], int nPoints)**
Draws the polygon defined by the specified set of points. `nPoints` represents the number of vertices on the polygon. Java will pair the first *n* coordinates of the arrays to create *n* ordered pairs that will serve as the vertices of the polygon.

◆ **abstract void drawString(String str, int x, int y)**
Draws a string at the specified coordinates using the current font.

◆ **void fill3DRect(int x, int y, int width, int height, boolean raised)**
Fills a rectangle at the specified coordinates that has the specified size. The `raised` variable will change the darkness of the rectangle—making it appear three-dimensional if `true`.

◆ **abstract void fillOval(int x, int y, int width, int height)**
Fills an oval defined by the x- and y-coordinates that will have the specified size.

◆ **abstract void fillRect(int x, int y, int width, int height)**
Fills a rectangle at the given coordinates with the specified size.

JAVA.AWT

Java Quick Reference

- ◆ **abstract void fillRoundRect(int x, int y, int width, int height, int arcWidth, int arcHeight)**
  Fills in a rectangle at the specified coordinates having the specified size. `arcWidth` and `arcHeight` determine the size and shape of the corners of the rectangle.

- ◆ **abstract void fillArc(int x, int y, int width, int height, int startAngle, int arcAngle)**
  Fills an arc at the given coordinates with the specified size. The arc will extend from the `startAngle` to the `arcAngle`, measured in degrees.

- ◆ **void fillPolygon(Polygon p)**
  Fills the polygon defined by the particular `Polygon` object.

- ◆ **abstract void fillPolygon(int xPoints[ ], int yPoints[ ], int nPoints)**
  Fills the polygon defined by the specified set of points. `nPoints` represents the number of vertices on the polygon. Java will pair the first *n* coordinates of the arrays to create *n* ordered pairs that will serve as the vertices of the polygon.

- ◆ **void finalize( )**
  Disposes of the specific `Graphics` object.

- ◆ **abstract Rectangle getClipRect( )**
  Returns the clipping rectangle set by the `clipRect( )` method.

- ◆ **abstract Color getColor( )**
  Returns the current color used by graphical operations.

- ◆ **abstract Font getFont( )**
  Returns the font used by all text-related operations.

- ◆ **abstract FontMetrics getFontMetrics(Font f)**
  Returns the `FontMetrics` for the specified `Font`.

◆ **FontMetrics getFontMetrics( )**
   Returns the `FontMetrics` for the current font.

◆ **abstract void setColor(Color c)**
   Sets the color to be used by all graphical operations.

◆ **abstract void setFont(Font font)**
   Sets the font for all graphical operations.

◆ **abstract void setPaintMode( )**
   Causes subsequent graphical commands to cover the
   locations with the current color.

◆ **abstract void setXORMode(Color otherColor)**
   This method will cause the `Graphics` object to XOR mode
   using the current color and the specified `otherColor`.
   When painting graphics, all figures in the current color will
   be painted with the `otherColor` and vice versa. Any
   figures not in either color will be displayed in a different,
   random color.

◆ **abstract void translate(int x, int y)**
   Makes the specified coordinates the new origin for graphical
   operations. As a result, all operations will be relative to this
   new origin.

◆ **String toString( )**
   Returns a string containing information about the `Graph-
   ics` object, including the current color and font.

GridBagConstraints Implements java.lang.Cloneable

The `GridBagConstraint` class enables you to customize the
layout attributes of each component in a `GridBagLayout`. By
first creating a `GridBagConstraint` and setting its fields, you
are able specify the shape, size, and behavior of the component
once added to the layout.

▶ *See "GridBagLayout Implements LayoutManager," p. 72*

Fields

▶ **int anchor**

Describes the location at which the component will be placed.

▶ **final static int BOTH**

A possible `fill` value. The component will fill as much space as allowed, both horizontally and vertically.

▶ **final static int CENTER**

A possible `anchor` value.

▶ **final static int EAST**

A possible `anchor` value.

▶ **int fill**

Determines how the component will behave if the container is resized. The component may expand horizontally, vertically, or in both directions.

▶ **int gridheight**

Sets the height of the component.

▶ **int gridwidth**

Sets the width of the component.

▶ **int gridx**

The x-coordinate of the component.

▶ **int gridy**

The y-coordinate of the component.

▶ **final static int HORIZONTAL**

A value for `fill`. Causes the component to expand horizontally when the area available for the component exceeds the size of the component.

JAVA.AWT

▶ **Insets insets**
Defines the amount of space to be placed around the outside of any components on the edge of the layout.

▶ **int ipadx**
The amount of horizontal space to be placed between components.

▶ **int ipady**
The amount of vertical space to be placed between components.

▶ **final static int NONE**
A value for `fill`. The component will not expand in any direction.

▶ **final static int NORTH**
A value for `anchor`.

▶ **final static int NORTHEAST**
A value for `anchor`.

▶ **final static int NORTHWEST**
A value for `anchor`.

▶ **final static int RELATIVE**
A value for `gridx` or `gridy`. The component will be placed just after the previous component. For `gridx` this means to the left. For `gridy`, this means directly beneath.

▶ **final static int REMAINDER**
A value for `gridwidth` or `gridheight`. The component will take up the remainder of the row or column, respectively.

▶ **final static int SOUTH**
A value for `anchor`.

▶ **final static int SOUTHEAST**
A value for `anchor`.

▶ **final static int SOUTHWEST**
A value for `anchor`.

▶ **final static int VERTICAL**
A value for `fill`. The component will expand vertically to fill the available area.

▶ **double weightx**
Defines the relative importance of the component. This attribute is used when resizing the container in which the component resides.

▶ **double weighty**
Defines the relative importance of the component. This attribute is used when resizing the container in which the component resides.

▶ **final static int WEST**
A value for `anchor`.

Methods

◆ **GridBagConstraints( )**
Creates a new `GridBagConstraints` object.

◆ **Object clone( )**
Returns a copy of the `GridBagConstraints` object.

GridBagLayout Implements LayoutManager

The `GridBagLayout` is the most versatile and commonly used layout manager for components. A `GridBagLayout` enables you to place any number of components in virtually any layout that you can imagine (see fig. 9).

To control the layout of components in a `GridBagLayout`, you must employ the `GridBagConstraints` class. After setting the values of the `GridBagConstraints` class, you can add a component to the layout using the constraints. This flexibility enables you to specify a great deal of information about how the components will be laid out.

▶ **See "GridBagConstraints Implements java.lang.Cloneable,"**
  p. 69

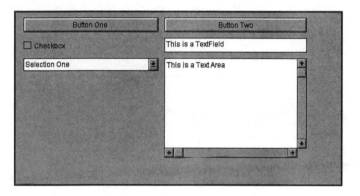

Fig. 9   The output of Listing 6.

The constraints for a `GridBagLayout` are set through the fields in the `GridBagLayout`, as described in the following table:

Fields	Purpose
anchor	Can be used to place the component in a particular region of the container (for example, SOUTHWEST).
fill	Determines how the component will act if the container provides it with room to grow. Valid values are NONE, HORIZONTAL, VERTICAL, and BOTH.

continues

JAVA.AWT

continued

Fields	Purpose
insets	Specifies the amount of space between components on the side of the container and the container edge.
ipadx, ipady	Specifies the amount of space between components.
gridx, gridy	Defines the upper left-hand corner of the component.
gridwidth, gridheight	Defines the size of the component.
weightx, weighty	Defines the relative importance of the components; to be used only when the container is resized.

Listing 6   GridbagLayout Example

```java
import java.applet.Applet;
import java.awt.*;

public class GridBagExample extends Applet
{
    GridBagLayout gridbag;
    GridBagConstraints c;

    public void init() {
        Button button;
        Checkbox checkbox;
        TextArea textarea;
        TextField textfield;
        Choice choice;

        gridbag = new GridBagLayout();
        c = new GridBagConstraints();
        setLayout(gridbag);

        c.ipadx=2;c.ipady=2;  // padding between components
        c.insets=new Insets(5,5,5,5);    /* padding
        between the components and the edge of the container*/
```

```
button = new Button("Button One");
gridbag.setConstraints(button,c);
add(button);

c.gridwidth = GridBagConstraints.REMAINDER;
/* Button will occupy the remainder of this row.
   Forces the next component onto the next row.    */

button = new Button("Button Two");
gridbag.setConstraints(button,c);
add(button);

c.gridwidth = 1;
// back to defaults - components continue on same row


checkbox = new Checkbox("Checkbox");
gridbag.setConstraints(checkbox,c);
add(checkbox);

c.gridwidth = GridBagConstraints.REMAINDER;
textfield = new TextField("This is a TextField");
gridbag.setConstraints(textfield,c);
add(textfield);

c.gridwidth = 1;
c.gridheight = GridBagConstraints.REMAINDER;
choice = new Choice();
choice.addItem("Selection One");
choice.addItem("Selection Two");
gridbag.setConstraints(choice,c);
add(choice);

textarea = new TextArea("This is a Text Area",10,3);
gridbag.setConstraints(textarea,c);
add(textarea);
    }
}
```

Fields

▶ **double columnWeights[ ]**
Stores the horizontal weights of the components in each column.

▶ **int columnWidths[ ]**
Stores the horizontal sizes of the components in each column.

▶ **protected Hashtable comptable**
A Hashtable to store the components.

▶ **protected GridBagConstraints defaultConstraints**
The default constraints for a component.

▶ **protected GridBagLayoutInfo layoutInfo**
The GridBagLayoutInfo class is a restricted class that facilitates management of the layout for the GridBagLayout class. It tracks the size of the layout, the minimum dimensions of the components, and the weights.

The class consists only of the following fields and one constructor method. Unless you are creating a new class in the java.awt package that extends the GridbagLayout class, you will not need to use this class—nor will you be able to.

```
int width, height;    // number of cells in each direction
int startx, starty;   // start of layout
int minWidth[];       // largest minWidth for each column
int minHeight[];      // largest minHeight for each row
double weightX[];     // largest weight for each column
double weightY[];     // largest weight for each row
```

▶ **protected final static int MAXGRIDSIZE**
The maximum number of rows or columns. Set to 128.

▶ **protected final static int MINSIZE**
The minimum number of rows or columns. Set to 1.

▶ **protected final static int PREFERREDSIZE**
The preferred size of a component. Set to 2.

▶ **int rowHeights[ ]**
Tracks the heights of the components in each row.

▶ **double rowWeights[ ]**
Tracks the weights of the components in each row.

Methods

◆ **GridBagLayout( )**
Creates a new `GridBagLayout`.

◆ **void addLayoutComponent(String name, Component comp)**
This function is required inasmuch as the `GridBagLayout` class implements the `LayoutManager` interface. It however has no function in this class.

◆ **protected void AdjustForGravity(GridBagConstraints constraints, Rectangle r)**
Adjusts the components according to their attributes within the specified `Rectangle`. This method is called by `ArrangeGrid()`.

◆ **protected void ArrangeGrid(Container parent)**
Arranges the parent container.

◆ **protected void DumpConstraints(GridBagConstraints constraints)**
Prints out the current constraints.

◆ **protected void DumpLayoutInfo(GridBagLayoutInfo string)**

Prints out the current layout info.

◆ **GridBagConstraints getConstraints(Component comp)**

Returns the current constraints.

◆ **int[ ][ ] getLayoutDimensions( )**

Returns an array of integers obtained for the arrays in the `LayoutInfo` object. If the returned array is named `arr`, then `arr[0]` is the array of minimum widths for each column and `arr[1]` is the array of minimum heights for each row.

◆ **protected GridBagLayoutInfo GetLayoutInfo(Container parent, int sizeflag)**

Returns the `GridBagLayoutInfo` object for the `GridBagLayout`.

◆ **Point getLayoutOrigin( )**

Returns the origin for the layout. This may not always be (0,0).

◆ **double[ ][ ] getLayoutWeights( )**

Returns the maximum weights of the components in each row and column. `arr[0]` is an array of the maximum weight in each column. `arr[1]` is an array of the maximum weight in each row.

◆ **protected Dimension GetMinSize(Container parent, GridBagLayoutInfo info)**

Returns the minimum size required for this layout. This value is based on the size of the components and the `insets` values for the parent container. This method is called by `perferredLayoutSize()` and `minimumLayoutSize()`, each with a different `info` parameter.

◆ **void layoutContainer(Container parent)**
Arranges the container in accordance with the
GridBagLayout parameters.

◆ **Point location(int x, int y)**
Returns the size of the rectangle occupied by all components
above and to the left of the point (x,y) on the grid. This value
is created by summing the minimum widths and minimum
heights for each component having an x-coordinate less than
or equal to x and a y-coordinate less than or equal to y.

◆ **protected GridBagConstraints
lookupConstraints(Component comp)**
Returns the constraints for the particular component.

◆ **Dimension minimumLayoutSize(Container parent)**
Returns the minimum layout size required for the container.
It is based on the minimum sizes for the components within
the layout.

◆ **Dimension preferredLayoutSize(Container parent)**
Returns the preferred size of the container. It is based on the
preferred sizes for the components within the layout.

◆ **void removeLayoutComponent(Component comp)**
Removes the specified component from the layout.

◆ **void setConstraints(Component comp,
GridBagConstraints constraints)**
Assigns the given component a new set of constraints.

◆ **String toString( )**
Returns the string java.awt.GridBagLayout.

GridLayout Implements
LayoutManager

A GridLayout provides you with slightly less control over the
layout than the GridBagLayout class. A GridLayout is
created by specifying a number of rows and columns. Each

subsequent add() statement will place the specified component in the layout, adjusting the size of all components. As a result, all components in a GridLayout are of the same size.

Methods

◆ **GridLayout(int rows, int cols)**
Constructs a GridLayout with the specified number of rows and columns. The hgap and vgap will be set to 0.

◆ **GridLayout(int rows, int cols, int hgap, int vgap)**
Constructs a GridLayout with the specified number of rows and columns, hgap, and vgap.

◆ **void addLayoutComponent(String name, Component comp)**
This method has no function.

◆ **void layoutContainer(Container parent)**
Arranges the container in accordance with the GridLayout model.

◆ **Dimension minimumLayoutSize(Container parent)**
Returns the minimum layout size required for the container. It is based on the preferred sizes for the components within the layout.

◆ **Dimension preferredLayoutSize(Container parent)**
Returns the preferred layout size requested for the container. Based on the preferred sizes for the components within the layout.

◆ **void removeLayoutComponent(Component comp)**
Removes the specified component.

◆ **String toString( )**
Returns a string containing the layout's name, hgap, vgaps, and the number of rows and columns.

Abstract Image

The Image class provides you with a platform-independent manner of handling images. Regardless of the source of the image or the platform, all the following methods may be used on all Images.

One problem encountered with images is that they often take some time to completely load. As a result, in all methods where this could be problematic, it is necessary to specify an ImageObserver (an object that implements the ImageObserver interface. If the method is unable to return the requested information, it will return a value of –1 or a null string. However, once the information does become available, the information will be sent along to the imageUpdate() method of the specified ImageObserver.

▶ *See "java.awt.Image," p. 120*

Field

▶ **final static Object UndefinedProperty**
This field is returned whenever you request a property not defined for the particular Image.

Methods

◆ **Image( )**
Creates a new Image.

◆ **abstract Graphics getGraphics( )**
Returns the Graphics object for this Image.

◆ **abstract int getHeight(ImageObserver observer)**
Returns the height of the Image. If the height is not currently known, this method will return a value of –1 and will inform the specified ImageObserver at a later time through the imageUpdate() method.

◆ **abstract Object getProperty(String propertyname, ImageObserver observer)**
Returns the requested property for this `Image`. If this property is undefined, the `UndefinedProperty` object will be returned. If the property is currently unknown, the method will return a value of `null`, and will later inform the `ImageObserver`.

◆ **abstract void flush( )**
Disposes of all memory being used by the `Image`. This contains cached information. If the `Image` is to be displayed again, it will be re-created for you, but this will take longer than if it were still cached.

◆ **abstract ImageProducer getSource( )**
Returns the source of the Image in the form of a class implementing the ImageProducer interface.

This method is useful when using `ImageFilters`. By first invoking this method, you can obtain the source of the `Image` to be used when creating a new `java.awt.image.FilteredImageSource`.

◆ **abstract int getWidth(ImageObserver observer)**
Returns the width of the `Image`. If the height is not currently known, this method will return a value of –1 and will later inform the specified `ImageObserver`.

Insets Implements Cloneable

The `Insets` class is a tool to be used by layout managers, particularly `GridBagLayoutManager`. An `Inset` may be used to set and track the amount of space that will be inserted between the components of the layout and the border of the container.

▶ *See Listing 6, "GridbagLayout Example," p. 74*

Fields

▶ **int bottom**
▶ **int left**
▶ **int right**
▶ **int top**

Methods

◆ **Insets(int top, int left, int bottom, int right)**
   Creates a new Insets object with the specified spacing values.

◆ **Object clone( )**
   Creates a copy of the *Insets* object.

◆ **String toString( )**
   Returns a string containing the class name and the four spacing values.

Label Extends Component

A Label is a convenient way of placing a single line of text on the screen (see fig. 10). Because it is a Component, it may be placed in a layout manager.

This is an example of a Label.

Fig. 10   Text as a label.

Fields

▶ **final static int CENTER**
   An alignment value for the text in the Label.

▶ **final static int LEFT**
   An alignment value for the text in the Label.

▶ **final static int RIGHT**
   An alignment value for the text in the Label.

Methods

◆ **Label( )**
   Constructs a new, empty label whose text will be left justified.

◆ **Label(String label)**
   Constructs a new label with the specified text. The text will be left justified.

◆ **Label(String label, int alignment)**
   Constructs a new label with the specified text and alignment. The alignment value may be either LEFT, CENTER, or RIGHT.

◆ **synchronized void addNotify( )**
   Creates the Label's peer.

◆ **int getAlignment( )**
   Returns the alignment for the Label.

◆ **String getText( )**
   Returns the current text for the Label.

◆ **protected String paramString( )**
   Returns a string containing the parameters for the Label including the alignment and the text.

◆ **void setAlignment(int alignment)**
   Sets the alignment for the displayed text. The parameter may be either LEFT, CENTER, or RIGHT.

◆ **void setText(String label)**
   Sets the text for the Label.

List Extends Component

A List is a useful scrollable index of textual headers (see fig. 11). When using a List, you may not only add items to the

end of the list, but may also insert them within the list. Furthermore, during execution, you can query the list for information
regarding the user's actions or even scroll the list yourself using
the `makeVisible()` method.

Fig. 11 A scrolling list.

Methods

◆ **List( )**

Creates a new `List` that contains no rows and does not
allow multiple selections.

◆ **List(int rows, boolean multipleSelections)**

Creates a new `List` with the specified number of rows. If
the `multipleSelection` argument is `true`, then more
than one item in the list can be selected at a given time.

◆ **synchronized void addItem(String itemTitle, int index)**

Adds an new item to the list at the specified index.
`itemTitle` specifies the title that will be displayed. If the
index is –1 or greater than the number of the items in the
`List`, the item will be added to the end of the `List`.

◆ **synchronized void addItem(String itemTitle)**

Adds an item with the specified title to the end of the `List`.

◆ **synchronized void addNotify( )**

Creates the `List`'s peer.

◆ **boolean allowsMultipleSelections( )**

Returns `true` if the user may select more than one item in
this list.

Java Quick Reference

◆ **synchronized void clear( )**
Clears the list. All items are erased.

◆ **int countItems( )**
Returns the number of items in the list.

◆ **String getItem(int index)**
Returns the title of the item at the specified index.

◆ **synchronized void delItem(int index)**
Deletes the item at the specified index.

◆ **synchronized void delItems(int start, int end)**
Deletes all items between and including the start and end
parameters.

◆ **synchronized void deselect(int index)**
Deselects the specified index. No item will be selected.

◆ **int getRows( )**
Returns the number of items that can be seen by the user.

◆ **synchronized int getSelectedIndex( )**
Returns the index of the currently selected item. Returns −1
if none is selected at the time.

◆ **synchronized int[ ] getSelectedIndexes( )**
Returns an array containing the indexes of all selected items.
This is only useful when multiple selections are permitted.

◆ **synchronized String getSelectedItem( )**
Returns the title of the currently selected item. Returns −1 if
none is selected at the time.

◆ **synchronized String[ ] getSelectedItems( )**
Returns an array containing the titles of all selected items.
This is only useful when multiple selections are permitted.

◆ **int getVisibleIndex( )**
Returns the index of the item that was made visible by the
last call to `makeVisible()`.

◆ **synchronized boolean isSelected(int index)**
Returns `true` if the specified item is visible.

◆ **void makeVisible(int index)**
Scrolls the list to make the specified index visible.

◆ **Dimension minimumSize( )**
Returns the minimum size required to properly display the
entire list. This value is based on either the size returned
from the `List`'s peer or the `Component` class.

◆ **Dimension minimumSize(int rows)**
Returns the minimum size required to properly display the
specified number of rows in this list. This value is based
on either the size returned from the `List`'s peer or the
`Component` class.

◆ **protected String paramString( )**
Returns a string containing information on the `List`
including the title of the selected item.

◆ **Dimension preferredSize( )**
Returns the size desired to display the entire list. This value is
based on either the size returned from the `List`'s peer or
the `Component` class.

◆ **Dimension preferredSize(int rows)**
Returns the size desired to display the specified number of
rows in the list. This value is based on either the size returned from the `List`'s peer or the `Component` class.

◆ **synchronized void removeNotify( )**
Removes the `List`'s peer.

◆ **synchronized void replaceItem(String newValue, int index)**
Changes the value of the item at the specified index. This is done by deleting the item at the specified index and then creating a new item with the specified title and index.

◆ **synchronized void select(int index)**
Selects the specified item.

◆ **void setMultipleSelections(boolean multipleSelections)**
If the `multipleSelections` parameter is `true`, then more than one item in the list can be selected at a time. If this is `false`, then only one item can be selected at a given moment.

MediaTracker

A `MediaTracker` is a means of managing a number of media objects, such as images and audio clips. (However, as of the 1.0.2 JDK, only `Images` were supported.) Somewhat like an array, the `MediaTracker` assigns each a reference number. However, it also keeps track of the status of each image, allowing you to determine the status of each or lock up the tracker until all images have been loaded.

Fields

▶ **final static int ABORTED**
A flag indicating that the loading of the media has been aborted.

▶ **final static int COMPLETE**
A flag indicating that the loading of the media has been successfully completed.

▶ **final static int ERRORED**
A flag indicating that an error has been encountered while loading the media.

Methods

◆ **MediaTracker(Component comp)**
Creates a new `MediaTracker` to report on the media in the specified component.

◆ **void addImage(Image image, int id)**
Adds an item to the `MediaTracker` with the specified id. This id value can later be used as a reference to a set of media items.

◆ **synchronized void addImage(Image image, int id, int width, int height)**
Adds an image with the specified dimensions to the `MediaTracker` with the specified id. This can later be used as a reference to a set of media items.

◆ **synchronized boolean checkAll(boolean load)**
Returns `true` if all media items have been successfully loaded, `false` otherwise. If the `load` parameter is `true`, this method will also load any non-loaded images.

◆ **boolean checkAll( )**
Returns `true` if all media items have been successfully loaded, `false` otherwise. This method will not affect non-loaded images.

◆ **synchronized boolean checkID(int id, boolean load)**
Returns `true` if all media items with the specified `id` have been successfully loaded, `false` otherwise. If the `load` parameter is `true`, this method will also load any non-loaded images.

◆ **boolean checkID(int id)**
Returns `true` if all media items with the specified `id` have been successfully loaded, `false` otherwise. This method has no effect on unloaded images.

Java Quick Reference

- ◆ **synchronized Object[ ] getErrorsAny( )**
  Returns an array of all media items that have encountered an error.

- ◆ **synchronized Object[ ] getErrorsID(int id)**
  Returns an array of all media items with the specified `id` that have encountered an error.

- ◆ **synchronized boolean isErrorAny( )**
  Returns `true` if any media items have encountered an error.

- ◆ **synchronized boolean isErrorID(int id)**
  Returns `true` if any media items with the specified `id` have encountered an error.

- ◆ **int statusAll(boolean load)**
  Returns the status for all media items in the `MediaTracker`. If the `load` parameter is `true`, any unloaded images will be loaded.

- ◆ **int statusID(int id, boolean load)**
  Returns the status for all media items with the specified `id`. If the `load` parameter is `true`, all unloaded items will be loaded.

- ◆ **void waitForAll( ) throws InterruptedException**
  Begins to load all media items and does not return until this process is complete. *Note that this method does not guarantee that these items will be loaded successfully,* and thus you are strongly encouraged to check for any errors.

- ◆ **synchronized boolean waitForAll(long ms) throws InterruptedException**
  Locks up the `MediaTracker` object and loads all media items. This method relinquishes control of the

`MediaTracker` only when the loading is complete or the specified number of milliseconds has expired. *Note that this method does not guarantee that these items will be loaded successfully,* and thus you are strongly encouraged to check for any errors.

◆ **void waitForID(int id) throws InterruptedException**
Begins to load all media items with the specified `id` and does not return until this process is complete. *Note that this method does not guarantee that these items will be loaded successfully,* and thus you are strongly encouraged to check for any errors.

◆ **synchronized boolean waitForID(int id, long ms) throws InterruptedException**
Begins to load all media items and does not return until this process is complete or the specified number of milliseconds has expired. *Note that this method does not guarantee that these items will be loaded successfully,* and thus you are strongly encouraged to check for any errors.

Menu Extends MenuItem Implements MenuContainer

A `Menu` is a column in a `MenuBar`. Like the standard "File" and "Help" headers in most applications, a `Menu` defines the title on the `MenuBar` as well as the headings in the column. When creating a menu, you must first create `Menu` items and then add them to your `MenuBar`.

▶ *See "MenuBar Extends MenuComponent Implements MenuContainer," p. 93*

▶ *See "Frame Extends Window Implements MenuContainer," p. 60*

Methods

◆ **Menu(String title)**
  Creates a new Menu with the specified title.

◆ **Menu(String title, boolean tearOff)**
  Creates a new Menu with the specified title. The effects of the tearOff parameter are platform-dependent. However, the idea of a tear-off menu is that it will remain as a separate window until the user selects an item from it.

◆ **void add(String label)**
  Adds a selection with the specified label to the Menu listing.

◆ **synchronized MenuItem add(MenuItem mitem)**
  Adds a MenuItem to the Menu listing.

◆ **synchronized void addNotify( )**
  Creates the Menu's peer.

◆ **void addSeparator( )**
  Inserts a line between the already added items in the Menu and any later items that you add.

◆ **int countItems( )**
  Returns the number of items in the menu listing.

◆ **MenuItem getItem(int index)**
  Returns the item at the specified index.

◆ **boolean isTearOff( )**
  Returns true if the menu is a tear-off menu.

◆ **synchronized void remove(MenuComponent item)**
  Removes the specified item from the menu listing.

◆ **synchronized void remove(int index)**
   Removes the item at the specified index from the menu listing.

◆ **synchronized void removeNotify( )**
   Removes the Menu's peer.

MenuBar Extends MenuComponent Implements MenuContainer

A MenuBar is a container for Menu items and serves as the head of the menu when displayed. In order to create a menu in your program, you must first create Menu items, and then add them to a MenuBar. By adding a MenuBar to the Frame, you are able to make the menu visible to the user.

▶ *See "Menu Extends MenuItem Implements MenuContainer,"*
   p. 91

▶ *See "Frame Extends Window Implements MenuContainer,"*
   p. 60

The menu shown in figure 12 was created with the code in Listing 7. Also note the use of the Display class to enable the applet to monitor the user's selections.

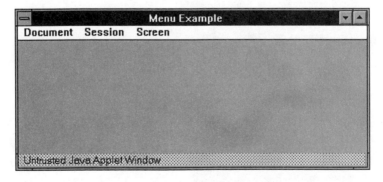

Fig. 12 The output of Listing 7.

Listing 7 Menu Example

```java
import java.applet.Applet;
import java.awt.*;

public class MenuExample extends Applet
{
    private Menu category;
    private MenuBar bar;
    private Display picture;

    public void init() {
        bar = new MenuBar();
        category = new Menu("Document");
        category.add("Option One");
        category.add("Option Two");
        category.add("Option Three");
        bar.add(category);

        category = new Menu("Session");
        category.add("Reset");
        category.add("Restart");
        bar.add(category);

        category = new Menu("Screen");
        category.add("Change colors");
        category.add("Display Titles");
        bar.add(category);


        picture = new Display();
        picture.setMenuBar(bar);
        picture.setTitle("Menu Example");
        picture.show();
    }
}

class Display extends Frame {
    public boolean action(Event evt, Object arg) {
        if(arg.equals("Option Two")) {
```

```
    System.out.println("Option Two was Selected");
    return true;
    }
  return super.handleEvent(evt);
  }

  public boolean handleEvent(Event evt) {
    if (evt.id == Event.WINDOW_DESTROY) {
      hide();   // closes the frame when appropriate
      return true;
    }
    return super.handleEvent(evt);
  }
}
```

Methods

◆ **MenuBar( )**
Creates a new MenuBar.

◆ **synchronized Menu add(Menu m)**
Adds a Menu to the MenuBar.

◆ **synchronized void addNotify( )**
Creates the MenuBar's peer.

◆ **int countMenus( )**
Returns the number of Menus in this MenuBar.

◆ **Menu getHelpMenu( )**
Returns the Help menu from this MenuBar.

◆ **Menu getMenu(int index)**
Returns the Menu at the specified index.

◆ **synchronized void remove(MenuComponent m)**
Removes the specified MenuComponent.

◆ **synchronized void remove(int index)**
Removes the `MenuComponent` at the specified index.

◆ **void removeNotify( )**
Removes the `MenuBar`'s peer.

◆ **synchronized void setHelpMenu(Menu m)**
Makes the specified `Menu` the Help menu for the `MenuBar`.

Abstract MenuComponent

`MenuComponent` is the superclass for all classes dealing with menu related components.

▶ *See "Menu Extends MenuItem Implements MenuContainer,"*
p. 91

Methods

◆ **MenuComponent( )**
Creates a new `MenuComponent`.

◆ **MenuContainer getParent( )**
Returns the container of this `MenuComponent`. This most likely will be the `Menu` in which the `MenuComponent` resides.

◆ **MenuComponentPeer getPeer( )**
Returns the peer of the `MenuComponent`.

◆ **Font getFont( )**
Returns the font of this `MenuComponent`.

◆ **protected String paramString( )**
Returns a string containing information on the `MenuComponent`. Although overridden in subclasses, this method returns an empty string.

◆ **boolean postEvent(Event evt)**
Posts the specified `Event` to the `MenuComponent`.

◆ **void removeNotify( )**
Removes the `MenuComponent`'s peer.

◆ **void setFont(Font f)**
Sets the font for the `MenuComponent`.

◆ **String toString( )**
Returns the object's name in addition to the information returned by `paramString()`.

MenuItem Extends MenuComponent

A `MenuItem` is a class that contains a string representation of an option on a menu. It is used and extended by the more useful menu classes.

▶   *See "CheckboxMenuItem Extends MenuItem," p. 28*

Methods

◆ **MenuItem(String label)**
Creates a new `MenuItem` with the specified text label.

◆ **synchronized void addNotify( )**
Creates the `MenuItem`'s peer.

◆ **void disable( )**
Prevents the user from selecting the `MenuItem`.

◆ **void enable(boolean cond)**
If `cond` is `true`, the user will be able to select the `MenuItem`. If `cond` is `false`, the user will be unable to select the item.

◆ **void enable( )**
Enables the user to select the `MenuItem`.

◆ **String getLabel( )**
Returns the textual label of this `MenuItem`.

◆ **boolean isEnabled( )**
Returns `true` if the `MenuItem` is enabled, meaning that the user will be able to select it.

◆ **String paramString( )**
Returns a string containing the item's label.

◆ **void setLabel(String label)**
Sets the label of this `MenuItem`.

Panel Extends Container

`Panel` is a simple container class that may be extended to create richer subclasses. `java.applet.Applet` is a subclass of `Panel`.

▶ *See Listing 3, "CardLayout Example Source Code," p. 24*

Methods
◆ **Panel( )**
Creates a new `Panel`.

◆ **synchronized void addNotify( )**
Creates the Panel's peer.

Point

`Point` is a simple class to keep track of and manage an ordered pair.

Fields
▶ **int x**
▶ **int y**

Methods

◆ **Point (int x, int y)**

Creates a new `Point` with the specified `x` and `y` values.

◆ **boolean equals(Object anotherobject)**

Compares a `Point` to another object. Two points are equal if their `x` and `y` values are equal.

◆ **int hashCode( )**

Returns the `hashcode` for the `Point` object. This value is dependent on the values of `x` and `y`.

◆ **void move(int x, int y)**

Sets the coordinates of the `Point` to the specified `x` and `y`.

◆ **String toString( )**

Returns a string containing the class name and the `x` and `y` values.

◆ **void translate(int x, Int y)**

Increments the x- and y-coordinates of the point by the specified amounts.

Polygon

A `Polygon` is a class that enables you to define an arbitrary polygon. This class does not draw a polygon on the screen, but rather specifies the coordinates that can be used by the methods in the `Graphics` class.

To track the vertices, the class maintains two parallel arrays (`xpoints[]` and `ypoints[]`). For example, if point #2 is (4,5), then `xpoints[3]` will equal 4 and `ypoints[3]` will equal 5.

▶ *See Listing 5, "Graphics Example," p. 63*

Fields

▶ **int npoints**

The number of points in the Polygon. Regardless of the number of values in the xpoints [] and ypoints [] arrays, this value will be used in defining the polygon.

▶ **int xpoints[ ]**

The x-coordinates of the vertices of the polygon. These values are paired with the corresponding values in the ypoints [] array to create the vertices of the polygon.

▶ **int ypoints[ ]**

The y-coordinates of the vertices of the polygon. These values are paired with the corresponding values in the xpoints [] array to create the vertices of the polygon.

Methods

◆ **Polygon( )**

Creates a new Polygon.

◆ **Polygon(int xpoints[ ], int ypoints[ ], int npoints)**

Creates a new Polygon with the specified points. npoints specifies the number of points that will be taken from the arrays.

◆ **void addPoint(int x, int y)**

Adds a point to the polygon.

◆ **Rectangle getBoundingBox( )**

Returns a Rectangle that encloses the polygon.

◆ **boolean inside(int x, int y)**

Returns true if the given point lies within the polygon.

Rectangle

The Rectangle class defines the vertices of a rectangle. While it does not actually draw the rectangle on the screen, it does enable you to create and track rectangular objects.

Fields
▶ **int height**
▶ **int width**
▶ **int x**
▶ **int y**

Methods

◆ **Rectangle( )**
Creates a new `Rectangle`.

◆ **Rectangle(Dimension d)**
Creates a new `Rectangle` with the specified dimensions.

◆ **Rectangle(int x, int y, int width, int height)**
Creates a new `Rectangle` with the specified coordinates
and dimensions.

◆ **Rectangle(int width, int height)**
Creates a new `Rectangle` with the specified coordinates.

◆ **Rectangle(Point p)**
Creates a new `Rectangle` with the specified coordinates.

◆ **Rectangle(Point p, Dimension d)**
Creates a new `Rectangle` with the specified coordinates
and dimensions.

◆ **void add(Rectangle r)**
Causes the current `Rectangle` to expand to enclose the
specified `Rectangle`.

◆ **void add(Point pt)**
Causes the current `Rectangle` to expand to enclose the
specified `Point`.

◆ **void add(int newx, int newy)**
Causes the current `Rectangle` to expand to enclose the
specified coordinates.

Java Quick Reference

◆ **boolean equals(Object anotherobject)**
Compares the Rectangle to another object. Two
Rectangles are equal if they have the same x- and y-
coordinates and dimensions.

◆ **void grow(int h, int v)**
Increases the size of the rectangle by the specified amount.

◆ **int hashCode( )**
Returns the hashcode for this Rectangle. This value is
dependent on the coordinates and dimensions of the
Rectangle.

◆ **boolean inside(int x, int y)**
Returns true if the coordinates lie within the rectangle.

◆ **Rectangle intersection(Rectangle r)**
Returns the Rectangle representing the intersection of the
rectangle and another specified rectangle.

◆ **boolean intersects(Rectangle r)**
Returns true if the rectangle intersects the specified
rectangle.

◆ **boolean isEmpty( )**
Returns true if both the width and the height of the
Rectangle are 0.

◆ **void move(int x, int y)**
Moves the rectangle to the specified location.

◆ **void reshape(int x, int y, int width, int height)**
Specifies a new set of coordinates and dimensions for the
rectangle.

◆ **void resize(int width, int height)**
Changes the dimensions of the Rectangle.

- ◆ **String toString( )**
  Returns a string containing the class name, the coordinates, and the dimensions of the rectangle.

- ◆ **void translate(int x, int y)**
  Increments the coordinates of the rectangle by the specified x and y values.

- ◆ **Rectangle union(Rectangle r)**
  Creates a new Rectangle object containing both the current and another Rectangle.

Scrollbar Extends Component

A Scrollbar is a versatile component used to create scrollbars in your programs. The Scrollbar class enables you to create both vertical and horizontal scrollbars and to set the value range for the scrollbar. Like any other Component, a Scrollbar can be placed by a layout manager.

The code in Listing 8 creates a very simple calculator that uses scrollbars to facilitate input (see fig. 13). Although the scrollbars adjust themselves automatically, note how the Calculate button updates the TextField.

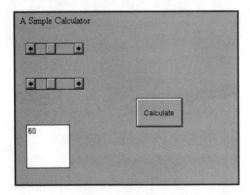

Fig. 13   A scrollbar calculator.

Java Quick Reference

Listing 8   Scrollbar Example

```java
import java.applet.Applet;
import java.awt.*;


public class ScrollbarExample extends Applet
{
    Scrollbar sb1, sb2;
    TextField info;
    Button trigger;

    public void init() {

        setLayout(null); // won't use one of the layout managers
        add(sb1);
        sb1.reshape(10,10,100,20);

        sb2 = new Scrollbar(Scrollbar.HORIZONTAL,30,20,0,100);
        add(sb2);
        sb2.reshape(10,70,100,20);

        trigger = new Button("Calculate");
        add(trigger);
        trigger.reshape(200,105,80,50);

        info = new TextField("0");
        add(info);
        info.reshape(10,150,75,75);

        refresh();
    }

    void refresh() {
        int sum = sb1.getValue() + sb2.getValue();
        info.setText("" + sum);
    }

    public boolean action(Event evt, Object arg) {
        if(arg.equals("Calculate")) {
```

```
        refresh();
        return true;
    }
    return false;
}
}
```

Fields

▶ **final static int HORIZONTAL**
A possible value for the orientation of the Scrollbar.
Produces a horizontal Scrollbar.

▶ **final static int VERTICAL**
A possible value for the orientation of the Scrollbar.
Produces a vertical Scrollbar.

Methods

◆ **Scrollbar( )**
Creates a new Scrollbar with an orientation set to
VERTICAL.

◆ **Scrollbar(int orientation)**
Creates a new Scrollbar with the specified
orientation.

◆ **Scrollbar(int orientation, int value, int visible,
int minimum, int maximum)**
Creates a new Scrollbar with the specified
orientation. value is the initial value of the
Scrollbar. visible is the amount of the Scrollbar
that will be visible—a property considered when the applet
screen is scrolled. minimum and maximum specify the
minimum and maximum values for the Scrollbar.

◆ **synchronized void addNotify( )**
Creates the Scrollbar's peer.

Java Quick Reference

◆ **int getLineIncrement( )**
Returns the amount that the scrollbar's value will change when the scrollbar is moved a "line." A request to move the scrollbar a line is created by a mouse click on one of the directional arrows at either end of the scrollbar.

◆ **int getMaximum( )**
Returns the maximum value for the scrollbar.

◆ **int getMinimum( )**
Returns the minimum value for the scrollbar.

◆ **int getOrientation( )**
Returns the orientation of the scrollbar—either HORIZONTAL or VERTICAL.

◆ **int getPageIncrement( )**
Returns the amount that the scrollbar's value will change when the scrollbar is moved a "page." A request to move the scrollbar a page is created by a mouse click within the scrollbar and to the side of the marker.

◆ **int getValue( )**
Returns the value of the scrollbar.

◆ **int getVisible( )**
Returns the amount of the scrollbar that is visible.

◆ **protected String paramString( )**
Returns a string containing information about the Scrollbar, including its value, visibility, maximum, and minimum values.

◆ **void setLineIncrement(int l)**
Sets amount that the scrollbar's value will change when the scrollbar is moved a "line." A request to move the scrollbar a line is created by a mouse click on one of the directional arrows at either side of the scrollbar.

◆ **void setPageIncrement(int I)**

Sets the amount that the scrollbar's value will change when the scrollbar is moved a "page." A request to move the scrollbar a page is created by a mouse click within the scrollbar and to the side of the marker.

◆ **void setValue(int value)**

Sets the value of the scrollbar. If the `value` parameter is out of range, the value of the scrollbar will be set to either the maximum or the minimum value of the scrollbar.

◆ **void setValues(int value, int visible, int minimum, int maximum)**

Sets the parameters for the scrollbar. `orientation`, either `VERTICAL` or `HORIZONTAL`, determines the appearance of the `Scrollbar`. `value` is the initial value of the `Scrollbar`. `visible` is the amount of the `Scrollbar` that will be visible—a property considered when the applet screen is scrolled. `minimum` and `maximum` specify the minimum and maximum values for the `Scrollbar`.

TextArea Extends TextComponent

A `TextArea` is used for displaying and editing multiple lines of text. Because of this, a `TextArea` is created with the capability of being scrolled (see fig. 14).

▶ *See Listing 6, "GridbagLayout Example," p. 74*

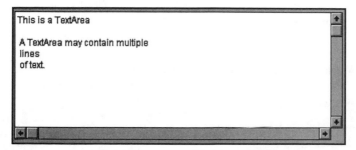

Fig. 14 A `TextArea` in Windows NT.

Methods

◆ **TextArea( )**
Creates a new `TextArea` that is empty.

◆ **TextArea(int rows, int cols)**
Creates a new `TextArea` with the specified number of rows and columns.

◆ **TextArea(String text)**
Creates a new `TextArea` with the specified text.

◆ **TextArea(String text, int rows, int cols)**
Creates a new `TextArea` with the specified number of rows and columns and specified text.

◆ **synchronized void addNotify( )**
Creates the `TextArea`'s peer.

◆ **void appendText(String newText)**
Adds the specified text to the end of the current text displayed.

◆ **int getColumns( )**
Returns the number of columns in the `TextArea`.

◆ **int getRows( )**
Returns the number of columns in the `TextArea`.

◆ **void insertText(String str, int pos)**
Inserts the text into the `TextArea` at the specified position.

◆ **Dimension minimumSize( )**
Returns the minimum size required by this entire component.

◆ **Dimension minimumSize(int rows, int cols)**
Returns the minimum size required by the specified number of rows and columns.

◆ **protected String paramString( )**
Returns a string that includes the text and the dimensions of
the TextArea.

◆ **Dimension preferredSize( )**
Returns the minimum size requested by the entire component.

◆ **Dimension preferredSize(int rows, int cols)**
Returns the minimum size desired by the specified number
of rows and columns.

◆ **void replaceText(String newText, int start, int end)**
Replaces the text from start to end with the newText.
The length of newText does not need to equal the length
of the text being replaced.

TextComponent Extends Component

TextComponent is the basic building block for the text
displaying components, TextArea and TextField (see fig.
15). Nevertheless, its constructor method has a restricted level of
access—preventing you from making use of it unless you are
developing within the java.awt package. Therefore, while
establishing several useful methods, this class is not usually used
directly.

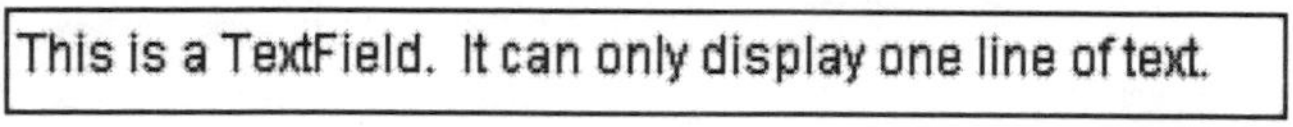

This is a TextField. It can only display one line of text.

Fig. 15 A TextField in Windows NT.

Methods

◆ **String getSelectedText( )**
Returns the text that is currently highlighted by the user.

◆ **int getSelectionEnd( )**
Returns the index of the last character in the highlighted
section.

◆ **int getSelectionStart( )**
Returns the index of the first character in the highlighted section.

◆ **boolean isEditable( )**
Returns `true` if the text displayed can be changed.

◆ **protected String paramString( )**
Returns a string including the text displayed, the beginning and ending indexes of the highlighted text, and whether or not the text can be edited.

◆ **void select(int start, int end)**
Selects all text between the specified indexes.

◆ **void selectAll( )**
Selects all text.

◆ **void setEditable(boolean editable)**
If `editable` is `true`, then the text can be changed by the user. If `editable` is `false`, then the text cannot be changed by the user.

TextField Extends TextComponent
A `TextField` is a simple component that is used to display and edit a single line of text.

Methods
◆ **TextField( )**
Creates a new `TextField`.

◆ **TextField(int cols)**
Creates a new `TextField` with the specified number of columns.

◆ **TextField(String text)**
Creates a new `TextField` with the specified text.

◆ **TextField(String text, int cols)**
Creates a new `TextField` with the specified text and
having the specified number of columns.

◆ **synchronized void addNotify( )**
Creates the peer of the `TextField`.

◆ **boolean echoCharIsSet( )**
Returns `true` if an echo character has been set for this
`TextField`. An echo character is a character that will be
displayed instead of the characters inputted by the user. This
feature is commonly used for `TextFields` that accept
passwords.

◆ **int getColumns( )**
Returns the number of columns in the `TextField`.

◆ **char getEchoChar( )**
Returns the echo character. The echo character is a character
displayed as a substitute for the characters entered by the
user.

◆ **Dimension minimumSize( )**
Returns the minimum size required by this component.

◆ **Dimension minimumSize(int cols)**
Returns the minimum size required by the specified number
of columns.

◆ **protected String paramString( )**
Returns a string containing the current text and the echo
character.

◆ **Dimension preferredSize( )**
Returns the size requested by this component.

◆ **Dimension preferredSize(int cols)**
Returns the size requested by the specified number of columns.

◆ **void setEchoCharacter(char c)**
Sets the echo character. This character will be displayed instead of the characters entered by the user.

Toolkit

The `Toolkit` class serves as the link between the abstract methods of the AWT and the platform-specific native implementation of these methods. Generally, you will not have to interact with the `Toolkit`. However, it is occasionally convenient to use some of the `Toolkit` methods, such as `getImage()`. In such cases, you must employ the `getToolkit()` method in the `Component` class to obtain the current `Toolkit`. Note that the `getToolkit()` method returns the `Toolkit` of the `Frame` in which the component resides.

Methods

◆ **Toolkit( )**
Creates a new Toolkit.

◆ **protected abstract ButtonPeer createButton(Button target)**
Creates the specified `Button` and returns its peer.

◆ **protected abstract CanvasPeer createCanvas(Canvas target)**
Creates the specified `Canvas` and returns its peer.

◆ **abstract int checkImage(Image image, int width, int height, ImageObserver observer)**
Returns the status of the specified `image` whose status will be updated through the `imageUpdate()` method in the specified `ImageObserver`.

◆ **abstract CheckboxPeer createCheckbox(Checkbox target)**
  Creates the specified Checkbox and returns its peer.

◆ **abstract Image createImage(ImageProducer producer)**
  Returns an Image created from the information supplied by the ImageProducer.

◆ **protected abstract CheckboxMenuItemPeer createCheckboxMenuItem(CheckboxMenuItem target)**
  Creates the specified CheckboxMenuItem and returns its peer.

◆ **protected abstract ChoicePeer createChoice(Choice target)**
  Creates the specified Choice and returns its peer.

◆ **protected abstract DialogPeer createDialog(Dialog target)**
  Creates the specified Dialog and returns its peer.

◆ **protected abstract FileDialogPeer createFileDialog(FileDialog target)**
  Creates the specified FileDialog and returns its peer.

◆ **protected abstract FramePeer createFrame(Frame target)**
  Creates the specified Frame and returns its peer.

◆ **protected abstract LabelPeer createLabel(Label target)**
  Creates the specified Label and returns its peer.

◆ **protected abstract ListPeer createList(List target)**
  Creates the specified List and returns its peer.

◆ **protected abstract MenuPeer createMenu(Menu target)**
  Creates the specified Menu and returns its peer.

Java Quick Reference

- ◆ **protected abstract MenuBarPeer createMenuBar(MenuBar target)**
  Creates the specified `MenuBar` and returns its peer.

- ◆ **protected abstract MenuItemPeer createMenuItem(MenuItem target)**
  Creates the specified `MenuItem` and returns its peer.

- ◆ **protected abstract PanelPeer createPanel(Panel target)**
  Creates the specified `Panel` and returns its peer.

- ◆ **protected abstract ScrollbarPeer createScrollbar(Scrollbar target)**
  Creates the specified `Scrollbar` and returns its peer.

- ◆ **protected abstract TextAreaPeer createTextArea(TextArea target)**
  Creates the specified `TextArea` and returns its peer.

- ◆ **protected abstract TextFieldPeer createTextField(TextField target)**
  Creates the specified `TextField` and returns its peer.

- ◆ **protected abstract WindowPeer createWindow(Window target)**
  Creates the specified `Window` and returns its peer.

- ◆ **abstract ColorModel getColorModel( )**
  Returns the `ColorModel` used when displaying the screen.

- ◆ **static synchronized Toolkit getDefaultToolkit( )**
  Returns the standard `Toolkit` used in this implementation.

- ◆ **abstract String[ ] getFontList( )**
  Returns an array containing all possible fonts in this implementation.

◆ **abstract FontMetrics getFontMetrics(Font font)**
Returns the `FontMetrics` for the current font based on native information.

◆ **abstract Image getImage(URL url)**
Returns the specified `Image`.

◆ **abstract Image getImage(String filename)**
Returns the specified `Image`.

◆ **abstract int getScreenResolution( )**
Returns the resolution of the screen in dots per inch.

◆ **abstract Dimension getScreenSize( )**
Returns the size of the screen in pixels.

◆ **abstract boolean prepareImage(Image image, int width, int height, ImageObserver observer)**
Prepares the specified image to be displayed with the specified width and height. The `ImageObserver` will be notified of the success or failure of this method.

◆ **abstract void sync( )**
Synchronizes some graphical operations.

Window Extends Container

A `Window` is a simple container that serves as a pop-up window spawned from a `Frame`. Because the `Frame` class extends the `Window` class and builds upon it, you may want to use a `Frame` instead of a `Window`.

Methods

◆ **Window(Frame parent)**
Creates a `Window` belonging to the specified `parent`.

◆ **synchronized void addNotify( )**
Creates the `Window`'s peer.

◆ **synchronized void dispose( )**
Disposes the Window's peer.

◆ **Toolkit getToolkit( )**
Returns the Toolkit for the Window.

◆ **final String getWarningString( )**
Returns the string warning to be displayed to the user. In Netscape, this string is "Untrusted Java Window."

◆ **synchronized void pack( )**
Shrinks the Window to the smallest size that will still display all components.

◆ **synchronized void show( )**
Makes the Window visible.

◆ **void toBack( )**
Places the Window behind its parent Frame.

◆ **void toFront( )**
Places the Window in front of its parent Frame.

Interfaces

LayoutManager

The LayoutManager defines a behavior that is implemented by all layout managers.

Methods

◆ **void addLayoutComponent(String name, Component comp)**
Adds the specified Component to the layout. The name parameter can be used to supply the layout manager with information regarding the component. The use of this parameter is different for each manager.

- ◆ **void layoutContainer(Container parent)**
  Arranges the specified `Container`.

- ◆ **Dimension minimumLayoutSize(Container parent)**
  Returns the minimum size required by the specified `Container` based on its `Components`.

- ◆ **Dimension preferredLayoutSize(Container parent)**
  Returns the size requested by the specified `Container` based on its `Components`.

- ◆ **void removeLayoutComponent(Component comp)**
  Removes the specified `Component` from the layout.

MenuContainer

The `MenuContainer` interface is implemented by all containers that deal with menus.

Methods

- ◆ **Font getFont( )**
  Returns the `Font` used in displaying the `MenuContainer`.

- ◆ **boolean postEvent(Event evt)**
  Posts an event to the `MenuContainer`.

- ◆ **void remove(MenuComponent comp)**
  Removes the specified `Component` from the `MenuContainer`.

JAVA.AWT.IMAGE

CLASSES AND INTERFACES

JAVA.AWT.IMAGE

Although related to the java.awt package, this package consists of tools designed to handle images coming across a network. Because all classes and interfaces in this package are closely related, you will see that many of the methods appear multiple times.

Classes

Abstract ColorModel

This abstract class declares the functionality necessary for any `ColorModel`—a class that translates a color identifier (red, green, blue, or alpha) into the actual color to be displayed.

Field

▶ **protected int pixel_bits**
   The number of bits per pixel.

Methods

◆ **ColorModel(int bits)**
   Creates a new `ColorModel` with the specified number of bits per pixel.

◆ **abstract int getAlpha(int pixel)**
   Returns the alpha value of the specified pixel.

◆ **abstract int getBlue(int pixel)**
   Returns the blue value of the specified pixel.

◆ **abstract int getGreen(int pixel)**
   Returns the green value of the specified pixel.

◆ **int getPixelSize( )**
   Returns the number of bits per pixel for this `ColorModel`.

◆ **abstract int getRed(int pixel)**
Returns the red value of the specified pixel.

◆ **int getRGB(int pixel)**
Returns the color of the pixel in the default RGB
`ColorModel`.

◆ **static ColorModel getRGBdefault( )**
Returns the default `ColorModel` used in displaying pixels
defined by RGB values.

CropImageFilter Extends ImageFilter

The `CropImageFilter` class is an image filter that enables
you to create a new image based on a portion of another
image.

The image in the upper left-hand corner of the applet shown in
figure 16 was created by extracting a portion of the larger
image in the middle using the `CropImageFilter` class in
Listing 9. Although each image filter is different, the steps taken
here are the general steps to make use of *any* image filter.

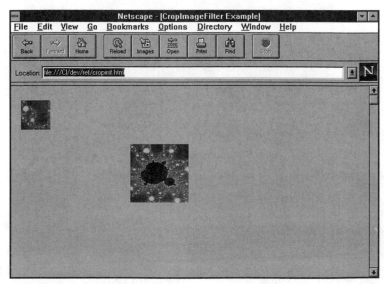

Fig. 16 The results of a `CropImageFilter`.

Listing 9   CropImageFilter Example

```
import java.applet.*;
import java.awt.*;
import java.awt.image.*;

public class CropImageFilterExample extends Applet {

    Image newimage, image;

    public void init() {

        image = getImage(getCodeBase(), "fract.jpg");
        ImageFilter filter = new CropImageFilter(0,0,50,50);
                                // set the properties for the filer

        /* The following statement creates an ImageProducer.
           producer will be able to produce a new image using
           the source of the old image and the specified filter*/

        ImageProducer producer = new
    FilteredImageSource(image.getSource(), filter);

        newimage = createImage(producer);
    }

    public void paint (Graphics g) {
        g.drawImage(newimage,10,10,50,50,this);
        g.drawImage(image,200,85,100,100,this);
    }
}
```

Methods

◆ **CropImageFilter(int x, int y, int w, int h)**
Creates a new `CropImageFilter`. The specified values do not pertain to a specific `Image`, but will be the values used when a filter is later employed to crop an `Image`.

◆ **void setDimensions(int width, int height)**
Sets the dimensions for the filter to be used when producing a cropped image.

◆ **void setPixels(int x, int y, int w, int h, ColorModel model, int pixels[ ], int offset, int scansize)**

A method used internally to create the desired Image.

◆ **void setPixels(int x, int y, int w, int h, ColorModel model, byte pixels[ ], int offset, int scansize)**

A method used internally to create the desired Image.

◆ **void setProperties(Hashtable props)**

Used to supply the ImageFilter.setProperties() method with information regarding the cropped region.

DirectColorModel Extends ColorModel

This class is used to translate machine-dependent pixel values into their alpha, red, green, and blue components.

Methods

◆ **DirectColorModel(int bits, int rmask, int gmask, int bmask)**

Creates a new DirectColorModel that will handle pixels with the specified number of bits. rmask, gmask, and bmask represent the location of the bits specifying the red, green, and blue components, respectively.

◆ **DirectColorModel(int bits, int rmask, int gmask, int bmask, int amask)**

Creates a new DirectColorModel that will handle pixels with the specified number of bits. rmask, gmask, bmask, and amask represent the location of the bits specifying the red, green, blue, and alpha components, respectively.

◆ **final int getAlpha(int pixel)**

Returns the alpha component of the specified pixel.

◆ **final int getAlphaMask( )**

Returns the alpha mask for the DirectColorModel.

◆ **final int getBlue(int pixel)**

Returns the blue component of the specified pixel.

◆ **final int getBlueMask( )**
Returns the blue mask for the `DirectColorModel`.

◆ **final int getGreen(int pixel)**
Returns the green component of the specified pixel.

◆ **final int getGreenMask( )**
Returns the green mask for the `DirectColorModel`.

◆ **final int getRed(int pixel)**
Returns the red component of the specified pixel.

◆ **final int getRedMask( )**
Returns the red mask for the `DirectColorModel`.

◆ **final int getRGB(int pixel)**
Obtains the color of the pixel according to the default RBG color model.

FilteredImageSource Extends Object Implements ImageProducer

A `FilterImageSource` enables you to pass the information that defines an image through a filter—somehow changing the appearance of the image. In most cases, the only method of this class that you will use is its constructor in conjunction with the `createImage()` method from the `java.awt.Component` class.

▶ *See Listing 9, "CropImageFilter Example," p. 122*

▶ *See Listing 10, "MyImageFilter Example," p. 126*

Methods

◆ **FilteredImageSource(ImageProducer source, ImageFilter filter)**
Creates a new `FilteredImageSource`. The information will be supplied by the `ImageProducer` and filtered by the specified `ImageFilter`.

◆ **synchronized void addConsumer(ImageConsumer ic)**
Adds a consumer to the objects retrieving information from this `ImageProducer`.

◆ **synchronized boolean isConsumer(ImageConsumer ic)**
Returns `true` if the specified `ImageConsumer` is a consumer of the information supplied by this `ImageProducer`.

◆ **void startProduction(ImageConsumer ic)**
Begins the process of delivering information to its consumers. The consumers notified include, but are not limited to, the specified `ImageConsumer`.

◆ **synchronized void removeConsumer(ImageConsumer ic)**
Removes the specified consumer from the list of objects obtaining information from this `ImageProducer`.

◆ **void requestTopDownLeftRightResend(ImageConsumer ic)**
Handles a request to send the pixels of the `Image` to the consumer in a top-down, left-right order.

ImageFilter Implements ImageConsumer, Cloneable

The `ImageFilter` class, as it is, does essentially nothing. It receives information from an `ImageProducer` and sends the same information on to an `ImageConsumer`. If you are simply loading and displaying images, you have no reason to explicitly use this class. However, the `ImageFilter` class also provides you with the framework on which you can build your own image filters: objects that will somehow transform the image after it is created by an `ImageProducer` and before it is received by an `ImageConsumer`.

To create your own image filter, you must extend the `ImageFilter` class and override at least one of its methods. The six methods that provide you with access to the image data are `setColorModel()`, `setDimensions()`, `setHints()`, `setPixels()` (two versions), `setProperties()`, and `imageComplete()`.

▶ *See Listing 9, "CropImageFilter Example," p. 122*

The two images in the applet shown in figure 17 were both created from the same source file. However, as you can see, the

Java Quick Reference

image in the upper left-hand corner has been transposed and shifted somewhat. This transformation was achieved with the code in Listing 10.

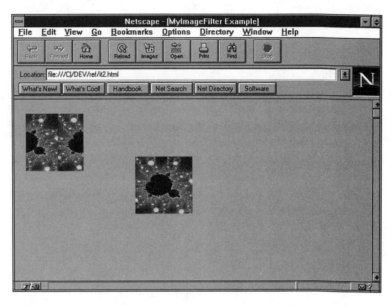

Fig. 17 Two images generated from one file.

Listing 10   MyImageFilter Example

```
import java.applet.*;
import java.awt.*;
import java.awt.image.*;

public class MyFilterExample extends Applet {

   Image newimage, image;

   public void init() {
      image = getImage(getCodeBase(), "fract.jpg");

      ImageFilter filter = new MyImageFilter(100);
      ImageProducer producer = new
➡FilteredImageSource(image.getSource(), filter);
```

```
      newimage = createImage(producer);
   }

   public void paint (Graphics g) {
      g.drawImage(newimage,10,10,100,100,this);
      g.drawImage(image,200,85,100,100,this);
   }
}


public class MyImageFilter extends ImageFilter {
   private int width ;
   private int shift;

   public MyImageFilter (int translation ) {
      shift = translation;
   }

   public void setDimensions(int width, int height) {
      consumer.setDimensions(width, height);
      this.width = width;
   }

/* This implementation of setPixels() shifts all columns
   over by the value of the shift field.  All columns that
   are pushed off the screen (to the left) are displayed on
   the right


  To do this, the method scrolls through each column on
     the screen.  If the column still fits once shifted, it is
     displayed in its new position.  If it is pushed off the
     screen, it is wrapped around relative to its original
     position.  */

   public void setPixels(int x, int y, int w, int h,
➥ColorModel model, byte pixels[], int off, int scansize) {
      for (int line = x; line < (x+w); line++) {
         if ( (line + shift) <= width)
            consumer.setPixels(line, y, 1, h, model, pixels,
➥off+shift, scansize);
```

Java Quick Reference

Listing 10   Continued

```
        else
            consumer.setPixels(line, y, 1, h, model, pixels,
    off -width + shift, scansize);
        }
    }


/* Shifts all columns over by the value of the shift field.
   All columns that are pushed off the screen (to the left)
   are displayed on the right */

    public void setPixels(int x, int y, int w, int h,
    ColorModel model, int pixels[], int off, int scansize) {
        for (int line = x; line < (x+w); line++) {
            if ( (line + shift) <= width)
                consumer.setPixels(line, y, 1, h, model, pixels,
    off+shift, scansize);
            else
                consumer.setPixels(line, y, 1, h, model, pixels,
    off -width + shift, scansize);
        }
    }
}
```

You will note that this image filter only uses three of the six available methods. In general, the most important method is the `setPixels()` method inasmuch as it assigns each pixel a location. All other methods may be useful, but are not as important as the `setPixels()` method.

Note   The shifting of pixels is the result of placing them in a different position in the array (`pixels[]`) that contains the image. As a rule, pixel (u,v) is stored in `pixels[ v * scansize + u + off]`. If you wanted to store (u,v) in (u,v), you could simply substitute the following statement in Listing 10:

```
consumer.setPixels(line, y, 1, h, model,
    pixels, off, scansize);
```

However, in this example you want to shift the pixels in the *x* direction. To advance each pixel to the left, use the following statement:

```
consumer.setPixels(line, y, 1, h, model,
➥pixels, off + shift, scansize);
```

Field

▶ **protected ImageConsumer consumer**

The `ImageConsumer` receiving information from this filter.

Methods

◆ **ImageFilter( )**

Creates a new `ImageFilter`.

◆ **Object clone( )**

Creates a copy of the `ImageFilter`.

◆ **ImageFilter getFilterInstance(ImageConsumer ic)**

Returns a copy of the `ImageFilter` that will provide information to the `ImageConsumer`.

◆ **void imageComplete(int status)**

Receives the information supplied by the `ImageProducer` before it is passed to the `ImageConsumer`. By default, this method simply passes the information along, but it may be overridden to do more.

◆ **void resendTopDownLeftRight(ImageProducer ip)**

Requests that the `ImageProducer` send the pixel information regarding the `Image` in a top-down, left-right order.

◆ **void setColorModel(ColorModel model)**

Receives the information supplied by the `setColorModel()` method of the `ImageConsumer` interface and provides you with an opportunity to make use of this information.

◆ **void setDimensions(int width, int height)**
Receives the information supplied by the
`setDimensions()` method in the `ImageConsumer`
interface.

◆ **void setHints(int hints)**
Receives the information supplied by the
`setDimensions()` method in the `ImageConsumer`
interface.

◆ **void setPixels(int x, int y, int width, int height,
ColorModel model, int pixels[ ], int offset, int scansize)**
Enables you to manipulate the pixels of the `Image`. This is
one of the more useful methods in this class.

◆ **void setPixels(int x, int y, int w, int h, ColorModel
model, byte pixels[ ], int offset, int scansize)**
Enables you to manipulate the pixels of the `Image`. This is
one of the more useful methods in this class.

◆ **void setProperties(Hashtable props)**
Adds information regarding the filter to the set of properties
before passing them along to the `ImageConsumer`.

IndexColorModel Extends ColorModel

This class enables you to create a lookup table for a set of
colors. The table will contain information regarding the individual components of the colors.

Methods

◆ **IndexColorModel(int bits, int size, byte r[ ], byte g[ ],
byte b[ ])**
Creates a new `IndexColorModel` with the specified
`size`. `bits` represents the number of bits per pixel representation. `r[]`, `g[]`, and `b[]` are the arrays of red, green,
and blue values.

◆ **IndexColorModel(int bits, int size, byte r[ ], byte g[ ], byte b[ ], int trans)**

Creates a new `IndexColorModel` with the specified `size`. `bits` represents the number of bits per pixel representation. `r[]`, `g[]`, and `b[]` are the arrays of red, green, and blue values. `trans` is the index in which the transparent color is stored.

◆ **IndexColorModel(int bits, int size, byte r[ ], byte g[ ], byte b[ ], byte a[ ])**

Creates a new `IndexColorModel` with the specified `size`. `bits` represents the number of bits per pixel representation. `r[]`, `g[]`, `b[]`, and `a[]` are the arrays of red, green, blue, and alpha values.

◆ **final int getAlpha(int index)**

Returns the alpha value for the pixel having the specified index.

◆ **final void getAlphas(byte a[ ])**

Returns the array of alpha values.

◆ **final int getBlue(int index)**

Returns the blue value for the pixel having the specified index.

◆ **final void getBlues(byte b[ ])**

Returns the array of blue values.

◆ **final int getGreen(int index)**

Returns the alpha value for the pixel having the specified index.

◆ **final void getGreens(byte g[ ])**

Returns the array of green values.

◆ **final int getMapSize( )**

Returns the number of values contained in each array.

◆ **final int getRed(int index)**
   Returns the red value for the pixel having the specified
   index.

◆ **final void getReds(byte r[ ])**
   Returns the array of red values.

◆ **final int getRGB(int index)**
   Returns an integer representation of the pixel value at the
   specified index based on the current RGB color model.

◆ **final int getTransparentPixel( )**
   Returns the index of the transparent pixel. Returns −1 if
   none is defined.

MemoryImageSource Implements ImageProducer

A `MemoryImageSource` enables you to create your own
images. After storing the "picture" in an array of either bytes or
integers, you are able to load the image from that array—not a
saved file.

Methods

◆ **MemoryImageSource(int w, int h, ColorModel cm, byte pix[ ], int offset, int scansize)**
   Creates a `MemoryImageSource` with the specified dimen-
   sions and `ColorModel`. `pix[]` is the source of the image.
   `offset` is the index at which the image begins. `scansize`
   is the number of bytes that each row occupies in the array.

◆ **MemoryImageSource(int w, int h, ColorModel cm, byte pix[ ], int offset, int scansize, Hashtable props)**
   Creates a `MemoryImageSource` with the specified dimen-
   sions and `ColorModel`. `pix[]` is the source of the image.
   `offset` is the index at which the image begins. `scansize`
   is the number of bytes that each row occupies in the array.
   `props` is a `Hashtable` of properties with which the image
   will be created.

◆ **MemoryImageSource(int w, int h, ColorModel cm, int pix[ ], int offset, int scan)**

Creates a MemoryImageSource with the specified dimensions and ColorModel. pix[] is the source of the image. offset is the index at which the image begins. scansize is the number of bytes that each row occupies in the array.

◆ **MemoryImageSource(int w, int h, ColorModel cm, int pix[ ], int offset, int scan, Hashtable props)**

Creates a MemoryImageSource with the specified dimensions and ColorModel. pix[] is the source of the image. offset is the index at which the image begins. scansize is the number of bytes that each row occupies in the array. props is a Hashtable of properties with which the image will be created.

◆ **MemoryImageSource(int w, int h, int pix[ ], int offset, int scan)**

Creates a MemoryImageSource with the specified dimensions of the default RGB color model. pix[] is the source of the image. offset is the index at which the image begins. scansize is the number of bytes that each row occupies in the array.

◆ **MemoryImageSource(int w, int h, int pix[ ], int offset, int scan, Hashtable props)**

Creates a MemoryImageSource with the specified dimensions of the default RGB color model. pix[] is the source of the image. offset is the index at which the image begins. scansize is the number of bytes that each row occupies in the array. props is a Hashtable of properties with which the image will be created.

◆ **synchronized void addConsumer(ImageConsumer ic)**

Adds a consumer to the list of objects retrieving information from this ImageProducer.

◆ **synchronized boolean isConsumer(ImageConsumer ic)**

Returns true if the ImageConsumer receives information from this ImageProducer.

JAVA.AWT.IMAGE

◆ **void startProduction(ImageConsumer ic)**
Begins the process of delivering information to its consumers. The consumers notified include, but are not limited to, the specified `ImageConsumer`.

◆ **synchronized void removeConsumer(ImageConsumer ic)**
Removes the specified consumer from the list of objects obtaining information from this `ImageProducer`.

◆ **void requestTopDownLeftRightResend(ImageConsumer ic)**
Handles a request to send the pixels of the `Image` to the consumer in a top-down, left-right order.

PixelGrabber Implements ImageConsumer

The `PixelGrabber` class is a special type of `ImageConsumer` designed to "grab" a rectangle of pixels belonging to an image. Note that you may grab pixels from either an `ImageProducer` or an already loaded image.

To grab a set of pixels, first create a pixel grabber, specifying what rectangle of pixels you want as well as the array in which you would like to store them. To actually grab the pixels, you must invoke the `grabPixels()` method.

Methods

◆ **PixelGrabber(Image img, int x, int y, int w, int h, int pix[ ], int offset, int scansize)**
Creates a new `PixelGrabber` object to capture the specified pixels from the `Image`. The pixels will be stored in the `pix[]` array, using the specified `offset` and `scansize`.

◆ **PixelGrabber(ImageProducer ip, int x, int y, int w, int h, int pix[ ], int offset, int scansize)**
Creates a new `PixelGrabber` object to capture the specified pixels from the `Image`. The pixels will be stored in the `pix[]` array, using the specified `offset` and `scansize`.

◆ **synchronized boolean grabPixels(long ms) throws InterruptedException**
Locks up the `PixelGrabber` object in requesting to grab the set of pixels. It returns when successful or after the specified number of milliseconds has expired.

◆ **boolean grabPixels( ) throws InterruptedException**
Requests the predetermined set of pixels from the image.

◆ **void setColorModel(ColorModel model)**
Required to implement the `ImageConsumer` interface. However, by default it does nothing.

◆ **void setDimensions(int width, int height)**
Required to implement the `ImageConsumer` interface. However, by default it does nothing.

◆ **void setHints(int hints)**
Required to implement the `ImageConsumer` interface. However, by default it does nothing.

◆ **void setPixels(int srcX, int srcY, int srcW, int srcH, ColorModel model, byte pixels[ ], int srcOff, int srcScan)**
The `PixelGrabber` class uses this method to place the desired pixels into the array specified in either the constructor method or the `setPixels()` method.

◆ **void setPixels(int srcX, int srcY, int srcW, int srcH, ColorModel model, int pixels[ ], int srcOff, int srcScan)**
The `PixelGrabber` class uses this method to place the desired pixels into the array specified in the constructor method.

◆ **void setProperties(Hashtable props)**
Required to implement the `ImageConsumer` interface. However, by default it does nothing.

◆ **synchronized int status( )**
Returns any flags produced in the lifetime of the `PixelGrabber`.

JAVA.AWT.IMAGE

◆ **synchronized void imageComplete(int status)**
Updates the internal `flags` field to reflect specified `status`. These flags may be returned via the `status()` method.

Abstract RGBImageFilter Extends ImageFilter

The `RGBImageFilter` class provides you with a very convenient way to manipulate the appearance of an image by changing the colors of individual pixels. To use the `RGBImageFilter` class, you must override the class, creating a new class and defining the `filterRGB()` method. This method can be used to adjust the display of the pixels by manipulating the individual color components, as shown in figure 18.

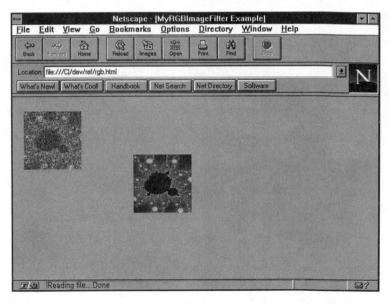

Fig. 18 Images created with `MyRGBImageFilter`.

What happened? As you can see, the appearance of the image in the upper left-hand corner of figure 18 has been changed. This was done with the code in Listing 11. (Note the resemblance to the `ImageFilter` example in fig. 17 and Listing 10.)

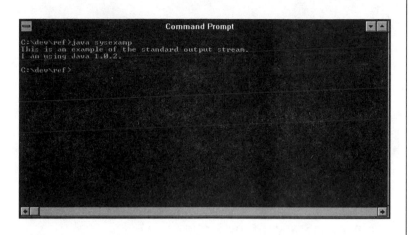

Fig. 22 The output of Listing 16.

Fields

▶ **static PrintStream err**
The standard stream for printing error messages. This is usually the same as out.

▶ **static InputStream in**
The standard input stream.

▶ **static PrintStream out**
The standard output stream. This is generally the prompt, or Java Console in Netscape.

Methods

◆ **static void arraycopy(Object src, int src_position, Object dst, int dst_posistion, int length)**
Copies length elements beginning at src[src_position] and places them in dst[dst_position].

◆ **static SecurityManager getSecurityManager( )**
Returns the security manager object for this context. This object can be handled via the SecurityManager interface.

◆ **static void setSecurityManager(SecurityManager s)**
Sets the security manager. This method can be invoked only once.

◆ **static void exit(int status)**
Causes the Virtual Machine to exit using the specified exit code.

◆ **static void gc( )**
Begins the garbage collection process. This does not cause immediate garbage collection.

◆ **static String getenv(String name)**
This method is no longer supported.

◆ **static Properties getProperties( )**
Returns a `Properties` object containing the properties of the system.

◆ **static String getProperty(String propName, String def)**
Returns the property specified by `propName`. If the property is undefined, the `String def` will be returned instead.

◆ **static String getProperty(String key)**
Returns the property specified by `propName`. If the property is not found, a null string will be returned instead.

◆ **static void load(String filename)**
Loads the specified library. `filename` represents the complete path and file name of the library.

◆ **static void loadLibrary(String libname)**
Loads the specified library. `libname` represents the library name.

◆ **static void runFinalization( )**
Runs the finalize( ) methods in any Objects pending garbage collection. The finalize( ) methods are automatically called before the Objects are collected. This method forces them all to be called at once.

◆ **static void setProperties(Properties props)**
Sets the system properties to the specified set of Properties.

Thread Implements Runnable

Threads are one of the most important topics in the Java language. Threads are individual processes that can run at the same time. By creating multiple threads, you are thus able to perform several tasks at once.

Threads are particularly useful in programs that deal with multiple sources of input. For example, you can create an applet that will accept input from both the user and a separate input stream, such as a networked socket. To do so, create the applet to deal with user input as you would normally, and then create a separate thread that reads and parses information from the stream.

Listing 17 and figure 23 demonstrate the use of a simple threaded class: Counter. While the threadex class is waiting for user input, the Counter class is counting in the background. Therefore, when the user presses the enter key, the value returned by the getCount( ) method has grown tremendously.

In particular, note the process used to create and begin the Counter class. To start execution of a thread, you must invoke the start( ) method. Furthermore, only the run( ) method of the threaded class has the ability to run concurrently.

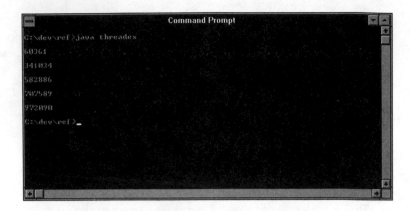

Fig. 23 The output of Listing 17.

▶ *See "Runnable," p. 245*

▶ *See "Runnable," p. 245*

Listing 17   Thread Example

```java
public class ThreadEx {

    public static void main(String argv[]) {
      Counter c = new Counter();
      c.start();                         // starts the counter

      for (int i = 1; i <= 5; i++) {
        try {
          System.in.read();
        }
        catch (Exception e) {
            System.out.println( e.toString() );
        }
        System.out.println(c.getCount() );
      } // end for loop

      c.stop();
      System.exit(1);
    }
}
```

```
class Counter extends Thread {
    private int count;

    public void run( ) {
      count = 0;
      while(true)          // creates a continual loop
        count++;
    }
    public int getCount( ) {
      return count;
    }
}
```

Fields

▶ final static int MAX_PRIORITY
The maximum priority of the Thread, which affects the amount of time that it receives to run.

▶ final static int MIN_PRIORITY
The minimum priority of the Thread, which affects the amount of time that it receives to run.

▶ final static int NORM_PRIORITY
The normal priority of the Thread, which affects the amount of time that it receives to run.

Methods

◆ Thread( )
Creates a new Thread.

◆ Thread(Runnable target)
Creates a new Thread that will use the run( ) method of the specified (target) class. This class must implement the Runnable interface.

◆ Thread(Runnable target, String name)
Creates a new Thread with the specified name that will use the run( ) method of the specified (target) class. This class must implement the Runnable interface.

◆ **Thread(ThreadGroup group, Runnable target)**
Creates a new `Thread` that will use the `run( )` method of the specified (`target`) class. This class must implement the `Runnable` interface. The new `Thread` will be placed in the specified thread group.

◆ **Thread(ThreadGroup group, Runnable target, String name)**
Creates a new `Thread` with the specified `name` that will use the `run( )` method of the specified (`target`) class. This class must implement the `Runnable` interface. The new `Thread` will be placed in the specified thread group.

◆ **Thread(ThreadGroup group, String name)**
Creates a new `Thread` with the specified name and places it in the specified thread group.

◆ **Thread(String name)**
Creates a new `Thread` with the specified name.

◆ **static int activeCount( )**
Returns the number of active threads in the current `ThreadGroup`.

◆ **void checkAccess( )**
Returns `true` if you are able to modify the `Thread`. Based on a value returned from the `SecurityManager`.

◆ **int countStackFrames( )**
Returns the number of stack frames in the thread.

◆ **static Thread currentThread( )**
Returns a reference to the executing `Thread` object.

◆ **void destroy( )**
Destroys the `Thread` without performing any cleanup.

◆ **static void dumpStack( )**

◆ **void setPixels(int x, int y, int width, int height, ColorModel model, int pixels[ ], int offset, int scansize)**
Passes the pixels through to the `ImageConsumer` after first filtering the pixels with the `filterRGB()` method.

◆ **void setPixels(int x, int y, int width, int height, ColorModel model, byte pixels[ ], int offset, int scansize)**
Passes the pixels through to the `ImageConsumer` after first filtering the pixels with the `filterRGB()` method.

◆ **abstract int filterRGB(int x, int y, int rgbpixel)**
This method is the most important method in the class. It must be overridden to create a functional `RGBColorModel`. To change the appearance of the specified `rgbpixel` that will be displayed at (x,y), create and return a new pixel value.

If x and y are equal to -1, the given pixel was obtained from an `IndexColorModel`.

Interfaces

ImageConsumer

The `ImageConsumer` interface defines a set of behaviors to be implemented by classes that will load ("consume") images. In addition to establishing the behavior of these classes, this class can also be used as a reference-type variable to refer to the following methods and fields that must be defined in *any* `ImageConsumer` class.

Fields

▶ **final static int COMPLETESCANLINES**
A hint value sent to `setHints()` to indicate that the pixels will be delivered in complete lines.

▶ **final static int IMAGEABORTED**
A status value sent to `imageComplete()` to indicate that the creation of the image was aborted.

▶ **final static int IMAGEERROR**
A status value sent to `imageComplete()` to indicate that the creation encountered an error.

▶ **final static int RANDOMPIXELORDER**
A value sent to `setHints()` to indicate that the pixels will be delivered in a random order.

▶ **final static int SINGLEFRAME**
A hint value sent to `setHints()` to indicate that the image contains a single frame.

▶ **final static int SINGLEFRAMEDONE**
A status value sent to `imageComplete()` to indicate that a frame of an image has been completely sent but more frames are yet to come.

▶ **final static int SINGLEPASS**
A value sent to `setHints()` to indicate that the image has been completely delivered.

▶ **final static int STATICIMAGEDONE**
A status value sent to `imageComplete()` to indicate that the entire image has been completely sent.

▶ **final static int TOPDOWNLEFTRIGHT**
A hint value sent to `setHints()` to indicate that the image will be delivered in a top-down, left-right manner.

Methods

◆ **abstract void imageComplete(int status)**
Called by the `ImageProducer` to indicate that the current image is complete. The `status` value will supply the `ImageConsumer` with more detailed information.

◆ **abstract void setColorModel(ColorModel model)**
Employed by the `ImageProducer` to set the default `ColorModel` for the pixels sent to this `ImageConsumer`.

◆ **abstract void setDimensions(int width, int height)**
   Employed by the `ImageProducer` to set the dimensions
   for the image being sent.

◆ **abstract void setHints(int hintflags)**
   Employed by the `ImageProducer` to inform
   `ImageConsumer` about various properties of the image
   about to be sent.

◆ **abstract void setPixels(int x, int y, int w, int h,
   ColorModel model, byte pixels[ ], int offset, int scansize)**
   Employed by the `ImageProducer` to set the pixel values.

◆ **abstract void setPixels(int x, int y, int w, int h,
   ColorModel model, int pixels[ ], int offset, int scansize)**
   Employed by the `ImageProducer` to set the pixel values.

ImageObserver

The `ImageObserver` interface defines a set of behaviors that
are implemented by classes that deal with images, and provides
for asynchronous updates of an `Image`. This is necessary
because not all information pertaining to an `Image` may be
available when it is first used. Specifying an `ImageObserver` in
such methods as `Graphics.drawImage()` will cause that
`Object` to receive updated information on the `Image` as it
arrives.

Fields

▶ **final static int ABORT**
   A value sent to `imageUpdate()` to denote that the
   loading of the image has been aborted.

▶ **final static int ALLBITS**
   A value sent to `imageUpdate()` to denote that a previously drawn image is now complete.

▶ **final static int ERROR**

A value sent to `imageUpdate()` to denote that an error has been encountered in the loading of the image.

▶ **final static int FRAMEBITS**

A value sent to `imageUpdate()` to denote that a complete frame of an image has been received.

▶ **final static int HEIGHT**

A value sent to `imageUpdate()` to denote that the height of the image cannot be obtained from the height parameter in the `imageUpdate()` method.

▶ **final static int PROPERTIES**

A value sent to `imageUpdate()` to denote that the properties of the image cannot be obtained from the parameters in the `imageUpdate()` method.

▶ **final static int SOMEBITS**

A value sent to `imageUpdate()` to denote that more pixels of the image are available.

▶ **final static int WIDTH**

A value sent to `imageUpdate()` to denote that the height of the image may not be obtained from the height parameter in the `imageUpdate()` method.

Method

◆ **abstract boolean imageUpdate(Image img, int infoflags, int x, int y, int width)**

This method is called when more information regarding an image being loaded becomes available. The `x`, `y`, `width`, and `height` values depend on the `infoflags` supplied. This method should return `true` if more updates are needed and `false` if all required information has been received.

ImageProducer

The `ImageProducer` class declares a set of behaviors common to any class that will produce an image, such as `FilteredImageSource` or `MemoryImageSource`.

▶ *See Listing 9, "CropImageFilter Example," p. 122*

▶ *See Listing 11, "MyRGBImageFilter Example," p. 137*

Methods

◆ **abstract void addConsumer(ImageConsumer ic)**
Records the specified `ImageConsumer` as one interested in the information supplied by this `ImageProducer`.

◆ **abstract boolean isConsumer(ImageConsumer ic)**
Returns `true` if the specified `ImageConsumer` is a registered consumer of this `ImageProducer` object.

◆ **abstract void removeConsumer(ImageConsumer ic)**
Removes the `ImageConsumer` from the list of consumers. This should be done once all necessary information has been received to prevent the consumer from receiving more copies of the information

◆ **abstract void requestTopDownLeftRightResend (ImageConsumer ic)**
Requests that the `ImageProducer` send the pixels in a top-down, left-right order.

◆ **abstract void startProduction(ImageConsumer ic)**
Adds the specified `ImageConsumer` to the list of consumers and sends pixel information to all registered consumers.

JAVA.AWT.IMAGE

JAVA.IO

CLASSES AND INTERFACES

 **JAVA.IO**

The java.io package serves as the standard input/output library for the Java language. Providing you with types as simple as a `StringBufferInputStream` or as complex as a `RandomAccessFile`, this package enables a virtually unlimited number of communication possibilities.

The java.io package is composed primarily of two types of classes: those that create streams and those that manage them. The following table is a summary showing where these classes fit into this model:

Stream Creators	Stream Managers
`ByteArrayInputStream`	`BufferedInputStream`
`ByteArrayOutputStream`	`BufferedOutputStream`
`FileInputStream`	`DataInputStream`
`FileOutputStream`	`DataOutputStream`
`PipedInputStream`	`FilterInputStream`
`PipedOutputStream`	`FilterOutputStream`
`StringBufferInputStream`	`LineNumberInputStream`
	`PrintStream`
	`PushbackInputStream`
	`RandomAccessFile`
	`SequenceInputStream`
	`StreamTokenizer`
	`StringBufferInputStream`

In general, a stream manager may be created using the syntax:

```
StreamManagerType    instanceofManager    = new
➥StreamManagerType(  StreamCreatorType);
```

where `StreamManagerType` and `StreamCreatorType` are both the names of classes.

Classes

BufferedInputStream Extends FilterInputStream

The buffered stream classes provide you with a more efficient way of reading information from an InputStream. Instead of allowing information to pile up on the stream and wait for you to read it, the BufferedInputStream will read in all data on the stream and place it in a buffer every time you invoke one of the read ( ) methods. Therefore, subsequent information may come from the buffer, not the stream—saving you time.

The BufferedInputStream will continue to read from the buffer until it becomes empty. If you attempt to read from an empty buffer, the BufferedInputStream will block it until there is sufficient data from the stream to satisfy your request. Any additional data waiting in the stream will be stored in the buffer.

Fields

▶ **protected byte buf[ ]**

The buffer in which the data is stored.

▶ **protected int count**

The number of bytes in the buffer.

▶ **protected int marklimit**

The limit on the number of bytes that you can advance before the BufferedInputStream looses track of your mark.

▶ **protected int markpos**

The marked position.

▶ **protected int pos**

The current position in the buffer.

Methods

◆ **BufferedInputStream(InputStream in)**
Creates a new `BufferedInputStream` based on the
specified `InputStream`.

◆ **BufferedInputStream(InputStream in, int size)**
Creates a new `BufferedInputStream` based on the
specified `InputStream`, specifying the buffer size.

◆ **synchronized int available( ) throws IOException**
Returns the number of available bytes that can be currently
read. This value will include both the number of unread
bytes in the buffer and the number of available bytes in the
`InputStream`.

◆ **synchronized void mark(int readlimit)**
Marks the current position in the stream. By calling the
`reset( )` method, you will be able to return to this spot
and read the same byte again. `readlimit` sets a boundary
on the number of bytes that may be read before you call
`reset( )`. Although larger values for `readlimit` give you
more flexibility, they also cause the storage buffer to grow
quite large.

◆ **boolean markSupported( )**
Because this is a `FilterInputStream`, this method
returns a `boolean` indicating whether or not this class
supports marks. For this class, this method simply returns
`true`.

◆ **synchronized int read(byte b[ ], int offset, int len)
throws IOException**
In addition to filling the storage buffer, this method places
the number of bytes specified by the `len` parameter in the
`b[ ]` array, beginning at the `offset` index.

◆ **synchronized int read( ) throws IOException**
Reads a byte of data.

◆ **synchronized void reset( ) throws IOException**
Returns to the last marked position, enabling you to read from this point on. Note that you lose your current position in the stream. If you have exceeded the `marklimit` (specified in `mark( )`) or if no mark has been specified, then an `IOException` will be thrown.

◆ **synchronized long skip(long num) throws IOException**
Skips the specified number of bytes in the stream.

BufferedOutputStream Extends FilterOutputStream

A `BufferedOutputStream` is an `OutputStream` manager that enables you to write to the stream in a more efficient manner. Instead of writing to the stream in small pieces every time you invoke a `write( )` method, a `BufferedOutputStream` will write your information to a temporary buffer. This information is then written to the stream either when the buffer becomes filled or when you invoke the `flush( )` method.

> **Caution** Make sure that you invoke the `flush( )` method before closing the `OutputStream`! If you fail to do so, some of your information may be caught in limbo—left in the buffer and never sent.

Fields

▶ **protected byte buf[ ]**
The temporary storage buffer.

▶ **protected int count**
The number of bytes currently in the buffer.

Methods

◆ **BufferedOutputStream(OutputStream out)**
Creates a new `BufferedOutputStream` that will use the specified `OutputStream`.

◆ **BufferedOutputStream(OutputStream out, int size)**
Creates a new `BufferedOutputStream` that will use the specified `OutputStream`. `size` specifies the size of the buffer array.

◆ **synchronized void flush( ) throws IOException**
Flushes the buffer, writing all bytes in the buffer to the `OutputStream`.

◆ **synchronized void write(byte b[ ], int offset, int len) throws IOException**
Writes the specified bytes to the buffer. The information written will begin at `b[offset]` and contain `len` bytes. If the buffer cannot contain the specified number of bytes, then both the buffer and the specified bytes will be written to the `OutputStream`.

◆ **synchronized void write(int b) throws IOException**
Writes the byte to the buffer. If the buffer has no room, the buffer will first be written to the stream. The specified byte will then be placed in the buffer.

ByteArrayInputStream Extends InputStream

A `ByteArrayInputStream` is a type of `InputStream` and thus can be handled like any other `InputStream`. However, a `ByteArrayInputStream` does not receive its information from a standard stream, but rather from an array that you have already created.

When you create a `ByteArrayInputStream`, you must specify the contents of the buffer that you want to use. This `InputStream` will then read from this buffer when read commands are invoked.

Fields
▶ **protected byte buf[ ]**
The buffer from which the information will be read. Note that this is not a copy of the array specified in the

constructor, but rather a reference (much like a C pointer) to the specified array.

❱ **protected int count**
The maximum number of bytes that should be read from the buffer.

❱ **protected int pos**
The current position in the buffer.

Methods

◆ **ByteArrayInputStream(byte buf[ ])**
Creates a new `ByteArrayInputStream` that will read from the specified buffer. The current position (`pos`) is set to 0, and the maximum number of bytes to be read is set to the length of the array.

◆ **ByteArrayInputStream(byte buf[ ], int offset, int length)**
Creates a new `ByteArrayInputStream` that will read from the specified buffer. The `pos` and `count` are set to the specified values.

◆ **synchronized int available( )**
Returns the number of available bytes to be read. This is equal to the total number of bytes minus the current position (`count-pos`).

◆ **synchronized int read(byte b[ ], int offset, int len)**
Reads up to `len` bytes from the array input stream, placing the read bytes in the `b [ ]` buffer beginning at the `offset` index.

◆ **synchronized int read( )**
Reads one byte from the buffer.

◆ **synchronized void reset( )**
Sets the current position to the beginning of the input buffer.

JAVA.IO

◆ **synchronized long skip(long num)**
Skips the specified number of bytes in the buffer.

ByteArrayOutputStream Extends OutputStream

A `ByteArrayOuputStream` is a special `OutputStream` that can be used to accumulate data. Instead of writing directly to a stream, the `ByteArrayOutputStream` will write to a temporary buffer that will grow as needed to accommodate your data.

After you have written your data to the buffer, you can

- Write the entire buffer to an `OutputStream` using the `writeTo( )` method;
- Retrieve all information in the buffer, storing it in a new array with the `toByteArray( )` method;
- Convert the buffer to a string using the `toString( )` method.

Fields

▶ **protected byte buf[ ]**
The temporary buffer used to store the data.

▶ **protected int count**
The number of bytes in the buffer.

Methods

◆ **ByteArrayOutputStream( )**
Creates a new `ByteArrayOutputStream` with a capacity of 32 bytes.

◆ **ByteArrayOutputStream(int size)**
Creates a new `ByteArrayOutputStream` with the specified capacity.

◆ **synchronized byte[ ] toByteArray( )**
Returns a copy of the buffer.

◆ **synchronized void reset( )**
◆ **int size( )**
Returns the number of bytes stored in the buffer.

◆ **String toString( )**
Returns the buffer as a string. (This is the same as using the following method with a `hibyte` value of 0.)

◆ **String toString(int hibyte)**
Returns the buffer as a string, setting the first eight bits of each character to `hibyte`.

◆ **synchronized void write(int b)**
Writes the specified byte to the temporary buffer, increasing its size if necessary.

◆ **synchronized void write(byte b[ ], int offset, int len)**
Writes the specified byte array to the temporary buffer, increasing its size if necessary.

◆ **synchronized void writeTo(OutputStream out) throws IOException**
Writes the entire buffer to the specified `OutputStream`.

DataInputStream Extends FilterInputStream Implements DataInput

A `DataInputStream` enables you to read basic data types from a stream. For example, instead of reading a string from a stream byte by byte, you may use the `readLine( )`, which will read until a newline character is encountered.

▶ *See "DataOutputStream Extends FilterOutputStream Implements DataOutput," p. 155*

Methods

◆ **DataInputStream(InputStream in)**
Creates a new `DataInputStream` to handle the specified `InputStream`.

JAVA.IO

◆ **final int read(byte b[ ], int offset, int len) throws IOException**
Reads `len` bytes from the stream, storing them in the b [ ] buffer beginning at b [offset].

◆ **final int read(byte b[ ]) throws IOException**
Reads data from the stream into the specified buffer, returning the number of bytes read.

◆ **final boolean readBoolean( ) throws IOException**
Reads the next byte from the stream assuming that it represents a `boolean` value.

◆ **final byte readByte( ) throws IOException**
Reads and returns a single byte from the stream.

◆ **final char readChar( ) throws IOException**
Reads and returns a character from the stream by combining the next two bytes to produce a 16-bit `char`.

◆ **final double readDouble( ) throws IOException**
Reads and returns a `double` value from the stream by combining the next eight bytes to produce a 64-bit `double`.

◆ **final float readFloat( ) throws IOException**
Reads and returns a `float` from the stream by combining the next four bytes to produce a 32-bit `char`.

◆ **final void readFully(byte b[ ], int offset, int len) throws IOException**
Reads from the stream, and does not return until the entire range (`offset` to `len`) in the buffer has been filled with new data.

◆ **final void readFully(byte b[ ]) throws IOException**
Reads from the stream and does not return until the entire buffer has been filled.

◆ **final int readInt( ) throws IOException**
Reads and returns a integer from the stream by combining the next four bytes to produce a 32-bit `int`.

◆ **final String readLine( ) throws IOException**
Reads a series of characters until encountering \n, \r, \r\n or EOF. Returns this complete string afterwards.

◆ **final long readLong( ) throws IOException**
Reads and returns a `long` from the stream by combining the next eight bytes to produce a 64-bit `char`.

◆ **final short readShort( ) throws IOException**
Reads and returns a short from the stream by combining the next four bytes to produce a 32-bit short.

◆ **final int readUnsignedByte( ) throws IOException**
Reads and returns a byte from the stream.

◆ **final int readUnsignedShort( ) throws IOException**
Reads and returns a unsigned short from the stream by combining the next two bytes to produce a 16-bit `char`.

◆ **final String readUTF( ) throws IOException**
Reads and returns a UTF string from the stream.

◆ **final static String readUTF(DataInput in) throws IOException**
Reads and returns a UTF string from the specified `DataInput`.

◆ **final int skipBytes(int num) throws IOException**
Skips the specified number of bytes.

DataOutputStream Extends FilterOutputStream Implements DataOutput

The counterpart of the `DataInputStream` class, the `DataOutputStream` class enables you to write data to a stream in the form of basic data types, such as characters or doubles rather than a series of bytes.

▶ *See "DataInputStream Extends FilterInputStream Implements DataInput," p. 153*

JAVA.IO

Field

▶ **protected int written**
   The number of bytes written to the stream.

Methods

◆ **DataOutputStream(OutputStream out)**
   Creates a new DataOutputStream to handle the specified
   OutputStream.

◆ **void flush( ) throws IOException**
   Flushes the stream. This only produces an action if the
   stream has been buffering output.

◆ **final int size( )**
   Returns the number of bytes written thus far to the
   stream—the written field.

◆ **synchronized void write(byte b[ ], int offset, int len)**
   throws IOException
   Writes the number of bytes specified by len to the stream.
   These bytes will be drawn from the specified array starting at
   the offset index.

◆ **synchronized void write(int b) throws IOException**
   Writes the byte to the stream.

◆ **final void writeBoolean(boolean v) throws IOException**
   Writes the boolean to the stream.

◆ **final void writeByte(int v) throws IOException**
   Writes the boolean to the stream—calls write( ).

◆ **final void writeBytes(String s) throws IOException**
   Writes the string as a series of bytes.

◆ **final void writeChar(int v) throws IOException**
   Writes the character to the stream.

◆ **final void writeChars(String s) throws IOException**
  Writes the string to the stream as a series of characters.

◆ **final void writeDouble(double v) throws IOException**
  Writes the `double` to the stream.

◆ **final void writeFloat(float v) throws IOException**
  Writes the `float` to the stream.

◆ **final void writeInt(int v) throws IOException**
  Writes the `int` value to the stream.

◆ **final void writeLong(long v) throws IOException**
  Writes the `long` to the stream.

◆ **final void writeShort(int v) throws IOException**
  Writes the short to the stream.

◆ **final void writeUTF(String str) throws IOException**
  Writes the string to the stream in UTF format.

File

The `File` class provides you with a means of performing basic
file management operations. Although it does not provide you
with direct access to the information contained in the files, it
does enable you to perform "housekeeping" operations, such
as making directories, finding the length of a file, or comparing
the versions of two separate files. Because of the nature of its
operations, this class relies heavily on native methods.

▶ *See "DataInputStream Extends FilterInputStream Implements
  DataInput," p. 153*

▶ *See "DataOutputStream Extends FilterOutputStream Implements DataOutput," p. 155*

▶ *See "FileDialog Extends Dialog," p. 51*

JAVA.IO

Caution Although Java per se has no problems with the
functionality in the class, many of the tasks performed by
the methods in this class raise several security concerns.

Java Quick Reference

> Therefore, while your code compiles, you may not be able to
> perform many of these tasks if you are running your code as
> an Applet in either the appletviewer or Netscape.

Fields

▶ **final static String pathSeparator**
The system dependent path separator (";" for Windows-
based machines).

▶ **final static char pathSeparatorChar**
The system dependent path separator as a character.

▶ **final static String separator**
The system dependent file separator ("\" for Windows-
based machines).

▶ **final static char separatorChar**
The system dependent file separator as a single character.

Methods

◆ **File(String path)**
Creates a new File object based on the file at the specified
path.

◆ **File(File dir, String name)**
Creates a new File object based on the file in the given
directory having the specified name. The directory will be
specified through another File object.

◆ **File(String path, String name)**
Creates a new File object based on the file in the given
directory with the specified name.

◆ **boolean canRead( )**
Returns true if the program can read from the given file.

◆ **boolean canWrite( )**
Returns true if the program can write to the given file.

◆ **boolean delete( )**
Deletes the file. It returns `true` if successful.

◆ **boolean equals(Object anotherObject)**
Compares the `File` object to another object. It returns `true` if the other object is a `File` having the same path.

◆ **boolean exists( )**
Returns `true` if the file exists.

◆ **String getAbsolutePath( )**
Returns the absolute path of the file.

◆ **String getName( )**
Returns the name of the file—the string following the last separator character in the path string.

◆ **String getParent( )**
Returns the name of the parent directory—everything but the file name.

◆ **String getPath( )**
Returns the entire path string consisting of the parent directory and the file name.

◆ **int hashCode( )**
Returns the `hashcode` for this `File` object. This value is based on the path string.

◆ **boolean isAbsolute( )**
Returns `true` if the path is absolute.

◆ **boolean isDirectory( )**
Returns `true` if a directory file exists.

◆ **boolean isFile( )**
Returns `true` if a file exists at the path.

◆ **long lastModified( )**
Returns the time last modified. The returned value has no meaning and should only be used when comparing two files.

◆ **long length( )**
Returns the length of the file.

◆ **String[ ] list( )**
Returns an array of the names of the files in the current path.

◆ **String[ ] list(FilenameFilter filter)**
Returns an array of the names of the files in the current path that meet the filter requirements.

◆ **boolean mkdir( )**
Creates the current directory. It returns `true` if successful.

◆ **boolean mkdirs( )**
Creates the current directory path. It returns `true` if successful.

◆ **boolean renameTo(File newName)**
Renames the current file.

◆ **String toString( )**
Returns the path of the file.

FileDescriptor

The `FileDescriptor` class is used internally by Java classes that deal with files. This class encapsulates the machine-based view of a file—describing each file as an integer. Uses of the `FileDescriptor` object, therefore, can be found in the `FileInputStream` and `FileOutputStream`. Due to the nature of the class, all fields and method are based on native properties.

Fields

▌ **final static FileDescriptor err**
A descriptor for the standard error output file.

▌ **final static FileDescriptor in**
A descriptor for the standard input file.

▌ **final static FileDescriptor out**
A descriptor for the standard output file.

Methods

◆ **FileDescriptor( )**
Creates a new `FileDescriptor`.

◆ **boolean valid( )**
Returns `true` if the `FileDescriptor` is valid.

FileInputStream Extends InputStream

A `FileInputStream`, as its name implies, is a specialized `InputStream` designed to obtain input from a file. In contrast to a standard `InputStream`, a `FileInputStream` does nothing more—save the capability to direct the input stream to a file.

Due to this limited capacity, `FileInputStream`s are generally managed with more robust input stream managers, such as `DataInputStream`. A `DataInputStream` can be created from a `FileInputStream` simply by specifying the `FileInputStream` as the parameter in the `DataInputStream` constructor.

▶ *See "DataInputStream Extends FilterInputStream Implements DataInput," p. 153*

Methods

◆ **FileInputStream(File file) throws FileNotFoundException**
Creates a `FileInputStream` that reads from the physical file managed by the specified `File` object.

JAVA.IO

Java Quick Reference

◆ **FileInputStream(String name) throws FileNotFoundException**
Creates a `FileInputStream` that reads from the file with the specified name.

◆ **FileInputStream(FileDescriptor descriptorObject)**
Creates a `FileInputStream` that reads from the file referred to by the specified `FileDescriptor`.

◆ **int available( ) throws IOException**
Returns the number of available bytes.

◆ **void close( ) throws IOException**
Closes the file.

◆ **protected void finalize( ) throws IOException**
Automatically called before the `FileInputStream` is destroyed. It closes the file.

◆ **final FileDescriptor getFD( ) throws IOException**
Returns the file descriptor for the file from which the `FileInputStream` is reading.

◆ **int read( ) throws IOException**
Reads and returns a single byte from the stream. It returns –1 if the end of the file is reached.

◆ **int read(byte b[ ]) throws IOException**
Reads into the specified array. It returns the number of bytes read or –1 if the end of the file is reached.

◆ **int read(byte b[ ], int offset, int len) throws IOException**
Reads at most `len` bytes into the specified buffer beginning at the `offset` index. It returns the number of bytes read or –1 if the end of the file is reached.

◆ **long skip(long num) throws IOException**
Skips the specified number of bytes in the stream.

FileOutputStream Extends OutputStream

A `FileOutputStream` is a simple extension of the `OutputStream` class than enables you to write data to a file. Like `FileInputStream`, `FileOutputStreams` are generally managed with a more robust stream manager, such as `DataOutputStream`.

▶ See "DataOutputStream Extends FilterOutputStream Implements DataOutput," p. 155

Methods

◆ **FileOutputStream(String name) throws IOException**
Creates a `FileOutputStream` that writes to the file with the specified name.

◆ **FileOutputStream(FileDescriptor fdObj)**
Creates a `FileOutputStream` that writes to the file referred to by the specified `FileDescriptor`.

◆ **FileOutputStream(File file) throws IOException**
Creates a `FileOutputStream` that writes to the physical file managed by the specified `File` object.

◆ **void close( ) throws IOException**
Closes the file.

◆ **protected void finalize( ) throws IOException**
This method is called just before the `FileOutputStream` is destroyed. It closes the file.

◆ **final FileDescriptor getFD( ) throws IOException**
Returns the `FileDescriptor` object for the output file.

◆ **void write(int b) throws IOException**
Writes a single byte.

JAVA.IO

◆ **void write(byte b[ ]) throws IOException**
   Write all bytes in the buffer.

◆ **void write(byte b[ ], int offset, int len) throws IOException**
   Writes `len` bytes from the specified array beginning at the `offset` index.

FilterInputStream Extends InputStream

A `FilterInputStream` is a non-abstract version of `InputStream`. It may be used to handle any input stream in a basic, yet useful, manner. Unfortunately, a `FilterInputStream` requires you to read your information as a series of bytes—complicating matters if you are reading more complex data types, such as `doubles` or even `Strings`. Therefore, `FilterInputStreams` are usually managed with more powerful stream managers, such as `DataInputStream`. `FilterInputStream` is also the basis for all other `InputStream` managers, such as `DataInputStream` and `PushBackInputStream`.

> **How does FilterInputStream Differ from InputStream?**
> Why can you create an instance of a `FilterInputStream`, but not an `InputStream`? You cannot create an instance of an `InputStream` because it is abstract—its `read( )` method is not defined. However, when creating a `FilterInputStream`, you must specify an `InputStream` that you want to manage, such as `FileInputStream` or `ByteArrayInputStream`. Because these classes have defined `read( )` methods, the `FilterInputStream` manager employs the methods of the `InputStream` class in accomplishing its tasks.

Field
▶ **protected InputStream in**
   The `InputStream` that will be read from.

Methods

◆ **FilterInputStream(InputStream in)**
Creates a `FilterInputStream` to manage the specified `InputStream`.

◆ **int available( ) throws IOException**
Returns the number of bytes available on the stream.

◆ **void close( ) throws IOException**
Closes the stream and calls the `close( )` method in the managed `InputStream`.

◆ **synchronized void mark(int readlimit)**
Places a mark at the current position in the `InputStream`. By invoking the `reset( )` method, you can return to the current position in the stream. `readlimit` specifies the number of bytes that can be read beyond the marked position before the mark is lost.

◆ **boolean markSupported( )**
Returns `true` if the current `InputStream` supports marking.

◆ **int read( ) throws IOException**
Reads and returns a single byte from the stream. It returns – 1 if the end of the file is reached.

◆ **int read(byte b[ ]) throws IOException**
Reads into the specified array. It returns the number of bytes read or −1 if the end of the file is reached.

◆ **int read(byte b[ ], int offset, int len) throws IOException**
Reads at most `len` bytes into the specified buffer beginning at the `offset` index. It returns the number of bytes read or −1 if the end of the file is reached.

◆ **synchronized void reset( ) throws IOException**
Returns to the marked position in the stream.

◆ **long skip(long num) throws IOException**
Skips the specified number of bytes in the stream.

FilterOutputStream Extends OutputStream

The FilterOutputStream class provides you with a simple but effective manner of managing OutputStreams. This class is the basis for all other classes designed to manage OutputStreams, such as BufferedOutputStream and DataOutputStream.

▶ *See "FilterInputStream Extends InputStream," p. 164*

Field
▌ **protected OutputStream out**
The OutputStream that is being managed.

Methods
◆ **FilterOutputStream(OutputStream out)**
Creates a new FilterOutputStream to manage the specified OutputStream.

◆ **void close( ) throws IOException**
Closes the OutputStream.

◆ **void flush( ) throws IOException**
Flushes any buffered information to the stream. This only produces a result in those OutputStreams that buffer information before writing it to the stream.

◆ **void write(int b) throws IOException**
Writes a single byte.

◆ **void write(byte b[ ]) throws IOException**
Write all bytes in the buffer.

◆ **void write(byte b[ ], int offset, int len) throws IOException**

Writes `len` bytes from the specified array beginning at the `offset` index.

Abstract InputStream

The `InputStream` class is a basic class for handling input across a stream. While it serves as the basis for all input stream classes, it is nevertheless abstract—which means that you cannot create an instance of an `InputStream`. However, because all input stream classes derive from the `InputStream` class, you can handle all `InputStreams` by using the methods found in the `InputStream` class.

You will see that the input stream handlers (such as `DataInputStream`) accept an `InputStream` as a parameter. Although it is impossible to supply these handlers with a pure `InputStream`, the stream that you do pass to a handler will be derived from the `InputStream` class and thus may be treated as a type of `InputStream`.

Methods

◆ **InputStream( )**

Creates a new `InputStream`.

◆ **int available( ) throws IOException**

Returns the number of bytes available on the stream.

◆ **void close( ) throws IOException**

Closes the stream. It calls the `close( )` method in the managed `InputStream`.

◆ **synchronized void mark(int readlimit)**

Places a mark at the current position in the `InputStream`. By invoking the `reset( )` method, you may return to the current position in the stream. `readlimit` specifies the number of bytes that may be read beyond the marked position before the mark is lost.

JAVA.IO

◆ **boolean markSupported( )**
Returns `true` if the current `InputStream` supports marking.

◆ **int read( ) throws IOException**
Reads and returns a single byte from the stream. It returns −1 if the end of the file is reached.

◆ **int read(byte b[ ]) throws IOException**
Reads into the specified array. It returns the number of bytes read or −1 if the end of the file is reached.

◆ **int read(byte b[ ], int offset, int len) throws IOException**
Reads at most `len` bytes into the specified buffer beginning at the `offset` index. It returns the number of bytes read or −1 if the end of the file is reached.

◆ **synchronized void reset( ) throws IOException**
Returns to the marked position in the stream.

◆ **long skip(long num) throws IOException**
Skips the specified number of bytes in the stream.

LineNumberInputStream Extends FilterInputStream

A `LineNumberInputStream` is an input stream manager. Slightly elaborating upon the `FilterInputStream`, it enables you not only to read information from the stream, but also to keep track of the number of lines that you have read from this stream.

Methods

◆ **LineNumberInputStream(InputStream in)**
Creates a new `LineNumberInputStream` to manage the specified `InputStream`.

◆ **int available( ) throws IOException**
Returns the number of available bytes.

◆ **int getLineNumber( )**
Returns the current line number.

◆ **void mark(int readlimit)**
Places a mark at the current position in the `InputStream`.
By invoking the `reset ( )` method, you can return to the
current position in the stream. `readlimit` specifies the
number of bytes that may be read beyond the marked
position before the mark is lost.

◆ **int read( ) throws IOException**
Reads and returns a byte from the stream.

◆ **int read(byte b[ ], int offset, int len) throws IOException**
Reads `len` bytes to the array beginning at the `offset`
index. It returns the number of bytes read.

◆ **void reset( ) throws IOException**
Returns to the marked position in the stream.

◆ **void setLineNumber(int lineNumber)**
Sets the current line number to the specified value.

◆ **long skip(long num) throws IOException**
Skips the specified number of bytes. It returns the number of
bytes actually skipped.

Abstract OutputStream

The `OutputStream` class is an abstract class that establishes
the foundation for all types of `OutputStream` classes. Although you cannot create an instance of an `OutputStream`—
because all output streams are based on this class—it provides
you with a convenient means of handling all types of output
streams.

Methods
◆ **OutputStream( )**
Creates a new `OutputStream`.

◆ **void close( ) throws IOException**
Closes the OutputStream.

◆ **void flush( ) throws IOException**
In subclasses, this method may be used to write any buffered bytes to the stream. However, in this class, the method
is empty.

◆ **abstract void write(int b) throws IOException**
Writes a single byte. This is the *essence* of the class that
must be overridden by any non-abstract subclasses.

◆ **void write(byte b[ ]) throws IOException**
Writes the array to the stream.

◆ **void write(byte b[ ], int offset, int len) throws
IOException**
Writes len bytes from the array beginning at the offset
index.

PipedInputStream Extends
InputStream

The PipedInputStream class works in conjunction with the
PipedOutputStream class. By connecting a
PipedInputStream to a PipedOutputStream, you are
able to create two separate threads—each running independently—with the capability to send information to each other in
an extremely convenient manner.

▶ *See "PipedOutputStream Extends OutputStream," p. 174*

The output shown in figure 19 was produced by linking instances of the PipedInputStream and
PipedOutputStream classes—each being managed by a
separate thread (see Listing 12). Due to the idiosyncrasies of
thread management, the sleep ( ) statement in the Writer
class is necessary to shift control to the Reader class. Without
the sleep ( ) statement, the Reader class would first write all
of its data, relinquish control to the Reader class, and then
allow it to read in all the data.

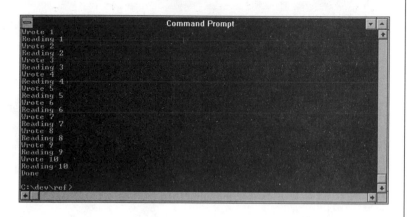

Fig. 19 The output of Listing 12.

Also note that in this example, I use the error handling of the
Reader class to exit the program. Once the Writer class
completes its task, the output pipe is shut down. This causes an
exception in the Reader class—terminating the entire program.

**Listing 12   An Example of PipedInputStream and
PipedOutputStream**

```
class Reader extends Thread {

    PipedInputStream in;
    boolean running;

    Reader(PipedOutputStream out) {
      try {
        in = new PipedInputStream(out);
        running = true;
      }
      catch (Exception e)
        System.out.println(e.toString() );
    }

    PipedInputStream getStream() {
      return (in);
    }
```

JAVA.IO

Java Quick Reference

Listing 12   Continued

```java
    public void run( ) {
      while (running) {
        try {
          System.out.println("Reading " +in.read( ));
        }
        catch(Exception e) {
          System.out.println("Done");
          System.exit(1);
        }
      }
    }
}


class Writer extends Thread {
    public PipedOutputStream out;
    boolean running;

    Writer( ) {
      out = new PipedOutputStream( );
      running = true;
    }

    PipedOutputStream getStream( ) {
      return (out);
    }

    void connectTo(PipedInputStream in) {
      try {
        out.connect(in);
      }
      catch (Exception e) {
        System.out.println(e.toString( ) );
        running = false;
      }
    }

    public void run( ) {
```

```
    try {
      for (int i = 1; i <= 10; i++)      {
        out.write(i);
        System.out.println("Wrote " + i + " ");
        yield();
        sleep(2000);
        }
    catch(Exception e) {
      System.out.println(e.toString() );
      }
    }
}


public class PipedExample {
    public static void main(String args[]) {
      Writer w = new Writer();
      Reader r = new Reader( w.getStream() );
      w.connectTo( r.getStream() );
      r.start();
      w.start();
    }
}
```

Methods

◆ PipedInputStream( )

Creates a `PipedInputStream`. This stream must be connected to a `PipedOutputStream` before it can be used.

◆ PipedInputStream(PipedOutputStream src) throws IOException

Creates a `PipedInputStream` and connects it to the specified `PipedOutputStream`.

◆ void close( ) throws IOException

Closes the stream by instructing it to no longer read from the `PipedOutputStream`.

◆ **void connect(PipedOutputStream src) throws IOException**

Connects the `PipedInputStream` to the specified `PipedOutputStream`.

◆ **synchronized int read( ) throws IOException**

Reads and returns a byte from the stream.

◆ **synchronized int read(byte b[ ], int offset, int len) throws IOException**

Reads `len` bytes from the stream, storing them in the specified array beginning at the `offset` index.

PipedOutputStream Extends OutputStream

Working with a `PipedInputStream`, a `PipedOutputStream` enables two concurrently running `Threads` to communicate via a stream.

▶ *See "PipedInputStream Extends InputStream," p. 170*

Methods

◆ **PipedOutputStream( )**

Creates a new `PipedOutputStream`. This must be connected to a `PipedInputStream` in order to function.

◆ **PipedOutputStream(PipedInputStream dest) throws IOException**

Creates a new `PipedOutputStream` and connects it to the specified `PipedInputStream`.

◆ **void close( ) throws IOException**

Informs the `PipedInputStream` that it has received its last byte—effectively closing the stream.

◆ **void connect(PipedInputStream dest) throws IOException**

Connects the `PipedOutputStream` to the specified `PipedInputStream`.

◆ **void write(int b) throws IOException**
Writes a single byte to the stream.

◆ **void write(byte b[ ], int offset, int len) throws IOException**
Writes `len` bytes from the specified buffer, beginning at the `offset` index.

PrintStream Extends FilterOutputStream

A `PrintStream` is a very straightforward stream manager that prints out all types of data as strings.

> **Caution**   Because a `PrintStream` prints everything as a `String`, all data types—even integers and doubles—will be printed as a string. Consequently, be careful when later reading this information: all data types except strings and characters must be first read as strings or bytes and then converted to their natural data types.

Methods

◆ **PrintStream(OutputStream out)**
Creates a new `PrintStream` to manage the specified `OutputStream`.

◆ **PrintStream(OutputStream out, boolean autoflush)**
Creates a new `PrintStream` to manage the specified `OutputStream`. If `autoflush` is `true`, the stream will be flushed every time a newline character (`'\n'`) is written.

◆ **boolean checkError( )**
Returns `true` if an error has been encountered in writing to the stream. Once an error has occurred, this method will continue to return a value of `true`.

Java Quick Reference

◆ **void close( )**
   Closes the stream.

◆ **void flush( )**
   Flushes any information being buffered by the
   `OutputStream`.

◆ **void print(boolean b)**
   Prints a `boolean`.

◆ **void print(double d)**
   Prints a `double`.

◆ **void print(float f)**
   Prints a `float`.

◆ **void print(long l)**
   Prints a `long`.

◆ **void print(int i)**
   Prints an `int`.

◆ **void print(char c)**
   Prints a `char`.

◆ **synchronized void print(char s[ ])**
   Prints the array of characters.

◆ **synchronized void print(String s)**
   Prints the string.

◆ **void print(Object obj)**
   Prints the value returned by `String.valueOf(obj)`.

◆ **synchronized void println(boolean b)**
   Prints a `boolean` followed by a newline character.

◆ **synchronized void println(double d)**
   Prints a `double` followed by a newline character.

◆ **synchronized void println(float f)**
Prints a `float` followed by a newline character.

◆ **synchronized void println(long l)**
Prints a `long` followed by a newline character.

◆ **synchronized void println(int i)**
Prints an `int` followed by a newline character.

◆ **synchronized void println(char c)**
Prints a `char` followed by a newline character.

◆ **synchronized void println(char s[ ])**
Prints the array of `chars` followed by a newline character.

◆ **synchronized void println(String s)**
Prints a string followed by a newline character.

◆ **synchronized void println(Object obj)**
Prints the value returned by `String.valueOf(obj)`
followed by a newline character.

◆ **void println( )**
Prints a newline character.

◆ **void write(int b)**
Writes a single byte.

◆ **void write(byte b[ ], int offset, int len)**
Writes all bytes in the specified array from `len` to
`len + offset`.

PushbackInputStream Extends
FilterInputStream

A `PushbackInputStream` is a stream manager that is quite
useful when parsing a stream. It enables you to "take a peek" at
the next byte in the stream without completely removing the
byte from the stream. If you decide that you don't want the
specific byte, you may return it to the stream via the `unread( )`

method. This will "push" the specified byte back onto the stream, making it the next character to be returned by any future read( ) statements.

How Do You Place a Character Back on a Stream?
You don't. A PushBackInputStream does not actually place the character back on the stream. However, it stores it in a protected field named pushBack. The next time you read from the stream, it will return the pushBack byte—not the next byte from the stream.

Field

▶ **protected int pushBack**

The byte that has been "pushed back."

Methods

◆ **PushbackInputStream(InputStream in)**

Creates a new PushBackInputStream to manage the specified stream.

◆ **int available( ) throws IOException**

Returns the number of bytes available on the stream.

◆ **boolean markSupported( )**

Returns false because this InputStream handler does not support the mark/reset procedure.

◆ **int read( ) throws IOException**

Reads and returns a single byte.

◆ **int read(byte b[ ], int offset, int len) throws IOException**

Reads len bytes from the array and places them in the specified buffer beginning at b[offset].

◆ **void unread(int ch) throws IOException**

Places the specified byte back on the stream.

RandomAccessFile Implements DataOutput DataInput

Closely resembling a random access file in C, the `RandomAccessFile` class provides you with an extremely flexible tool for file input and output. Furthermore, by enabling you to specify the type of access allowed—either read-only or read and write—this class supplies you with a degree of security.

Methods

◆ **RandomAccessFile(File file, String mode) throws IOException**

Creates a new `RandomAccessFile` object to handle the physical file managed by the `File` object. `mode` specifies the type of file access permitted. "`r`" allows read-only and "`rw`" allows both reading and writing.

◆ **RandomAccessFile(String name, String mode) throws IOException**

Creates a new `RandomAccessFile` object to handle the file with the specified name. `mode` specifies the type of file access permitted. "`r`" allows read-only and "`rw`" allows both reading and writing.

◆ **void close( ) throws IOException**

Closes the file.

◆ **final FileDescriptor getFD( ) throws IOException**

Returns the `FileDescriptor` of the file being accessed.

◆ **long getFilePointer( ) throws IOException**

Returns the current location of the file pointer in the file.

◆ **long length( ) throws IOException**

Returns the length of the file.

◆ **int read( ) throws IOException**

Reads and returns a single byte.

◆ **int read(byte b[ ]) throws IOException**
Reads to the specified byte array, returning the number of bytes read.

◆ **int read(byte b[ ], int offset, int len) throws IOException**
Reads `len` bytes and places them in the array beginning at the `offset` index. It returns the actual number of bytes read.

◆ **final boolean readBoolean( ) throws IOException**
Reads a `boolean` from the file.

◆ **final byte readByte( ) throws IOException**
Reads a byte from the file.

◆ **final char readChar( ) throws IOException**
Reads a `char` from the file.

◆ **final double readDouble( ) throws IOException**
Reads a `double` from the file.

◆ **final float readFloat( ) throws IOException**
Reads a `float` from the file.

◆ **final void readFully(byte b[ ], int offset, int len) throws IOException**
Reads from the stream, waiting until `len` bytes have been read from the stream. The bytes will be written to the array beginning at the specified `offset`.

◆ **final void readFully(byte b[ ]) throws IOException**
Reads from the stream, placing bytes in the specified array until the array is full.

◆ **final int readInt( ) throws IOException**
Reads and returns an `int` from the stream.

◆ **final String readLine( ) throws IOException**
Reads and returns a string from the stream terminated by `'\n'` or `EOF`.

◆ **final long readLong( ) throws IOException**
Reads and returns a `long` from the stream.

◆ **final short readShort( ) throws IOException**
Reads and returns a `short` from the stream.

◆ **final int readUnsignedByte( ) throws IOException**
Reads and returns an unsigned byte from the stream.

◆ **final int readUnsignedShort( ) throws IOException**
Reads and returns an unsigned short from the stream.

◆ **final String readUTF( ) throws IOException**
Reads and returns a string in UTF format from the stream.

◆ **void seek(long pos) throws IOException**
Places the file pointer at the specified location in the file.

◆ **int skipBytes(int num) throws IOException**
Advances the file pointer the specified number of bytes.

◆ **void write(byte b[ ]) throws IOException**
Writes the specified buffer to the file.

◆ **void write(byte b[ ], int offset, int len) throws
IOException**
Writes `len` bytes from the buffer to the file beginning at the
`offset`.

◆ **final void writeBoolean(boolean v) throws IOException**
Writes the `boolean` to the file.

◆ **final void writeByte(int v) throws IOException**
Writes the byte to the file.

◆ **final void writeBytes(String s) throws IOException**
Writes the string to the file as a series of bytes.

◆ **final void writeChar(int v) throws IOException**
Writes the `char` to the file.

◆ **final void writeChars(String s) throws IOException**
Writes the string to the file as a sequence of `chars`.

◆ **final void writeDouble(double v) throws IOException**
Writes the `double` to the file.

◆ **final void writeFloat(float v) throws IOException**
Writes the `float` to the file.

◆ **final void writeInt(int v) throws IOException**
Writes the `int` to the file.

◆ **final void writeLong(long v) throws IOException**
Writes the `long` to the file.

◆ **final void writeShort(int v) throws IOException**
Writes the `short` to the file.

◆ **final void writeUTF(String str) throws IOException**
Writes the string to the file in UTF format.

SequenceInputStream Extends InputStream

A `SequenceInputStream` enables you to link multiple `InputStreams` to form one pseudo-stream. The `SequenceInputStream` will read from one stream until completion, at which time it will read from the next stream.

Methods

◆ **SequenceInputStream(InputStream s1, InputStream s2)**
Creates a new `SequenceInputStream`, linking the specified `InputStream`.

◆ **SequenceInputStream(Enumeration e)**
Creates a `SequenceInputStream`, linking all `InputStreams` in the specified `Enumeration`.

◆ **void close( ) throws IOException**
Effectively closes the stream by scrolling through all remaining streams until the last stream has been marked as read.

◆ **int read( ) throws IOException**
Reads and returns a byte from the current stream.

◆ **int read(byte b[ ], int offset, int len) throws IOException**
Reads `len` bytes from the sequence of streams, placing them in the array (b [ ]) beginning at the specified `offset`.

StreamTokenizer

A `StreamTokenizer` is a heavy-duty tool used for parsing streams. Using the `nextToken ( )` method, you are able to scan the stream for any *tokens*—characters defined by you to be important. When such a character is encountered, the `StreamTokenizer` will return a flag. The flag will either be the character itself or a special flag, such as `TT_EOF` (which signifies the end of the stream).

Fields

▶ **double nval**
If `TT_NUMBER` is the returned token, this is the recently read number.

▶ **String sval**
If `TT_WORD` is the returned token, this is the recently read string.

▶ **final static int TT_EOF**
The end of file token.

▶ **final static int TT_EOL**
The end of line token.

▶ **final static int TT_NUMBER**
A token indicating a number has just been read.

▶ **final static int TT_WORD**
A token indicating a word (string) has just been read.

Methods

◆ **StreamTokenizer(InputStream in)**
Creates a `StreamTokenizer` to manage the specified `InputStream`.

◆ **void commentChar(int ch)**
Sets the comment character.

◆ **void eolIsSignificant(boolean flag)**
If `flag` is `true`, then end-of-line characters will be returned as tokens.

◆ **int lineno( )**
Returns the current line number. This is useful when end-of-line tokens are not significant.

◆ **void lowerCaseMode(boolean flag)**
If `flag` is `true`, then the string placed in `sval` will be converted to lowercase characters.

◆ **int nextToken( ) throws IOException**
Advances in the stream until the next token is reached. It returns this token.

◆ **void ordinaryChar(int ch)**
Makes the specified character an *ordinary* character. This means that it will not be returned as a token.

◆ **void ordinaryChars(int low, int hi)**
The range of characters from `low` to `hi` are now considered ordinary. They will not be returned as tokens.

◆ **void parseNumbers( )**
Forces parsing of numbers. This method is called by default when a `StreamTokenizer` is created, but if you reset the syntax, you must call this method again. This task is accomplished by making the numeric characters (0–9), the period (.), and the hyphen (-) special characters that will be handled differently by the `tokenizer`.

◆ **void pushBack( )**
Effectively returns the current token to the stream. As a result, the next call to `nextToken( )` will return the same token with the same `nval` or `sval` if appropriate.

◆ **void quoteChar(int ch)**
Sets the quote character.

◆ **void resetSyntax( )**
Resets the syntax for the `tokenizer`. All characters are set to ordinary status.

◆ **void slashSlashComments(boolean flag)**
If `flag` is `true`, the slash-slash flag (`//`) will denote comments.

◆ **void slashStarComments(boolean flag)**
If `flag` is `true`, the slash-star flag (`/*` to `*/`) denotes comments.

◆ **String toString( )**
Returns a string containing the current token and `sval` or `nval` if appropriate.

◆ **void whitespaceChars(int low, int hi)**
All characters between `low` and `hi` are considered whitespace. By default, characters 0 to 32 are considered whitespace.

◆ **void wordChars(int low, int hi)**
All characters between `low` and `hi` are considered a part of a word.

StringBufferInputStream Extends InputStream

A `StringBufferInputStream` enables you to read information from a `String` as if it were an `InputStream`.

▶ *See "PushbackInputStream Extends FilterInputStream," p. 177*

JAVA.IO

Fields

▶ **protected String buffer**

A reference to the `String` specified in the constructor method.

▶ **protected int count**

The length of the buffer.

▶ **protected int pos**

The current position in the buffer.

Methods

◆ **StringBufferInputStream(String s)**

Creates a new `StringBufferInputStream` to read from the specified string.

◆ **synchronized int available( )**

Returns the number of bytes remaining in the string buffer.

◆ **synchronized int read( )**

Reads and returns a single byte. It returns –1 if no bytes remain.

◆ **synchronized int read(byte b[ ], int offset, int len)**

Reads at most `len` bytes from string buffer, storing them in the array beginning at the `offset` index. It returns the number of bytes read and –1 if no bytes remain.

◆ **synchronized void reset( )**

Returns to the beginning of the buffer.

◆ **synchronized long skip(long num)**

Skips at most `num` bytes in the stream. It returns the number of bytes skipped.

Interfaces

DataInput

This interface declares a set of methods defining the behavior of a machine-independent input stream. It is implemented by the `DataInputStream` class.

Methods

◆ **abstract boolean readBoolean( ) throws IOException**
Reads and returns a `boolean` from the stream.

◆ **abstract byte readByte( ) throws IOException**
Reads and returns a byte from the stream.

◆ **abstract char readChar( ) throws IOException**
Reads and returns a `char` from the stream.

◆ **abstract double readDouble( ) throws IOException**
Reads and returns a `double` from the stream.

◆ **abstract float readFloat( ) throws IOException**
Reads and returns a `float` from the stream.

◆ **abstract void readFully(byte b[ ]) throws IOException**
Reads from the stream, waiting until the entire array is filled.

◆ **abstract void readFully(byte b[ ], int offset, int len) throws IOException**
Reads from the stream, waiting until `len` bytes have been read. It places the bytes in the array, beginning at the specified `offset`.

◆ **abstract int readInt( ) throws IOException**
Reads and returns an `int` from the stream.

◆ **abstract long readLong( ) throws IOException**
Reads and returns a `long` from the stream.

JAVA.IO

◆ **abstract short readShort( ) throws IOException**
Reads and returns a short from the stream.

◆ **abstract int readUnsignedByte( ) throws IOException**
Reads and returns an unsigned byte from the stream.

◆ **abstract int readUnsignedShort( ) throws IOException**
Reads and returns an unsigned short from the stream.

◆ **abstract String readUTF( ) throws IOException**
Reads and returns a string from the stream in UTF format.

◆ **abstract int skipBytes(int num) throws IOException**
Skips at most num bytes in the stream. It returns the actual
number of bytes skipped.

DataOutput

This class declares a set of methods that enable machine-
independent output of data. It is implemented by the
DataOutputStream class.

Methods

◆ **abstract void write(byte b[ ], int offset, int len) throws
IOException**
Writes bytes from the array to the stream, beginning at
b[offset] and continuing to b[offset + len].

◆ **abstract void write(byte b]) throws IOException**
Writes the entire array to the stream.

◆ **abstract void write(int b) throws IOException**
Writes an int to the stream.

◆ **abstract void writeBoolean(boolean v) throws
IOException**
Writes a boolean to the stream.

◆ **abstract void writeByte(int v) throws IOException**
Writes a byte to the stream.

◆ **abstract void writeBytes(String s) throws IOException**
Writes a string to the stream as a series of bytes.

◆ **abstract void writeChar(int v) throws IOException**
Writes a `char` to the stream.

◆ **abstract void writeChars(String s) throws IOException**
Writes a string to the stream as a series of `chars`.

◆ **abstract void writeDouble(double v) throws IOException**
Writes a `double` to the stream.

◆ **abstract void writeFloat(float v) throws IOException**
Writes a `float` to the stream.

◆ **abstract void writeInt(int v) throws IOException**
Writes an `int` to the stream.

◆ **abstract void writeLong(long v) throws IOException**
Writes a `long` to the stream.

◆ **abstract void writeShort(int v) throws IOException**
Writes a `short` to the stream.

◆ **abstract void writeUTF(String str) throws IOException**
Writes a string to the stream in UTF format.

FilenameFilter

A `FilenameFilter` is a tool to be used when screening directories. It is used in the `File` and `java.awt.FileDialog` classes.

Method

◆ **abstract boolean accept(File dir, String name)**
Returns `true` if the specified file satisfies the requirements of the filter.

JAVA.IO

JAVA.LANG

CLASSES AND INTERFACES

JAVA.LANG

These classes are essentially the *heart* of the java language. This package includes not only wrappers for the basic data types, such as `Integer` and `String`, but also a means of handling errors through the `Throwable` and `Error` classes. Furthermore, the `SecurityManager` and `System` classes supply you with some degree of control over the client's system, albeit the command prompt or the Java Console in Netscape.

Classes

Boolean

Although a `boolean` is a primitive data type, the `Boolean` class serves as a wrapper class—providing you with a means of better handling `boolean` values. Wrapper classes for primitive data types are also useful in using `hashtables`, which only accept objects—not primitive data types.

Fields

▶ **final static Boolean FALSE**
A `Boolean` object created with a value of `false`.

▶ **final static char MAX_VALUE**
The maximum value of a character: 65535. These values were accidentally placed in the `Boolean` class.

▶ **final static char MIN_VALUE**
The minimum value of a character: 0. These values were accidentally placed in the `Boolean` class.

▶ **final static Boolean TRUE**
A `Boolean` object created with a value of `true`.

Methods

◆ **Boolean(String s)**

Creates a Boolean object with the specified value: true if s equals true and false otherwise.

◆ **Boolean(boolean value)**

Creates a Boolean object with the specified boolean value.

◆ **boolean booleanValue( )**

Returns the value of the Boolean object.

◆ **boolean equals(Object anotherObject)**

Returns true if the anotherObject is a boolean with the same value.

◆ **static boolean getBoolean(String s)**

Returns true if s equals true. Otherwise, it returns false.

◆ **int hashCode( )**

Returns the hashcode for the Boolean object—a value dependent on the boolean value of the object.

◆ **String toString( )**

Returns either true or false depending on the value of the boolean value of the object.

◆ **static Boolean valueOf(String s)**

Returns a Boolean object whose value is the value of the specified string.

Character

The Character class serves as a wrapper class for handling char values.

Fields

▶ **final static int MAX_RADIX**

The maximum radix that can be used in converting a number, represented by a character, to an int. The radix refers to the mathematical *base* of the number, denoting the value of each position. MAX_RADIX is 36.

▶ **final static int MIN_RADIX**

The maximum radix that can be used in converting a number, represented by a character, to an int. The radix refers to the mathematical *base* of the number, denoting the value of each position. MIN_RADIX is 2.

Methods

◆ **Character(char value)**

Creates a Character object with the specified character value.

◆ **char charValue( )**

Returns the value of the Character object.

◆ **static int digit(char ch, int base)**

Converts a number, represented by ch, to an int value in the specified base.

◆ **boolean equals(Object anotherObject)**

Returns true if anotherObject is a Character object with the same char value.

◆ **static char forDigit(int digit, int base)**

Returns a char representing the value of the digit in the specified base.

◆ **int hashCode( )**
Returns the hashcode of the Character object—the char value casted to an int.

◆ **static boolean isDigit(char ch)**
Returns true if the char value is between 0 and 9.

◆ **static boolean isJavaLetter(char ch)**
Returns true if ch is a *Java letter*—meaning that it can be used as the first letter of an identifier. This includes all characters, the dollar sign ('$'), and the underscore character ('_').

◆ **static boolean isJavaLetterOrDigit(char ch)**
Returns true if ch is a valid character within a Java identifier. This includes all letters and digits as well as the dollar sign ('$'), and the underscore character ('_'). It will return true if ch equals '$', '_', or if isLetterOrDigit(ch) is true.

◆ **static boolean isLetter(char ch)**
Returns true if ch is a letter.

◆ **static boolean isLetterOrDigit(char ch)**
Returns true if ch is a letter or a digit.

◆ **static boolean isLowerCase(char ch)**
Returns true if the char value is a lowercase letter.

◆ **static boolean isSpace(char ch)**
Returns true if the char value is ' ', '\t', '\f', '\n', or '\r'.

◆ **static boolean isSpace(char ch)**
Returns true if ch is one of the five white space characters: ' ', '\t', '\f', '\n', or '\r'.

◆ **static boolean isTitleCase(char ch)**
Returns `true` if ch is one of four special Unicode characters. These characters are special because they resemble two
ASCII characters together, such as *Lj*. This method will return
`true` only if ch is one of these four characters and its first
letter is capitalized.

◆ **static boolean isUpperCase(char ch)**
Returns `true` if the char value is an uppercase letter.

◆ **static char toLowerCase(char ch)**
Returns the lowercase value of the specified `char`.

◆ **String toString( )**
Returns the char value as a string.

◆ **static char toTitleCase(char ch)**
Returns the title case of a ch. For all but four characters, this
is simply their uppercase form. For the four special Latin
Unicode characters resembling two ASCII characters, this
capitalizes the first letter and leaves the second unchanged.

◆ **static char toUpperCase(char ch)**
Returns the uppercase value of the specified `char`.

Class

To the Virtual Machine, every class is an `Object`. However,
within the Virtual Machine, every class (and interface) is handled
with the `Class` class. While the `Object` class gives you
information regarding an instance of the class (the actual
object), this class gives you information regarding the code used
in creating the class. Because you cannot create an instance of a
`Class`, you must use the `forName( )` method to return a
`Class` object.

Methods

◆ **static Class forName(String className) throws ClassNotFoundException**
Returns the `Class` object descriptor for the specified class.

◆ **ClassLoader getClassLoader( )**
Returns the `ClassLoader` for this class.

◆ **Class[ ] getInterfaces( )**
Returns an array containing the interfaces implemented by this class.

◆ **String getName( )**
Returns the name of this class.

◆ **Class getSuperclass( )**
Returns the `Class` object for the superclass of this class.

◆ **boolean isInterface( )**
Returns `true` if this "class" is actually an interface.

◆ **Object newInstance( ) throws InstantiationException, IllegalAccessException**
Creates a instance of the class described by this `Class` object.

◆ **String toString( )**
Returns a string containing either the word *class* or *interface* along with the class/interface name.

Abstract ClassLoader

A class loader can be used to load a class from a source other than the current server—such as a network. Because the process depends heavily on your particular circumstances, the actual loading of the class is left up to you.

Because the `ClassLoader` class is abstract, you must first extend the class and override the `loadClass( )` method if you want to use a `ClassLoader`. Once this is done, you must employ the `defineClass( )` method to create a `Class` object describing the class—which also enables you to create an instance of the class.

Methods

◆ **protected ClassLoader( )**

Creates a new `ClassLoader`.

◆ **abstract Class loadClass(String name, boolean resolve) throws ClassNotFoundException**

This method must be overridden in your own class. `resolve` represents the need to "resolve" the class: loading all classes referred to by the newly loaded class.

◆ **final Class defineClass(byte data[ ], int offset, int length)**

Returns a `Class` object describing the class created from the specified set of bytes. The class will be created from the bytes beginning at `data[offset]` and continuing to `data[offset + length]`.

◆ **final Class findSystemClass(String name) throws ClassNotFoundException**

Loads a class from the system. This employs the default (null) class loader.

◆ **final void resolveClass(Class c)**

Resolves the specified class by loading all classes referred to by the specified class. This must be done before the class can be used.

Compiler

This class is designed to provide an interface with future Java technology that will provide you with more control over the Java compiler. However, there is no complete set of libraries or means of creating a `Compiler` object as of the 1.0.2 JDK.

Methods

◆ **static Object command(Object any)**

Executes the specified command.

◆ **static boolean compileClass(Class class)**
Compiles the specified class.

◆ **static boolean compileClasses(String string)**
Compiles the specified classes.

◆ **static void disable( )**
Disables the compiler.

◆ **static void enable( )**
Enables the compiler.

Double Extends Number

`Double` is a wrapper class designed to handle `double` values.

Fields

▶ **final static double MAX_VALUE**
The maximum value of a `double` is
$1.79769313486231570 * 10^{308}$.

▶ **final static double MIN_VALUE**
The minimum value of a `double` is
$-4.94065645841246544e * 10^{324}$.

▶ **final static double NaN**
This special value represents a `double` that is *Not a Number*.
It is set equal to 0.0 / 0.0. It is not equal to *anything*—even
itself.

▶ **final static double NEGATIVE_INFINITY**
Negative infinity: -1.0/0.0.

▶ **final static double POSITIVE_INFINITY**
Positive infinity: 1.0/0.0.

Methods

◆ **Double(double value)**
Creates a new `Double` object based on the specified
`double` value.

◆ **Double(String s) throws NumberFormatException**
Creates a new `Double` object, assuming `s` represents a valid `double` value.

◆ **static long doubleToLongBits(double value)**
Returns a bit representation of the specified value.

◆ **double doubleValue( )**
Returns the value of the `Double` object.

◆ **boolean equals(Object anotherObject)**
Returns `true` if `anotherObject` is a `Double` with the same value.

◆ **float floatValue( )**
Returns the `double` value of the object as a `float`.

◆ **int hashCode( )**
Returns the `hashcode` of the `Double` object—the `double` value casted to an `int`.

◆ **int intValue( )**
Returns the `double` value casted to an `int`.

◆ **boolean isInfinite( )**
Returns `true` if the `double` value equals either `POSITIVE_INFINITY` or `NEGATIVE_INFINITY`.

◆ **static boolean isInfinite(double v)**
Returns `true` if the specified `double` value equals either `POSITIVE_INFINITY` or `NEGATIVE_INFINITY`.

◆ **boolean isNaN( )**
Returns `true` if the `double` value is equal to the special `NaN` value.

◆ **static boolean isNaN(double v)**
Returns `true` if the specified `double` value is equal to the special `NaN` value.

◆ **static double longBitsToDouble(long bits)**
Returns the `double` representation of a given bit representation.

◆ **long longValue( )**
Returns the `double` value as a `long`.

◆ **String toString( )**
Returns the `double` value as a string.

◆ **static String toString(double d)**
Converts the specified `double` to a string.

◆ **static Double valueOf(String s) throws NumberFormatException**
Converts the specified string into a `Double` object.

Float Extends Number
`Float` is a wrapper class designed to handle float values.

Fields
▶ **final static float MAX_VALUE**
The maximum value for a `float` is
$3.40282346638528860 * 10^{38}$.

▶ **final static float MIN_VALUE**
The minimum value of a `float` is
$1.40129846432481707 * 10^{-45}$.

▶ **final static float NaN**
This special value represents a `double` that is *Not a Number*. It is set equal to 0.0 / 0.0. It is not equal to *anything*—even itself.

▶ **final static float NEGATIVE_INFINITY**
Negative infinity: −1.0/0.0.

▶ **final static float POSITIVE_INFINITY**
Positive infinity: 1.0/0.0.

Methods

◆ **Float(String s) throws NumberFormatException**
  Creates a `Float` object whose `float` value will be that of
  the specified string.

◆ **Float(double value)**
  Creates a `Float` object whose initial value will be the value
  of the specified `double`.

◆ **Float(float value)**
  Creates a `Float` object whose initial value will be the value
  of the specified `float`.

◆ **double doubleValue( )**
  Returns the `float` value as a `double`.

◆ **boolean equals(Object anotherObject)**
  Returns `true` if `anotherObject` is a `Float` with the
  same value.

◆ **static int floatToIntBits(float value)**
  Returns a bit representation of the specified `float`.

◆ **float floatValue( )**
  Returns the `float` value of the `Float`.

◆ **int hashCode( )**
  Returns the `hashcode` of the `Float`: the float value
  casted to an `int`.

◆ **static float intBitsToFloat(int bits)**
  Returns the `float` value of the bit representation.

◆ **int intValue( )**
  Returns the `float` value as a `float`.

◆ **boolean isInfinite( )**
  Returns `true` if the `float` value is equal to either
  `POSITIVE_INFINITY` or `NEGATIVE_INFINITY`.

◆ **static boolean isInfinite(float v)**
Returns `true` if the specified `float` is equal to positive or negative infinity.

◆ **boolean isNaN( )**
Returns `true` if the `float` value is not a number.

◆ **static boolean isNaN(float v)**
Returns `true` if the specified `float` is not a number.

◆ **long longValue( )**
Returns the `float` value as a `long`.

◆ **String toString( )**
Returns the `float` value in a string.

◆ **static String toString(float f)**
Converts the specified `float` into a string.

◆ **static Float valueOf(String s) throws NumberFormatException**
Returns a `Float` object whose initial value is equal to the `float` contained in the string.

Integer Extends Number

`Integer` is a wrapper class designed to handle `int` values. Often, `Integer` objects are returned by methods in the API as a means of providing you with a number and a means to manage it.

Fields

▶ **final static int MAX_VALUE**
The maximum value for an `Integer` is 2147483647.

▶ **final static int MIN_VALUE**
The minimum value for an `Integer` is –2147483648.

Methods

◆ **Integer(int value)**
Creates a new Integer object with the specified value.

◆ **Integer(String s) throws NumberFormatException**
Creates a new Integer object whose initial value will be equal to the int contained in the specified string.

◆ **double doubleValue( )**
Returns the int value as a double.

◆ **boolean equals(Object anotherObject)**
Returns true if anotherObject is an Integer with the same int value.

◆ **float floatValue( )**
Returns the int value as a float.

◆ **static Integer getInteger(String propName)**
Returns a system property whose value is an int that may be stored in hexadecimal or octal format.

◆ **static Integer getInteger(String propName, int val)**
Returns a system property whose value is an int that may be stored in hexadecimal or octal format. If this process fails, the method returns an Integer with the value of val.

◆ **static Integer getInteger(String propName, Integer val)**
Returns a system property whose value is an int that may be stored in hexadecimal or octal format. If this process fails, the method returns val.

◆ **int hashCode( )**
Returns the hashcode of the Integer: its int value.

◆ **int intValue( )**
Returns the int value.

◆ **long longValue( )**
Returns the int value as a long.

◆ **static int parseInt(String s) throws NumberFormatException**

Returns the `int` represented by the specified string.

◆ **static int parseInt(String s, int base) throws NumberFormatException**

Returns the `int` specified by the string in base `base`. For example `parseInt("101",2) = 5` and `parseInt("101",10) = 10`.

◆ **static String toBinaryString(int)**

Returns a `String` representing `num` as an unsigned binary number.

◆ **static String toHexString(int)**

Returns a `String` representing `num` as an unsigned hexadecimal number.

◆ **static String toOctalString(int)**

Returns a `String` representing `num` as an unsigned octal number.

◆ **String toString( )**

Returns the `int` value in a string.

◆ **static String toString(int i)**

Returns a string containing the specified `int`.

◆ **static String toString(int i, int base)**

Returns the string represented by `i` in the specified `base`. For example, `toString(5,2) = 101` and `toString(5,10) = 5`.

◆ **static Integer valueOf(String s) throws NumberFormatException**

Returns an `Integer` object with a value equal to the `int` contained in the string.

◆ **static Integer valueOf(String s, int base) throws NumberFormatException**
Returns the value of the string in the specified base.

Long Extends Number

Long is a wrapper class designed to handle long values.

Fields

❯ **final static long MAX_VALUE**
The maximum value for a Long is 9223372036854775807.

❯ **final static long MIN_VALUE**
The minimum value for a Long is –9223372036854775808.

Methods

◆ **Long(String s) throws NumberFormatException**
Creates a Long object with an initial value of the long contained in the string.

◆ **Long(long value)**
Creates a new Long with the specified initial value.

◆ **double doubleValue( )**
Returns the long value as a double.

◆ **boolean equals(Object anotherObject)**
Returns true if anotherObject is a Long with the same long value.

◆ **float floatValue( )**
Returns the long value of the object as a float.

◆ **static Long getLong(String name)**
Returns a system property represented by name.

◆ **static Long getLong(String name, long val)**
Returns a system property represented by name. If unable to do so, returns a Long object with a value of val.

◆ **static Long getLong(String name, Long val)**

Returns a system property represented by `name`. If unable to do so, returns `val`.

◆ **int hashCode( )**

Returns the `hashcode` of the `Long`—its value casted to an `int`.

◆ **int intValue( )**

Returns the `long` value as an `int`.

◆ **long longValue( )**

Returns the `long` value of the object.

◆ **static long parseLong(String s) throws NumberFormatException**

Returns the `long` value contained in the string.

◆ **static long parseLong(String s, int base) throws NumberFormatException**

Returns a `long` with a value equal to the number in `s`. `base` specifies the base in which the number is written. Thus, if you want to parse a string containing a `long` in base 10, use a `base` value of 10.

◆ **static String toBinaryString(long num)**

Returns a `String` representing `num` as an unsigned binary number.

◆ **static String toHexString(long num)**

Returns a `String` representing `num` as an unsigned hexadecimal number.

◆ **static String toOctalString(long num)**

Returns a `String` representing `num` as an unsigned octal number.

◆ **String toString( )**

Returns the `long` value as a string.

◆ **static String toString(long val)**
Converts the specified `long` to a string.

◆ **static String toString(long val, int base)**
Returns a string containing the specified `long` stored in the specified `base`.

◆ **static Long valueOf(String s) throws NumberFormatException**
Returns a `Long` object with a value determined by the number contained in the specified string.

◆ **static Long valueOf(String s, int base) throws NumberFormatException**
Returns a `Long` containing the value of the string assuming that the string contains a number in the specified `base`.

Math

The `Math` class provides you with a wide variety of mathematical methods as well as some handy constants, such as e and pi.

Fields

▶ **final static double E**
The constant e: 2.7182818284590452354.

▶ **final static double PI**
The constant pi: 3.14159265358979323846.

Methods

◆ **static double abs(double val)**
Returns the absolute value of a `double`.

◆ **static float abs(float val)**
Returns the absolute value of a `float`.

◆ **static long abs(long val)**
Returns the absolute value of a `long`.

◆ **static int abs(int val)**
Returns the absolute value of an `int`.

◆ **static double acos(double val)**
Returns the inverse cosine of the specified number.

◆ **static double asin(double val)**
Returns the inverse sin of the specified angle in radians.

◆ **static double atan(double val)**
Returns the inverse tangent of the specified number.

◆ **static double atan2(double u, double v)**
Returns the angle defined by the rectangular coordinates
(u,v).

◆ **static double ceil(double val)**
Returns the smallest integer greater than or equal to val.
(This is the "Least-Integer Function" $\lceil val \rceil$.)

◆ **static double cos(double val)**
Returns the cosine of the specified angle in radians.

◆ **static double exp(double x)**
Returns $e^{\wedge x}$.

◆ **static double floor(double val)**
Returns the greatest integer less than or equal to val. (This is
the "Greatest-Integer Function" $\lfloor val \rfloor$.)

◆ **static double IEEEremainder(double v1, double v2)**
Returns the remainder of the operation v1/v2.

◆ **static double log(double val) throws
ArithmeticException**
Returns the mathematical log of the specified value.

◆ **static double max(double v1, double v2)**
Returns the maximum value: either v1 or v2.

- ◆ **static float max(float v1, float v2)**
  Returns the maximum value: either v1 or v2.

- ◆ **static long max(long v2, long v2)**
  Returns the maximum value: either v1 or v2.

- ◆ **static int max(int v1, int v2)**
  Returns the maximum value: either v1 or v2.

- ◆ **static double min(double v1, double v2)**
  Returns the minimum value: either v1 or v2.

- ◆ **static float min(float v1, float v2)**
  Returns the minimum value: either v1 or v2.

- ◆ **static long min(long v1, long v2)**
  Returns the minimum value: either v1 or v2.

- ◆ **static int min(int v1, int v2)**
  Returns the minimum value: either v1 or v2.

- ◆ **static double pow(double base, double exp) throws ArithmeticException**
  Returns the value of base^{exp}.

- ◆ **static synchronized double random( )**
  Returns a random number by using the
  `java.util.Random` class.

- ◆ **static double rint(double val)**
  Rounds val to the nearest integer, returning the value as a
  double. (e.g., `rint(5.3)` = 5.0).

- ◆ **static long round(double val)**
  Rounds the `double`, returning it as a `float`.

- ◆ **static int round(float val)**
  Rounds the specified number.

◆ **static double sin(double val)**
Returns the sine of the specified angle in radians.

◆ **static double sqrt(double val) throws**
ArithmeticException
Returns the square root of the number.

◆ **static double tan(double val)**
Returns the tangent of the specified angle in radians.

Abstract Number

The Number class serves as the basis for all wrapper classes designed to handle number data types, such as Integer, Float, and Double.

Although int, double, and float are data types in their own right, they are considered *primitive data types* because they are much more basic that the richer objects used in Java. Although these primitive types facilitate more efficient code, they are often not robust enough for certain circumstances, such as hashtables, where it is necessary to treat each item as a full Object. Furthermore, each of these Number-type classes provides you with a means of handing data in a class-dependent nature. This gives you a very simple means of obtaining primitive values from more complex objects, such as Strings.

Methods

◆ **Number( )**
Creates a new Number.

◆ **abstract double doubleValue( )**
Returns the Number's value as a double.

◆ **abstract float floatValue( )**
Returns the Number's value as a float.

◆ **abstract int intValue( )**
Returns the Number's value as an int.

◆ **abstract long longValue( )**
Returns the Number's value as a long.

Object

The Object class is the basis for all classes in the Java programming language. Every class, even if you don't declare a superclass, will be derived from the Object class. Therefore, *all* methods in this class are accessible to all classes. However, this is not to say that you will ever have need to actually work with these methods.

Methods

◆ **Object( )**
Creates a new Object.

◆ **protected Object clone( ) throws CloneNotSupportedException**
Creates a copy of the Object.

◆ **boolean equals(Object anotherObject)**
Returns true if the two Objects are equal.

◆ **protected void finalize( ) throws Throwable**
This method will be called before the Object is collected by the Java environment. Empty by default, *any* class may override this method to add functionality. Throwing an exception from this method will halt garbage collection.

◆ **final Class getClass( )**
Returns the class of the Object as a Class object.

◆ **int hashCode( )**
Returns the hashcode of the Object. This value is dependent on the specific object.

◆ **final void notify( )**
Notifies a thread (paused with wait ( )) that it may regain control.

◆ **final void notifyAll( )**
Notifies all threads (paused with `wait ( )`) that they may regain control.

◆ **String toString( )**
Returns the class name and its *uniqufier:* a special integer tag used to distinguish separate instances of the same class.

◆ **final void wait( ) throws InterruptedException**
Causes a thread to wait indefinitely until it is notified.

◆ **final void wait(long millisec) throws InterruptedException**
Causes a thread to wait the specified number of milliseconds, or until notified.

◆ **final void wait(long millisec, int nanos) throws InterruptedException**
Causes a thread to wait the specified number of milliseconds and nanoseconds, or until notified.

Abstract Process

The `Process` class provides a handle for managing operations begun by Java programs. Returned by the `exec ( )` methods in the `Runtime` class, the `Process` class is generally used to monitor—not to control—the ongoing operation.

▶ *See "Runtime," p. 214*

Methods

◆ **Process( )**
Creates a new `Process`.

◆ **abstract void destroy( )**
Destroys the sub-process.

JAVA.LANG

◆ **abstract int exitValue( )**
Returns the exit value of the `Process`. It throws an `IllegalThreadStateException` if the `Process` has not completed.

◆ **abstract InputStream getErrorStream( )**
Returns the stream used by the `Process` for standard error output.

◆ **abstract InputStream getInputStream( )**
Returns the stream used by the `Process` for standard input.

◆ **abstract OutputStream getOutputStream( )**
Returns the stream used by the `Process` for standard output.

◆ **abstract int waitFor( ) throws InterruptedException**
Waits until the `Process` is completed and returns its exit value.

Runtime

The `Runtime` class enables you to interface with the system on which your program is running as well as the Java Virtual Machine.

> **Caution** Although the `exec ( )` method is allowed under the appletviewer, it will cause a security restriction in Netscape.

The `Runtime` class enables you to perform tasks normally associated with the prompt, such as starting a file. In figure 20, the `Runtime` class is used to begin a game of Solitaire (see Listing 13).

▶ *See "Abstract Process," p. 213*

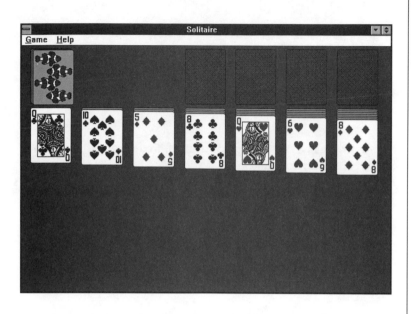

Fig. 20 The output of Listing 13.

Listing 13 Runtime Example

```java
public class RuntimeExample {
   public static void main(String argv()) {
     Runtime r=java.lang.Runtime.getRuntime();
     try{
       r.exec("\\winnt\\system32\\sol.exe");
     }
     catch (Exception e) {
       {System.out.println(e.toString() );
     }
   }
}
```

Methods

◆ **Process exec(String command) throws IOException**
Executes the specified command.

◆ **Process exec(String cmdarray[ ]) throws IOException**
Executes the commands found in the cmdarray.

◆ **Process exec(String cmdarray[ ], String envp[ ]) throws IOException**
Executes the commands in the `cmdarray` using the environment parameters specified in the `envp` array. The parameters should be specified in the format, `parameter = value`.

◆ **Process exec(String command, String envp[ ]) throws IOException**
Executes the command using the environment parameters specified in the `envp` array. The parameters should be specified in the format, `parameter = value`.

◆ **void exit(int status)**
Terminates all code and exits the Java Virtual Machine. `status` is the exit code for the entire operation.

◆ **long freeMemory( )**
Returns the number of free bytes in memory.

◆ **void gc( )**
Calls the garbage collector. This method frees any objects in memory that are no longer in use—no references to the objects remain. Garbage collection is automatically done by the system during lulls in activity or as you run out of memory.

◆ **InputStream getLocalizedInputStream(InputStream in)**
The purpose of this method is to return an `InputStream` that will translate input into UNICODE format. However, this method simply returns the `in` parameter.

◆ **OutputStream getLocalizedOutputStream(OutputStream out)**
The purpose of this method is to return an `OutputStream` that will translate to UNICODE format. However, this method simply returns the `out` parameter.

◆ **static Runtime getRuntime( )**
Returns the current `Runtime` object. This method must be used to obtain a `Runtime` object inasmuch as the constructor method for this class is not public.

◆ **synchronized void load(String filename)**
Loads a dynamic library.

◆ **synchronized void loadLibrary(String libname)**
Loads a dynamic library.

◆ **void runFinalization( )**
Runs the `finalize( )` method in any object being collected. The `finalize( )` methods are automatically called during garbage collection.

◆ **long totalMemory( )**
Returns the total number of bytes in memory.

◆ **void traceInstructions(boolean on)**
If `on` is `true`, instructions will be traced.

◆ **void traceMethodCalls(boolean on)**
If `on` is `true`, method calls will be traced.

Abstract SecurityManager

The `SecurityManager` provides you with a means of instituting and configuring many security inspections that monitor the power of your programs. These checks are necessary when you consider that Java applets have the ability to run on both intranets and the Internet—networks where security and privacy are important issues.

To create your own security restrictions, it is necessary to subclass this class and define those methods that are important to your program. You will note that most methods in this class that check the validity of an action do not return any data types. Instead, they throw `SecurityExceptions` when the action is not allowed.

Field

▶ **protected boolean inCheck**

True only if the SecurityManager is in the middle of a security check.

Methods

◆ **protected SecurityManager( )**

Creates a new SecurityManager.

◆ **void checkAccept(String host, int port)**

Determines the success of an attempted connection to the specified host at the given port.

◆ **void checkAccess(ThreadGroup g)**

Checks if the current Thread can modify the specified ThreadGroup.

◆ **void checkAccess(Thread t)**

Checks to see if the specified Thread can modify the current ThreadGroup, throwing an exception if it cannot.

◆ **void checkConnect(String host, int port)**

Checks to see if a socket has connected to the specified port on the specified host, throwing an exception if it has not.

◆ **void checkConnect(String host, int port, Object executionContext)**

Checks to see if the current executing code and the specified executionContext can connect to the specified port on the specified host, throwing an exception if it cannot.

◆ **void checkCreateClassLoader( )**

Checks to see if the ClassLoader has been created, throwing an exception if not.

◆ **void checkDelete(String file)**

Checks to see if the specified file can be deleted, throwing an exception if it cannot.

◆ **void checkExec(String cmd)**

Checks to see if the specified command will be run by trusted code, throwing an exception if not.

◆ **void checkExit(int status)**

Checks to see if the runtime system has exited with the specified exit code, throwing an exception if not.

◆ **void checkLink(String lib)**

Checks to see if the library exists, throwing an exception if not.

◆ **void checkListen(int port)**

Checks to see if the server socket on the specified `port` is listening, throwing an exception if not.

◆ **void checkPackageAccess(String packageName)**

Checks to see if the applet can access the specified package, throwing an exception if not.

◆ **void checkPackageDefinition(String packageName)**

Checks to see if the applet can create classes in the specified package, throwing an exception if not.

◆ **void checkPropertiesAccess( )**

Checks to see if the program has access to the set of system properties, throwing an exception if not.

◆ **void checkPropertyAccess(String property)**

Checks to see if the applet can access the specified system `property`, throwing an exception if not.

◆ **void checkPropertyAccess(String property, String default)**

Checks to see if the applet can access the specified system property, throwing an exception if not. `default` is used when subclassing this class to specify a value that should be used if the value of `property` is unattainable.

◆ **void checkRead(String file)**
Checks to see if the applet can read from the specified file, throwing an exception if not.

◆ **void checkRead(FileDescriptor fd)**
Checks to see if the applet can read from the specified file, throwing an exception if not.

◆ **void checkRead(String file, Object executionContext)**
Checks to see if the applet and the specified `executionContext` can read from the specified file, throwing an exception if not.

◆ **void checkSetFactory( )**
Checks to see if the applet can set an object factory, throwing an exception if not.

◆ **boolean checkTopLevelWindow(Object window)**
Checks to see if the applet can create trusted top-level windows. A return value of `false` means that a warning message should be displayed along with the window.

◆ **void checkWrite(String file)**
Checks to see if the applet can write to the specified file, throwing an exception if not.

◆ **void checkWrite(FileDescriptor fd)**
Checks to see if the applet can write to the specified file, throwing an exception if not.

◆ **protected int classDepth(String name)**
Returns the first position in the stack frame of the specified class name.

◆ **protected int classLoaderDepth( )**
Returns the first position in the stack frame of the specified class loader.

◆ **protected ClassLoader currentClassLoader( )**
Returns the current class loader on top of the execution stack.

◆ **protected Class[ ] getClassContext( )**
Returns the context of the class.

◆ **boolean getInCheck( )**
Returns `true` if a security check is underway.

◆ **Object getSecurityContext( )**
Returns an `Object` containing information regarding the current context that may be used for later security checks. Currently, this method returns a null string.

◆ **protected boolean inClass(String className)**
Returns `true` if the specified `className` can be found in the execution stack.

◆ **protected boolean inClassLoader( )**
Returns `true` if the current `ClassLoader` is not null.

String

The `String` class provides the basic nature and functionality for a string. Because the value of a `String` cannot change once created, this class is therefore primarily used for parsing, handling, and obtaining string values—not creating them. Although there are some methods that enable you to somewhat modify and add to the value of the string, these methods do not modify the `String` itself, but rather return a new `String` with the desired value.

Methods
◆ **String( )**
Creates a new `String`.

◆ **String(StringBuffer buffer)**
Creates a new `String`, copying the contents of the `buffer`.

JAVA.LANG

Java Quick Reference

◆ **String(byte ascii[ ], int hibyte)**
Creates a new String based on the specified array.
hibyte will be the top byte of each character.

◆ **String(byte ascii[ ], int hibyte, int offset, int count)**
Creates a new String based on the specified array. offset specifies the first element to be added to the String;
count is the number of bytes to be added; and hibyte
will be the top byte of each character.

◆ **String(char value[ ], int offset, int count)**
Creates a new String based on the specified array. offset specifies the first element to be added to the String,
and count is the number of bytes to be added.

◆ **String(char value[ ])**
Creates a new String based on the specified array.

◆ **String(String value)**
Creates a new String with the specified value.

◆ **char charAt(int index)**
Returns the character at the specified index.

◆ **int compareTo(String anotherString)**
Returns an integer indicating whether the String is less
than, equal to, or greater than another String. If the
return value is less than 0, the String is less than
anotherString. If it is 0, the String is equal to
anotherString. If the return value is greater than 0,
the String is greater than anotherString.

◆ **String concat(String str)**
Returns the combination of this String and str.

◆ **boolean equals(Object anotherObject)**
Returns true if anotherObject is a String with the
same value.

◆ **boolean equalsIgnoreCase(String anotherString)**
Compares the String with anotherString without case
sensitivity. It returns true if they are equal.

◆ **void getBytes(int srcBegin, int srcEnd, byte dst[ ], int dstBegin)**
Copies characters between srcBegin and srcEnd in the
String to the specified array beginning at dstBegin.

◆ **void getChars(int srcBegin, int srcEnd, char dst[ ], int dstBegin)**
Copies characters between srcBegin and srcEnd in the
String to the specified array beginning at dstBegin.

◆ **int length( )**
Returns the length of the String.

◆ **static String copyValueOf(char data[ ])**
Returns a String equal to the specified characters.

◆ **static String copyValueOf(char data[ ], int offset, int count)**
Returns a String equal to the characters in data [ ]
between offset and offset + count.

◆ **boolean endsWith(String suffix)**
Returns true if the String ends with the specified
suffix.

◆ **int hashCode( )**
Returns the hashcode of the String—a value based on
some (but not necessarily all) characters of the String.

◆ **int indexOf(String str)**
Returns the first index of str within this String.

◆ **int indexOf(String str, int fromIndex)**
Returns the first index of str within this String after
fromIndex.

◆ **int indexOf(int ch)**
Returns the first index of the `ch` in this `String`.

◆ **int indexOf(int ch, int fromIndex)**
Returns the first index of the `ch` in this `String` following `fromIndex`.

◆ **String intern( )**
Returns a `String` equal to this `String`. The new `String` will be taken from a `Hashtable` pool based on the value of the `String`.

◆ **int lastIndexOf(String str)**
Returns the last index of `str` in this `String`.

◆ **int lastIndexOf(String str, int fromIndex)**
Returns the last index of `str` in this `String` that is before `fromIndex`.

◆ **int lastIndexOf(int ch)**
Returns the last index of `ch` in this `String`.

◆ **int lastIndexOf(int ch, int fromIndex)**
Returns the last index of `ch` in this `String` that is before `fromIndex`.

◆ **boolean regionMatches(boolean ignoreCase, int toffset, String another, int offset, int len)**
Compares a portion of this string with an equally sized portion of `another`. If `ignoreCase` is `true`, the case of the characters will be ignored. `len` is the number of characters to be compared; `toffset` is the first character to be checked in this `String`; and `offset` is the first character to be checked in `another`.

◆ **boolean regionMatches(int toffset, String other, int offset, int len)**
Compares a portion of this string with an equally sized portion of `another` with case sensitivity. `len` is the number

of characters to be compared; `toffset` is the first character to be checked in this `String`; and `offset` is the first character to be checked in `another`.

◆ **String replace(char oldChar, char newChar)**
Replaces all instances of `oldChar` in the `String` with `newChar`.

◆ **boolean startsWith(String prefix)**
Returns `true` if the `String` begins with the specified `prefix` string.

◆ **boolean startsWith(String prefix, int toffset)**
Returns `true` if the substring following `toffset` is equal to `prefix`.

◆ **String substring(int beginIndex, int endIndex)**
Returns the substring of this `String` from `beginIndex` to `endIndex`.

◆ **String substring(int beginIndex)**
Returns the portion of the `String` extending from `beginIndex` to the end.

◆ **char[ ] toCharArray( )**
Returns the `String` as an array of characters.

◆ **String toLowerCase( )**
Returns a copy of this `String` in which all characters are in lowercase.

◆ **String toString( )**
Returns the `String`.

◆ **String toUpperCase( )**
Returns a copy of this `String` in which all characters are in uppercase.

◆ **String trim( )**
Returns a copy of this `String` in which any leading or trailing whitespace is removed.

◆ **static String valueOf(double d)**
Returns a `String` containing the `double`.

◆ **static String valueOf(float f)**
Returns a `String` containing the `float`.

◆ **static String valueOf(long l)**
Returns a `String` containing the `long`.

◆ **static String valueOf(int i)**
Returns a `String` containing the `int`.

◆ **static String valueOf(char c)**
Returns a `String` containing the `char`.

◆ **static String valueOf(boolean b)**
Returns a `String` containing the `boolean`.

◆ **static String valueOf(char data[ ], int offset, int num)**
Returns a `String` containing `num` characters from `data[ ]` array beginning at `offset`.

◆ **static String valueOf(char data[ ])**
Returns a `String` containing characters in the array.

◆ **static String valueOf(Object obj)**
Returns a `String` containing string representation of the `Object`. This value is obtained using `obj.toString( )`.

StringBuffer

A `StringBuffer` is a dynamic string class that enables you to modify and add to string values. Extremely flexible, this class is used in creating string values—especially those obtained from a separate source, such as a socket connection or the applet tag parameters, as shown in Listing 14 and Listing 15 (see fig. 21).

API Reference

Listing 14   StringBuffer Example Using Applet Tag Parameters—HTML

```
<HEAD>
<TITLE>StringBuffer Example</TITLE>

<BODY>

<applet code="sbufe.class" width=300 height=300 >
<param name=linenum0 value="This is the">
<param name=linenum1 value="message I'm">
<param name=linenum2 value="trying to show.">
</applet>
</BODY>
```

Listing 15   StringBuffer Example

```java
import java.applet.Applet;
import java.awt.Graphics;

public class StringBufferExample extends Applet {
   String message;

   /* This method parses the applet parameters, and returns
      them in one string separated by spaces */
   public  void init() {
     StringBuffer mes;
     String val;
     int i = 0;

     mes = new StringBuffer();

     do {
       String paramName = "linenum" + i++;
       val = getParameter(paramName);
       if (val != null) {          // continues until end
         mes.append(val);          // adds the message
         mes.append(' ');          // adds the space
```

Java Quick Reference

Listing 15   Continued

```
    }
  } while (val != null);
  message = mes.toString();  // saves the message
                             // as a String
}

public void paint(Graphics g) {
  g.drawString(message,10,10);
}
}
```

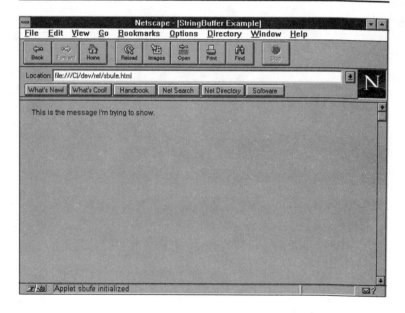

Fig. 21   The output of Listing 15 when used with Listing 14.

Methods

◆ **StringBuffer(String str)**

Creates a `StringBuffer` based on the specified `String`.

◆ **StringBuffer(int length)**

Creates a `StringBuffer` with the specified length.

◆ **StringBuffer( )**
Creates a `StringBuffer` initially 16 characters in size.

◆ **int capacity( )**
Returns the number of characters that can be added to the `StringBuffer` without requiring additional memory.

◆ **synchronized char charAt(int index)**
Returns the character at the specified index.

◆ **synchronized void ensureCapacity(int minimumCapacity)**
Increases the size of the `StringBuffer` if necessary to make sure that at least `minimumCapacity` characters can be added.

◆ **synchronized void getChars(int srcBegin, int srcEnd, char dst[ ], int dstBegin)**
Copies all characters between the `srcBegin` and `srcEnd` indexes. It places them in the `dest` array, beginning at `dstBegin`.

◆ **synchronized void setLength(int newLength)**
Sets the length of the `StringBuffer`.

Caution If the length is reduced, data may be lost.

◆ **StringBuffer append(double d)**
Appends a `double` to the `StringBuffer`, increasing its size if necessary.

◆ **StringBuffer append(float f)**
Appends a `float` to the `StringBuffer`, increasing its size if necessary.

◆ **StringBuffer append(long l)**
Appends a `long` to the `StringBuffer`, increasing its size if necessary.

JAVA.LANG

◆ **StringBuffer append(int i)**
  Appends an `int` to the `StringBuffer`, increasing its size if necessary.

◆ **synchronized StringBuffer append(char c)**
  Appends a `char` to the `StringBuffer`, increasing its size if necessary.

◆ **StringBuffer append(boolean b)**
  Appends a `boolean` to the `StringBuffer`, increasing its size if necessary.

◆ **synchronized StringBuffer append(char str[ ], int offset, int len)**
  Appends a series of characters to the `StringBuffer`, increasing its size if necessary.

◆ **synchronized StringBuffer append(char str[ ])**
  Appends an array of characters to the `StringBuffer`, increasing its size if necessary.

◆ **synchronized StringBuffer append(String str)**
  Appends a `String` to the `StringBuffer`, increasing its size if necessary.

◆ **synchronized StringBuffer append(Object obj)**
  Appends an `Object` to the `StringBuffer`, increasing its size if necessary. The actual string appended will be equal to the value returned by the `String.valueOf(obj)` method.

◆ **StringBuffer insert(int offset, double d)**
  Inserts a `double` into the `StringBuffer` at the specified `offset`, increasing the size of the buffer if necessary.

◆ **StringBuffer insert(int offset, float f)**
  Inserts a `float` into the `StringBuffer` at the specified `offset`, increasing the size of the buffer if necessary.

◆ **StringBuffer insert(int offset, long l)**
Inserts a `long` into the `StringBuffer` at the specified `offset`, increasing the size of the buffer if necessary.

◆ **StringBuffer insert(int offset, int i)**
Inserts an `int` into the `StringBuffer` at the specified `offset`, increasing the size of the buffer if necessary.

◆ **synchronized StringBuffer insert(int offset, char c)**
Inserts a character into the `StringBuffer` at the specified `offset`, increasing the size of the buffer if necessary.

◆ **StringBuffer insert(int offset, boolean b)**
Inserts a `boolean` into the `StringBuffer` at the specified `offset`, increasing the size of the buffer if necessary.

◆ **synchronized StringBuffer insert(int offset, char str[ ])**
Inserts an array of characters into the `StringBuffer` at the specified `offset`, increasing the size of the buffer if necessary.

◆ **synchronized StringBuffer insert(int offset, Object obj)**
Inserts a `double` into the `StringBuffer` at the specified `offset`, increasing the size of the buffer if necessary. The string added will be equal to the value returned by the `String.valueOf(obj)` method.

◆ **synchronized StringBuffer insert(int offset, String str)**
Inserts a `String` into the `StringBuffer` at the specified `offset`, increasing the size of the buffer if necessary.

◆ **int length( )**
Returns the length of the `StringBuffer`.

◆ **synchronized void setCharAt(int index, char ch)**
Sets the character at the specified `index` to `ch`.

◆ **String toString( )**
Returns the contents of the `StringBuffer` as a `String`.

System

Java programs, especially applets, are handled by the Java Virtual Machine in a manner that hides a great deal of functionality from you, the programmer. This is primarily the result of Java's aim to be completely platform-independent. However, in conjunction with the `Runtime` class, the `System` class enables you gain control of some system-related functions—such as garbage collection—all in a system-independent manner.

To use the `System` class, it is not necessary (and in fact impossible) to create a `System` object. However, because all methods in the class are static, you may use the methods shown in Listing 16 (see fig. 22).

Listing 16   System Example

```
public class SystemExample {

    public static void main(String argv()) {

        System.out.print("This is an example of the standard");
        System.out.println("output stream.");

        String s = System.getProperty("java.version");
        System.out.println("I am using Java " + s + ".");
    }
}
```

You will see that the only important method in the
`RGBFilterClass` is the `filterRGB()` method.
Implementing it in the `MyRGBImageFilter` class not only
makes this class non-abstract, but also performs the actual chore
of changing the value of the pixels.

Listing 11   MyRGBImageFilter Example

```
public class ImageFilterExample extends Applet {

    Image newimage, image;

    public void init() {

        image = getImage(getCodeBase(), "fract.jpg");
        ImageFilter filter = new MyRGBFilter();
        ImageProducer producer = new
➥FilteredImageSource(image.getSource(), filter);
        newimage = createImage(producer);
    }

    public void paint (Graphics g) {
        g.drawImage(newimage,10,10,100,100,this);
        g.drawImage(image,200,85,100,100,this);
    }
}

public class MYRGBFilter extends RGBImageFilter {
    private int width;
    private int shift;

    public int filterRGB(int x, int y, int rgb) {
        return( rgb >> 1);
    }
}
```

Fields

▶ **protected boolean canFilterIndexColorModel**

If `true`, enables the filter to handle pixel values from
`IndexColorModel` tables. If your `filterRGB()` method

is independent of the coordinates of the pixel, this field
should be true.

▶ **protected ColorModel newmodel**
Set by the substituteColorModel( ) method.

▶ **protected ColorModel origmodel**
Set by the substituteColorModel( ) method.

Methods

◆ **RGBImageFilter( )**
Creates a new RGBImageFilter.

◆ **IndexColorModel**
filterIndexColorModel(IndexColorModel icm)
Filters the specified IndexColorModel tables, returning a
modified version of the model.

◆ **void filterRGBPixels(int x, int y, int w, int h, int pixels[ ],**
int offset, int scansize)
Filters a portion of the pixel[] array by passing each pixel
through the filterRGB() method. offset defines the
beginning of the portion to be filtered. x and y define the
coordinates of this pixel. w and h specify the size of the area
to be filtered. scansize defines the number of pixels per
row.

◆ **void setColorModel(ColorModel model)**
If this filter class can handle IndexColorModels and the
specified ColorModel is an IndexColorModel, this
method will cause the specified model to be replaced by its
filtered version whenever encountered in the setPixels()
methods.

◆ **void substituteColorModel(ColorModel oldcm,**
ColorModel newcm)
Causes the oldcm to be substituted for the newcm when-
ever it is encountered in the setPixels() methods.

◆ **static int enumerate(Thread tarray[ ])**
Places in the array every active `Thread` in the
`ThreadGroup` of this `Thread`. It returns the number of
`Threads` placed in the array.

◆ **final String getName( )**
Returns the name of this thread.

◆ **final int getPriority( )**
Returns the priority of this `Thread`.

◆ **final ThreadGroup getThreadGroup( )**
Returns the `ThreadGroup` to which this `Thread` belongs.

◆ **void interrupt( )**
Interrupts the thread. This method must be overridden, or it
will return a `NoSuchMethodException`.

◆ **static boolean interrupted( )**
Used to determine if this `Thread` has been interrupted. This
method must be overridden, or it will return a
`NoSuchMethodException`.

◆ **boolean isInterrupted( )**
Used to determine if another `Thread` has been interrupted.
This method must be overridden, or it will return a
`NoSuchMethodException`.

◆ **final boolean isDaemon( )**
Returns `true` if the `Thread` is a daemon.

◆ **final void join( ) throws InterruptedException**
Waits an unlimited amount of time for the thread to die.

◆ **final synchronized void join(long millis, int nanos)
throws InterruptedException**
Waits the specified amount of time for the thread to die. It
uses `java.lang.wait( )`.

◆ **final synchronized void join(long millis) throws InterruptedException**
Waits the specified amount of time for the thread to die. It uses `java.lang.wait( )`.

◆ **final void resume( )**
Used to restart a thread after it has been suspended.

◆ **void run( )**
The body of execution for the thread. Although the `run( )` method can use other methods, it is the only method that can run concurrently with other operations. Any method in the thread intended to run while another operation is occurring must be called from the `run( )` method.

◆ **final void setDaemon(boolean on)**
If `on` is `true`, the `Thread` is "daemonized," allowing it to run in the background independently from Java operations.

◆ **final void setName(String name)**
Sets the name of the `Thread`.

◆ **final void setPriority(int newPriority)**
Sets the priority of the `Thread`.

◆ **static void sleep(long millis, int nanos) throws InterruptedException**
Causes the `Thread` to pause for the specified amount of time.

◆ **static void sleep(long millis) throws InterruptedException**
Causes the `Thread` to pause for the specified amount of time.

◆ **synchronized void start( )**
Causes the `run( )` method to begin.

◆ **final synchronized void stop(Throwable obj)**
Stops the thread, specifying a `Throwable` object as a reason for termination.

◆ **final void stop( )**
Calls the `stop(Throwable)` method with an instance of `ThreadDeath` as the argument.

◆ **final void suspend( )**
Suspends the current thread. To restart it, use the `resume( )` method.

◆ **static void yield( )**
Yields time to any waiting `Threads`.

◆ **String toString( )**
Returns a string containing the `Thread`'s name, priority, and `ThreadGroup`.

ThreadGroup

Because threads are somewhat independent processes, it is often advantageous to place some constraints on them in order to manage them better. The `ThreadGroup` class enables you to create collections of `Threads`. Furthermore, it enables you to create a hierarchy of `ThreadGroups` in which a `Thread` can access all `Threads` in the same group, but no `Threads` above it in the current hierarchy.

Methods

◆ **ThreadGroup(String name)**
Creates a `ThreadGroup` with the specified name. The current `ThreadGroup` will become the parent of the new `ThreadGroup`.

◆ **ThreadGroup(ThreadGroup parent, String name)**
Creates a new `ThreadGroup` with the specified name and parent.

◆ **synchronized int activeCount( )**
Returns the number of active threads in this group.

◆ **synchronized int activeGroupCount( )**
Returns the number of active thread groups in this group.

◆ **final void checkAccess( )**
Sees if the current thread can modify this `ThreadGroup`.
Uses the `checkAccess( )` method in the current
`SecurityManager`.

◆ **final synchronized void destroy( )**
Destroys the `ThreadGroup`, but does not harm the individual threads.

◆ **int enumerate(Thread list[ ])**
Places a reference to every active `Thread` in this group in
the `list[ ]` array. It returns the number of elements in the
array.

◆ **int enumerate(Thread list[ ], boolean recurse)**
Places a reference to every active `Thread` in this group in
the `list[ ]` array. If `recurse` is `true`, this method also
transverses and adds all `Threads` in all `ThreadGroups`
that are in this group. It returns the number of elements in
the array.

◆ **int enumerate(ThreadGroup list[ ])**
Places a reference to every active `ThreadGroup` in this
group in the `list[ ]` array. It returns the number of
elements in the array.

◆ **int enumerate(ThreadGroup list[ ], boolean recurse)**
Places a reference to every active `Thread` in this group in
the `list[ ]` array. If `recurse` is `true`, this method also
transverses and adds the `ThreadsGroups` in all
`ThreadGroups` that are in this group. It returns the
number of elements in the array.

◆ **final int getMaxPriority( )**
Returns the maximum priority of all the methods in this group.

◆ **final String getName( )**
Returns the name of the group.

◆ **final ThreadGroup getParent( )**
Returns the parent of the group.

◆ **final boolean isDaemon( )**
Returns the value of the `daemon` flag in this `ThreadGroup`. All `Threads` created by a `Thread` in this `ThreadGroup` will inherit the same flag.

◆ **synchronized void list( )**
Prints all `Threads` and `ThreadGroups` in this `ThreadGroup` to `System.out`.

◆ **final boolean parentOf(ThreadGroup anotherGroup)**
Returns `true` if this `ThreadGroup` is the parent of, or equal to, `anotherGroup`.

◆ **final synchronized void resume( )**
Invokes the `resume( )` method in all `Threads` belonging to this `ThreadGroup` and any of its child `ThreadGroups`.

◆ **final void setDaemon(boolean daemon)**
Sets the `daemon` flag for this `ThreadGroup`.

◆ **final synchronized void setMaxPriority(int level)**
Sets the maximum priority level for any new `Threads` created in this group.

◆ **final synchronized void stop( )**
Invokes the `stop( )` method in all `Threads` belonging to this `ThreadGroup` and any of its child `ThreadGroups`.

◆ **final synchronized void suspend( )**
   Invokes the `suspend( )` method in all `Threads` belonging
   to this `ThreadGroup` and any of its child `ThreadGroups`.

◆ **String toString( )**
   Returns a string containing the name of this group and its
   maximum priority level.

◆ **void uncaughtException(Thread t, Throwable e)**
   Called by the system to handle uncaught exceptions.

Throwable

A `Throwable` object can be thrown by a method. The
`Throwable` class defines a common set of behaviors for all
objects that are thrown from methods. All exceptions and errors
are derived from the `Throwable` class.

▶ *See "Exceptions," p. 298*

▶ *See "Errors," p. 304*

Methods

◆ **Throwable( )**
   Creates a new `Throwable` object.

◆ **Throwable(String message)**
   Creates a new `Throwable` object with the specified error
   message.

◆ **Throwable fillInStackTrace( )**
   Fills the stack trace for this `Throwable` object.

◆ **String getMessage( )**
   Returns the `detailmessage` message of the object. This
   can only be set in the constructor method.

◆ **void printStackTrace( )**
   Prints the stack trace to the standard error output stream
   (`System.err`). This is the error message that is displayed by

the browser when you fail to catch an exception. It is useful in finding the source of your errors, and looks something like the following:

```
java.lang.ArithmeticException: / by zero
        at appletname.init(appletname.java:6)
        at sun.applet.AppletPanel.run(AppletPanel.java:243)
        at java.lang.Thread.run(Thread.java:289)
```

◆ **void printStackTrace(PrintStream s)**
Prints the stack trace to the specified `PrintStream`.

◆ **String toString( )**
Returns a string, including the name of the `Throwable` object and its error message (if any).

Interfaces

Cloneable

Although this interface consists of no methods, it nevertheless provides you with a lot of flexibility. It serves as a flag to the `Object` class. If a class used implements the `Cloneable` interface, you can create a copy of such an object.

Runnable

The `Runnable` interface is a chief example of the power of interfaces. By implementing the `Runnable` interface, you can create a class—most often an applet—that can also serve as a thread.

In Listing 18 and Listing 19, a simple applet class is created that serves as a message scroller (see fig. 24). Using the status bar at the bottom of the browser screen, you are able to scroll through a series
of messages that have been obtained from the applet tag parameters.

▶ *See "Thread Implements Runnable," p. 235*

JAVA.LANG

Java Quick Reference

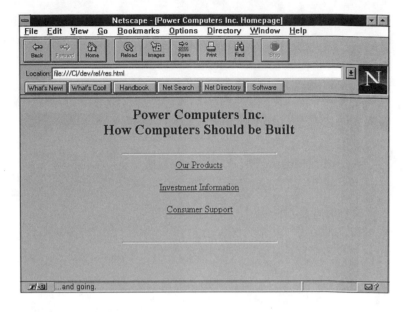

Fig. 24 The output of Listing 18 and Listing 19.

Listing 18 Runnable Example—HTML

```
<HTML>
<HEAD>


<TITLE>Power Computers Inc. Homepage</TITLE>
</HEAD>


<center>
<h2>Power Computers Inc.<br>
How Computers Should be Built</h2>

<hr width=45%>

<a href="\products.html">Our Products</a><P>
<a href="\stocks.html">Investment Information</a><P>
<a href="\operators.html">Consumer Support</a><P>
</center>
```

```
<applet code="runne.class" width=0 height=0 >
<param name=linenum0 value="This is the message.">
<param name=linenum1 value="It keeps going,">
<param name=linenum2 value="and going...">
<param name=linenum3 value="...and going.">
</applet>
<hr width=45%>
</BODY>
</HTML>
```

Listing 19   Runnable Example—Java Code

```java
import java.applet.Applet;

public class RunnableEx extends Applet implements Runnable
{
   Thread display;
   int pos, max_mes;
   String message[];

   /* This method obtains the applet parameters and stores
      them in message[].  It also sets the max_mes value */

   public void init() {
     String val;
     int i = 0;

     message = new String[30];
                             // can accept up to 30 messages
     do {
       String paramName = "linenum" + i;
       val = getParameter(paramName);
       if (val != null) {
         message[i] = val;
        i++;
       }
     } while (val != null);
```

continues

Java Quick Reference

Listing 19   Continued

```
  max_mes = i-1;     /* we don't want to display the null
          message that caused the do loop to terminate */
  pos = 0;

  for (int j = 0; j <= max_mes; j++)
  System.out.println(j+message[j]);
}

/* This method creates and begins the thread. */
public void start() {
  if (display == null)
    display = new Thread(this);
    display.start();
}

public void stop() {
  if (display != null) {
    display.stop();
    display = null;
  }
}

public void run() {
/* We don't want the scroller to receive too
  much attention. */
Thread.currentThread().setPriority(Thread.MIN_PRIORITY);

while (display != null) {
  getAppletContext().showStatus( message[pos++]);
  if (pos > max_mes)
    pos = 0;

    try {
      Thread.sleep(1000);    // pauses
    }
    catch (Exception e) {
      System.out.println( e.toString() );
```

```
        }  // end catch
      }  // end while
    }  // end method
  }  // end class
```

For the sake of simplicity, an array of `Strings` is used to store the lines of text. To create a more efficient and flexible model, it would be advisable to use a more adaptive construct, such as a `Vector`.

Method
◆ **abstract void run( )**

JAVA.NET

CLASSES AND INTERFACES

JAVA.NET

Because Java is a network-based language, this comparatively small package is very useful. Most importantly, it provides you with the capability to communicate with other sources of information by creating or connecting to sockets or making use of URLs and Internet addresses.

Classes

Abstract ContentHandler

This class is used to return a specific type of Object from a URL. It is called by the ContentHandlerFactory when an appropriate object is found in a URL.

Methods

◆ **ContentHandler( )**

Creates a new ContentHandler object.

◆ **abstract Object getContent(URLConnection contentSource) throws IOException**

Assuming that the contentSource contains a particular MIME type, this method parses the information from the contentSource and returns the particular Object.

DatagramPacket

A DatagramPacket is a bundle of information that can be transmitted across a networking stream. Such an object encapsulates a lot of information about the bundle, including the information contained, its length, and the host from which it was sent.

The following are private fields within the class:

```
private byte[] buf;
private int length;
private InetAddress address;
private int port;
```

These fields cannot be accessed explicitly in your code; however, it is advantageous to know what a `DatagramPacket` does and does not contain.

▶ *See "DatagramSocket," below.*

Methods

◆ **DatagramPacket(byte buf[ ], int length)**

Creates a `DatagramPacket` that will receive information. The data of the packet will be stored in the `buf[ ]` array. `length` specifies the number of bytes to be received. The `address` will be set to `null` and the `port` to −1.

◆ **DatagramPacket(byte buf[ ], int length, InetAddress destAddr, int destPort)**

Creates a `DatagramPacket` to send information. The information packet will consist of the first `length` bytes of the `buf[ ]` array. `destAddr` and `destPort` specify the recipient of the packet.

◆ **InetAddress getAddress( )**

Returns `address` field—the host to which the information will be sent or the host from which the information was received.

◆ **byte[ ] getData( )**

Returns information contained in the packet—either the information that has been received or that will be sent.

◆ **int getLength( )**

Returns the `length` field set in the constructor method.

◆ **int getPort( )**

Returns the `port` field to which the packet will be sent or from which the packet was received.

DatagramSocket

A `DatagramSocket` is a socket that is used in transmitting a `DatagramPacket`. A `DatagramSocket` is different from a standard `Socket` in that it implements no means of error checking. It does not ensure that all packets are sent or received in their entirety. Therefore, it is referred to as *unreliable.*

▶ *See "DatagramPacket," p. 252*

Methods

◆ **DatagramSocket(int port) throws SocketException**
Creates a `DatagramSocket` to listen to a given port.

◆ **DatagramSocket( ) throws SocketException**
Creates a `DatagramSocket` whose port number will be assigned by the system.

◆ **protected synchronized void finalize( )**
Used to perform cleanup. As is, this method closes the socket.

◆ **int getLocalPort( )**
Returns the port to which the socket is bound on the system.

◆ **synchronized void receive(DatagramPacket p) throws IOException**
Reads a `DatagramPacket` from the stream, waiting until one is available.

◆ **void send(DatagramPacket p) throws IOException**
Sends a `DatagramPacket` across the stream.

Final InetAddress

An `InetAddress` is a convenient manner of handling Internet addresses. It can be used to store both raw IP addresses as well as more friendly host names.

Methods

◆ **static synchronized InetAddress[ ] getAllByName(String hostName) throws UnknownHostException**
Returns all addresses for the specified `hostName`.

◆ **static InetAddress getLocalHost( ) throws UnknownHostException**
Returns an `InetAddress` object representing the local host.

◆ **boolean equals(Object anotherObject)**
Returns `true` if `anotherObject` is an `InetAddress` with the same address as this `InetAddress`.

◆ **byte[ ] getAddress( )**
Returns the raw IP address of this `InetAddress`. The returned array will consist of four bytes.

◆ **static synchronized InetAddress getByName(String hostName) throws UnknownHostExction**
Returns a single address for the specified `hostName`.

◆ **String getHostName( )**
Returns the host name of this `InetAddress`.

◆ **int hashCode( )**
Returns the `hashcode` value of this `InetAddress`: the IP address.

◆ **String toString( )**
Returns a string containing the host name and the IP address of this `InetAddress`.

ServerSocket

`ServerSocket` creates a server-side socket to be used in communications. By default, it is created based on the `PlainSocket SocketImpl`, which performs no security checks. However, you can specify the `socketImpl` for the `ServerSocket` to enhance security restrictions.

Methods

◆ **ServerSocket(int port) throws IOException**
Creates a new socket on the specified `port` using the current `SocketImplFactory`.

♦ **ServerSocket(int port, int count) throws IOException**
Creates a new socket on the specified `port` using the
current `SocketImplFactory`. `count` specifies the
amount of time that the socket will wait for a connection.

♦ **Socket accept( ) throws IOException**
Waits for a request and then properly handles a request for a
connection. It returns the `Socket` that contains the actual
connection.

♦ **void close( ) throws IOException**
Closes the socket connection.

♦ **InetAddress getInetAddress( )**
Returns the `InetAddress` to which the socket is connected.

♦ **int getLocalPort( )**
Returns the port number to which the socket is listening.

♦ **String toString( )**
Returns a string containing the address and port to which
the socket is bound as well as the local port number.

♦ **static synchronized void
setSocketFactory(SocketImplFactory fac) throws
IOException**
Sets the `SocketImplFactory` for this `ServerSocket`
object. All future sockets that are created with this
`ServerSocket` object will employ the specified
`SocketImplFactory`. This method can be used only
once on a `ServerSocket` object.

Socket

`Socket` creates a client-side socket to be used in communications. By default, it is based on the `PlainSocket`
`SocketImpl`, which performs no security checks. However,
you can specify the `socketImpl` for the `ServerSocket` to
enhance security.

When using a `Socket`, you must consider *who* you will be speaking to. In general, you will communicate with a socket server residing on a specific port. In such a case, will you be writing the server? What protocol will be used? Will the host name and port be fixed?

Furthermore, you must remember to use the `getInputStream( )` and `getOutputStream( )` methods to communicate with the socket, inasmuch as these streams are not accessible outside of the sun packages.

The code in Listing 20 lays the foundation for a standard socket communication. The `DataInputStream` in and the `OutputStream` out will enable you to freely communicate over the socket if the connection has been successful.

Listing 20   Socket Example

```
import java.net.Socket;
import java.io.*;
public class Client {
    String host = "host.name.com";
    int port = 1500;

    try {
      me = new Socket(host,port);
      in = new DataInputStream(me.getInputStream( ));
      out = me.getOutputStream( );
    }
    catch (Exception e) {
        System.out.prinln( e.toString( )  );
    }

      .
      .
      .

    }
```

Methods

◆ **Socket(String host, int port) throws UnknownHostException, IOException**

Creates a Socket and attempts to connect it to the specified port on the specified host.

◆ **Socket(InetAddress host, int port) throws IOException**

Creates a Socket and attempts to connect it to the specified port on the specified host.

◆ **Socket(String host, int port, boolean stream) throws IOException**

Creates a Socket and attempts to connect it to the specified port on the specified host. If stream is true, then the information will be read as a stream. If stream is false, then it will be read in packets as a DatagramSocket would.

◆ **Socket(InetAddress address, int port, boolean stream) throws IOException**

Creates a Socket and attempts to connect it to the specified port on the specified host. If stream is true, then the information will be read as a stream. If stream is false, then it will be read in packets as a DatagramSocket would.

◆ **synchronized void close( ) throws IOException**

Closes the socket.

◆ **InetAddress getInetAddress( )**

Returns the InetAddress of the host to which the Socket is connected.

◆ **InputStream getInputStream( ) throws IOException**

Returns the InputStream for this Socket. This method is necessary if you want to read from the stream.

◆ **int getLocalPort( )**

Returns the local port to which the socket is connected.

◆ **OutputStream getOutputStream( ) throws IOException**
Returns the OutputStream for this Socket. This method
is necessary if you want to write to the stream.

◆ **int getPort( )**
Returns the port to which the socket is connected on the
remote machine.

◆ **static synchronized void
setSocketImplFactory(SocketImplFactory fac) throws
IOException**
Sets the SocketImplFactory for this object. Future
Sockets created by this object will be based on this factory.
This method can be called only once.

◆ **String toString( )**
Returns a string containing the host and the port to which
the socket is connected as well as the local port.

Abstract SocketImpl

The SocketImpl class defines a set of behaviors necessary for
communication between sockets. This functionality is integral to
socket communication and is used by the Socket and
ServerSocket classes. However, most programmers find little
need to use it explicitly.

Fields

❱ **protected InetAddress address**
The address to which the socket is connected.

❱ **protected FileDescriptor fd**
A *FileDescriptor* object used internally when reading
and writing from a socket. This is because the socket
interface is based on the FileInputStream and
FileOutputStream classes.

❱ **protected int localport**
The local port used by the socket.

> ▶ **protected int port**
> The port on the remote system to which the socket is connected.

Methods

◆ **SocketImpl( )**
Creates a new SocketImpl.

◆ **protected abstract void accept(SocketImpl connection) throws IOException**
Accepts the specified connection.

◆ **protected abstract int available( ) throws IOException**
Returns the number of bytes available in the stream.

◆ **protected abstract void bind(InetAddress host, int port) throws IOException**
Binds the socket to the specified host and port.

◆ **protected abstract void close( ) throws IOException**
Closes the socket.

◆ **protected abstract void connect(InetAddress host, int port) throws IOException**
Connects the socket to the specified host and port.

◆ **protected abstract void connect(String host, int port) throws IOException**
Connects the socket to the specified host and port.

◆ **protected abstract void create(boolean stream) throws IOException**
Creates a socket. If stream is true, then the socket will read information as a stream. If it is false, then information will be read in packets.

◆ **FileDescriptor getFileDescriptor( )**
Returns the FileDescriptor object for this socket. This descriptor is used in creating the stream interaction.

◆ **protected InetAddress getInetAddress( )**
   Returns the `InetAddress` to which the socket is connected.

◆ **protected abstract InputStream getInputStream( ) throws IOException**
   Returns the `InputStream` that will obtain information from the socket stream.

◆ **protected int getLocalPort( )**
   Returns the local port number connected to the socket.

◆ **protected abstract OutputStream getOutputStream( ) throws IOException**
   Returns the `OutputStream` that will write information to the socket stream.

◆ **protected int getPort( )**
   Returns the port number to which the socket is connected.

◆ **protected abstract void listen(int time) throws IOException**
   Listens to the socket for the specified amount of `time`, awaiting requests for connections.

◆ **String toString( )**
   Returns a string containing the host and the port to which the socket is connected as well as the local port.

URL

The function of the `URL` class is twofold. Most simply, it enables you to handle the semantic operations of `URL`, such as parsing the file or host name of the URL. More importantly, however, it also serves as a handle for the retrieval of the information stored at the specific URL.

Methods

◆ **URL(String link) throws MalformedURLException**
   Creates a `URL` object from the specified string containing a complete URL.

◆ **URL(URL context, String fileName) throws MalformedURLException**

Creates a URL object with the same host name and protocol as context, but using the fileName specified.

For example, examine the following code:

```
URL u1 = new
URL("http","www.xyz.com",1500,"/
➥foo.html#abc");
URL u = new URL(u1, "funny.html");
System.out.println( u1.toString() );
System.out.println( u.toString() );
```

The output will look as follows:

```
http://www.xyz.com:1500/foo.html#abc
http://www.xyz.com:1500/funny.html
```

◆ **URL(String protocol, String host, String file) throws MalformedURLException**

Creates a new URL that will use the specified protocol to interact with the specified host. file is the name of the file to which the URL pertains, such as a HTML document or a file to be received via FTP.

◆ **URL(String protocol, String host, int port, String file) throws MalformedURLException**

Creates a new URL that will use the specified protocol to interact with the specified host on the specified port. file is the name of the file to which the URL pertains, such as a HTML document or a file to be received via FTP.

◆ **int getPort( )**

Returns the port from which the URL will obtain its information.

◆ **String getProtocol( )**

Returns the port from which the URL will obtain its information.

◆ **boolean equals(Object anotherObject)**

Returns `true` if `anotherObject` is a URL object express-ing an interest in the same file in the same manner. This means that `anotherObject` must have the same protocol, host, port, and file. However, any "#ref" fields at the end of the URL are ignored. (This is the value that is returned by the `sameFile( )` method.)

◆ **final Object getContent( ) throws IOException**
◆ **String getFile( )**

Returns the name of the file that the URL is interested in.

◆ **String getHost( )**

Returns the host from which the URL will obtain its informa-tion.

◆ **String getRef( )**

Returns the `ref` of the URL—anything following the pound sign (#).

◆ **int hashCode( )**

Returns the `hashcode` of the URL object—a value depen-dent on the `hashcode` of the protocol, host, and file name.

◆ **URLConnection openConnection( ) throws IOException**

Opens a connection to obtain the information contained in the file specified by the URL. It returns an appropriate `URLConnection` based on the current `URLStreamHandler`.

◆ **final InputStream openStream( ) throws IOException**

Opens an `InputStream` to the URL. This is done by first creating a `URLConnection` object and then obtaining the `InputStream` via the `URLConnection.getInputStream( )` method.

◆ **boolean sameFile(URL otherURL)**
Returns `true` if the `otherURL` refers to the same file in the same manner. This means that `otherURL` must have the same protocol, host, port, and file. However, any "#ref" fields at the end of the URL are ignored.

◆ **protected void set(String protocol, String host, int port, String file, String ref)**
Sets the fields of the `URL`. This method is protected to enable only `URLStreamHandlers` to change these fields.

◆ **static synchronized void setURLStreamHandlerFactory(URLStreamHandlerFactory fac)**
Sets the `URLStreamHandlerFactory` for this `URL`. The `URLStreamHandlerFactory` will determine how to handle the content of the `URL`'s document.

◆ **String toExternalForm( )**
Combines the various fields to create a URL in *standard* format.

◆ **String toString( )**
Combines the various fields to create a URL in *standard* format.

Abstract URLConnection

The `URLConnection` class is an abstract class that can be used to assist in managing a connection based on a `URL` object.

Fields

▶ **protected boolean allowUserInteraction**
Some URLs require user input—such as in filling out a password box. It is initially set to `false`, meaning any requests to obtain user interaction will cause an exception.

▶ **protected boolean connected**
Tracks the status of the `URLConnection`—connected or not.

❯ **protected boolean doInput**

True if the URLConnection is to be used as a source of input. It is initially set as true.

❯ **protected boolean doOutput**

True if the URLConnection is to be used as a source of input. It is initially set as false.

❯ **protected long ifModifiedSince**

This field may be used to make the connection more efficient by not loading old information. It is initially set to 0 and further requires you to implement it yourself in any subclasses.

❯ **protected URL url**

The URL with which the connection has been made.

❯ **protected boolean useCaches**

If useCaches is true, the connection will make use of cached information whenever possible. This field is initially true.

Methods

◆ **protected URLConnection(URL url)**

Creates a URLConnection to the specified URL.

◆ **abstract void connect( ) throws IOException**

Creates a connection to the specified URL of this object.

◆ **boolean getAllowUserInteraction( )**

Returns the allowUserInteraction flag.

◆ **Object getContent( ) throws IOException**

Returns the object referred to by the URL.

◆ **String getContentEncoding( )**

Returns the "content encoding" field from the headers of this URL.

Java Quick Reference

◆ **int getContentLength( )**
   Returns the "content length" from the headers of the URL.

◆ **String getContentType( )**
   Returns the "content type" field from the list of headers of
   this URL.

◆ **long getDate( )**
   Returns the "date" field from the list of headers of this URL.

◆ **boolean getDoInput( )**
   Returns the doInput field of this object.

◆ **boolean getDoOutput( )**
   Returns the doOutput field of this object.

◆ **long getExpiration( )**
   Returns the "expires" field from the headers of the URL.

◆ **String getHeaderField(int n)**
   Returns the title of the nth field from the header list. Returns
   null if there are less than n headers. Currently returns a
   null string.

◆ **String getHeaderField(String name)**
   Returns the value of the header with the specified name.

◆ **long getHeaderFieldDate(String name, long Default)**
   Returns the value of the header with the specified name as a
   date.

◆ **int getHeaderFieldInt(String name, int Default)**
   Returns the value of the specified header field as an int.

◆ **String getHeaderFieldKey(int n)**
   Returns the value of the nth field in the header list. It returns
   null if there are fewer than n headers.

◆ **InputStream getInputStream( ) throws IOException**
   Returns the InputStream for this URLConnection.

◆ **long getLastModified( )**

Returns the value of the "last modified" field, or 0 if undefined.

◆ **OutputStream getOutputStream( ) throws IOException**

Returns the OutputStream for this URLConnection.

◆ **URL getURL( )**

Returns the URL from which this URLConnection is obtaining its information.

◆ **void setAllowUserInteraction(boolean allow)**

Sets the allowUserInteraction field to the specified allow value.

◆ **static void setDefaultAllowUserInteraction(boolean default)**

Sets the default value for the allowUserInteraction field.

◆ **void setDoInput(boolean doinput)**

Sets the value of the doInput field.

◆ **void setDoOutput(boolean dooutput)**

Sets the value of the doOutput field.

◆ **String toString( )**

Returns a string containing the class name and the name of the URL to which this URLConnection is connected.

◆ **static boolean getDefaultAllowUserInteraction( )**

Returns the default value for the allowUserInteraction field.

◆ **static String getDefaultRequestProperty(String key)**

Returns the default value for the allowUserInteraction field. By default, this returns a null string and thus must be overridden.

◆ **boolean getDefaultUseCaches( )**
Returns the default value for the `useCaches` field.

◆ **long getIfModifiedSince( )**
Returns the `isModifiedSince` field.

◆ **String getRequestProperty(String key)**
Returns the general request property whose name is `key`.

◆ **boolean getUseCaches( )**
Returns the `useCaches` field.

◆ **static synchronized void
setContentHandlerFactory(ContentHandlerFactory fac)**
Specifies the `ContentHandlerFactory` for this object.

◆ **static void setDefaultRequestProperty(String key, String
value)**
This method can be used to set the default value of a
request property for the `URLConnection`. Unless overridden this method does nothing.

◆ **void setDefaultUseCaches(boolean defaultusecaches)**
Sets the default value for the `useCaches` field.

◆ **void setIfModifiedSince(long ifmodifiedsince)**
Sets the value of the `ifModifiedSince` field.

◆ **void setRequestProperty(String key, String value)**
This method can be used to set a request property to be
used by this `URLConnection`. Currently, the method does
nothing.

◆ **void setUseCaches(boolean usecaches)**
Sets the value for the `useCaches` field.

◆ **static String guessContentTypeFromName(String
fileName)**
Returns a string containing the MIME type that is most likely
contained in the file with the specified `fileName`. This

method is already implemented for you and recognizes a total of 39 content-type-specifying extensions, including .exe, .zip, .gif, and .html.

◆ **static String guessContentTypeFromStream(InputStream is) throws IOException**
This method can be used to guess at the content type based on the first six bytes of the stream. This method recognizes image/gif, image/jpg, image/x-bitmap, and text/html data MIME types.

URLEncoder

This class is simply a means of translating standard strings into x-www-form-urlencoded format. This process involves such conversions as changing spaces to '+' symbols and representing non-alphanumeric characters with hexadecimal numbers. This is the format that you will see used in standard URLs when passing information to CGI scripts.

Method

◆ **static String encode(String s)**
Translates a string in standard format to one in x-www-form-urlencoded format. All spaces become '+' symbols and all characters except digits, characters, and the underscore character '_' are translated into numerical representations in hex format.

Abstract URLStreamHandler

A `URLStreamHandler` is a rather simple class used to transform a `URL` into a `URLConnection`.

Methods

◆ **URLStreamHandler( )**
Creates a new `URLStreamHandler`.

◆ **abstract URLConnection openConnection(URL url) throws IOException**
This method creates an `InputStream` to receive information from the specified URL. It must be overridden to make the class non-abstract.

◆ **void parseURL(URL url, String spec, int start, int limit)**
Parses the `spec` string between (and including) characters `start` and `limit` and stores their values in the `URL` object. Note that although no new `URL` is returned, the fields in the specified `URL` will change inasmuch as this method sets the internal fields of the `URL`.

◆ **void setURL(URL url, String protocol, String host, int port, String file, String ref)**
Sets the fields of the specified `URL` object. Note that although no new `URL` is returned, the fields in the specified `URL` will change inasmuch as this method sets the internal fields of the `URL`.

◆ **String toExternalForm(URL url)**
Returns a string representing the specified URL from which this object is retrieving its information.

Interfaces

ContentHandlerFactory

A `ContentHandlerFactory` can be used to create a manager that will return the appropriate `ContentHandler` for a specified MIME type. Such classes are used by the `URLConnection` class to correctly handle incoming data.

Method

◆ **abstract ContentHandler createContentHandler(String mimetype)**
Returns the `ContentHandler` specific for the distinct MIME type.

SocketImplFactory

The `SocketImplFactory` enables you to make use of the `SocketImpl` class. The `SocketImplFactory` class will return a `SocketImpl` in response to a request to create a socket. By using the `setSocketFactory` in the `java.net.severSocket` class, you can specify which `SocketImplFactory` you want to use and thus which `SocketImpl` will be employed.

Method

◆ **abstract SocketImpl createSocketImpl( )**

Creates a new `SocketImpl` object to be used in creating a socket.

URLStreamHandlerFactory

By means of the `CreateURLStreamHandler( )` method, the `URLStreamHandlerFactory` class creates `URLStreamHandlers` for specific types of data streams. This class is generally not explicitly used in programs.

Method

◆ **abstract URLStreamHandler CreateURLStreamHandler(String protocol)**

Creates a `URLStreamHandler` to handle a URL with the specified protocol.

JAVA.UTIL

CLASSES AND INTERFACES

 **JAVA.UTIL**

This package is essentially a smorgasbord of useful classes that do not truly fit into any of the other packages. Among these handy classes are the Date class, designed to manage and handle operations with dates, the Hashtable class, and ADTs, such as Stack and Vector.

Classes

BitSet Implements java.lang.Cloneable

A Bitset is a dynamic collection of bits that has the added capability of basic logical operations. Although you may perform some logical operations on a BitSet, the methods do not return a new BitSet, but rather modify the current BitSet. As demonstrated in Listing 21 and shown in figure 25, the logical operation will result in a change of the original BitSet.

```
Command Prompt

C:\dev\ref>java bitsetex
This is the first set: {0, 1, 2}
This is the second set: {0, 1, 8, 9}
The following elements are in both sets: {0, 1}

C:\dev\ref>
```

Fig. 25 The output of Listing 21.

Listing 21   BitSet Example

```java
import java.util.BitSet;

public class BitsetExample {
    public static void main(String argv[]) {

        BitSet a = new BitSet();
        BitSet b = new BitSet();

        a.set(0);
        a.set(1);
        a.set(2);
```

```
    b.set(0);
    b.set(1);
    b.set(8);
    b.set(9);

    System.out.println("This is the first set: " + a);
    System.out.println("This is the second set: " + b);
    a.and(b);    // places all elements in both sets into a
    System.out.print("The following elements are in both");
    System.our.println(" sets: " + a );
  }
}
```

Methods

◆ **BitSet( )**

Creates a new BitSet with a size of 64.

◆ **BitSet(int nbits)**

Creates a new BitSet with the specified size.

◆ **vold and(BitSet set)**

Places all elements of both sets into the original set—the logical intersection of the two.

◆ **void clear(int bit)**

Removes all instances of the specified bit from the set.

◆ **Object clone( )**

Creates a copy of the current set.

◆ **boolean equals(Object anotherObject)**

Returns true if anotherObject is a BitSet with the same elements.

◆ **boolean get(int bit)**

Returns true if the specified bit can be found in this BitSet.

◆ **int hashCode( )**
Returns the `hashcode` of the set—a value based on its elements.

◆ **void or(BitSet set)**
Places all elements of either this `BitSet` or the specified `set` into this set—the logical union.

◆ **void set(int bit)**
Places the specified bit in the set.

◆ **int size( )**
Returns the size of the set.

◆ **String toString( )**
Returns a string containing the set in standard set notation, for example, {1, 2, 3}.

◆ **void xor(BitSet set)**
Places all elements of one, but not both, sets into the current set. This contains all elements in the union but not the intersection.

Date

The `Date` class provides you with a convenient means of managing dates and times. Rather flexible, this class enables you to set and manipulate the date in a number of ways, and can handle time zone and daylight-savings time conversions.

Methods

◆ **Date( )**
Creates a `Date` based on the current time.

◆ **Data(long date)**
Creates a `Date` based on the specified `date`, representing the number of milliseconds since 00:00:00 GMT, January 1, 1970. Although this may seem a rather abstruse manner of specifying a time, this compacted format is extremely efficient.

To obtain the current time in milliseconds since 00:00:00 GMT, January 1, 1970, use the `System.currentTimeMillis()`.

◆ **Date(int year, int month, int date)**
Creates a `Date` with the specified `year`, `month`, and `date`. The year must be later than 1900.

◆ **Date(int year, int month, int date, int hours, int min)**
Creates a `Date` with the specified `year`, `month`, `date`, `hours`, and `min` values. The year must be later than 1900.

◆ **Date(String dateString)**
Creates a `Date` with values specified in `dateString`. This relies on `parse()`, which accepts dates in such formats as "`Tue, 26 Mar 1996 04:05:00 GMT+1900`".

◆ **Date(int year, int month, int date, int hrs, int min, int sec)**
Creates a `Date` with the specified values.

◆ **boolean after(Date when)**
Returns `true` if this `Date` is chronologically after `when`.

◆ **boolean before(Date when)**
Returns `true` if this `Date` is chronologically before `when`.

◆ **boolean equals(Object anotherObject)**
Returns `true` if `anotherObject` is a `Date` with the same `value` field (the number of milliseconds since 1/1/70).

◆ **int getDate( )**
Returns the date of the `Date`: an `int` between 1 and 31.

◆ **int getDay( )**
Returns the weekday of the `Date`: an `int` between 0 and 6 with 0 representing Sunday.

◆ **int getHours( )**
Returns the hour value of the Date: an int between 0 and 23.

◆ **int getMinutes( )**
Returns the minute value of the Date: an int between 0 and 59.

◆ **int getMonth( )**
Returns the month value of the Date: an int between 1 and 12.

◆ **int getSeconds( )**
Returns the seconds value of the Date: an int between 0 and 59.

◆ **long getTime( )**
Returns the date specified by this Date object as a long representing the number of milliseconds since 00:00:00 GMT, January 1, 1970.

◆ **int getTimezoneOffset( )**
Returns the offset of this time zone as the number of minutes from Greenwich mean time.

◆ **int getYear( )**
Returns the year value of this Date offset from 1900. (Thus 100 would represent 2000.)

◆ **int hashCode( )**
Returns the hashcode of the Date: a value based on the number of elapsed seconds since 00:00:00 GMT, January 1, 1970.

◆ **static long parse(String s)**
Parses a string representing a date, returning the number of seconds between that time and 00:00:00 GMT, January 1, 1970.

◆ **void setDate(int date)**
Sets the date (the day of the month) of this Date object.

◆ **void setHours(int hours)**
Sets the hour value of this Date object.

◆ **void setMinutes(int minutes)**
Sets the minutes value of this Date object.

◆ **void setMonth(int month)**
Sets the month value of this Date object.

◆ **void setSeconds(int seconds)**
Sets the seconds value of this Date object.

◆ **void setTime(long time)**
Sets the value of this Date object by specifying a time in milliseconds relative to 00:00:00 GMT, January 1, 1970.

◆ **void setYear(int year)**
Sets the year value for this Date.

◆ **String toGMTString( )**
Returns a string containing the date in GMT format, adjusted for the specified time zone (e.g., 25 Mar 1996 09:05:00 GMT).

◆ **String toLocaleString( )**
Returns a string containing the date in *locale* format, not adjusting for the time zone (e.g., 03/25/96 04:05:00).

◆ **String toString( )**
Returns a string representing the time in a system dependent format.

◆ **static long UTC(int year, int month, int date, int hrs, int min, int sec)**
Returns the time in milliseconds between 00:00:00 GMT, January 1, 1970, and the specified time.

Abstract Dictionary

This class defines the behavior of a Hashtable. While all of its methods serve a purpose in a Hashtable, they are all abstract in this class.

Methods

◆ **Dictionary( )**

Creates a new Dictionary.

◆ **abstract Enumeration elements( )**

Returns an Enumeration of the elements for sequential viewing.

◆ **abstract Object get(Object key)**

Returns the element with the specified key.

◆ **abstract boolean isEmpty( )**

Returns true if the Dictionary is empty.

◆ **abstract Enumeration keys( )**

Returns an Enumeration of the keys for sequential viewing.

◆ **abstract Object put(Object key, Object element)**

Places the specified element in the Dictionary under the specified key.

◆ **abstract Object remove(Object key)**

Removes the key and its corresponding element.

◆ **abstract int size( )**

Returns the number of elements in the Dictionary.

Hashtable Extends Dictionary Implements java.lang.Cloneable

The Hashtable class is a simple implementation of a hashtable ADT. A hashtable provides you with a convenient and efficient means of storing information based on a distinct relationship. Similar to an array, whose elements are

each paired with a specific index, each element in a
hashtable is paired with a specific *key*. By using this key, you
are able to retrieve the information stored in the table.

One important consideration when using the Hashtable class
is that every key and element *must* be an Object. As you can
see in figure 26, this is not a problem when dealing with strings
(see Listing 22).

Fig. 26 The output of Listing 22.

Listing 22   Hashtable Example Using String Objects

```
import java.util.*;
import java.io.DataInputStream;

public class HashtableExample {

    public static void main(String argv[]) {
        Hashtable phones = new Hashtable();
        String name = null;
        String phone = null;

        phones.put("Danny", "555-0718" );
        phones.put("Jason", "555-0031" );
        phones.put("Jaime", "555-2191" );
        phones.put("Jeff",  "555-1391" );
```

continues

Listing 22   Continued

```
System.out.print("Please enter a name ==> ");
System.out.flush(); // forces the prompt to be displayed
DataInputStream din = new DataInputStream(System.in);

try {
  name = din.readLine();
}
catch (Exception e) {
  System.out.println( e.toString() );
}

if (phones.containsKey(name)) {        /* checks to see if
                                          the name is valid */
  phone = (String)phones.get(name);
  System.out.println(name + "'s phone number is " +phone
➡+ "." );
  }
  else {
    System.out.print("Sorry.  I don't know who ");
    System.out.println(name + " is.");
  }
}
```

The requirement to use full-blown Objects poses a slight problem when dealing with primitive data types, such as an int or a float. As shown in Listing 23, whose output can be found in figure 27, it is necessary to create a wrapper Object to handle such primitive data types. This wrapper must be used initially to store the value and again used when retrieving the information.

Fig. 27   The output of Listing 23.

Listing 23   Hashtable Example Using Integer Objects

```java
import java.util.*;
import java.io.DataInputStream;

public class HashtableExample2  {

  public static void main(String argv[]) {
    Hashtable ages = new Hashtable();
    String name = null;
    Integer age = null;

    ages.put("Danny", new Integer(13) );
    ages.put("Jason", new Integer(7)  );
    ages.put("Jaime", new Integer(39) );
    ages.put("Jeff", new Integer(54)  );

    System.out.print("Please enter a name ==> ");
    System.out.flush();
    DataInputStream din = new DataInputStream(System.in);


    try {
      name = din.readLine();
    }
    catch (Exception e) {
      System.out.println( e.toString() );
    }

    if (ages.containsKey(name)) {
      age = (Integer)ages.get(name);
      System.out.print(name + "is " +age.intValue())';
      System.out.println(" years old." );             }
    }
    else {
      System.out.print("Sorry.  I don't know who ");
      System.out.println(name + " is.");
    }
  }
}
```

Methods

◆ **Hashtable( )**

Creates a new Hashtable. The capacity will be set to 101 and the loadFactor will be set to 0.75.

◆ **Hashtable(int initialCapacity)**

Creates a new Hashtable with the specified capacity and a loadFactor of 0.75.

◆ **Hashtable(int initialCapacity, float loadFactor)**

Creates a new Hashtable. initialCapacity is the number of entries that the Hashtable will be able to contain and loadFactor is a number between 0.0 and 1.0 that represents the percentage of the hashtable that may be filled before it is resized via the rehash() method.

◆ **synchronized void clear( )**

Clears the Hashtable, removing all keys and elements.

◆ **synchronized Object clone( )**

Creates a clone of the Hashtable. However, the contents of the new table will be references to the old objects, not new objects.

◆ **synchronized boolean contains(Object value)**

Returns true if value is an element in the hashtable.

◆ **synchronized boolean containsKey(Object key)**

Returns true if key is a key in the hashtable.

◆ **synchronized Enumeration elements( )**

Returns an Enumeration of the elements for sequential viewing.

◆ **synchronized Object get(Object key)**

Returns the element with the specified key.

◆ **boolean isEmpty( )**

Returns true if the hashtable is empty.

◆ **synchronized Enumeration keys( )**
Returns an `Enumeration` of the keys for sequential viewing.

◆ **synchronized Object put(Object key, Object element)**
Places the specified `element` into the `hashtable` with the specified `key`.

◆ **protected void rehash( )**
Resizes the `hashtable`. This is automatically triggered when the size of the `hashtable` exceeds the threshold specified in the `constructor` method. The new `hashtable` will be one more than twice the current size.

◆ **synchronized Object remove(Object key)**
Removes the `key` and its corresponding element. Returns the `key` if properly removed, or `null` if it could not be found.

◆ **int size( )**
Returns the number of elements in the `hashtable`.

◆ **synchronized String toString( )**
Returns a string containing all key-element pairs.

Observable

The `Observable` class enables you to create an `Object` containing data that will be manipulated in close connection with other objects. To use this class, you must extend it to create your own "observable" class. This class will have the ability to communicate with a number of `Observer` classes via the `notifyObservers()` method. As a result, any change in the `Observable` class can trigger an appropriate response in all `Observers`.

▶ *See "Observer," p. 296*

JAVA.UTIL

Methods

◆ **Observable( )**
Creates a new Observable object.

◆ **synchronized void addObserver(Observer o)**
Adds an observer to the list of observers of this object.

◆ **protected synchronized void clearChanged( )**
Sets the changed flag to false.

◆ **synchronized int countObservers( )**
Returns the number of observers.

◆ **synchronized void deleteObserver(Observer o)**
Removes the specified Observer from the list of observers.

◆ **synchronized void deleteObservers( )**
Removes all observers from the observer list.

◆ **synchronized boolean hasChanged( )**
Returns the value of the changed flag.

◆ **synchronized void notifyObservers(Object information)**
Sends the specified information object to all observers.

◆ **void notifyObservers( )**
Sends a null object to all observers.

◆ **protected synchronized void setChanged( )**
Sets the changed flag to true.

Properties Extends Hashtable

The Properties class is a Hashtable that may be saved
and/or loaded. It is generally used to handle system properties,
inasmuch as it is often necessary to retrieve these properties and
sometimes convenient to be able to store them.

▶ *See "System," p. 232*

Field
▶ **protected Properties defaults**
A set of properties that will be used when a property cannot be found in the new `Properties` set.

Methods
◆ **Properties( )**
Creates a new `Properties` object with no set of defaults.

◆ **Properties(Properties defaults)**
Creates a new `Properties` object with the specified set of defaults.

◆ **String getProperty(String key, String defaultValue)**
Returns the property element with the specified `key`. If it cannot be found, the method will then check the default `Properties`. If it is still unable to find the specified `key`, it will return the `defaultValue`.

◆ **String getProperty(String key)**
Returns the property element with the specified `key`. If it cannot be found, the method will then check the default `Properties`.

◆ **void list(PrintStream out)**
Prints out the properties to the specified `PrintStream`.

◆ **synchronized void load(InputStream in) throws IOException**
Retrieves a set of `Properties` from the specified `InputStream`.

◆ **Enumeration propertyNames( )**
Returns an `Enumeration` of all the keys in this `Properties` table.

◆ **synchronized void save(OutputStream out, String header)**

Saves the `Properties` table to the specified `OutputStream` using the `header`.

Random

The `Random` class encapsulates the behavior necessary for creating random numbers.

Methods

◆ **Random( )**

Creates a new `Random` object using the current time in milliseconds as the `seed`.

◆ **Random(long seed)**

Creates a new `Random` object using the specified `seed`.

◆ **double nextDouble( )**

Returns a random number between 0.0 and 1.0.

◆ **float nextFloat( )**

Returns a random number between 0.0 and 1.0.

◆ **synchronized double nextGaussian( )**

Returns a randomly generated `double` centered around 0 but with a standard deviation of 1.0. This means that you will get some numbers above 1.

◆ **int nextInt( )**

Returns a random `int` value.

◆ **long nextLong( )**

Returns a randomly generated `long` value.

◆ **synchronized void setSeed(long seed)**

Sets the `seed` used in generating the random numbers.

Stack Extends Vector

The `Stack` class implements a standard stack ADT. A stack follows the *Last In First Out* (LIFO) algorithm in which new items are placed on top of the stack—thereby making them the first items removed. In Java, each *item* in a stack must be a full-blown `Object`.

Methods
◆ **Stack( )**
Creates an empty `Stack`.

◆ **boolean empty( )**
Returns `true` if the stack is empty.

◆ **Object peek( )**
Returns the top item in the stack without removing it.

◆ **Object pop( )**
Returns the top item in the stack and removes it from the stack.

◆ **Object push(Object item)**
Places the specified `item` at the top of the stack.

◆ **int search(Object item)**
Returns the position of the `item` relative to the top of the stack, or –1 if it is not in the stack.

StringTokenizer Implements Enumeration

The `StringTokenizer` class enables you to parse a string consisting of several sub-strings.

In using a `StringTokenizer`, there are two internal fields that may be altered: the `delimiters` string and the value `retTokens`. The `delimiters` string contains all tokens that are important. When parsing the string, the `StringTokenizer` will return a string if the current characters are in `delimiters`. `retTokens` is a flag that specifies whether or not to return the delimiter characters as separate tokens.

Methods

◆ **StringTokenizer(String str)**

Creates a new `StringTokenizer`. By default,
"\t\n\r" will be used as the delimiter string (making ' ',
'\t', '\n', and '\r' token delimiters), and the
retTokens flag will be set to `false`.

◆ **StringTokenizer(String str, String delim)**

Creates a new `StringTokenizer` with the specified set of
delimiting characters.

◆ **StringTokenizer(String str, String delim, boolean returnTokens)**

Creates a new `StringTokenizer` with the specified set of
delimiting characters. If `returnTokens` is `true`, all tokens
will be returned as well as the separate strings.

◆ **int countTokens( )**

Counts the number of tokens in this string.

◆ **boolean hasMoreElements( )**

Returns `true` if elements remain in the string. By default, it
simply returns the value of `hasMoreTokens()`. This
method is necessary to satisfy the requirements of implementing the `Enumeration` interface.

◆ **boolean hasMoreTokens( )**

Returns `true` if more tokens exist in the string.

◆ **Object nextElement( )**

Returns the string returned by `nextToken()`. This method
is necessary to satisfy the requirements of implementing the
`Enumeration` interface.

◆ **String nextToken(String delim)**

Makes `delim` the new set of delimiters and then returns the
next token.

◆ **String nextToken( )**
Returns the next token in the string.

Vector Implements java.lang.Cloneable

A `Vector` is a dynamic array, most useful when dealing with an unknown quantity of data that will be changed frequently. Although based on the structure of an array, a `Vector` will automatically grow to provide new memory when needed. Furthermore, this capability enables you to perform more manipulative tasks, such as removing an element from a `Vector` or inserting an element into the middle of the `Vector`.

When using a `Vector`, keep in mind that—like a `Hashtable`—all elements must be `Objects`. Therefore, if you want to store simple data, such as an `int` or `float`, you must use the wrapper classes in the `java.lang` package.

Fields

▶ **protected int capacityIncrement**
The amount that the `Vector` array will grow each time that expansion is required. If `capacityIncrement` is 0, then the array will double in size.

▶ **protected int elementCount**
The number of elements in the `Vector`.

▶ **protected Object elementData[ ]**
The array of the stored elements.

Methods

◆ **Vector( )**
Creates a new `Vector` object with an initial capacity of 10. When the `Vector` needs to grow, it will double in size.

◆ **Vector(int initialCapacity)**
Creates a new `Vector` object with the specified `initalCapacity`. When the `Vector` needs to grow, it will double in size.

JAVA.UTIL

◆ **Vector(int initialCapacity, int capacityIncrement)**
   Creates a new `Vector` object with the specified
   `initalCapacity`. When the `Vector` needs to grow, it
   will do so by the specified amount.

◆ **final synchronized void addElement(Object element)**
   Adds the specified `element` to the end of the `Vector`
   array, growing in size as required.

◆ **final int capacity( )**
   Returns the total capacity of the `Vector`: the length of the
   `elementData[]` array.

◆ **synchronized Object clone( )**
   Clones the `Vector` object itself, but not its elements. This
   means that the elements of both the new and the old
   `Vector` objects will be references to the same objects.

◆ **final boolean contains(Object element)**
   Returns `true` if the `Vector` contains the specified
   `element`.

◆ **final synchronized void copyInto(Object anArray[ ])**
   Copies the elements in the `Vector` into a static (standard)
   array.

◆ **final synchronized Object elementAt(int index)**
   Returns the element at the specified `index`.

◆ **final synchronized Enumeration elements( )**
   Returns an `Enumeration` of the elements in the `Vector`.

◆ **final synchronized void ensureCapacity(int elements)**
   Checks to see if the `Vector` can contain at least the
   specified number of `elements`.

◆ **final synchronized Object firstElement( )**
   Returns the first element in the `Vector` array.

◆ **final int indexOf(Object element)**
Returns the first index at which the specified `element` is located. It returns −1 if the element was not found.

◆ **final synchronized int indexOf(Object elem, int start)**
Returns the first index at which the specified `element` is located. It begins searching at the specified `start` and returns −1 if the element is not found.

◆ **final synchronized void insertElementAt(Object object, int index)**
Inserts the specified `object` at the specified `index`.

◆ **final boolean isEmpty( )**
Returns `true` if the `Vector` array is empty.

◆ **final synchronized Object lastElement( )**
Returns the last element at the last index in the array.

◆ **final int lastIndexOf(Object elem)**
Returns the last index at which the specified `element` is located. It returns −1 if the element is not found.

◆ **final synchronized int lastIndexOf(Object elem, int start)**
Returns the first index at which the specified `element` is located. It begins the backwards search at the specified `start` and returns −1 if the element is not found.

◆ **final synchronized void removeAllElements( )**
Erases all elements in the `Vector`.

◆ **final synchronized boolean removeElement(Object element)**
Removes the first instance of the specified `element` from the `Vector` array.

◆ **final synchronized void removeElementAt(int index)**
Removes the element at the specified `index` from the `Vector` array.

♦ **final synchronized void setElementAt(Object obj, int index)**
Sets the element at the specified `index`, overwriting any value previously stored at the index.

♦ **final synchronized void setSize(int newSize)**
Sets the size of the `Vector` array. If `newSize` is greater than the current size, the array will be shrunk to the `newSize`. If `newSize` is larger than the current size, the array will be enlarged to the `newSize`.

♦ **final int size( )**
Returns the size of the `Vector` array.

♦ **final synchronized String toString( )**
Returns a string containing all the elements in the `Vector` array.

♦ **final synchronized void trimToSize( )**
Shrinks the array to the minimum size that is capable of containing all the elements in the `Vector`.

Interfaces

Enumeration

An `Enumeration` is a simple way to handle a set of items without having to worry about the number of items contained in the set. This is necessary when dealing with many groups of data that do not provide you with a simple manner of dealing with each element in a sequential manner, such as `Hashtables` and the applets in an `AppletContext` (see fig. 28). By using an `Enumeration`, you are able to scroll through the items—such as the keys in a set of `Properties`, the applets in an `AppletContext`, or the sub-strings in a `StringTokenizer`—in a very simple manner.

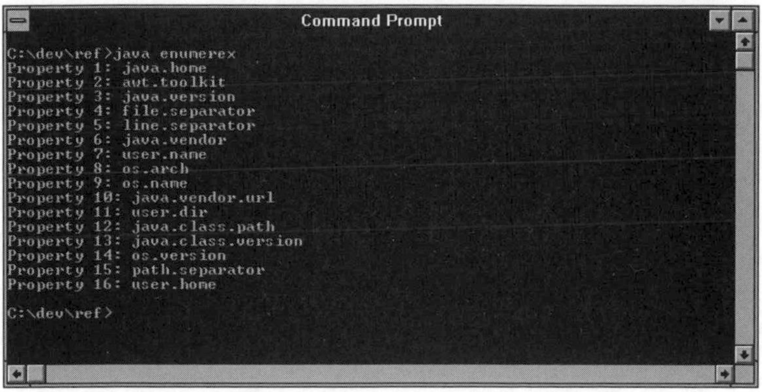

Fig. 28 The output of Listing 24.

Listing 24   Enumeration Example

```
import java.util.Enumeration;
import java.util.Properties;

public class EnumerationExample {

   public static void main(String args[]) {

     Enumeration propNames =
➥System.getProperties().propertyNames();
     int index = 1;

      while (propNames.hasMoreElements() )
        System.out.print("Property " + (index++) + ": ");
        System.out.println(propNames.nextElement() );
      }
}
```

Methods
◆ **abstract boolean hasMoreElements( )**
   Returns true if the Enumeration contains more elements.

◆ **abstract Object nextElement( )**
Returns the next element in the Enumeration.

Observer

The Observer interface is used in conjunction with an Observable class. By adding an Observer to the Observable class list of observers, the Observable class will be informed of any important changes in the Observable class. (This communication transpires whenever the notifyObservers() method is invoked in the Observable class.)

Method

◆ **abstract void update(Observable o, Object arg)**

▶ *See "Observable," p. 285*

EXCEPTIONS

EXCEPTIONS

Exceptions provide you with a means of managing the ordinary runtime problems that may be encountered during execution of your program. All exceptions are derived from the java.lang.Exception class and most consist only of two constructor methods. Consequently, only the constructor methods for the java.lang.Exception class are listed here.

Unless otherwise noted, all exceptions may be created with no parameters or with a descriptive string as a parameter. Exceptions are handled by using the try...catch construct. Once an exception has been caught, it may be dealt with or thrown to the calling method. Listing 25 is an example of a simple division method that sets the result equal to 0 if division by 0 occurs.

Listing 25   Catching an Exception

```
int divide(int a, int b) {
   int val;
   try {
      val = a / b;
   }
   catch(ArithmeticException e) {
     System.out.println("Invalid data.  val set to 0.");
     val = 0;
   }
   return (val);
}
```

To throw an exception, you must use the throw statement, as shown in Listing 26 and Listing 27.

Listing 26   Throwing a Caught Exception

```
void connect(String host, int port) throws IOException {
  try {
    s = new Socket(host,port);
```

```
    }
    catch(IOException e) {
      throw e;
    }
}
```

Listing 27 Throwing a New Exception

```
static void connect(String host, int port) throws IOException {
  /* Makes sure the port satisfies our system policy */
  if (port < 1600)
    throw new SocketException("Port under 1600");

  try {
    s = new Socket(host,port);
  }
  catch(IOException e) {
    throw e;
  }
}
```

EXCEPTIONS

java.awt

AWTException
AWTException(String message)

java.io

EOFException Extends IOException
FileNotFoundException Extends IOException
IOException Extends java.lang.Exception
InterruptedIOException Extends IOException
UTFDataFormatException Extends IOException

java.lang

ArithmeticException Extends RuntimeException

ArrayIndexOutOfBoundsException Extends IndexOutOfBoundsException

Constructors

ArrayIndexOutOfBoundsException( )

ArrayIndexOutOfBoundsException(int invalid_index)

ArrayIndexOutOfBoundsException(String message)

ArrayStoreException Extends RuntimeException

ClassCastException Extends RuntimeException

ClassNotFoundException Extends Exception

CloneNotSupportedException Extends Exception

Exception Extends Throwable

Methods

Exception(String message)

Exception( )

IllegalAccessException Extends Exception

IllegalArgumentException Extends RuntimeException

IllegalMonitorStateException Extends RuntimeException

IllegalThreadStateException Extends RuntimeException

IndexOutOfBoundsException Extends RuntimeException

InstantiationException Extends Exception

InterruptedException Extends Exception

NegativeArraySizeException Extends RuntimeException

NoSuchMethodException Extends Exception

NullPointerException Extends RuntimeException

NumberFormatException Extends IllegalArgumentException

RuntimeException Extends Exception

SecurityException Extends RuntimeException

StringIndexOutOfBoundsException Extends IndexOutOfBoundsException

Constructors

StringIndexOutOfBoundsException( )

StringIndexOutOfBoundsException(int invalid_index)

StringIndexOutOfBoundsException(String)

java.net

MalformedURLException Extends java.lang.IOException

ProtocolException Extends java.lang.IOException

SocketException Extends java.lang.IOException

UnknownHostException Extends java.lang.IOException

UnknownServiceException Extends java.lang.IOException

java.util

EmptyStackException Extends java.lang.RuntimeException

Constructors

EmptyStackException( )

NoSuchElementException Extends java.lang.RuntimeException

EXCEPTIONS

ERRORS

 ERRORS

Although errors and exceptions are both based on the
`java.lang.Throwable` class, errors are designed to manage
more critical runtime errors. Errors may be handled in a similar
manner to exceptions. However, unless you clearly understand
the problem and have devised a suitable way of resolving it,
error handling is not something that should be used in your
code.

Similar to exceptions, all errors are derived from
`java.lang.Error`. All errors contain only constructor
methods and most contain only two: `ErrorName()` and
`ErrorName(String message)`. Although all errors are listed
here, only those errors whose constructors conform to the
above pattern are listed in detail.

java.awt

AWTError Extends java.lang.Error
Constructors
    AWTError( )

java.lang

AbstractMethodError Extends IncompatibleClassChangeError

ClassCircularityError Extends LinkageError

ClassFormatError Extends LinkageError

Error Extends Throwable

Methods
    Error(String message)
    Error( )

**IlegalAccessError Extends
IncompatibleClassChangeError**

**IncompatibleClassChangeError Extends
LinkageError**

**InstantiationError Extends
IncompatibleClassChangeError**

InternalError Extends VirtualMachineError

LinkageError Extends Error

NoClassDefFoundError Extends LinkageError

**NoSuchFieldError Extends
IncompatibleClassChangeError**

**NoSuchMethodError Extends
IncompatibleClassChangeError**

OutOfMemoryError Extends VirtualMachineError

**StackOverflowError Extends
VirtualMachineError**

ThreadDeath Extends Error
Constructors
    ThreadDeath( )

UnknownError Extends VirtualMachineError

UnsatisfiedLinkError Extends LinkageError

VerifyError Extends LinkageError

VirtualMachineError Extends Error

SYNTAX
REFERENCE

SYNTAX REFERENCE

This section serves as a reference for the Java language itself. All keywords and operators in the language are listed in alphabetical order, each followed by a complete explanation of the term, its syntax, and an example of how it might be used in actual code. Further, for ease of identification, the terms are set in bold in the code samples.

Abstract

An `abstract` class or method is one that is not complete. Interfaces are automatically `abstract`.

Syntax:
```
abstract class className {
     abstract returnType
methodName(optionalParameters);
}
```

Example:
```
abstract class Grapher

abstract void displayImage(Image im);
```

Break

This is used to exit a loop.

Syntax:
```
break;
```

Example:
```
while (true) {
     if ( connection.isClosed() )
```

```
        break;
    else
     // code goes here
    }
```

Catch

The `catch` statement is used to handle any exceptions thrown by code within a `try` block.

Syntax:
```
try {
    statement(s)
}
catch(Exception list) {
  statement(s)
}
```

Example:
```
InputStream in;
int val;
...
try {
  val = in.read() / in.read();
}
catch(ArithmeticException e) {
    System.out.println("Invalid data.  val set to
0.");
    val = 0;
  }
catch(Exception e) {
    System.out.println("Exception encountered, but
not handled.");
  }
```

Class

This is used in a class declaration to denote that the following code defines a class.

Syntax:
```
modifiers class className extends SuperClassName
implements InterfaceNames
```

Example:
```
class MyClass

public class GraphAnimator extends Applet

public class Calculator implements Runnable,
Cloneable
```

Continue

This returns the program to the top of a loop.

Syntax:
```
continue;
```

Example:
```
Enumeration enum;
Object value;
...
while ( enum.hasMoreElements() ) {
     value = enum.nextElement();
     if ( value.equals("Invalid") )
          continue;
     else
          System.out.println( value);
     }
```

Do...While

This is used to perform operations while a condition is met. The loop
body will be executed at least once.

Syntax:
```
do
   statement(s)
while (booleanVariable);
```

Do...While

```
do
  statement(s)
while (booleanExpression);
```

Example:
```
do {
    val = in.readByte();
    System.out.println(val);
} while (val != '\n');

boolean valid = true;
do {
    val = in.readByte();
    if (val == '\n')
        valid = false;
    else
        System.out.println(val);
} while (valid);
```

Else

This is used in conjunction with the if statement to perform operations only when the requirements of the if statement are not met.

Syntax:
```
if (booleanVariable)
    statement(s)
else
    statement(s)
if (booleanExpression)
    statement(s)
else
    statement(s)
```

Example:
```
if (stillRunning) {
    System.out.println("Still Running");
    advanceCounter();
}
```

```
else {
    System.out.println("We're all done.");
    closeConnection();
}

if (size >= 5)
    System.out.println("Too big");
else
    System.out.println("Just Right");
```

Extends

This is used to make the current class or interface a subclass of another class or interface.

Syntax:

```
modifiers class className extends superClassName

interface interfaceName extends superInterfaceName
```

Example:

```
public class Clock extends Applet

public interface carefulObserver extends Observer
```

Final

The **final** modifier makes a class or method final, meaning that it cannot be changed in a subclass. Interfaces cannot be final.

Syntax:

```
final class className

final returnType methodName(optionalParameters)
```

Example:

```
final class LogoAnimator

final Color getCurrentColor()
```

Finally

The `finally` statement is used in error handling to ensure the execution of a section of code. Regardless of whether an exception is thrown within a `try` statement, the code in the finally block will be executed.

Syntax:

```
try {
     statement(s)
     }
finally {
     cleanUpStatement(s)
     }

try {
     statement(s)
     }
catch (Exception) {
     exceptionHandlingStatement(s)
     }
finally {
     cleanUpStatement(s)
     }
```

Example:

```
public static void testMath(int numerator, int
divisor) throws ArithmeticException {
try {
        if (divisor == 0)
          throw new ArithmeticException("Division
by Zero.");
        }
        finally {
          System.out.println("The fraction was " +
numerator + "/" + divisor);
        }
}

try {
```

```
        percent_over = quantity / number_ordered *
100;        // could cause division by 0
    }
catch (ArithmeticException e) {
    percent_over = 0;
    }
finally {  // regardless of the success of the try,
we still need to print the info
    System.out.println("Quantity = " + quantity);
    System.out.println("Ordered = " + ordered);
    System.out.println("Percent Over = " +
percent_over);
    }
```

For

This is used to execute a block of code a specific number of times.

Syntax:
```
for (counterInitialization ; counterCheck   ;
counterChange)
    statement(s)
```

Example:
```
String name;
...
for (pos = 0; pos < name.length(); I++)
    System.out.println(name.charAt(i));
```

If

This is used to perform operations only if a certain condition is met.

Syntax:
```
if (booleanVariable)
    statement(s)

if (booleanExpression)
    statement(s)
```

Example:
```
if (ValidNumbersOnly)
   checkInput(Answer);

if (area >= 2*PI) {
  System.out.println("The size of the loop is still
too big.");
   reduceSize(area);
}
```

Implements

This is used to force a class to implement the methods defined in an interface.

Syntax:
```
modifiers class className implements interfaceName
```

Example:
```
public class Clock implements Runnable, Cloneable
```

Import

This is used to include other libraries.

Syntax:
```
import packageName;
```
```
import className;
```
```
import interfaceName;
```

Example:
```
import java.io.*;
```
```
import java.applet.Applet;
```
```
import java.applet.AppletContext;
```

Instanceof

The `instanceof` operator returns `true` if the object to the left of the expression is an instance of the class to the right of the expression.

Syntax:
```
object instanceof ClassName
```

Example:
```
void testType(Object instance) {
    if (instance instanceof String) {
        System.out.println("This is a string.")
        System.out.println("It is " +
((String)i).length() );  // casts the Object to a
String first
```

Modifiers

Access modifiers are used to control the accessibility and behavior of classes, interfaces, methods, and fields.

Modifier	Effect on Classes	Effect on Methods	Effect on Fields
none (friendly)	Visible to subclasses and classes within the same package.	Can be called by methods belonging to classes within the same package.	Accessible only to classes within the same package.
public	Visible to subclasses and other classes regardless of their package.	Can be called by methods in subclasses and all classes regardless of their package.	Accessible only to subclasses and all classes regardless of their package.
private	Classes cannot be private.	Can only be called by methods within the current class.	Accessible only to methods within the current class.
static	Not applicable to classes.	Method is shared by all instances of the current class.	Field is shared by all instances of the current class.

continues

Modifiers

continued

Modifier	Effect on Classes	Effect on Methods	Effect on Fields
abstract	Some methods are not defined. These methods must be implemented in subclasses.	Contains no body and must be overridden in subclasses.	Not applicable to fields.
final	The class cannot be used as a superclass.	The method cannot be overridden in any subclasses.	Variable's value cannot be changed.
native	Not applicable to classes.	This method's implementation will be defined by code written in another language.	Not applicable to fields.
synchronized	Not applicable to classes.	This method will seize control of the class while running. If another method has already seized control, it will wait until the first has completed.	Not applicable to fields.

Native

A `native` method will be defined by code written in another language.

Syntax:
```
native returnType methodName(optionalParameters)
```

Example:
```
native long sumSeries();
```

New

The new operator allocates memory for an object, such as a `String`, a `Socket`, an array, or an instance of any other class.

Syntax:
```
dataType arrayName[] = new dataType[ number ];
dataType fieldName = new dataType( constructor parameters)
```

Example:
```
int sizes[] = new int[9];
String name = new String("Hello");
```

Package

This is used to place the current class within the specified package.

Syntax:
```
package packageName;
```

Example:
```
package java.lang;
package mytools;
```

Public

`Public` makes the class, method, or field accessible to all classes.

Syntax:
```
public class className;
public interface interfaceName;
public returnType methodName(optionalParameters)
public dataType fieldName;
```

Public

Example:
```
public class GraphicsExample;

public interface Graph;

public boolean checkStatus(int x, int y)

public int size;
```

Private

The modifier `private` makes the method or field accessible only to methods in the current class.

Syntax:
```
private returnType methodName(optionalParameters)

private dataType fieldName;
```

Example:
```
private int changeStatus(int index);

private int count;
```

Return

The `return` statement is used to return a value from a method. The data type returned must correspond to the data type specified in the method declaration.

Syntax:
```
return value;
```

Example:
```
float calculateArea(float circumference) {
     float radius, area;
     radius = circumference / (2 * PI);
     area = radius * radius * PI;
     return(area);
}
```

Super

This is used to refer to the superclass of this class.

Syntax:
```
super

super.methodName()

super.fieldName
```

Example:
```
class FloorManager extends Manager {
    FloorManager() {
        type = floor;
        super();          // calls the Manager
constructor
        }
    void organize() {
        size = name.getSize();
        super.organize(size);  // calls the orga
nize method in the Manager method
        ....      }
}
```

This

This is used to refer to the current class.

Syntax:
```
this

this.methodName()

this.fieldName
```

Example:
```
ticker = new Thread(this);
```

Throw

The `throw` statement is used to throw an exception within the body of a method. The exception must be a subclass of one of the exceptions declared with the `throws` statement in the method declaration.

Syntax:
```
throw exceptionObject
```

Example:
```
float calculateArea(float radius) throws
IllegalArgumentException {
    if (radius < 0)
        throw(new
IllegalArgumentException("Radius less than 0.");
    else
        return(radius*radius*PI);
}
```

Throws

The `throws` keyword specifies the types of exceptions that can be thrown from a method.

Syntax:
```
modifiers returnType methodName(optionalParameters)
throws ExceptionNames
```

Example:
```
String getName(InputStream in) throws IOException
```

Static

The `static` modifier makes a method or field static. Regardless of the number of instances that are created of a given class, only one copy of a static method or field will be created.

Syntax:
```
static returnType methodName(optionalParameters)

static dataType fieldName;
```

Example:
```
static void haltChanges(optionalParameters)

static Color backgroundColor;
```

Static

A static block is a set of code that is executed immediately after object creation. It can only handle static methods and static fields.

Syntax:
```
static
   statement(s)
```

Example:
```
static {
        type = prepare();
        size = 25;
    }
```

Switch

The `switch` statement is a conditional statement with many options.

Syntax:
```
switch (variableName) {
   case (valueExpression1)  :   statement(s)
   case (valueExpression2)  :   statement(s)
   default  :  statement(s)
  }
```

Example:
```
char ans;
...
switch (ans) {
```

```
    case 'Y'   :    startOver();
                    break;
    case 'n'   :
    case 'N'   :    cleanUp();
    default    :    System.out.println("Invalid
response.");
}
```

Synchronized

Every object has a "lock" that can be seized by an operation. Any synchronized operation seizes this lock, preventing other synchronized processes from beginning until it has finished.

Syntax:
Synchronized Method:

```
synchronized returnType
methodName(optionalParameters)
```

```
synchronized (objectName)
    statement(s)
```

Example:
```
synchronized void changeValues(int size, int shape,
String name)
```

```
synchronized (runningThread) {
    runningThread.name = newName;
}
```

Try

The try statement is used to enclose code that can throw an exception. It should be used with the catch() statement and may be used with the finally statement.

Syntax:
```
try
    statement(s)
catch(Exception list)
  statement(s)
finally
  statement(s)
```

Example:
```
InputStream in;
int val;
...
try
  val = in.read() / in.read();
catch(ArithmeticException e) {
    System.out.println("Invalid data.  val set to
0.");
    val = 0;
  }
catch(Exception e)
    System.out.println("Exception encountered, but
not handled.");
finally {
    in.close();
    System.out.println("Stream closed.");
  }
```

While

This is used to perform a loop operation while a certain condition is met.

Syntax:
```
while (booleanVariable)
    statement(s)

while (booleanExpression)
    statement(s)
```

While

Example:

```
FileInputStream din;
byte info;

while (info = din.read() != -1) // End of File
     System.out.println(info);

while (stillValidData) {
     info = din.read();
     stillValidData = checkData(info);  // returns
false if data is not valid
}
```

ACTION INDEX

ACTION INDEX

This is a table for problem solving. Common questions are posed in the first column. The second column provides keys to the solutions. The page numbers refer you to a detailed explanation for each entry.

Animation

Question	Solution	Page
How do I display my graphics?	`Graphics`	62
How do I enable my applet to run on its own?	`Runnable`	245
How do I begin the animation?	`Thread`	235
Is there an animation example in this manual?	`Runnable`	245

Applets

Question	Solution	Page
How do I create an applet?	`Applet`	10
How do I interact with the browser?	`AppletContext`	16
How do I handle user interactions?	`Event`	46
Which methods catch user interactions?	`Component`	33

Action Index

Applications

Question	Solution	Page
How do I display text on the screen?	System.out	177
How do I start other programs on the client's side?	Runtime	214
How do I handle files?	File	157
How do I read from a file?	FileInputStream	161
How do I write to a file?	FileOutputStream	163

Communication

Question	Solution	Page
How do I display a URL?	AppletContext.show ➥Document()	17
How do I handle URLs?	URL	261
How do I load information from a URL?	URLConnection	264
How do I communicate with a server?	Socket	256
How do I create a TCP socket?	ServerSocket	255
How can I continually communicate with a socket?	Thread	235

Image Processing

Question	Solution	Page
How do I load an image in an applet?	Applet.getImage()	14
How do I load an image in an application?	Toolkit.getImage()	115
How do I manipulate an image?	ImageFilter	125

How do I crop an image?	`CropImageFilter`	121
How do I create an image from pixel data?	`MemoryImageSource`	132

Input and Output

Question	Solution	Page
Is there a class that's like `printf()` in C?	`PrintStream`	175
Is there an easy way to parse streams?	`StreamTokenizer`	183
How do I read doubles, strings, etc., from a stream?	`DataInputStream`	153
How do I write doubles, strings, etc., to a stream?	`DataOutputStream`	155
How do I link `InputStreams` together?	`SequenceInputStream`	182
How do I interact with the environment (either the prompt of the Java console or a browser)?	`System`	232

Math

Question	Solution	Page
How do I perform standard mathematical functions?	`Math`	208
How do I create random numbers?	`Random`	288
How do I handle a `char` as an `Object`?	`Character`	194
How do I handle an `int` as an `Object`?	`Integer`	203

Action Index

User Interfaces

Question	Solution	Page
Where can I find the window components?	`java.awt` package	20
How do I create a pop-up menu?	`Frame`	60
How do I position components on the screen?	`GridBagLayout`	72
How do I handle user interactions?	`Event`	46
Which methods catch user interactions?	`Component`	33
How do I scroll through a series of screens?	`CardLayout`	23
How do I create a toolbar menu?	`Menu`	91

INDEX OF FIELDS

INDEX OF FIELDS

This is a complete alphabetical listing of all public and protected fields in the Java API. For a thorough explanation of each field, refer to the specified page number. Note that all field names set in italics are *protected* fields.

Field	Class or Interface	Page
ABORT	java.awt.image.ImageObserver	141
ABORTED	java.awt.MediaTracker	88
ACTION_EVENT	java.awt.Event	46
address	java.net.SocketImpl	259
ALLBITS	java.awt.image.ImageObserver	141
allowUser ➡*Interaction*	java.net.URLConnection	264
ALT_MASK	java.awt.Event	47
anchor	java.awt.GridBagConstraints	70
arg	java.awt.Event	47
black	java.awt.Color	31
blue	java.awt.Color	31
BOLD	java.awt.Font	56
BOTH	java.awt.GridBagConstraints	70
bottom	java.awt.Insets	83
buf[]	java.io.BufferedInputStream	147
buf[]	java.io.BufferedOutputStream	149
buf[]	java.io.ByteArrayInputStream	150
buf[]	java.io.ByteArrayOutputStream	152

continues

Index of Fields

continued

Field	Class or Interface	Page
buffer	java.io. ➥StringBufferInputStream	186
canFilterIndex ➥*ColorModel*	java.awt.Image.RGBImageFilter	137
capacityIncrement	java.util.Vector	291
CENTER	java.awt.FlowLayout	54
CENTER	java.awt.GridBagConstraints	70
CENTER	java.awt.Label	83
clickCount	java.awt.Event	47
columnWeights[]	java.awt.GridBagLayout	76
columnWidths[]	java.awt.GridBagLayout	76
COMPLETE	java.awt.MediaTracker	88
COMPLETESCANLINES	java.awt.image.ImageConsumer	139
comptable	java.awt.GridBagLayout	76
connected	java.net.URLConnection	264
consumer	java.awt.Image.ImageFilter	129
count	java.io.BufferedInputStream	147
count	java.io.BufferedOutputStream	149
count	java.io.ByteArrayInputStream	151
count	java.io.ByteArrayOutputStream	152
count	java.io. ➥StringBufferInputStream	186
CROSSHAIR_CURSOR	java.awt.Frame	60
CTRL_MASK	java.awt.Event	47
cyan	java.awt.Color	31
darkGray	java.awt.Color	31
DEFAULT_CURSOR	java.awt.Frame	60
defaultConstraints	java.awt.GridBagLayout	76
defaults	java.util.Properties	287

Index of Fields

doInput	java.net.URLConnection	265
doOutput	java.net.URLConnection	265
DOWN	java.awt.Event	47
E	java.lang.Math	208
E_RESIZE_CURSOR	java.awt.Frame	60
EAST	java.awt.GridBagConstraints	70
elementCount	java.util.Vector	291
elementData[]	java.util.Vector	291
err	java.io.FileDescriptor	161
err	java.lang.System	233
ERROR	java.awt.image.ImageObserver	142
ERRORED	java.awt.MediaTracker	88
evt	java.awt.Event	47
F1	java.awt.Event	47
F2	java.awt.Event	47
F3	java.awt.Event	47
F4	java.awt.Event	47
F5	java.awt.Event	47
F6	java.awt.Event	47
F7	java.awt.Event	47
F8	java.awt.Event	47
F9	java.awt.Event	47
F10	java.awt.Event	47
F11	java.awt.Event	47
F12	java.awt.Event	47
FALSE	java.lang.Boolean	192
fd	java.net.SocketImpl	259
fill	java.awt.GridBagConstraints	70
font	java.awt.FontMetrics	58

continues

Index of Fields

continued

Field	Class or Interface	Page
FRAMEBITS	java.awt.image.ImageObserver	142
GOT_FOCUS	java.awt.Event	47
gray	java.awt.Color	31
green	java.awt.Color	31
gridheight	java.awt.GridBagConstraints	70
gridwidth	java.awt.GridBagConstraints	70
gridx	java.awt.GridBagConstraints	70
gridy	java.awt.GridBagConstraints	70
HAND_CURSOR	java.awt.Frame	60
height	java.awt.Dimension	45
HEIGHT	java.awt.image.ImageObserver	142
height	java.awt.Rectangle	101
HOME	java.awt.Event	48
HORIZONTAL	java.awt.GridBagConstraints	70
HORIZONTAL	java.awt.Scrollbar	105
id	java.awt.Event	48
ifModifiedSince	java.net.URLConnection	265
IMAGEABORTED	java.awt.image.ImageConsumer	139
IMAGEERROR	java.awt.image.ImageConsumer	140
in	java.io.FileDescriptor	161
in	java.io.FilterInputStream	164
in	java.lang.System	233
inCheck	java.lang.SecurityManager	218
insets	java.awt.GridBagConstraints	71
ipadx	java.awt.GridBagConstraints	71
ipady	java.awt.GridBagConstraints	71
ITALIC	java.awt.Font	56
key	java.awt.Event	48

Index of Fields

KEY_ACTION	java.awt.Event	48
KEY_ACTION_RELEASE	java.awt.Event	48
KEY_PRESS	java.awt.Event	48
KEY_RELEASE	java.awt.Event	48
layoutInfo	java.awt.GridBagLayout	76
LEFT	java.awt.Event	48
LEFT	java.awt.FlowLayout	54
left	java.awt.Insets	83
LEFT	java.awt.Label	83
lightGray	java.awt.Color	31
LIST_DESELECT	java.awt.Event	48
LIST_SELECT	java.awt.Event	48
LOAD	java.awt.FileDialog	52
LOAD_FILE	java.awt.Event	49
localport	java.net.SocketImpl	259
LOST_FOCUS	java.awt.Event	49
magenta	java.awt.Color	31
marklimit	java.io.BufferedInputStream	147
markpos	java.io.BufferedInputStream	147
MAX_PRIORITY	java.lang.Thread	237
MAX_RADIX	java.lang.Character	194
MAX_VALUE	java.lang.Boolean	192
MAX_VALUE	java.lang.Double	199
MAX_VALUE	java.lang.Float	201
MAX_VALUE	java.lang.Integer	203
MAX_VALUE	java.lang.Long	206
MAXGRIDSIZE	java.awt.GridBagLayout	77
META_MASK	java.awt.Event	49
MIN_PRIORITY	java.lang.Thread	237

continues

Index of Fields

continued

Field	Class or Interface	Page
MIN_RADIX	java.lang.Character	194
MIN_VALUE	java.lang.Boolean	192
MIN_VALUE	java.lang.Double	199
MIN_VALUE	java.lang.Float	201
MIN_VALUE	java.lang.Integer	203
MIN_VALUE	java.lang.Long	206
MINSIZE	java.awt.GridBagLayout	77
modifiers	java.awt.Event	49
MOUSE_DOWN	java.awt.Event	49
MOUSE_DRAG	java.awt.Event	49
MOUSE_ENTER	java.awt.Event	49
MOUSE_EXIT	java.awt.Event	49
MOUSE_MOVE	java.awt.Event	49
MOUSE_UP	java.awt.Event	49
MOVE_CURSOR	java.awt.Frame	60
N_RESIZE_CURSOR	java.awt.Frame	60
name	java.awt.Font	56
NaN	java.lang.Double	199
NaN	java.lang.Float	201
NE_RESIZE_CURSOR	java.awt.Frame	60
NEGATIVE_INFINITY	java.lang.Double	199
NEGATIVE_INFINITY	java.lang.Float	201
newmodel	java.awt.Image.RGBImageFilter	138
NONE	java.awt.GridBagConstraints	71
NORM_PRIORITY	java.lang.Thread	237
NORTH	java.awt.GridBagConstraints	71
NORTHEAST	java.awt.GridBagConstraints	71

NORTHWEST	java.awt.GridBagConstraints	71
npoints	java.awt.Polygon	100
nval	java.io.StreamTokenizer	183
NW_RESIZE_CURSOR	java.awt.Frame	60
orange	java.awt.Color	31
origmodel	java.awt.Image.RGBImageFilter	138
out	java.io.FileDescriptor	161
out	java.io.FilterOutputStream	166
out	java.lang.System	233
pathSeparator	java.io.File	158
pathSeparatorChar	java.io.File	158
PGDN	java.awt.Event	49
PGUP	java.awt.Event	49
PI	java.lang.Math	208
pink	java.awt.Color	31
pixel_bits	java.awt.image.ColorModel	120
PLAIN	java.awt.Font	56
port	java.net.SocketImpl	260
pos	java.io.BufferedInputStream	147
pos	java.io.ByteArrayInputStream	151
pos	java.io.↳StringBufferInputStream	186
POSITIVE_INFINITY	java.lang.Double	199
POSITIVE_INFINITY	java.lang.Float	201
PREFERREDSIZE	java.awt.GridBagLayout	77
PROPERTIES	java.awt.image.ImageObserver	142
pushBack	java.io.PushBackInputStream	178
RANDOMPIXELORDER	java.awt.image.ImageConsumer	140
red	java.awt.Color	31

continues

Index of Fields

continued

Field	Class or Interface	Page
RELATIVE	java.awt.GridBagConstraints	71
REMAINDER	java.awt.GridBagConstraints	71
RIGHT	java.awt.Event	49
RIGHT	java.awt.FlowLayout	54
right	java.awt.Insets	83
RIGHT	java.awt.Label	83
rowHeights[]	java.awt.GridBagLayout	77
rowWeights[]	java.awt.GridBagLayout	77
S_RESIZE_CURSOR	java.awt.Frame	60
SAVE	java.awt.FileDialog	53
SAVE_FILE	java.awt.Event	49
SCROLL_ABSOLUTE	java.awt.Event	49
SCROLL_LINE_DOWN	java.awt.Event	49
SCROLL_LINE_UP	java.awt.Event	49
SCROLL_PAGE_DOWN	java.awt.Event	49
SCROLL_PAGE_UP	java.awt.Event	49
SE_RESIZE_CURSOR	java.awt.Frame	60
separator	java.io.File	158
separatorChar	java.io.File	158
SHIFT_MASK	java.awt.Event	50
SINGLEFRAME	java.awt.image.ImageConsumer	140
SINGLEFRAMEDONE	java.awt.image.ImageConsumer	140
SINGLEPASS	java.awt.image.ImageConsumer	140
size	java.awt.Font	56
SOMEBITS	java.awt.image.ImageObserver	142
SOUTH	java.awt.GridBagConstraints	71
SOUTHEAST	java.awt.GridBagConstraints	72
SOUTHWEST	java.awt.GridBagConstraints	72

Index of Fields

STATICIMAGEDONE	java.awt.image.ImageConsumer	140
style	java.awt.Font	56
sval	java.io.StreamTokenizer	183
SW_RESIZE_CURSOR	java.awt.Frame	60
target	java.awt.Event	50
TEXT_CURSOR	java.awt.Frame	60
top	java.awt.Insets	83
TOPDOWNLEFTRIGHT	java.awt.image.ImageConsumer	140
TRUE	java.lang.Boolean	192
TT_EOF	java.io.StreamTokenizer	183
TT_EOL	java.io.StreamTokenizer	183
TT_NUMBER	java.io.StreamTokenizer	183
TT_WORD	java.io.StreamTokenizer	183
UndefinedProperty	java.awt.Image	81
UP	java.awt.Event	50
URL	*java.net.URLConnection*	265
useCaches	java.net.URLConnection	265
VERTICAL	java.awt.GridBagConstraints	72
VERTICAL	java.awt.Scrollbar	105
W_RESIZE_CURSOR	java.awt.Frame	60
WAIT_CURSOR	java.awt.Frame	60
weightx	java.awt.GridBagConstraints	72
weighty	java.awt.GridBagConstraints	72
WEST	java.awt.GridBagConstraints	72
white	java.awt.Color	31
width	java.awt.Dimension	45
WIDTH	java.awt.image.ImageObserver	142
width	java.awt.Rectangle	101

continues

Index of Fields

continued

Field	Class or Interface	Page
WINDOW_DEICONIFY	java.awt.Event	50
WINDOW_DESTROY	java.awt.Event	50
WINDOW_EXPOSE	java.awt.Event	50
WINDOW_ICONIFY	java.awt.Event	50
WINDOW_MOVED	java.awt.Event	50
written	java.io.DataOutputStream	156
x	java.awt.Event	50
x	java.awt.Point	98
x	java.awt.Rectangle	101
xpoints[]	java.awt.Polygon	100
y	java.awt.Event	50
y	java.awt.Point	98
y	java.awt.Rectangle	101
yellow	java.awt.Color	31
ypoints[]	java.awt.Polygon	100

INDEX OF
METHODS

INDEX OF METHODS

This index is an alphabetical listing of all methods found in the Java API. The page numbers refer you to the complete explanations of the methods and their classes.

Method Name	Class Name	Page
abs(double)	java.lang.Math	208
abs(float)	java.lang.Math	208
abs(int)	java.lang.Math	209
abs(long)	java.lang.Math	208
AbstractMethodError()	java.lang. ➥AbstractMethodError	304
AbstractMethodError(String)	java.lang. ➥AbstractMethodError	304
accept()	java.net.ServerSocket	256
accept(File, String)	java.io.FilenameFilter	189
accept(SocketImpl)	java.net.SocketImpl	260
acos(double)	java.lang.Math	209
action(Event, Object)	java.awt.Component	34
activeCount()	java.lang.Thread	238
activeCount()	java.lang.ThreadGroup	242
activeGroupCount()	java.lang.ThreadGroup	242
add(Component)	java.awt.Container	42
add(Component, int)	java.awt.Container	42
add(int, int)	java.awt.Rectangle	101
add(Menu)	java.awt.MenuBar	95

continues

Index of Methods

continued

Method Name	Class Name	Page
add(MenuItem)	java.awt.Menu	92
add(Point)	java.awt.Rectangle	101
add(Rectangle)	java.awt.Rectangle	101
add(String)	java.awt.Menu	92
add(String, Component)	java.awt.Container	42
addConsumer(ImageConsumer)	java.awt.image. ➥FilteredImageSource	124
addConsumer(ImageConsumer)	java.awt.image.ImageProducer	143
addConsumer(ImageConsumer)	java.awt.image. ➥MemoryImageSource	133
addElement(Object)	java.util.Vector	292
addImage(Image, int)	java.awt.MediaTracker	89
addImage(Image, int, ➥int, int)	java.awt.MediaTracker	89
addItem(String)	java.awt.Choice	30
addItem(String)	java.awt.List	85
addItem(String, int)	java.awt.List	85
addLayoutComponent ➥(String, Component)	java.awt.BorderLayout	20
addLayoutComponent ➥(String, Component)	java.awt.CardLayout	25
addLayoutComponent ➥(String, Component)	java.awt.FlowLayout	54
addLayoutComponent ➥(String, Component)	java.awt.GridBagLayout	77
addLayoutComponent ➥(String, Component)	java.awt.GridLayout	80
addLayoutComponent ➥(String, Component)	java.awt.LayoutManager	116
addNotify()	java.awt.Button	22
addNotify()	java.awt.Canvas	23

Index of Methods

addNotify()	java.awt.Checkbox	27
addNotify()	java.awt.CheckboxMenuItem	29
addNotify()	java.awt.Choice	30
addNotify()	java.awt.Component	34
addNotify()	java.awt.Container	42
addNotify()	java.awt.Dialog	45
addNotify()	java.awt.FileDialog	53
addNotify()	java.awt.Frame	60
addNotify()	java.awt.Label	84
addNotify()	java.awt.List	85
addNotify()	java.awt.Menu	92
addNotify()	java.awt.MenuBar	95
addNotify()	java.awt.MenuItem	97
addNotify()	java.awt.Panel	98
addNotify()	java.awt.Scrollbar	105
addNotify()	java.awt.TextArea	108
addNotify()	java.awt.TextField	111
addNotify()	java.awt.Window	115
addObserver(Observer)	java.util.Observable	286
addPoint(int, int)	java.awt.Polygon	100
addSeparator()	java.awt.Menu	92
AdjustForGravity(GridBag Constraints,Rectangle)	java.awt.GridBagConstraints	77
after(Date)	java.util.Date	277
allowsMultipleSelections()	java.awt.List	85
and(BitSet)	java.util.BitSet	275
append(boolean)	java.lang.StringBuffer	230
append(char)	java.lang.StringBuffer	230
append(char[])	java.lang.StringBuffer	230
append(char[], int, int)	java.lang.StringBuffer	230

continues

Index of Methods

continued

Method Name	Class Name	Page
append(double)	java.lang.StringBuffer	229
append(float)	java.lang.StringBuffer	229
append(int)	java.lang.StringBuffer	230
append(long)	java.lang.StringBuffer	229
append(Object)	java.lang.StringBuffer	230
append(String)	java.lang.StringBuffer	230
appendText(String)	java.awt.TextArea	108
appletResize(int, int)	java.applet.AppletStub	18
ArithmeticException()	java.lang.➡ArithmeticException	299
ArithmeticException(String)	java.lang.➡ArithmeticException	299
ArrangeGrid(Container)	java.awt.GridBagLayout	77
arraycopy(Object, int, ➡Object, int, int)	java.lang.System	233
ArrayIndexOutOfBounds➡Exception()	java.lang.ArrayIndex➡OutOfBoundsException	300
ArrayIndexOutOfBounds➡Exception(int)	java.lang.ArrayIndex➡OutOfBoundsException	300
ArrayIndexOutOfBounds➡Exception(String)	java.lang.ArrayIndex➡OutOfBoundsException	300
ArrayStoreException()	java.lang.➡ArrayStoreException	300
ArrayStoreException(String)	java.lang.➡ArrayStoreException	300
asin(double)	java.lang.Math	209
atan(double)	java.lang.Math	209
atan2(double, double)	java.lang.Math	209
available()	java.io.BufferedInputStream	148
available()	java.io.➡ByteArrayInputStream	151

351

Index of Methods

available()	java.io.FileInputStream	162
available()	java.io.FilterInputStream	165
available()	java.io.InputStream	167
available()	java.io.➡LineNumberInputStream	168
available()	java.io.PushbackInputStream	178
available()	java.io.➡StringBufferInputStream	186
available()	java.net.SocketImpl	260
AWTError(String)	java.awt.AWTError	304
AWTException(String)	java.awt.AWTException	299
before(Date)	java.util.Date	277
bind(InetAddress, int)	java.net.SocketImpl	260
BitSet()	java.util.BitSet	275
BitSet(int)	java.util.BitSet	275
Boolean(boolean)	java.lang.Boolean	193
Boolean(String)	java.lang.Boolean	193
booleanValue()	java.lang.Boolean	193
BorderLayout()	java.awt.BorderLayout	20
BorderLayout(int, int)	java.awt.BorderLayout	20
bounds()	java.awt.Component	34
brighter()	java.awt.Color	31
BufferedInputStream➡(InputStream)	java.io.BufferedInputStream	148
BufferedInputStream➡(InputStream, int)	java.io.BufferedInputStream	148
BufferedOutputStream➡(OutputStream)	java.io.BufferedOutputStream	149
BufferedOutputStream➡(OutputStream, int)	java.io.BufferedOutputStream	150
Button()	java.awt.Button	22
Button(String)	java.awt.Button	22

continues

Index of Methods

continued

Method Name	Class Name	Page
ByteArrayInputStream(byte[])	java.io.ByteArrayInputStream	151
ByteArrayInputStream ➡(byte[], int, int)	java.io.ByteArrayInputStream	151
ByteArrayOutputStream()	java.io. ➡ByteArrayOutputStream	152
ByteArrayOutputStream(int)	java.io. ➡ByteArrayOutputStream	152
bytesWidth(byte[], int, int)	java.awt.FontMetrics	58
canRead()	java.io.File	158
Canvas()	java.awt.Canvas	22
canWrite()	java.io.File	158
capacity()	java.lang.StringBuffer	229
capacity()	java.util.Vector	292
CardLayout()	java.awt.CardLayout	25
CardLayout(int, int)	java.awt.CardLayout	25
ceil(double)	java.lang.Math	209
Character(char)	java.lang.Character	194
charAt(int)	java.lang.String	222
charAt(int)	java.lang.StringBuffer	229
charsWidth(char[], int, int)	java.awt.FontMetrics	58
charValue()	java.lang.Character	194
charWidth(char)	java.awt.FontMetrics	58
charWidth(int)	java.awt.FontMetrics	58
checkAccept(String, int)	java.lang.SecurityManager	218
checkAccess()	java.lang.Thread	238
checkAccess()	java.lang.ThreadGroup	242
checkAccess(Thread)	java.lang.SecurityManager	218
checkAccess(ThreadGroup)	java.lang.SecurityManager	218
checkAll()	java.awt.MediaTracker	89

Index of Methods

checkAll(boolean)	java.awt.MediaTracker	89
Checkbox()	java.awt.Checkbox	27
Checkbox(String)	java.awt.Checkbox	27
Checkbox(String, ➥CheckboxGroup, boolean)	java.awt.Checkbox	27
CheckboxGroup()	java.awt.CheckboxGroup	28
CheckboxMenuItem(String)	java.awt.CheckboxMenuItem	29
checkConnect(String, int)	java.lang.SecurityManager	218
checkConnect(String, ➥int, Object)	java.lang.SecurityManager	218
checkCreateClassLoader()	java.lang.SecurityManager	218
checkDelete(String)	java.lang.SecurityManager	218
checkError()	java.io.PrintStream	175
checkExec(String)	java.lang. ➥SecurityManager	219
checkExit(int)	java.lang. ➥SecurityManager	219
checkID(int)	java.awt.MediaTracker	89
checkID(int, boolean)	java.awt.MediaTracker	89
checkImage(Image, ➥ImageObserver)	java.awt.Component	34
checkImage(Image, int, ➥int, ImageObserver)	java.awt.Component	34
checkImage(Image, int, ➥int, ImageObserver)	java.awt.Toolkit	112
checkLink(String)	java.lang.SecurityManager	219
checkListen(int)	java.lang.SecurityManager	219
checkPackageAccess ➥(String)	java.lang.SecurityManager	219
checkPackageDefinition ➥(String)	java.lang.SecurityManager	219
checkPropertiesAccess()	java.lang.SecurityManager	219

continues

Index of Methods

continued

Method Name	Class Name	Page
checkPropertyAccess ➥(String)	java.lang.SecurityManager	219
checkPropertyAccess ➥(String, String)	java.lang.SecurityManager	219
checkRead(FileDescriptor)	java.lang.SecurityManager	220
checkRead(String)	java.lang.SecurityManager	220
checkRead(String, Object)	java.lang.SecurityManager	220
checkSetFactory()	java.lang.SecurityManager	220
checkTopLevelWindow ➥(Object)	java.lang.SecurityManager	220
checkWrite ➥(FileDescriptor)	java.lang.SecurityManager	220
checkWrite(String)	java.lang.SecurityManager	220
Choice()	java.awt.Choice	30
ClassCastException()	java.lang. ➥ClassCastException	300
ClassCastException(String)	java.lang.ClassCastException	300
ClassCircularityError()	java.lang. ➥ClassCircularityError	304
ClassCircularityError ➥(String)	java.lang. ➥ClassCircularityError	304
classDepth(String)	java.lang.SecurityManager	220
ClassFormatError()	java.lang.ClassFormatError	304
ClassFormatError(String)	java.lang.ClassFormatError	304
ClassLoader()	java.lang.ClassLoader	198
classLoaderDepth()	java.lang.SecurityManager	220
ClassNotFoundException()	java.lang. ➥ClassNotFoundException	300
ClassNotFoundException ➥(String)	java.lang. ➥ClassNotFoundException	300
clear()	java.awt.List	86

clear()	java.util.Hashtable	284
clear(int)	java.util.BitSet	275
clearChanged()	java.util.Observable	286
clearRect(int, int, ➡int, int)	java.awt.Graphics	64
clipRect(int, int, int, int)	java.awt.Graphics	64
clone()	java.awt.GridBagConstraints	72
clone()	java.awt.image.ImageFilter	129
clone()	java.awt.Insets	83
clone()	java.lang.Object	212
clone()	java.util.BitSet	275
clone()	java.util.Hashtable	284
clone()	java.util.Vector	292
CloneNotSupportedException()	java.lang.Clone ➡NotSupportedException	300
CloneNotSupported ➡Exception(String)	java.lang.CloneNotSupported	300
close()	java.io.FileInputStream	162
close()	java.io.FileOutputStream	163
close()	java.io.FilterInputStream	165
close()	java.io.FilterOutputStream	166
close()	java.io.InputStream	167
close()	java.io.OutputStream	170
close()	java.io.PipedInputStream	173
close()	java.io.PipedOutputStream	174
close()	java.io.PrintStream	176
close()	java.io.RandomAccessFile	179
close()	java.io.SequenceInputStream	182
close()	java.net.ServerSocket	256
close()	java.net.Socket	258
close()	java.net.SocketImpl	260

continues

Index of Methods

continued

Method Name	Class Name	Page
Color(float, float, float)	java.awt.Color	31
Color(int)	java.awt.Color	31
Color(int, int, int)	java.awt.Color	31
ColorModel(int)	java.awt.image.ColorModel	120
command(Object)	java.lang.Compiler	198
commentChar(int)	java.io.StreamTokenizer	184
compareTo(String)	java.lang.String	222
compileClass(Class)	java.lang.Compiler	199
compileClasses(String)	java.lang.Compiler	199
concat(String)	java.lang.String	222
connect()	java.net.URLConnection	265
connect(InetAddress, int)	java.net.SocketImpl	260
connect(PipedInputStream)	java.io.PipedOutputStream	174
connect(PipedOutputStream)	java.io. ➥java.io.PipedInputStream	174
connect(String, int)	java.net.SocketImpl	260
contains(Object)	java.util.Hashtable	284
contains(Object)	java.util.Vector	292
containsKey(Object)	java.util.Hashtable	284
ContentHandler()	java.net.ContentHandler	252
controlDown()	java.awt.Event	51
copyArea(int, int, int, ➥int, int, int)	java.awt.Graphics	64
copyInto(Object[])	java.util.Vector	292
copyValueOf(char[])	java.lang.String	223
copyValueOf(char[], ➥int, int)	java.lang.String	223
cos(double)	java.lang.Math	209
countComponents()	java.awt.Container	43

Index of Methods

`countItems()`	`java.awt.Choice`	30
`countItems()`	`java.awt.List`	86
`countItems()`	`java.awt.Menu`	92
`countMenus()`	`java.awt.MenuBar`	95
`countObservers()`	`java.util.Observable`	286
`countStackFrames()`	`java.lang.Thread`	238
`countTokens()`	`java.util.StringTokenizer`	290
`create()`	`java.awt.Graphics`	64
`create(boolean)`	`java.net.SocketImpl`	260
`create(int, int, int, int)`	`java.awt.Graphics`	64
`createButton(Button)`	`java.awt.Toolkit`	112
`createCanvas(Canvas)`	`java.awt.Toolkit`	112
`createCheckbox(Checkbox)`	`java.awt.Toolkit`	113
`createCheckboxMenuItem` `➥(CheckboxMenuItem)`	`java.awt.Toolkit`	113
`createChoice(Choice)`	`java.awt.Toolkit`	113
`createContentHandler(String)`	`java.net.` `➥ContentHandlerFactory`	270
`createDialog(Dialog)`	`java.awt.Toolkit`	113
`createFileDialog(FileDialog)`	`java.awt.Toolkit`	113
`createFrame(Frame)`	`java.awt.Toolkit`	113
`createImage(ImageProducer)`	`java.awt.Component`	34
`createImage(ImageProducer)`	`java.awt.Toolkit`	113
`createImage(int, int)`	`java.awt.Component`	34
`createLabel(Label)`	`java.awt.Toolkit`	113
`createList(List)`	`java.awt.Toolkit`	113
`createMenu(Menu)`	`java.awt.Toolkit`	113
`createMenuBar(MenuBar)`	`java.awt.Toolkit`	114
`createMenuItem(MenuItem)`	`java.awt.Toolkit`	114
`createPanel(Panel)`	`java.awt.Toolkit`	114
`createScrollbar(Scrollbar)`	`java.awt.Toolkit`	114

continues

Index of Methods

continued

Method Name	Class Name	Page
createSocketImpl()	java.net.SocketImplFactory	271
createTextArea(TextArea)	java.awt.Toolkit	114
createTextField(TextField)	java.awt.Toolkit	114
createURLStreamHandler ➥(String)	java.net. ➥URLStreamHandlerFactory	271
createWindow(Window)	java.awt.Toolkit	114
CropImageFilter(int, int, ➥int, int)	java.awt.image. ➥CropImageFilter	122
currentClassLoader()	java.lang.SecurityManager	221
currentThread()	java.lang.Thread	238
currentTimeMillis()	java.lang.System	277
darker()	java.awt.Color	31
DatagramPacket(byte[], int)	java.net.DatagramPacket	253
DatagramPacket(byte[], ➥int,InetAddress, int)	java.net.DatagramPacket	253
DatagramSocket()	java.net.DatagramSocket	254
DatagramSocket(int)	java.net.DatagramSocket	254
DataInputStream(InputStream)	java.io.DataInputStream	153
DataOutputStream ➥(OutputStream)	java.io.DataOutputStream	156
Date()	java.util.Date	276
Date(int, int, int)	java.util.Date	277
Date(int, int, int, ➥int, int)	java.util.Date	277
Date(int, int, int, ➥int, int, int)	java.util.Date	277
Date(long)	java.util.Date	276
Date(String)	java.util.Date	277
defineClass(byte[], ➥int, int)	java.lang.ClassLoader	198

Index of Methods

`delete()`	`java.io.File`	159
`deleteObserver(Observer)`	`java.util.Observable`	286
`deleteObservers()`	`java.util.Observable`	286
`delItem(int)`	`java.awt.List`	86
`delItems(int, int)`	`java.awt.List`	86
`deliverEvent(Event)`	`java.awt.Component`	34
`deliverEvent(Event)`	`java.awt.Container`	43
`deselect(int)`	`java.awt.List`	86
`destroy()`	`java.applet.Applet`	14
`destroy()`	`java.lang.Process`	213
`destroy()`	`java.lang.Thread`	238
`destroy()`	`java.lang.ThreadGroup`	242
`Dialog(Frame, boolean)`	`java.awt.Dialog`	45
`Dialog(Frame, String,` `➥boolean)`	`java.awt.Dialog`	45
`Dictionary()`	`java.util.Dictionary`	280
`digit(char, int)`	`java.lang.Character`	194
`Dimension()`	`java.awt.Dimension`	46
`Dimension(Dimension)`	`java.awt.Dimension`	46
`Dimension(int, int)`	`java.awt.Dimension`	46
`DirectColorModel(int,` `➥int, int, int)`	`java.awt.image.` `➥DirectColorModel`	123
`DirectColorModel(int, int,` `➥int, int, int)`	`java.awt.image.` `➥DirectColorModel`	123
`disable()`	`java.awt.Component`	35
`disable()`	`java.awt.MenuItem`	97
`disable()`	`java.lang.Compiler`	199
`dispose()`	`java.awt.Frame`	61
`dispose()`	`java.awt.Graphics`	65
`dispose()`	`java.awt.Window`	116
`Double(double)`	`java.lang.Double`	199

continues

Index of Methods

continued

Method Name	Class Name	Page
Double(String)	java.lang.Double	200
doubleToLongBits(double)	java.lang.Double	200
doubleValue()	java.lang.Double	200
doubleValue()	java.lang.Float	202
doubleValue()	java.lang.Integer	204
doubleValue()	java.lang.Long	206
doubleValue()	java.lang.Number	211
draw3DRect(int, int, ➡int, int, boolean)	java.awt.Graphics	65
drawArc(int, int, int, ➡int, int, int)	java.awt.Graphics	65
drawBytes(byte[], int, ➡int, int, int)	java.awt.Graphics	65
drawChars(char[], int, ➡int, int, int)	java.awt.Graphics	65
drawImage(Image, int, int, ➡Color, ImageObserver)	java.awt.Graphics	66
drawImage(Image, int, int, ➡ImageObserver)	java.awt.Graphics	66
drawImage(Image, int, int, ➡int, int, Color, ➡ImageObserver)	java.awt.Graphics	65
drawImage(Image, int, int, ➡int, int, ImageObserver)	java.awt.Graphics	66
drawLine(int, int, int, ➡int)	java.awt.Graphics	66
drawOval(int, int, int, ➡int)	java.awt.Graphics	66
drawPolygon(int[], int[], ➡int)	java.awt.Graphics	67
drawPolygon(Polygon)	java.awt.Graphics	67
drawRect(int, int, int, int)	java.awt.Graphics	66

Index of Methods

drawRoundRect(int, int, ➥int, int, int, int)	java.awt.Graphics	67
drawString(String, int, int)	java.awt.Graphics	67
DumpConstraints ➥(GridBagConstraints)	java.awt.GridBagLayout	77
DumpLayoutInfo ➥(GridBagLayoutInfo)	java.awt.GridBagLayout	78
dumpStack()	java.lang.Thread	238
echoCharIsSet()	java.awt.TextField	111
elementAt(int)	java.util.Vector	292
elements()	java.util.Dictionary	280
elements()	java.util.Hashtable	284
elements()	java.util.Vector	292
empty()	java.util.Stack	289
EmptyStackException()	java.util. ➥EmptyStackException	301
enable()	java.awt.Component	35
enable()	java.awt.MenuItem	97
enable()	java.lang.Compiler	199
enable(boolean)	java.awt.Component	35
enable(boolean)	java.awt.MenuItem	97
encode(String)	java.net.URLEncoder	269
endsWith(String)	java.lang.String	223
ensureCapacity(int)	java.lang.StringBuffer	229
ensureCapacity(int)	java.util.Vector	292
enumerate(Thread[])	java.lang.Thread	239
enumerate(Thread[])	java.lang.ThreadGroup	242
enumerate(Thread[], boolean)	java.lang.ThreadGroup	242
enumerate(ThreadGroup[])	java.lang.ThreadGroup	242
enumerate(ThreadGroup[], ➥boolean)	java.lang.ThreadGroup	242

continues

Index of Methods

continued

Method Name	Class Name	Page
EOFException()	java.io.EOFException	299
EOFException(String)	java.io.EOFException	299
eolIsSignificant(boolean)	java.io.StreamTokenizer	184
equals(Object)	java.awt.Color	32
equals(Object)	java.awt.Font	56
equals(Object)	java.awt.Point	99
equals(Object)	java.awt.Rectangle	102
equals(Object)	java.io.File	159
equals(Object)	java.lang.Boolean	193
equals(Object)	java.lang.Character	194
equals(Object)	java.lang.Double	200
equals(Object)	java.lang.Float	202
equals(Object)	java.lang.Integer	204
equals(Object)	java.lang.Long	206
equals(Object)	java.lang.Object	212
equals(Object)	java.lang.String	222
equals(Object)	java.net.InetAddress	255
equals(Object)	java.net.URL	263
equals(Object)	java.util.BitSet	275
equals(Object)	java.util.Date	277
equalsIgnoreCase(String)	java.lang.String	223
Error()	java.lang.Error	305
Error(String)	java.lang.Error	305
Event(Object, int, Object)	java.awt.Event	50
Event(Object, long, int, ➡int, int, int, int)	java.awt.Event	51
Event(Object, long, int, ➡int, int, int, int, Object)	java.awt.Event	51

Index of Methods

`Exception()`	`java.lang.Exception`	300
`Exception(String)`	`java.lang.Exception`	300
`exec(String)`	`java.lang.Runtime`	215
`exec(String, String[])`	`java.lang.Runtime`	216
`exec(String[])`	`java.lang.Runtime`	215
`exec(String[], String[])`	`java.lang.Runtime`	216
`exists()`	`java.io.File`	159
`exit(int)`	`java.lang.Runtime`	216
`exit(int)`	`java.lang.System`	234
`exitValue()`	`java.lang.Process`	214
`exp(double)`	`java.lang.Math`	209
`File(File, String)`	`java.io.File`	158
`File(String)`	`java.io.File`	158
`File(String, String)`	`java.io.File`	158
`FileDescriptor()`	`java.io.FileDescriptor`	161
`FileDialog(Frame, String)`	`java.awt.FileDialog`	53
`FileDialog(Frame,` ➥`String, int)`	`java.awt.FileDialog`	53
`FileInputStream(File)`	`java.io.FileInputStream`	161
`FileInputStream` ➥`(FileDescriptor)`	`java.io.FileInputStream`	162
`FileInputStream(String)`	`java.io.FileInputStream`	162
`FileNotFoundException()`	`java.io.` ➥`FileNotFoundException`	299
`FileNotFoundException(String)`	`java.io.` ➥`FileNotFoundException`	299
`FileOutputStream(File)`	`java.io.FileOutputStream`	163
`FileOutputStream` ➥`(FileDescriptor)`	`java.io.FileOutputStream`	163
`FileOutputStream(String)`	`java.io.FileOutputStream`	163
`fill3DRect(int, int,` ➥`int, int, boolean)`	`java.awt.Graphics`	67

continues

Index of Methods

continued

Method Name	Class Name	Page
fillArc(int, int, int, ➥int, int, int)	java.awt.Graphics	68
fillInStackTrace()	java.lang.Throwable	244
fillOval(int, int, int, int)	java.awt.Graphics	67
fillPolygon(int[], ➥int[], int)	java.awt.Graphics	68
fillPolygon(Polygon)	java.awt.Graphics	68
fillRect(int, int, int, int)	java.awt.Graphics	67
fillRoundRect(int, int, ➥int, int, int, int)	java.awt.Graphics	68
FilteredImageSource ➥(ImageProducer, ➥ImageFilter)	java.awt. ➥FilteredImageSource	124
filterIndexColorModel ➥(IndexColorModel)	java.awt.image.RGBImage	138
FilterInputStream ➥(InputStream)	java.io.FilterInputStream	165
FilterOutputStream ➥(OutputStream)	java.io.FilterOutputStream	166
filterRGB(int, int, int)	java.awt. ➥image.RGBImageFilter	139
filterRGBPixels(int, int, ➥int, int, int[], int, int)	java.awt.image. ➥RGBImageFilter	138
finalize()	java.awt.Graphics	68
finalize()	java.io.FileInputStream	162
finalize()	java.io.FileOutputStream	163
finalize()	java.lang.Object	212
finalize()	java.net.DatagramSocket	254
findSystemClass(String)	java.lang.ClassLoader	198
first(Container)	java.awt.CardLayout	25
firstElement()	java.util.Vector	292
Float(double)	java.lang.Float	202

Index of Methods

Method	Class	Page
Float(float)	java.lang.Float	202
Float(String)	java.lang.Float	202
floatToIntBits(float)	java.lang.Float	202
floatValue()	java.lang.Double	200
floatValue()	java.lang.Float	202
floatValue()	java.lang.Integer	204
floatValue()	java.lang.Long	206
floatValue()	java.lang.Number	211
floor(double)	java.lang.Math	209
FlowLayout()	java.awt.FlowLayout	54
FlowLayout(int)	java.awt.FlowLayout	54
FlowLayout(int, int, int)	java.awt.FlowLayout	54
flush()	java.awt.Image	82
flush()	java.io.➡BufferedOutputStream	150
flush()	java.io.DataOutputStream	156
flush()	java.io.FilterOutputStream	166
flush()	java.io.OutputStream	170
flush()	java.io.PrintStream	176
Font(String, int, int)	java.awt.Font	56
FontMetrics(Font)	java.awt.FontMetrics	58
forDigit(int, int)	java.lang.Character	194
forName(String)	java.lang.Class	197
Frame()	java.awt.Frame	60
Frame(String)	java.awt.Frame	60
freeMemory()	java.lang.Runtime	216
gc()	java.lang.Runtime	216
gc()	java.lang.System	234
get(int)	java.util.BitSet	275
get(Object)	java.util.Dictionary	280

continues

Index of Methods

continued

Method Name	Class Name	Page
get(Object)	java.util.Hashtable	284
getAbsolutePath()	java.io.File	159
getAddress()	java.net.DatagramPacket	253
getAddress()	java.net.InetAddress	255
getAlignment()	java.awt.Label	84
getAllByName(String)	java.net.InetAddress	254
getAllowUserInteraction()	java.net.URLConnection	265
getAlpha(int)	java.awt.image.ColorModel	120
getAlpha(int)	java.awt.image.➡DirectColorModel	123
getAlpha(int)	java.awt.image.➡IndexColorModel	131
getAlphaMask()	java.awt.image.➡DirectColorModel	123
getAlphas(byte[])	java.awt.image.➡IndexColorModel	131
getApplet(String)	java.applet.AppletContext	16
getAppletContext()	java.applet.Applet	14
getAppletContext()	java.applet.AppletStub	18
getAppletInfo()	java.applet.Applet	14
getApplets()	java.applet.AppletContext	16
getAscent()	java.awt.FontMetrics	58
getAudioClip(URL)	java.applet.Applet	14
getAudioClip(URL)	java.applet.AppletContext	16
getAudioClip(URL, String)	java.applet.Applet	14
getBackground()	java.awt.Component	35
getBlue()	java.awt.Color	32
getBlue(int)	java.awt.image.ColorModel	120
getBlue(int)	java.awt.image.➡DirectColorModel	123
getBlue(int)	java.awt.image.➡IndexColorModel	131

Index of Methods

getBlueMask()	java.awt.image.➡DirectColorModel	124
getBlues(byte[])	java.awt.image.➡IndexColorModel	131
getBoolean(String)	java.lang.Boolean	193
getBoundingBox()	java.awt.Polygon	100
getByName(String)	java.net.InetAddress	255
getBytes(int, int, ➡byte[], int)	java.lang.String	223
getChars(int, int, ➡char[], int)	java.lang.String	223
getChars(int, int, ➡char[], int)	java.lang.StringBuffer	229
getCheckboxGroup()	java.awt.Checkbox	27
getClass()	java.lang.Object	212
getClassContext()	java.lang.SecurityManager	221
getClassLoader()	java.lang.Class	197
getClipRect()	java.awt.Graphics	68
getCodeBase()	java.applet.Applet	14
getCodeBase()	java.applet.AppletStub	18
getColor()	java.awt.Graphics	68
getColor(String)	java.awt.Color	32
getColor(String, Color)	java.awt.Color	32
getColor(String, int)	java.awt.Color	32
getColorModel()	java.awt.Component	35
getColorModel()	java.awt.Toolkit	114
getColumns()	java.awt.TextArea	108
getColumns()	java.awt.TextField	111
getComponent(int)	java.awt.Container	43
getComponents()	java.awt.Container	43
getConstraints(Component)	java.awt.GridBagLayout	78

continues

Index of Methods

continued

Method Name	Class Name	Page
getContent()	java.net.URL	263
getContent()	java.net.URLConnection	265
getContent(URLConnection)	java.net.ContentHandler	252
getContentEncoding()	java.net.URLConnection	265
getContentLength()	java.net.URLConnection	266
getContentType()	java.net.URLConnection	266
getCurrent()	java.awt.CheckboxGroup	28
getCursorType()	java.awt.Frame	61
getData()	java.net.DatagramPacket	253
getDate()	java.net.URLConnection	266
getDate()	java.util.Date	277
getDay()	java.util.Date	277
getDefaultAllowUser ➥Interaction()	java.net.URLConnection	267
getDefaultRequestProperty ➥(String)	java.net.URLConnection	267
getDefaultToolkit()	java.awt.Toolkit	114
getDefaultUseCaches()	java.net.URLConnection	268
getDescent()	java.awt.FontMetrics	59
getDirectory()	java.awt.FileDialog	53
getDocumentBase()	java.applet.Applet	14
getDocumentBase()	java.applet.AppletStub	18
getDoInput()	java.net.URLConnection	266
getDoOutput()	java.net.URLConnection	266
getEchoChar()	java.awt.TextField	111
getenv(String)	java.lang.System	234
getErrorsAny()	java.awt.MediaTracker	90
getErrorsID(int)	java.awt.MediaTracker	90
getErrorStream()	java.lang.Process	214

Index of Methods

getExpiration()	java.net.URLConnection	266
getFamily()	java.awt.Font	56
getFD()	java.io.FileInputStream	162
getFD()	java.io.FileOutputStream	163
getFD()	java.io.RandomAccessFile	179
getFile()	java.awt.FileDialog	53
getFile()	java.net.URL	263
getFileDescriptor()	java.net.SocketImpl	260
getFilenameFilter()	java.awt.FileDialog	53
getFilePointer()	java.io.RandomAccessFile	179
getFilterInstance ➡(ImageConsumer)	java.awt.image.ImageFilter	129
getFont()	java.awt.Component	35
getFont()	java.awt.FontMetrics	59
getFont()	java.awt.Graphics	68
getFont()	java.awt.MenuComponent	96
getFont()	java.awt.MenuContainer	117
getFont(String)	java.awt.Font	56
getFont(String, Font)	java.awt.Font	56
getFontList()	java.awt.Toolkit	114
getFontMetrics()	java.awt.Graphics	69
getFontMetrics(Font)	java.awt.Component	35
getFontMetrics(Font)	java.awt.Graphics	68
getFontMetrics(Font)	java.awt.Toolkit	115
getForeground()	java.awt.Component	35
getGraphics()	java.awt.Component	35
getGraphics()	java.awt.Image	81
getGreen()	java.awt.Color	32
getGreen(int)	java.awt.image.ColorModel	120
getGreen(int)	java.awt.image. ➡DirectColorModel	124

continues

Index of Methods

continued

Method Name	Class Name	Page
getGreen(int)	java.awt.image.➥IndexColorModel	131
getGreenMask()	java.awt.image.➥DirectColorModel	124
getGreens(byte[])	java.awt.image.➥IndexColorModel	131
getHeaderField(int)	java.net.URLConnection	266
getHeaderField(String)	java.net.URLConnection	266
getHeaderFieldDate(String,➥long)	java.net.URLConnection	266
getHeaderFieldInt(String,➥int)	java.net.URLConnection	266
getHeaderFieldKey(int)	java.net.URLConnection	266
getHeight()	java.awt.FontMetrics	59
getHeight(ImageObserver)	java.awt.Image	81
getHelpMenu()	java.awt.MenuBar	95
getHost()	java.net.URL	263
getHostName()	java.net.InetAddress	255
getHours()	java.util.Date	278
getHSBColor(float,➥float, float)	java.awt.Color	32
getIconImage()	java.awt.Frame	61
getIfModifiedSince()	java.net.URLConnection	268
getImage(String)	java.awt.Toolkit	115
getImage(URL)	java.applet.Applet	14
getImage(URL)	java.applet.AppletContext	17
getImage(URL)	java.awt.Toolkit	115
getImage(URL, String)	java.applet.Applet	15
getInCheck()	java.lang.SecurityManager	221
getInetAddress()	java.net.ServerSocket	256
getInetAddress()	java.net.Socket	258

getInetAddress()	java.net.SocketImpl	261
getInputStream()	java.lang.Process	214
getInputStream()	java.net.Socket	258
getInputStream()	java.net.SocketImpl	261
getInputStream()	java.net.URLConnection	266
getInteger(String)	java.lang.Integer	204
getInteger(String, int)	java.lang.Integer	204
getInteger(String, Integer)	java.lang.Integer	204
getInterfaces()	java.lang.Class	197
getItem(int)	java.awt.Choice	30
getItem(int)	java.awt.List	86
getItem(int)	java.awt.Menu	92
getLabel()	java.awt.Button	22
getLabel()	java.awt.Checkbox	27
getLabel()	java.awt.MenuItem	98
getLastModified()	java.net.URLConnection	267
getLayout()	java.awt.Container	43
getLayoutDimensions()	java.awt.GridBagLayout	78
GetLayoutInfo(Container, ➥int)	java.awt.GridBagLayout	78
getLayoutOrigin()	java.awt.GridBagLayout	78
getLayoutWeights()	java.awt.GridBagLayout	78
getLength()	java.net.DatagramPacket	253
getLineIncrement()	java.awt.Scrollbar	106
getLineNumber()	java.io.LineNumberInputStream	169
getLocalHost()	java.net.InetAddress	255
getLocalizedInputStream ➥(InputStream)	java.lang.Runtime	216
getLocalizedOutputStream ➥(OutputStream)	java.lang.Runtime	216
getLocalPort()	java.net.DatagramSocket	254

continues

Index of Methods

continued

Method Name	Class Name	Page
getLocalPort()	java.net.ServerSocket	256
getLocalPort()	java.net.Socket	258
getLocalPort()	java.net.SocketImpl	261
getLong(String)	java.lang.Long	206
getLong(String, Long)	java.lang.Long	207
getLong(String, long)	java.lang.Long	206
getMapSize()	java.awt.image.➥IndexColorModel	131
getMaxAdvance()	java.awt.FontMetrics	59
getMaxAscent()	java.awt.FontMetrics	59
getMaxDescent()	java.awt.FontMetrics	59
getMaximum()	java.awt.Scrollbar	106
getMaxPriority()	java.lang.ThreadGroup	243
getMenu(int)	java.awt.MenuBar	95
getMenuBar()	java.awt.Frame	61
getMessage()	java.lang.Throwable	244
getMinimum()	java.awt.Scrollbar	106
GetMinSize(Container, ➥GridBagLayoutInfo)	java.awt.GridBagLayout	78
getMinutes()	java.util.Date	278
getMode()	java.awt.FileDialog	53
getMonth()	java.util.Date	278
getName()	java.awt.Font	57
getName()	java.io.File	159
getName()	java.lang.Class	197
getName()	java.lang.Thread	239
getName()	java.lang.ThreadGroup	243
getOrientation()	java.awt.Scrollbar	106
getOutputStream()	java.lang.Process	214

getOutputStream()	java.net.Socket	259
getOutputStream()	java.net.SocketImpl	261
getOutputStream()	java.net.URLConnection	267
getPageIncrement()	java.awt.Scrollbar	106
getParameter(String)	java.applet.Applet	15
getParameter(String)	java.applet.AppletStub	18
getParameterInfo()	java.applet.Applet	15
getParent()	java.awt.Component	35
getParent()	java.awt.MenuComponent	96
getParent()	java.io.File	159
getParent()	java.lang.ThreadGroup	243
getPath()	java.io.File	159
getPeer()	java.awt.Component	36
getPeer()	java.awt.MenuComponent	96
getPixelSize()	java.awt.image.ColorModel	120
getPort()	java.net.DatagramPacket	253
getPort()	java.net.Socket	259
getPort()	java.net.SocketImpl	261
getPort()	java.net.URL	262
getPriority()	java.lang.Thread	239
getProperties()	java.lang.System	234
getProperty(String)	java.lang.System	234
getProperty(String)	java.util.Properties	287
getProperty(String, ImageObserver)	java.awt.Image	82
getProperty(String, String)	java.lang.System	234
getProperty(String, String)	java.util.Properties	287
getProtocol()	java.net.URL	262
getRed()	java.awt.Color	32
getRed(int)	java.awt.image.ColorModel	121

continues

Index of Methods

continued

Method Name	Class Name	Page
getRed(int)	java.awt.image. ➥DirectColorModel	124
getRed(int)	java.awt.image. ➥IndexColorModel	132
getRedMask()	java.awt.image. ➥DirectColorModel	124
getReds(byte[])	java.awt.image. ➥IndexColorModel	132
getRef()	java.net.URL	263
getRequestProperty(String)	java.net.URLConnection	268
getRGB()	java.awt.Color	32
getRGB(int)	java.awt.image.ColorModel	121
getRGB(int)	java.awt.image. ➥DirectColorModel	124
getRGB(int)	java.awt.image. ➥IndexColorModel	132
getRGBdefault()	java.awt.image.ColorModel	121
getRows()	java.awt.List	86
getRows()	java.awt.TextArea	108
getRuntime()	java.lang.Runtime	217
getScreenResolution()	java.awt.Toolkit	115
getScreenSize()	java.awt.Toolkit	115
getSeconds()	java.util.Date	278
getSecurityContext()	java.lang.SecurityManager	221
getSecurityManager()	java.lang.System	233
getSelectedIndex()	java.awt.Choice	30
getSelectedIndex()	java.awt.List	86
getSelectedIndexes()	java.awt.List	86
getSelectedItem()	java.awt.Choice	30
getSelectedItem()	java.awt.List	86

Index of Methods

getSelectedItems()	java.awt.List	86
getSelectedText()	java.awt.TextComponent	109
getSelectionEnd()	java.awt.TextComponent	109
getSelectionStart()	java.awt.TextComponent	110
getSize()	java.awt.Font	57
getSource()	java.awt.Image	82
getState()	java.awt.Checkbox	27
getState()	java.awt.CheckboxMenuItem	29
getStyle()	java.awt.Font	57
getSuperclass()	java.lang.Class	197
getText()	java.awt.Label	84
getThreadGroup()	java.lang.Thread	239
getTime()	java.util.Date	278
getTimezoneOffset()	java.util.Date	278
getTitle()	java.awt.Frame	61
getToolkit()	java.awt.Component	36
getToolkit()	java.awt.Window	116
getTransparentPixel()	java.awt.image. ➥IndexColorModel	132
getURL()	java.net.URLConnection	267
getUseCaches()	java.net.URLConnection	268
getValue()	java.awt.Scrollbar	106
getVisible()	java.awt.Scrollbar	106
getVisibleIndex()	java.awt.List	87
getWarningString()	java.awt.Window	116
getWidth(ImageObserver)	java.awt.Image	82
getWidths()	java.awt.FontMetrics	59
getYear()	java.util.Date	278

continues

Index of Methods

continued

Method Name	Class Name	Page
gotFocus(Event, Object)	java.awt.Component	36
grabPixels()	java.awt.image.PixelGrabber	135
grabPixels(long)	java.awt.image.PixelGrabber	135
Graphics()	java.awt.Graphics	64
GridBagConstraints()	java.awt.GridBagConstraints	72
GridBagLayout()	java.awt.GridBagLayout	77
GridLayout(int, int)	java.awt.GridLayout	80
GridLayout(int, int, ➥int, int)	java.awt.GridLayout	80
grow(int, int)	java.awt.Rectangle	102
guessContentTypeFromName ➥(String)	java.net.URLConnection	268
guessContentTypeFromStream ➥(InputStream)	java.net.URLConnection	269
handleEvent(Event)	java.awt.Component	36
hasChanged()	java.util.Observable	286
hashCode()	java.awt.Color	33
hashCode()	java.awt.Font	57
hashCode()	java.awt.Point	99
hashCode()	java.awt.Rectangle	102
hashCode()	java.io.File	159
hashCode()	java.lang.Boolean	193
hashCode()	java.lang.Character	195
hashCode()	java.lang.Double	200
hashCode()	java.lang.Float	202
hashCode()	java.lang.Integer	204
hashCode()	java.lang.Long	207
hashCode()	java.lang.Object	212
hashCode()	java.lang.String	223
hashCode()	java.net.InetAddress	255
hashCode()	java.net.URL	263

Index of Methods

hashCode()	java.util.BitSet	276
hashCode()	java.util.Date	278
Hashtable()	java.util.Hashtable	284
Hashtable(int)	java.util.Hashtable	284
Hashtable(int, float)	java.util.Hashtable	284
hasMoreElements()	java.util.Enumeration	295
hasMoreElements()	java.util.StringTokenizer	290
hasMoreTokens()	java.util.StringTokenizer	290
hide()	java.awt.Component	36
HSBtoRGB(float, float, ➥float)	java.awt.Color	33
IEEEremainder(double, ➥double)	java.lang.Math	209
IllegalAccessError()	java.lang. ➥IllegalAccessError	305
IllegalAccessError(String)	java.lang. ➥IllegalAccessError	305
IllegalAccessException()	java.lang. ➥IllegalAccessException	300
IllegalAccessException ➥(String)	java.lang. ➥IllegalAccessException	300
IllegalArgumentException()	java.lang. ➥IllegalArgumentException	300
IllegalArgumentException ➥(String)	java.lang. ➥IllegalArgumentException	300
IllegalMonitorState ➥Exception()	java.lang.Illegal ➥MonitorStateException	300
IllegalMonitorStateException ➥(String)	java.lang.Illegal ➥MonitorStateException	300
IllegalThreadStateException()	java.lang.Illegal ➥ThreadStateException	300
IllegalThreadStateException ➥(String)	java.lang.Illegal ➥ThreadStateException	300
Image()	java.awt.Image	81

continues

Index of Methods

continued

Method Name	Class Name	Page
imageComplete(int)	java.awt.image.ImageConsumer	140
imageComplete(int)	java.awt.image.ImageFilter	129
imageComplete(int)	java.awt.image.PixelGrabber	136
ImageFilter()	java.awt.image.ImageFilter	129
imageUpdate(Image, int, ➥int, int, int, int)	java.awt.Component	36
imageUpdate(Image, int, ➥int, int, int, int)	java.awt.image.ImageObserver	142
inClass(String)	java.lang.SecurityManager	221
inClassLoader()	java.lang.SecurityManager	221
IncompatibleClassChange ➥Error()	java.lang.Incompatible ➥ClassChangeError	305
IncompatibleClassChange ➥Error(String)	java.lang.Incompatible ➥ClassChangeError	305
IndexColorModel(int, int, ➥byte[], byte[], byte[])	java.lang.IndexColorModel	130
IndexColorModel(int, int, ➥byte[], byte[], byte[], ➥byte[])	java.lang.IndexColorModel	131
IndexColorModel(int, int, ➥byte[], byte[], byte[], int)	java.lang.IndexColorModel	131
indexOf(int)	java.lang.String	224
indexOf(int, int)	java.lang.String	224
indexOf(Object)	java.util.Vector	293
indexOf(Object, int)	java.util.Vector	293
indexOf(String)	java.lang.String	223
indexOf(String, int)	java.lang.String	223
IndexOutOfBoundsException()	java.lang. ➥IndexOutOfBoundsException	300
IndexOutOfBoundsException ➥(String)	java.lang. ➥IndexOutOfBoundsException	300
init()	java.applet.Applet	15

Index of Methods

InputStream()	java.io.InputStream	167
insert(int, boolean)	java.lang.StringBuffer	231
insert(int, char)	java.lang.StringBuffer	231
insert(int, char[])	java.lang.StringBuffer	231
insert(int, double)	java.lang.StringBuffer	230
insert(int, float)	java.lang.StringBuffer	230
insert(int, int)	java.lang.StringBuffer	231
insert(int, long)	java.lang.StringBuffer	231
insert(int, Object)	java.lang.StringBuffer	231
insert(int, String)	java.lang.StringBuffer	231
insertElementAt(Object, int)	java.util.Vector	293
insertText(String, int)	java.awt.TextArea	108
Insets(int, int, int, int)	java.awt.Insets	83
inside(int, int)	java.awt.Component	36
inside(int, int)	java.awt.Polygon	100
inside(int, int)	java.awt.Rectangle	102
InstantiationError()	java.lang.⟶InstantiationError	305
InstantiationError(String)	java.lang.⟶InstantiationError	305
InstantiationException()	java.lang.⟶InstantiationException	300
InstantiationException⟶(String)	java.lang.⟶InstantiationException	300
intBitsToFloat(int)	java.lang.Float	202
Integer(int)	java.lang.Integer	204
Integer(String)	java.lang.Integer	204
intern()	java.lang.String	224
InternalError()	java.lang.InternalError	305
InternalError(String)	java.lang.InternalError	305
interrupt()	java.lang.Thread	239

continues

Index of Methods

continued

Method Name	Class Name	Page
interrupted()	java.lang.Thread	239
InterruptedException()	java.lang.InterruptedException	300
InterruptedException(String)	java.lang.InterruptedException	300
InterruptedIOException()	java.io.InterruptedIOException	299
InterruptedIOException ➥(String)	java.io.InterruptedIOException	299
intersection(Rectangle)	java.awt.Rectangle	102
intersects(Rectangle)	java.awt.Rectangle	102
intValue()	java.lang.Double	200
intValue()	java.lang.Float	202
intValue()	java.lang.Integer	204
intValue()	java.lang.Long	207
intValue()	java.lang.Number	211
invalidate()	java.awt.Component	37
IOException()	java.io.IOException	299
IOException(String)	java.io.IOException	299
isAbsolute()	java.io.File	159
isActive()	java.applet.Applet	15
isActive()	java.applet.AppletStub	18
isBold()	java.awt.Font	57
isConsumer(ImageConsumer)	java.awt.image. ➥FilteredImageSource	125
isConsumer(ImageConsumer)	java.awt.image. ➥ImageProducer	143
isConsumer(ImageConsumer)	java.awt.image. ➥MemoryImageSource	133
isDaemon()	java.lang.Thread	239
isDaemon()	java.lang.ThreadGroup	243
isDigit(char)	java.lang.Character	195

isDirectory()	java.io.File	159
isEditable()	java.awt.TextComponent	110
isEmpty()	java.awt.Rectangle	102
isEmpty()	java.util.Dictionary	280
isEmpty()	java.util.Hashtable	284
isEmpty()	java.util.Vector	293
isEnabled()	java.awt.Component	37
isEnabled()	java.awt.MenuItem	98
isErrorAny()	java.awt.MediaTracker	90
isErrorID(int)	java.awt.MediaTracker	90
isFile()	java.io.File	159
isInfinite()	java.lang.Double	200
isInfinite()	java.lang.Float	202
isInfinite(double)	java.lang.Double	200
isInfinite(float)	java.lang.Float	903
isInterface()	java.lang.Class	197
isInterrupted()	java.lang.Thread	239
isItalic()	java.awt.Font	57
isJavaLetter(char)	java.lang.Character	195
isJavaLetterOrDigit(char)	java.lang.Character	195
isLetter(char)	java.lang.Character	195
isLetterOrDigit(char)	java.lang.Character	195
isLowerCase(char)	java.lang.Character	195
isModal()	java.awt.Dialog	45
isNaN()	java.lang.Double	200
isNaN()	java.lang.Float	203
isNaN(double)	java.lang.Double	200
isNaN(float)	java.lang.Float	203
isPlain()	java.awt.Font	57
isResizable()	java.awt.Dialog	45

continues

Index of Methods

continued

Method Name	Class Name	Page
isResizable()	java.awt.Frame	61
isSelected(int)	java.awt.List	87
isShowing()	java.awt.Component	37
isSpace(char)	java.lang.Character	195
isTearOff()	java.awt.Menu	92
isUpperCase(char)	java.lang.Character	196
isValid()	java.awt.Component	37
isVisible()	java.awt.Component	37
join()	java.lang.Thread	239
join(long)	java.lang.Thread	240
join(long, int)	java.lang.Thread	239
keyDown(Event, int)	java.awt.Component	37
keys()	java.util.Dictionary	280
keys()	java.util.Hashtable	285
keyUp(Event, int)	java.awt.Component	37
Label()	java.awt.Label	84
Label(String)	java.awt.Label	84
Label(String, int)	java.awt.Label	84
last(Container)	java.awt.CardLayout	25
lastElement()	java.util.Vector	293
lastIndexOf(int)	java.lang.String	224
lastIndexOf(int, int)	java.lang.String	224
lastIndexOf(Object)	java.util.Vector	293
lastIndexOf(Object, int)	java.util.Vector	293
lastIndexOf(String)	java.lang.String	224
lastIndexOf(String, int)	java.lang.String	224
lastModified()	java.io.File	160
layout()	java.awt.Component	37

Index of Methods

`layout()`	`java.awt.Container`	43
`layoutContainer(Container)`	`java.awt.BorderLayout`	21
`layoutContainer(Container)`	`java.awt.CardLayout`	26
`layoutContainer(Container)`	`java.awt.FlowLayout`	55
`layoutContainer(Container)`	`java.awt.GridBagLayout`	79
`layoutContainer(Container)`	`java.awt.GridLayout`	80
`layoutContainer(Container)`	`java.awt.LayoutManager`	116
`length()`	`java.io.File`	160
`length()`	`java.io.RandomAccessFile`	179
`length()`	`java.lang.String`	223
`length()`	`java.lang.StringBuffer`	231
`lineno()`	`java.io.StreamTokenizer`	184
`LineNumberInputStream` ➥`(InputStream)`	`java.io.` ➥`LineNumberInputStream`	168
`LinkageError()`	`java.lang.LinkageError`	305
`LinkageError(String)`	`java.lang.LinkageError`	305
`list()`	`java.awt.Component`	37
`List()`	`java.awt.List`	85
`list()`	`java.io.File`	160
`list()`	`java.lang.ThreadGroup`	243
`list(FilenameFilter)`	`java.io.File`	160
`List(int, boolean)`	`java.awt.List`	85
`list(PrintStream)`	`java.awt.Component`	38
`list(PrintStream)`	`java.util.Properties`	287
`list(PrintStream, int)`	`java.awt.Component`	38
`list(PrintStream, int)`	`java.awt.Container`	43
`listen(int)`	`java.net.SocketImpl`	261
`load(InputStream)`	`java.util.Properties`	287
`load(String)`	`java.lang.Runtime`	217
`load(String)`	`java.lang.System`	234

continues

Index of Methods

continued

Method Name	Class Name	Page
loadClass(String, boolean)	java.lang.ClassLoader	198
loadLibrary(String)	java.lang.Runtime	217
loadLibrary(String)	java.lang.System	234
locate(int, int)	java.awt.Component	38
locate(int, int)	java.awt.Container	43
location()	java.awt.Component	38
location(int, int)	java.awt.GridBagLayout	79
log(double)	java.lang.Math	209
Long(long)	java.lang.Long	206
Long(String)	java.lang.Long	206
longBitsToDouble(long)	java.lang.Double	201
longValue()	java.lang.Double	201
longValue()	java.lang.Float	203
longValue()	java.lang.Integer	204
longValue()	java.lang.Long	207
longValue()	java.lang.Number	212
lookupConstraints(Component)	java.awt.GridBagLayout	79
loop()	java.applet.AudioClip	18
lostFocus(Event, Object)	java.awt.Component	38
lowerCaseMode(boolean)	java.io.StreamTokenizer	184
makeVisible(int)	java.awt.List	87
MalformedURLException()	java.net.MalformedURLException	301
MalformedURLException(String)	java.net.MalformedURLException	301
mark(int)	java.io.BufferedInputStream	148
mark(int)	java.io.FilterInputStream	165
mark(int)	java.io.InputStream	167
mark(int)	java.io.LineNumberInputStream	169
markSupported()	java.io.BufferedInputStream	148

Index of Methods

markSupported()	java.io.FilterInputStream	165
markSupported()	java.io.InputStream	168
markSupported()	java.io.PushbackInputStream	178
max(double, double)	java.lang.Math	209
max(float, float)	java.lang.Math	210
max(int, int)	java.lang.Math	210
max(long, long)	java.lang.Math	210
MediaTracker(Component)	java.awt.MediaTracker	89
MemoryImageSource(int, int, ➥ColorModel, byte[], ➥int, int)	java.awt.image.MemoryImageSource	132
MemoryImageSource(int, int, ➥ColorModel, byte[], int, ➥int, Hashtable)	java.awt.image.MemoryImageSource	132
MemoryImageSource(int, int, ➥ColorModel, int[], ➥int, int)	java.awt.image.MemoryImageSource	133
MemoryImageSource(int, int, ➥ColorModel, int[], int, ➥int, Hashtable)	java.awt.image.MemoryImageSource	133
MemoryImageSource(int, int, ➥int[], int, int)	java.awt.image.MemoryImageSource	133
MemoryImageSource(int, int, ➥int[], int, int, Hashtable)	java.awt.image.MemoryImageSource	133
Menu(String)	java.awt.Menu	92
Menu(String, boolean)	java.awt.Menu	92
MenuBar()	java.awt.MenuBar	95
MenuComponent()	java.awt.MenuComponent	96
MenuItem(String)	java.awt.MenuItem	97
metaDown()	java.awt.Event	51
min(double, double)	java.lang.Math	210
min(float, float)	java.lang.Math	210
min(int, int)	java.lang.Math	210
min(long, long)	java.lang.Math	210

continues

Index of Methods

continued

Method Name	Class Name	Page
minimumLayoutSize(Container)	java.awt.BorderLayout	21
minimumLayoutSize(Container)	java.awt.CardLayout	26
minimumLayoutSize(Container)	java.awt.FlowLayout	55
minimumLayoutSize(Container)	java.awt.GridBagLayout	79
minimumLayoutSize(Container)	java.awt.GridLayout	80
minimumLayoutSize(Container)	java.awt.LayoutManager	117
minimumSize()	java.awt.Component	39
minimumSize()	java.awt.Container	43
minimumSize()	java.awt.List	87
minimumSize()	java.awt.TextArea	108
minimumSize()	java.awt.TextField	111
minimumSize(int)	java.awt.List	87
minimumSize(int)	java.awt.TextField	111
minimumSize(int, int)	java.awt.TextArea	108
mkdir()	java.io.File	160
mkdirs()	java.io.File	160
mouseDown(Event, int, int)	java.awt.Component	38
mouseDrag(Event, int, int)	java.awt.Component	38
mouseEnter(Event, int, int)	java.awt.Component	38
mouseExit(Event, int, int)	java.awt.Component	38
mouseMove(Event, int, int)	java.awt.Component	38
mouseUp(Event, int, int)	java.awt.Component	39
move(int, int)	java.awt.Component	39
move(int, int)	java.awt.Point	99
move(int, int)	java.awt.Rectangle	102
NegativeArraySizeException()	java.lang.➥NegativeArraySizeException	300
NegativeArraySizeException➥(String)	java.lang.➥NegativeArraySizeException	300

newInstance()	java.lang.Class	197
next(Container)	java.awt.CardLayout	26
nextDouble()	java.util.Random	288
nextElement()	java.util.Enumeration	296
nextElement()	java.util.StringTokenizer	290
nextFloat()	java.util.Random	288
nextFocus()	java.awt.Component	39
nextGaussian()	java.util.Random	288
nextInt()	java.util.Random	288
nextLong()	java.util.Random	288
nextToken()	java.io.StreamTokenizer	184
nextToken()	java.util.StringTokenizer	291
nextToken(String)	java.util.StringTokenizer	290
NoClassDefFoundError()	java.lang.➥NoClassDefFoundError	305
NoClassDefFoundError(String)	java.lang.➥NoClassDefFoundError	305
NoSuchElementException()	java.util.➥NoSuchElementException	301
NoSuchElementException➥(String)	java.util.➥NoSuchElementException	301
NoSuchFieldError()	java.lang.NoSuchFieldError	305
NoSuchFieldError(String)	java.lang.NoSuchFieldError	305
NoSuchMethodError()	java.lang.NoSuchMethodError	305
NoSuchMethodError(String)	java.lang.NoSuchMethodError	305
NoSuchMethodException()	java.lang.➥NoSuchMethodException	300
NoSuchMethodException(String)	java.lang.➥NoSuchMethodException	300
notify()	java.lang.Object	212
notifyAll()	java.lang.Object	213
notifyObservers()	java.util.Observable	286

continues

Index of Methods

continued

Method Name	Class Name	Page
`notifyObservers(Object)`	`java.util.Observable`	286
`NullPointerException()`	`java.lang.` ➡`NullPointerException`	300
`NullPointerException(String)`	`java.lang.` ➡`NullPointerException`	300
`Number()`	`java.lang.Number`	211
`NumberFormatException()`	`java.lang.` ➡`NumberFormatException`	300
`NumberFormatException(String)`	`java.lang.` ➡`NumberFormatException`	300
`Object()`	`java.lang.Object`	212
`Observable()`	`java.util.Observable`	286
`openConnection()`	`java.net.URL`	263
`openConnection(URL)`	`java.net.URLStreamHandler`	269
`openStream()`	`java.net.URL`	263
`or(BitSet)`	`java.util.BitSet`	276
`ordinaryChar(int)`	`java.io.StreamTokenizer`	184
`ordinaryChars(int, int)`	`java.io.StreamTokenizer`	184
`OutOfMemoryError()`	`java.lang.OutOfMemoryError`	305
`OutOfMemoryError(String)`	`java.lang.OutOfMemoryError`	305
`OutputStream()`	`java.io.OutputStream`	169
`pack()`	`java.awt.Window`	116
`paint(Graphics)`	`java.awt.Canvas`	23
`paint(Graphics)`	`java.awt.Component`	39
`paintAll(Graphics)`	`java.awt.Component`	39
`paintComponents(Graphics)`	`java.awt.Container`	44
`Panel()`	`java.awt.Panel`	98
`paramString()`	`java.awt.Button`	22
`paramString()`	`java.awt.Checkbox`	27
`paramString()`	`java.awt.CheckboxMenuItem`	29

paramString()	java.awt.Choice	30
paramString()	java.awt.Component	39
paramString()	java.awt.Container	44
paramString()	java.awt.Dialog	45
paramString()	java.awt.Event	51
paramString()	java.awt.FileDialog	53
paramString()	java.awt.Frame	61
paramString()	java.awt.Label	84
paramString()	java.awt.List	87
paramString()	java.awt.MenuComponent	96
paramString()	java.awt.MenuItem	98
paramString()	java.awt.Scrollbar	106
paramString()	java.awt.TextArea	109
paramString()	java.awt.TextComponent	110
paramString()	java.awt.TextField	111
parentOf(ThreadGroup)	java.lang.ThreadGroup	243
parse(String)	java.util.Date	278
parseInt(String)	java.lang.Integer	205
parseInt(String, int)	java.lang.Integer	205
parseLong(String)	java.lang.Long	207
parseLong(String, int)	java.lang.Long	207
parseNumbers()	java.io.StreamTokenizer	184
parseURL(URL, String, ➥int, int)	java.net.URLStreamHandler	270
peek()	java.util.Stack	289
PipedInputStream()	java.io.PipedInputStream	173
PipedInputStream ➥(PipedOutputStream)	java.io.PipedInputStream	173
PipedOutputStream()	java.io.PipedOutputStream	174
PipedOutputStream ➥(PipedInputStream)	java.io.PipedOutputStream	174

continues

Index of Methods

continued

Method Name	Class Name	Page
PixelGrabber(Image, int, int, ➥int, int, int[], int, int)	java.awt.Image.PixelGrabber	134
PixelGrabber(ImageProducer, ➥int, int, int, int, ➥int[], int, int)	java.awt.Image.PixelGrabber	134
play()	java.applet.AudioClip	18
play(URL)	java.applet.Applet	15
play(URL, String)	java.applet.Applet	15
Point(int, int)	java.awt.Point	99
Polygon()	java.awt.Polygon	100
Polygon(int[], int[], int)	java.awt.Polygon	100
pop()	java.util.Stack	289
postEvent(Event)	java.awt.Component	39
postEvent(Event)	java.awt.MenuComponent	97
postEvent(Event)	java.awt.MenuContainer	117
pow(double, double)	java.lang.Math	210
preferredLayoutSize ➥(Container)	java.awt.BorderLayout	21
preferredLayoutSize ➥(Container)	java.awt.CardLayout	26
preferredLayoutSize ➥(Container)	java.awt.FlowLayout	55
preferredLayoutSize ➥(Container)	java.awt.GridBagLayout	79
preferredLayoutSize ➥(Container)	java.awt.GridLayout	80
preferredLayoutSize ➥(Container)	java.awt.LayoutManager	117
preferredSize()	java.awt.Component	39
preferredSize()	java.awt.Container	44
preferredSize()	java.awt.List	87
preferredSize()	java.awt.TextArea	109

Index of Methods

`preferredSize()`	`java.awt.TextField`	111
`preferredSize(int)`	`java.awt.List`	87
`preferredSize(int)`	`java.awt.TextField`	112
`preferredSize(int, int)`	`java.awt.TextArea`	109
`prepareImage(Image,` `➡ImageObserver)`	`java.awt.Component`	40
`prepareImage(Image, int,` `➡int, ImageObserver)`	`java.awt.Component`	40
`prepareImage(Image, int,` `➡int, ImageObserver)`	`java.awt.Toolkit`	115
`previous(Container)`	`java.awt.CardLayout`	26
`print(boolean)`	`java.io.PrintStream`	176
`print(char)`	`java.io.PrintStream`	176
`print(char[])`	`java.io.PrintStream`	176
`print(double)`	`java.io.PrintStream`	176
`print(float)`	`java.io.PrintStream`	176
`print(Graphics)`	`java.awt.Component`	40
`print(int)`	`java.io.PrintStream`	176
`print(long)`	`java.io.PrintStream`	176
`print(Object)`	`java.io.PrintStream`	176
`print(String)`	`java.io.PrintStream`	176
`printAll(Graphics)`	`java.awt.Component`	40
`printComponents(Graphics)`	`java.awt.Container`	44
`println()`	`java.io.PrintStream`	177
`println(boolean)`	`java.io.PrintStream`	177
`println(char)`	`java.io.PrintStream`	177
`println(char[])`	`java.io.PrintStream`	177
`println(double)`	`java.io.PrintStream`	177
`println(float)`	`java.io.PrintStream`	177
`println(int)`	`java.io.PrintStream`	177
`println(long)`	`java.io.PrintStream`	177

continues

Index of Methods

continued

Method Name	Class Name	Page
println(Object)	java.io.PrintStream	177
println(String)	java.io.PrintStream	177
printStackTrace()	java.lang.Throwable	244
printStackTrace(PrintStream)	java.lang.Throwable	245
PrintStream(OutputStream)	java.io.PrintStream	175
PrintStream ➡(OutputStream, boolean)	java.io.PrintStream	175
Process()	java.lang.Process	213
Properties()	java.util.Properties	287
Properties(Properties)	java.util.Properties	287
propertyNames()	java.util.Properties	287
ProtocolException()	java.net.ProtocolException	301
ProtocolException(String)	java.net.ProtocolException	301
push(Object)	java.util.Stack	289
pushBack()	java.io.StreamTokenizer	185
PushbackInputStream ➡(InputStream)	java.io.PushbackInputStream	178
put(Object, Object)	java.util.Dictionary	280
put(Object, Object)	java.util.Hashtable	285
quoteChar(int)	java.io.StreamTokenizer	185
random()	java.lang.Math	210
Random()	java.util.Random	288
Random(long)	java.util.Random	288
RandomAccessFile ➡(File, String)	java.io.RandomAccessFile	179
RandomAccessFile ➡(String, String)	java.io.RandomAccessFile	179
read()	java.io.BufferedInputStream	148
read()	java.io.ByteArrayInputStream	151
read()	java.io.FileInputStream	162

read()	java.io.FilterInputStream	165
read()	java.io.InputStream	168
read()	java.io.LineNumberInputStream	169
read()	java.io.PipedInputStream	174
read()	java.io.PushbackInputStream	178
read()	java.io.RandomAccessFile	179
read()	java.io.SequenceInputStream	183
read()	java.io.➥StringBufferInputStream	186
read(byte[])	java.io.DataInputStream	154
read(byte[])	java.io.FileInputStream	162
read(byte[])	java.io.FilterInputStream	165
read(byte[])	java.io.InputStream	168
read(byte[])	java.io.RandomAccessFile	180
read(byte[], int, int)	java.io.BufferedInputStream	148
read(byte[], int, int)	java.io.➥ByteArrayInputStream	151
read(byte[], int, int)	java.io.DataInputStream	154
read(byte[], int, int)	java.io.FileInputStream	162
read(byte[], int, int)	java.io.FilterInputStream	165
read(byte[], int, int)	java.io.InputStream	168
read(byte[], int, int)	java.io.➥LineNumberInputStream	169
read(byte[], int, int)	java.io.PipedInputStream	174
read(byte[], int, int)	java.io.PushbackInputStream	178
read(byte[], int, int)	java.io.RandomAccessFile	180
read(byte[], int, int)	java.io.SequenceInputStream	183
read(byte[], int, int)	java.io.➥StringBufferInputStream	186
readBoolean()	java.io.DataInput	187
readBoolean()	java.io.DataInputStream	154

continues

Index of Methods

continued

Method Name	Class Name	Page
readBoolean()	java.io.RandomAccessFile	180
readByte()	java.io.DataInput	187
readByte()	java.io.DataInputStream	154
readByte()	java.io.RandomAccessFile	180
readChar()	java.io.DataInput	187
readChar()	java.io.DataInputStream	154
readChar()	java.io.RandomAccessFile	180
readDouble()	java.io.DataInput	187
readDouble()	java.io.DataInputStream	154
readDouble()	java.io.RandomAccessFile	180
readFloat()	java.io.DataInput	187
readFloat()	java.io.DataInputStream	154
readFloat()	java.io.RandomAccessFile	180
readFully(byte[])	java.io.DataInput	187
readFully(byte[])	java.io.DataInputStream	154
readFully(byte[])	java.io.RandomAccessFile	180
readFully(byte[], int, int)	java.io.DataInput	187
readFully(byte[], int, int)	java.io.DataInputStream	154
readFully(byte[], int, int)	java.io.RandomAccessFile	180
readInt()	java.io.DataInput	187
readInt()	java.io.DataInputStream	154
readInt()	java.io.RandomAccessFile	180
readLine()	java.io.DataInputStream	155
readLine()	java.io.RandomAccessFile	180
readLong()	java.io.DataInput	187
readLong()	java.io.DataInputStream	155
readLong()	java.io.RandomAccessFile	181
readShort()	java.io.DataInput	188

readShort()	java.io.DataInputStream	155
readShort()	java.io.RandomAccessFile	181
readUnsignedByte()	java.io.DataInput	188
readUnsignedByte()	java.io.DataInputStream	155
readUnsignedByte()	java.io.RandomAccessFile	181
readUnsignedShort()	java.io.DataInput	188
readUnsignedShort()	java.io.DataInputStream	155
readUnsignedShort()	java.io.RandomAccessFile	181
readUTF()	java.io.DataInput	188
readUTF()	java.io.DataInputStream	155
readUTF()	java.io.RandomAccessFile	181
readUTF(DataInput)	java.io.DataInputStream	155
receive(DatagramPacket)	java.net.DatagramSocket	254
Rectangle()	java.awt.Rectangle	101
Rectangle(Dimension)	java.awt.Rectangle	101
Rectangle(int, int)	java.awt.Rectangle	101
Rectangle(int, int, int, int)	java.awt.Rectangle	101
Rectangle(Point)	java.awt.Rectangle	101
Rectangle(Point, Dimension)	java.awt.Rectangle	101
regionMatches(boolean, int, ➥String, int, int)	java.lang.String	224
regionMatches(int, ➥String, int, int)	java.lang.String	224
rehash()	java.util.Hashtable	285
remove(Component)	java.awt.Container	44
remove(int)	java.awt.Menu	93
remove(int)	java.awt.MenuBar	96
remove(MenuComponent)	java.awt.Frame	61
remove(MenuComponent)	java.awt.Menu	92
remove(MenuComponent)	java.awt.MenuBar	95
remove(MenuComponent)	java.awt.MenuContainer	117

continues

continued

Method Name	Class Name	Page
remove(Object)	java.util.Dictionary	280
remove(Object)	java.util.Hashtable	285
removeAllElements()	java.util.Vector	293
removeConsumer(ImageConsumer)	java.awt.image. ➡FilteredImageSource	125
removeConsumer(ImageConsumer)	java.awt.image. ➡ImageProducer	143
removeConsumer(ImageConsumer)	java.awt.image. ➡MemoryImageSource	134
removeElement(Object)	java.util.Vector	293
removeElementAt(int)	java.util.Vector	293
removeLayoutComponent ➡(Component)	java.awt.BorderLayout	21
removeLayoutComponent ➡(Component)	java.awt.CardLayout	26
removeLayoutComponent ➡(Component)	java.awt.FlowLayout	55
removeLayoutComponent ➡(Component)	java.awt.GridBagLayout	79
removeLayoutComponent ➡(Component)	java.awt.GridLayout	80
removeLayoutComponent ➡(Component)	java.awt.LayoutManager	117
removeNotify()	java.awt.Component	40
removeNotify()	java.awt.Container	44
removeNotify()	java.awt.List	87
removeNotify()	java.awt.Menu	93
removeNotify()	java.awt.MenuBar	96
removeNotify()	java.awt.MenuComponent	97
renameTo(File)	java.io.File	160
repaint()	java.awt.Component	41
repaint(int, int, int, int)	java.awt.Component	40

Index of Methods

repaint(long)	java.awt.Component	40
repaint(long, int, int, ➡int, int)	java.awt.Component	40
replace(char, char)	java.lang.String	225
replaceItem(String, int)	java.awt.List	88
replaceText(String, ➡int, int)	java.awt.TextArea	109
requestFocus()	java.awt.Component	41
requestTopDownLeft ➡RightResend(ImageConsumer)	java.awt.image. ➡FilteredImageSource	125
requestTopDownLeft ➡RightResend(ImageConsumer)	java.awt.image.ImageProducer	143
requestTopDownLeft ➡RightResend(ImageConsumer)	java.awt.image. ➡MemoryImageSource	134
resendTopDownLeftRight ➡(ImageProducer)	java.awt.image.ImageFilter	129
reset()	java.io.BufferedInputStream	149
reset()	java.io.ByteArrayInputStream	151
reset()	java.io.ByteArrayOutputStream	153
reset()	java.io.FilterInputStream	165
reset()	java.io.InputStream	168
reset()	java.io. ➡LineNumberInputStream	169
reset()	java.io. ➡StringBufferInputStream	186
resetSyntax()	java.io.StreamTokenizer	185
reshape(int, int, int, int)	java.awt.Component	41
reshape(int, int, int, int)	java.awt.Rectangle	102
resize(Dimension)	java.applet.Applet	15
resize(Dimension)	java.awt.Component	41
resize(int, int)	java.applet.Applet	15
resize(int, int)	java.awt.Component	41

continues

Index of Methods

continued

Method Name	Class Name	Page
resize(int, int)	java.awt.Rectangle	102
resolveClass(Class)	java.lang.ClassLoader	198
resume()	java.lang.Thread	240
resume()	java.lang.ThreadGroup	243
RGBImageFilter()	java.awt.image. ➥RGBImageFilter	138
RGBtoHSB(int, int, ➥int, float[])	java.awt.Color	33
rint(double)	java.lang.Math	210
round(double)	java.lang.Math	210
round(float)	java.lang.Math	210
run()	java.lang.Runnable	249
run()	java.lang.Thread	240
runFinalization()	java.lang.Runtime	217
runFinalization()	java.lang.System	235
RuntimeException()	java.lang.RuntimeException	300
RuntimeException(String)	java.lang.RuntimeException	300
sameFile(URL)	java.net.URL	264
save(OutputStream, String)	java.util.Properties	288
Scrollbar()	java.awt.Scrollbar	105
Scrollbar(int)	java.awt.Scrollbar	105
Scrollbar(int, int, int, ➥int, int)	java.awt.Scrollbar	105
search(Object)	java.util.Stack	289
SecurityException()	java.lang.SecurityException	300
SecurityException(String)	java.lang.SecurityException	300
SecurityManager()	java.lang.SecurityManager	218
seek(long)	java.io.RandomAccessFile	181
select(int)	java.awt.Choice	30

select(int)	java.awt.List	88
select(int, int)	java.awt.TextComponent	110
select(String)	java.awt.Choice	30
selectAll()	java.awt.TextComponent	110
send(DatagramPacket)	java.net.DatagramSocket	254
SequenceInputStream ➥(Enumeration)	java.io.SequenceInputStream	182
SequenceInputStream ➥(InputStream, InputStream)	java.io.SequenceInputStream	182
ServerSocket(int)	java.net.ServerSocket	255
ServerSocket(int, int)	java.net.ServerSocket	256
set(int)	java.util.BitSet	276
set(String, String, int, ➥String, String)	java.net.URL	264
setAlignment(int)	java.awt.Label	84
setAllowUserInteraction ➥(boolean)	java.net.URLConnection	267
setBackground(Color)	java.awt.Component	41
setChanged()	java.util.Observable	286
setCharAt(int, char)	java.lang.StringBuffer	231
setCheckboxGroup ➥(CheckboxGroup)	java.awt.Checkbox	27
setColor(Color)	java.awt.Graphics	69
setColorModel(ColorModel)	java.awt.image.ImageConsumer	140
setColorModel(ColorModel)	java.awt.image.ImageFilter	129
setColorModel(ColorModel)	java.awt.image.PixelGrabber	135
setColorModel(ColorModel)	java.awt.image.➥RGBImageFilter	138
setConstraints(Component, ➥GridBagConstraints)	java.awt.GridBagLayout	79
setContentHandlerFactory ➥(ContentHandlerFactory)	java.net.URLConnection	268

continues

continued

Method Name	Class Name	Page
setCurrent(Checkbox)	java.awt.CheckboxGroup	28
setCursor(int)	java.awt.Frame	61
setDaemon(boolean)	java.lang.Thread	240
setDaemon(boolean)	java.lang.ThreadGroup	243
setDate(int)	java.util.Date	279
setDefaultAllowUser ➡Interaction(boolean)	java.net.URLConnection	267
setDefaultRequestProperty ➡(String, String)	java.net.URLConnection	268
setDefaultUseCaches(boolean)	java.net.URLConnection	268
setDimensions(int, int)	java.awt.image. ➡CropImageFilter	122
setDimensions(int, int)	java.awt.image. ➡ImageConsumer	141
setDimensions(int, int)	java.awt.image.ImageFilter	130
setDimensions(int, int)	java.awt.image.PixelGrabber	135
setDirectory(String)	java.awt.FileDialog	53
setDoInput(boolean)	java.net.URLConnection	267
setDoOutput(boolean)	java.net.URLConnection	267
setEchoCharacter(char)	java.awt.TextField	112
setEditable(boolean)	java.awt.TextComponent	110
setElementAt(Object, int)	java.util.Vector	294
setFile(String)	java.awt.FileDialog	53
setFilenameFilter ➡(FilenameFilter)	java.awt.FileDialog	54
setFont(Font)	java.awt.Component	41
setFont(Font)	java.awt.Graphics	69
setFont(Font)	java.awt.MenuComponent	97
setForeground(Color)	java.awt.Component	41
setHelpMenu(Menu)	java.awt.MenuBar	96

setHints(int)	java.awt.image.ImageConsumer	141
setHints(int)	java.awt.image.ImageFilter	130
setHints(int)	java.awt.image.PixelGrabber	135
setHours(int)	java.util.Date	279
setIconImage(Image)	java.awt.Frame	61
setIfModifiedSince(long)	java.net.URLConnection	268
setLabel(String)	java.awt.Button	22
setLabel(String)	java.awt.Checkbox	28
setLabel(String)	java.awt.MenuItem	98
setLayout(LayoutManager)	java.awt.Container	44
setLength(int)	java.lang.StringBuffer	229
setLineIncrement(int)	java.awt.Scrollbar	106
setLineNumber(int)	java.io.LineNumberInputStream	169
setMaxPriority(int)	java.lang.ThreadGroup	243
setMenuBar(MenuBar)	java.awt.Frame	61
setMinutes(int)	java.util.Date	279
setMonth(int)	java.util.Date	279
setMultipleSelections ➥(boolean)	java.awt.List	88
setName(String)	java.lang.Thread	240
setPageIncrement(int)	java.awt.Scrollbar	107
setPaintMode()	java.awt.Graphics	69
setPixels(int, int, int, ➥int, ColorModel, byte[], ➥int, int)	java.awt.image. ➥CropImageFilter	123
setPixels(int, int, int, ➥int, ColorModel, byte[], ➥int, int)	java.awt.image.ImageConsumer	141
setPixels(int, int, int, ➥int, ColorModel, byte[], ➥int, int)	java.awt.image.ImageFilter	130

continues

Index of Methods

continued

Method Name	Class Name	Page
setPixels(int, int, int, ➡int, ColorModel, byte[], ➡int, int)	java.awt.image.PixelGrabber	135
setPixels(int, int, int, ➡int, ColorModel, byte[], ➡int, int)	java.awt.image. ➡RGBImageFilter	139
setPixels(int, int, int, ➡int, ColorModel, int[], ➡int, int)	java.awt.image. CropImageFilter	123
setPixels(int, int, int, ➡int, ColorModel, int[], ➡int, int)	java.awt.image.ImageConsumer	141
setPixels(int, int, int, ➡int, ColorModel, int[], ➡int, int)	java.awt.image.ImageFilter	130
setPixels(int, int, int, ➡int, ColorModel, int[], ➡int, int)	java.awt.image.PixelGrabber	135
setPixels(int, int, int, ➡int, ColorModel, int[], ➡int, int)	java.awt.image. ➡RGBImageFilter	139
setPriority(int)	java.lang.Thread	240
setProperties(Hashtable)	java.awt.image. ➡CropImageFilter	123
setProperties(Hashtable)	java.awt.image. ➡ImageFilter	130
setProperties(Hashtable)	java.awt.image.PixelGrabber	135
setProperties(Properties)	java.lang.System	235
setRequestProperty(String, ➡String)	java.net.URLConnection	268
setResizable(boolean)	java.awt.Frame	62
setSeconds(int)	java.util.Date	279
setSecurityManager ➡(SecurityManager)	java.lang.System	234
setSeed(long)	java.util.Random	288

Index of Methods

`setSize(int)`	`java.util.Vector`	294
`setSocketFactory` ➥`(SocketImplFactory)`	`java.net.ServerSocket`	256
`setSocketImplFactory` ➥`(SocketImplFactory)`	`java.net.Socket`	259
`setState(boolean)`	`java.awt.Checkbox`	28
`setState(boolean)`	`java.awt.CheckboxMenuItem`	29
`setStub(AppletStub)`	`java.applet.Applet`	15
`setText(String)`	`java.awt.Label`	84
`setTime(long)`	`java.util.Date`	279
`setTitle(String)`	`java.awt.Dialog`	45
`setTitle(String)`	`java.awt.Frame`	62
`setURL(URL, String, String,` ➥`int, String, String)`	`java.net.URLStreamHandler`	270
`setURLStreamHandlerFactory` ➥`(URLStreamHandlerFactory)`	`java.net.URL`	264
`setUseCaches(boolean)`	`java.net.URLConnection`	268
`setValue(int)`	`java.awt.Scrollbar`	107
`setValues(int, int, int, int)`	`java.awt.Scrollbar`	107
`setXORMode(Color)`	`java.awt.Graphics`	69
`setYear(int)`	`java.util.Date`	279
`shiftDown()`	`java.awt.Event`	51
`show()`	`java.awt.Component`	41
`show()`	`java.awt.Window`	116
`show(boolean)`	`java.awt.Component`	41
`show(Container, String)`	`java.awt.CardLayout`	26
`showDocument(URL)`	`java.applet.AppletContext`	17
`showDocument(URL, String)`	`java.applet.AppletContext`	17
`showStatus(String)`	`java.applet.Applet`	16
`showStatus(String)`	`java.applet.AppletContext`	17

continues

404

Index of Methods

continued

Method Name	Class Name	Page
sin(double)	java.lang.Math	211
size()	java.awt.Component	41
size()	java.io.➡ByteArrayOutputStream	153
size()	java.io.DataOutputStream	156
size()	java.util.BitSet	276
size()	java.util.Dictionary	280
size()	java.util.Hashtable	285
size()	java.util.Vector	294
skip(long)	java.io.➡BufferedInputStream	149
skip(long)	java.io.➡ByteArrayInputStream	152
skip(long)	java.io.FileInputStream	162
skip(long)	java.io.FilterInputStream	166
skip(long)	java.io.InputStream	168
skip(long)	java.io.➡LineNumberInputStream	169
skip(long)	java.io.➡StringBufferInputStream	186
skipBytes(int)	java.io.DataInput	188
skipBytes(int)	java.io.DataInputStream	155
skipBytes(int)	java.io.RandomAccessFile	181
slashSlashComments(boolean)	java.io.StreamTokenizer	185
slashStarComments(boolean)	java.io.StreamTokenizer	185
sleep(long)	java.lang.Thread	240
sleep(long, int)	java.lang.Thread	240
Socket(InetAddress, int)	java.net.Socket	258
Socket(InetAddress, ➡int, boolean)	java.net.Socket	258

Index of Methods

Socket(String, int)	java.net.Socket	258
Socket(String, int, boolean)	java.net.Socket	258
SocketException()	java.net.SocketException	301
SocketException(String)	java.net.SocketException	301
SocketImpl()	java.net.SocketImpl	260
sqrt(double)	java.lang.Math	211
Stack()	java.util.Stack	289
StackOverflowError()	java.lang.StackOverflowError	305
StackOverflowError(String)	java.lang.StackOverflowError	305
start()	java.applet.Applet	16
start()	java.lang.Thread	240
startProduction ➥(ImageConsumer)	java.awt.image. ➥FilteredImageSource	125
startProduction ➥(ImageConsumer)	java.awt.image.ImageProducer	143
startProduction ➥(ImageConsumer)	java.awt.image. ➥MemoryImageSource	134
startsWith(String)	java.lang.String	225
startsWith(String, int)	java.lang.String	225
status()	java.awt.image.PixelGrabber	135
statusAll(boolean)	java.awt.MediaTracker	90
statusID(int, boolean)	java.awt.MediaTracker	90
stop()	java.applet.Applet	16
stop()	java.applet.AudioClip	18
stop()	java.lang.Thread	241
stop()	java.lang.ThreadGroup	243
stop(Throwable)	java.lang.Thread	241
StreamTokenizer(InputStream)	java.io.StreamTokenizer	184
String()	java.lang.String	221
String(byte[], int)	java.lang.String	222
String(byte[], int, int, int)	java.lang.String	222

continues

Index of Methods

continued

Method Name	Class Name	Page
`String(char[])`	`java.lang.String`	222
`String(char[], int, int)`	`java.lang.String`	222
`String(String)`	`java.lang.String`	222
`String(StringBuffer)`	`java.lang.String`	221
`StringBuffer()`	`java.lang.StringBuffer`	229
`StringBuffer(int)`	`java.lang.StringBuffer`	228
`StringBuffer(String)`	`java.lang.StringBuffer`	228
`StringBufferInputStream ➡(String)`	`java.io. ➡StringBufferInputStream`	186
`StringIndexOutOfBounds ➡Exception()`	`java.lang.String ➡IndexOutOfBoundsException`	300
`StringIndexOutOfBounds ➡Exception(int)`	`java.lang.String ➡IndexOutOfBoundsException`	300
`StringIndexOutOfBounds ➡Exception(String)`	`java.lang.String ➡IndexOutOfBoundsException`	301
`StringTokenizer(String)`	`java.util.StringTokenizer`	290
`StringTokenizer(String, ➡String)`	`java.util.StringTokenizer`	290
`StringTokenizer(String, ➡String, boolean)`	`java.util.StringTokenizer`	290
`stringWidth(String)`	`java.awt.FontMetrics`	59
`substituteColorModel ➡(ColorModel, ColorModel)`	`java.awt.image. ➡RGBImageFilter`	138
`substring(int)`	`java.lang.String`	225
`substring(int, int)`	`java.lang.String`	225
`suspend()`	`java.lang.Thread`	241
`suspend()`	`java.lang.ThreadGroup`	244
`sync()`	`java.awt.Toolkit`	115
`tan(double)`	`java.lang.Math`	211
`TextArea()`	`java.awt.TextArea`	108
`TextArea(int, int)`	`java.awt.TextArea`	108

Index of Methods

TextArea(String)	java.awt.TextArea	108
TextArea(String, int, int)	java.awt.TextArea	108
TextField()	java.awt.TextField	110
TextField(int)	java.awt.TextField	110
TextField(String)	java.awt.TextField	110
TextField(String, int)	java.awt.TextField	111
Thread()	java.lang.Thread	237
Thread(Runnable)	java.lang.Thread	237
Thread(Runnable, String)	java.lang.Thread	237
Thread(String)	java.lang.Thread	238
Thread(ThreadGroup, Runnable)	java.lang.Thread	238
Thread(ThreadGroup, ➥Runnable, String)	java.lang.Thread	238
Thread(ThreadGroup, String)	java.lang.Thread	238
ThreadDeath()	java.lang.ThreadDeath	305
ThreadGroup(String)	java.lang.ThreadGroup	241
ThreadGroup(ThreadGroup, ➥String)	java.lang.ThreadGroup	241
Throwable()	java.lang.Throwable	244
Throwable(String)	java.lang.Throwable	244
toBack()	java.awt.Window	116
toBinaryString(int)	java.lang.Integer	205
toBinaryString(long)	java.lang.Long	207
toByteArray()	java.io.ByteArrayOutputStream	152
toCharArray()	java.lang.String	225
toExternalForm()	java.net.URL	264
toExternalForm(URL)	java.net.URLStreamHandler	270
toFront()	java.awt.Window	116
toGMTString()	java.util.Date	279
toHexString(int)	java.lang.Integer	205
toHexString(long)	java.lang.Long	207

continues

Index of Methods

continued

Method Name	Class Name	Page
toLocaleString()	java.util.Date	279
toLowerCase()	java.lang.String	225
toLowerCase(char)	java.lang.Character	196
toOctalString(int)	java.lang.Integer	205
toOctalString(long)	java.lang.Long	207
Toolkit()	java.awt.Toolkit	112
toString()	java.awt.BorderLayout	21
toString()	java.awt.CardLayout	26
toString()	java.awt.CheckboxGroup	28
toString()	java.awt.Color	33
toString()	java.awt.Component	42
toString()	java.awt.Dimension	46
toString()	java.awt.Event	51
toString()	java.awt.FlowLayout	55
toString()	java.awt.Font	57
toString()	java.awt.FontMetrics	59
toString()	java.awt.Graphics	69
toString()	java.awt.GridBagLayout	79
toString()	java.awt.GridLayout	80
toString()	java.awt.Insets	83
toString()	java.awt.MenuComponent	97
toString()	java.awt.Point	99
toString()	java.awt.Rectangle	103
toString()	java.io.ByteArrayOutputStream	153
toString()	java.io.File	160
toString()	java.io.StreamTokenizer	185
toString()	java.lang.Boolean	193
toString()	java.lang.Character	196

Index of Methods

toString()	java.lang.Class	197
toString()	java.lang.Double	201
toString()	java.lang.Float	203
toString()	java.lang.Integer	205
toString()	java.lang.Long	207
toString()	java.lang.Object	213
toString()	java.lang.String	225
toString()	java.lang.StringBuffer	232
toString()	java.lang.Thread	241
toString()	java.lang.ThreadGroup	244
toString()	java.lang.Throwable	245
toString()	java.net.InetAddress	255
toString()	java.net.ServerSocket	256
toString()	java.net.Socket	259
toString()	java.net.SocketImpl	261
toString()	java.net.URL	264
toString()	java.net.URLConnection	267
toString()	java.util.BitSet	276
toString()	java.util.Date	279
toString()	java.util.Hashtable	285
toString()	java.util.Vector	294
toString(double)	java.lang.Double	201
toString(float)	java.lang.Float	203
toString(int)	java.io.ByteArrayOutputStream	153
toString(int)	java.lang.Integer	205
toString(int, int)	java.lang.Integer	205
toString(long)	java.lang.Long	208
toString(long, int)	java.lang.Long	208
totalMemory()	java.lang.Runtime	217
toTitleCase(char)	java.lang.Character	196

continues

Index of Methods

continued

Method Name	Class Name	Page
toUpperCase()	java.lang.String	225
toUpperCase(char)	java.lang.Character	196
traceInstructions(boolean)	java.lang.Runtime	217
traceMethodCalls(boolean)	java.lang.Runtime	217
translate(int, int)	java.awt.Event	51
translate(int, int)	java.awt.Graphics	69
translate(int, int)	java.awt.Point	99
translate(int, int)	java.awt.Rectangle	103
trim()	java.lang.String	226
trimToSize()	java.util.Vector	294
uncaughtException(Thread, ➥Throwable)	java.lang.ThreadGroup	244
union(Rectangle)	java.awt.Rectangle	103
UnknownError()	java.lang.UnknownError	305
UnknownError(String)	java.lang.UnknownError	305
UnknownHostException()	java.net.UnknownHostException	301
UnknownHostException(String)	java.net.➥UnknownHostException	301
UnknownServiceException()	java.net.➥UnknownServiceException	301
UnknownServiceException ➥(String)	java.net.➥UnknownServiceException	301
unread(int)	java.io.➥PushbackInputStream	178
UnsatisfiedLinkError()	java.lang.➥UnsatisfiedLinkError	305
UnsatisfiedLinkError(String)	java.lang.➥UnsatisfiedLinkError	305
update(Graphics)	java.awt.Component	42
update(Observable, Object)	java.util.Observer	296

Index of Methods

URL(String)	java.net.URL	261
URL(String, String, ➡int, String)	java.net.URL	262
URL(String, String, String)	java.net.URL	262
URL(URL, String)	java.net.URL	262
URLConnection(URL)	java.net.URLConnection	265
URLStreamHandler()	java.net.URLStreamHandler	269
UTC(int, int, int, ➡int, int, int)	java.util.Date	279
UTFDataFormatException()	java.io. ➡UTFDataFormatException	299
UTFDataFormatException ➡(String)	java.io. ➡UTFDataFormatException	299
valid()	java.io.FileDescriptor	161
validate()	java.awt.Component	42
validate()	java.awt.Container	44
valueOf(boolean)	java.lang.String	226
valueOf(char)	java.lang.String	226
valueOf(char[])	java.lang.String	226
valueOf(char[], int, int)	java.lang.String	226
valueOf(double)	java.lang.String	226
valueOf(float)	java.lang.String	226
valueOf(int)	java.lang.String	226
valueOf(long)	java.lang.String	226
valueOf(Object)	java.lang.String	226
valueOf(String)	java.lang.Boolean	193
valueOf(String)	java.lang.Double	201
valueOf(String)	java.lang.Float	203
valueOf(String)	java.lang.Integer	205
valueOf(String)	java.lang.Long	208
valueOf(String, int)	java.lang.Integer	206
valueOf(String, int)	java.lang.Long	208

Index of Methods

continued

Method Name	Class Name	Page
Vector()	java.util.Vector	291
Vector(int)	java.util.Vector	291
Vector(int, int)	java.util.Vector	292
VerifyError()	java.lang.VerifyError	305
VerifyError(String)	java.lang.VerifyError	305
VirtualMachineError()	java.lang.VirtualMachineError	305
VirtualMachineError(String)	java.lang.VirtualMachineError	305
wait()	java.lang.Object	213
wait(long)	java.lang.Object	213
wait(long, int)	java.lang.Object	213
waitFor()	java.lang.Process	214
waitForAll()	java.awt.MediaTracker	90
waitForAll(long)	java.awt.MediaTracker	90
waitForID(int)	java.awt.MediaTracker	91
waitForID(int, long)	java.awt.MediaTracker	91
whitespaceChars(int, int)	java.io.StreamTokenizer	185
Window(Frame)	java.awt.Window	115
wordChars(int, int)	java.io.StreamTokenizer	185
write(byte[])	java.io.DataOutput	188
write(byte[])	java.io.FileOutputStream	164
write(byte[])	java.io.FilterOutputStream	166
write(byte[])	java.io.OutputStream	170
write(byte[])	java.io.RandomAccessFile	181
write(byte[], int, int)	java.io.➥BufferedOutputStream	150
write(byte[], int, int)	java.io.➥ByteArrayOutputStream	153
write(byte[], int, int)	java.io.DataOutput	188
write(byte[], int, int)	java.io.DataOutputStream	156

write(byte[], int, int)	java.io.FileOutputStream	164
write(byte[], int, int)	java.io.FilterOutputStream	166
write(byte[], int, int)	java.io.OutputStream	170
write(byte[], int, int)	java.io.PipedOutputStream	175
write(byte[], int, int)	java.io.PrintStream	177
write(byte[], int, int)	java.io.RandomAccessFile	181
write(int)	java.io. ➥BufferedOutputStream	150
write(int)	java.io. ➥ByteArrayOutputStream	153
write(int)	java.io.DataOutput	188
write(int)	java.io.DataOutputStream	156
write(int)	java.io.FileOutputStream	163
write(int)	java.io.FilterOutputStream	166
write(int)	java.io.OutputStream	170
write(int)	java.io.PipedOutputStream	175
write(int)	java.io.PrintStream	177
writeBoolean(boolean)	java.io.DataOutput	188
writeBoolean(boolean)	java.io.DataOutputStream	156
writeBoolean(boolean)	java.io.RandomAccessFile	181
writeByte(int)	java.io.DataOutput	188
writeByte(int)	java.io.DataOutputStream	156
writeByte(int)	java.io.RandomAccessFile	181
writeBytes(String)	java.io.DataOutput	189
writeBytes(String)	java.io.DataOutputStream	156
writeBytes(String)	java.io.RandomAccessFile	181
writeChar(int)	java.io.DataOutput	189
writeChar(int)	java.io.DataOutputStream	156
writeChar(int)	java.io.RandomAccessFile	181
writeChars(String)	java.io.DataOutput	189
writeChars(String)	java.io.DataOutputStream	157

continues

Index of Methods

continued

Method Name	Class Name	Page
writeChars(String)	java.io.RandomAccessFile	182
writeDouble(double)	java.io.DataOutput	189
writeDouble(double)	java.io.DataOutputStream	157
writeDouble(double)	java.io.RandomAccessFile	182
writeFloat(float)	java.io.DataOutput	189
writeFloat(float)	java.io.DataOutputStream	157
writeFloat(float)	java.io.RandomAccessFile	182
writeInt(int)	java.io.DataOutput	189
writeInt(int)	java.io.DataOutputStream	157
writeInt(int)	java.io.RandomAccessFile	182
writeLong(long)	java.io.DataOutput	189
writeLong(long)	java.io.DataOutputStream	157
writeLong(long)	java.io.RandomAccessFile	182
writeShort(int)	java.io.DataOutput	189
writeShort(int)	java.io.DataOutputStream	157
writeShort(int)	java.io.RandomAccessFile	182
writeTo(OutputStream)	java.io.ByteArrayOutputStream	153
writeUTF(String)	java.io.DataOutput	189
writeUTF(String)	java.io.DataOutputStream	157
writeUTF(String)	java.io.RandomAccessFile	182
xor(BitSet)	java.util.BitSet	276
yield()	java.lang.Thread	241

INDEX OF CLASSES
AND INTERFACES

INDEX OF CLASSES AND INTERFACES

This is a complete alphabetical listing of all classes and interfaces found in this manual. The page numbers refer you to the complete documentation for each entry. Each interface is indicated by an asterisk (*).

Class or Interface	Page	Class or Interface	Page
Applet	10	Choice	29
AppletContext*	16	Class	196
AppletStub*	17	ClassLoader	197
AudioClip*	18	Cloneable*	245
BitSet	274	Color	30
Boolean	192	ColorModel	120
BorderLayout	20	Compiler	198
BufferedInputStream	147	Component	33
BufferedOutputStream	149	Container	42
Button	21	ContentHandler	252
ByteArrayInputStream	150	ContentHandlerFactory*	270
ByteArrayOutputStream	152	CropImageFilter	121
Canvas	22	DatagramPacket	252
CardLayout	23	DatagramSocket	253
Character	194	DataInput*	187
Checkbox	26	DataInputStream	153
CheckboxGroup	28	DataOutput*	188
CheckboxMenuItem	28	DataOutputStream	155

continues

Index of Classes and Interfaces

continued

Class or Interface	Page	Class or Interface	Page
Date	276	GridBagLayout	72
Dialog	44	GridLayout	79
Dictionary	280	Hashtable	280
Dimension	45	Image	81
DirectColorModel	123	ImageConsumer*	139
Double	199	ImageFilter	125
Enumeration*	294	ImageObserver*	141
Errors	304	ImageProducer*	143
Event	46	IndexColorModel	130
Exceptions	298	InetAddress	254
File	157	InputStream	167
FileDescriptor	160	Insets	82
FileDialog	51	Integer	203
FileInputStream	161	Label	83
FilenameFilter*	189	LayoutManager*	116
FileOutputStream	163	LineNumberInputStream	168
FilteredImageSource	124	List	84
FilterInputStream	164	Long	206
FilterOutputStream	166	Math	208
Float	201	MediaTracker	88
FlowLayout	54	MemoryImageSource	132
Font	55	Menu	91
FontMetrics	57	MenuBar	93
Frame	60	MenuComponent	96
Graphics	62	MenuContainer	117
GridBagConstraints	69	MenuItem	97

Index of Classes and Interfaces

Class or Interface	Page	Class or Interface	Page
Number	211	SocketImplFactory*	270
Object	212	Stack	288
Observable	285	StreamTokenizer	183
Observer*	296	String	221
OutputStream	169	StringBuffer	226
Panel	98	StringBuffer ➥InputStream	185
PipedInputStream	170		
PipedOutputStream	174	StringTokenizer	289
PixelGrabber	134	System	232
Point	98	TextArea	107
Polygon	99	TextComponent	109
PrintStream	175	TextField	110
Process	213	Thread	235
Properties	206	ThreadGroup	241
PushbackInputStream	177	Throwable	244
Random	288	Toolkit	112
RandomAccessFile	179	URL	261
Rectangle	100	URLConnection	264
RGBImageFilter	136	URLEncoder	269
Runnable	245	URLStreamHandler	269
Runtime*	214	URLStreamHandler ➥Factory*	271
Scrollbar	103		
SecurityManager	217	Vector	291
SequenceInputStream	182	Window	115
ServerSocket	255		
Socket	256		
SocketImpl	259		